BUILDING THE CORPORATE INTRANET

STEVE GUENGERICH

DOUGLAS GRAHAM

MITRA MILLER

SKIPPER McDONALD

WILEY COMPUTER PUBLISHING

John Wiley & Sons, Inc.

New York ◆ Chichester ◆ Brisbane ◆ Toronto ◆ Singapore ◆ Weinheim

Executive Publisher: Katherine Schowalter
Editor: Robert M. Elliott
Managing Editor: Carl Germann
Text Design & Composition: North Market Street Graphics

Designations used by companies to distinguish their products are often claimed as trademarks. In all instances where John Wiley & Sons, Inc., is aware of a claim, the product names appear in initial capital or ALL CAPITAL LETTERS. Readers, however, should contact the appropriate companies for more complete information regarding trademarks and registration.

This text is printed on acid-free paper.

This publication is designed to provide accurate and authoritative information in regard to the subject matter covered. It is sold with the understanding that the publisher is not engaged in rendering legal, accounting, or other professional service. If legal advice or other expert assistance is required, the services of a competent professional person should be sought.

Library of Congress Cataloging-in-Publication Data:

Guengerich, Steven L.
    Building the corporate intranet / Steve Guengerich, Skipper
McDonald, Douglas Graham.
       p. cm.
    "Wiley Computer Publishing."
    Includes bibliographical references (p.).
    ISBN 0-471-16268-X (alk. paper)
    1. Intranets (Computer networks)—Design and construction.
I. McDonald, Skipper. II. Graham, Douglas, 1950– . III. Title.
HD30.385.G83   1996
004'.36—dc20   96-38422
                                                   CIP

Printed in the United States of America
10 9 8 7 6 5 4 3 2 1

CONTENTS

Chapter 4—Organizational Issues   77

Chapter 5—Intranet Architectures   105

Chapter 7—Intranet Design   159

Chapter 10—The User Interface   251

Chapter 11—Back-End Applications   293

Chapter 12—Implementing an Intranet   313

ACKNOWLEDGMENTS

The experience of writing a book is at once vastly energizing and deeply humbling. Both feelings come from the realization that there are so many people who know as much as or more than you do about the subject at hand. You are energized by all that you are learning from (and teaching to) others; at the same time, though, you are humbled by how much you rely on others to complete your book. The real challenge for an author is to bring together the network of all these clever minds—with their bits of individual brilliance—to create a single work that has value for the reader.

As we hope you will come to see in these pages, this book has been enriched by many brilliant minds—and a selfless attitude held in common—drawn from the extended family at BSG Corporation.

From the beginning, this book was a team effort. Steve Guengerich provided the initial energy and writing to get the book going, as well as overall management throughout the project. Douglas Graham, however, provided the overall vision and the majority of the writing for the book. As BSG's leader for new media and Inter/intranet services, Douglas is the real soul of the book. Mitra Miller's organization, writing, and ideas made the difference, especially at the end, in getting this book into your hands. And, Skipper McDonald was early-in, contributing ideas, writing, and reviewing several of the technical chapters. A team effort indeed!

First and foremost we appreciatively acknowledge Andy Roehr for his overall technical vision and advice, and his generous contribution of time and counsel when we needed it most. We also thank Ben Bernard for his knowledge and contributions on the subjects of technical architecture models and tools. Kudos to Paul Leonhirth, Ed Cowden, and Matt Greenhouse for their generous helpings of advice, technical material, and "gotchas" worked into the book. Likewise, thanks to Dermot Grady and Milo Chan for their assistance with the material in the ORBs chapter. Also, Doron Etzioni, Dan Neiman, Pascal Antoine, and Bill Acheson deserve applause for their ongoing, critical yet supportive feedback. A special note of thanks goes to Jim Long, Morgan Pierce, and BSG's New York office for all of the wonderful executive and staff support they provided, from the very beginning and all the way through the "crunch" writing period!

A major thanks to Keith Nickerson, who wrote the first draft of the user interface chapter, and was always there to help with a figure or an idea when needed. Thanks, as well, to Angela Montz, Cynthia Schultz, and Tiffany Russell for pulling together various figures, research, and permissions where needed.

A special thanks to Steve Telleen and Amdahl Corporation for their contributions to Chapter 4, in the section on "Integrating the Intranet with IS Organizational Structure." The majority of the section on the Web Information Network is drawn from their publication, *The Intranet Methodology: Concepts and Rationale* (Copyright Amdahl Corporation 1995).

For their sage advice on I-Net legal issues we wish to thank George Brencher IV, Newton Brenner, and Wayne Martino of Brenner, Saltzman & Wallace.

Big "Thank You's" go to Alex Sharpe of Rapid Systems Solutions, Steve Champeon of Imonics, and Doug Gentile of Medaphis, and the members of their respective teams, who—whether they know it or not—were helpful in providing ideas, thoughts, resources, and words of inspiration toward key portions of the book. Our gratitude also to Tom Patterson, the Chief Internet Strategist for IBM Corporation, for his help in describing the intranet security issues.

Deepest thanks to our managing editor, Jan Wright, for the unending patience, encouragement, and attention to detail that we believe makes this book the best that it could be. Jan, we couldn't have done it without you!

Finally, with grateful appreciation, we acknowledge the editorial review, vision, and overall support from Bob Elliott, our editor at John Wiley & Sons, who first picked up the project and drove it to the printed page before you.

Writing even another word about internet computing at this point would seem to be an exercise in repetition. In our experience, however, we have yet to find a book that walked through the steps of *building* an application system for business using internet computing technology. That's what BSG's *Building the Corporate Intranet* is all about.

BSG Corporation is known as one of the leading client/server systems integrators in the professional services industry. So much of what we do, however, goes beyond the insert-notch-A-into-slot-B kind of integrating that many people visualize—for that reason we prefer to call BSG an information technology (IT) services company.

In fact, what is most obvious—yet overlooked in typical new technology initiatives—is the importance of nontechnology factors in the success of the initiative. All of the systems integration skill in the world won't help a company that has no clue about its strategy or understanding of the true motivations of its customers. The issues in linking business and IT strategy, changing business processes to match rapid time-to-market imperatives, and organizing a motivated, resilient workforce that can adapt as the technology changes (as it most assuredly will) are the ones that IT services companies help their customers tackle.

At BSG, we call this blending together of business, technology, and human factors *High Performance IT.* The result of High Performance IT is an enterprise (whether you define an enterprise as a single department within a company, or the entire company itself) that exceeds its goals, beats the competition, generates rewards and recognition for its people, and has a deep, pervasive focus on customer service.

For *Building the Corporate Intranet,* we've done our best to weave in the elements of High Performance IT where they can make a difference for you, as you lead your company through an intranet planning or implementation. You'll see questions and pointers about seemingly nontechnological issues in our workplans, checklists, and other writings. When you do, it's because experience has taught us that the ultimate success of your corporate intranet will have far more to do with who uses it, the expectations of its functionality over time, and the benefits it is perceived to deliver.

We hope you enjoy *Building the Corporate Intranet*. We look forward to hearing from you on our World Wide Web site, where we are committed to building on the body of knowledge that we've begun with this book.

Steven G. Papermaster
CEO and President
BSG Corporation, September 1996
www.bsginc.com

INTRODUCTION

"1995—The Year of the Internet"
Newsweek Cover, January 1, 1996

"1996—The Year of the Intranet"
Newsweek, January 15, 1996

What will *Newsweek*'s cover headline be in early January 1997? Perhaps, a turn of the tables . . .

"1997—Intranet of the Year: [put your company's name here]"
Newsweek Cover, January 1997

At least, that's the purpose of this book—to help you build a corporate intranet that can begin to make a significant impact for your company. Our goal is to strip away the hype of the last couple of years and show how to build and manage intranet technology for real business applications. To do this, we've come up with what we consider to be a novel approach to building an intranet.

Fundamentally, *Building the Corporate Intranet* is designed around a 12-step program. Our thinking was twofold. First, while there can be a tremendous amount of complexity at various points along the way, there should be no mystery about intranet deployment. It is very straightforward and can more or less be narrowed down to such a simple series of steps.

Second, with tongue in cheek, the analogy of working your way to the perfect intranet has the same appeal as other mass-market approaches to better fitness, personal wealth creation, and improved love lives. Thus, we present to you the Intranet 12-Step Program:

Step 1: Should We Implement?

Step 2: Do We Need Help?

Step 3: Enlist User Support

Step 4: Address Organizational Issues

Step 5: Determine Technical Architecture

Step 6: Decide on Applications and Prototype

Step 7: Complete Registration and IP Addressing

Step 8: Finalize the Plan

Step 9: Implement the Architecture

Step 10: Design and Develop the Applications

Step 11: Implement Intranet Policies and Procedures

Step 12: Manage the Intranet

Chapter 2, "The 12-Step Program," provides a detailed roadmap for relating the other chapters of the book to the 12-step program. So, readers who are familiar with intranet technology and are anxious to begin building the corporate intranet may want to skip the roadmap. But, understand that it sets the context for the 12-step program and contains many references to other sections of the book, so it's a good place to start if you're not sure where a particular topic is dealt with or how it fits into the overall program for establishing an intranet. Regardless of your technical proficiency, however, we recommend that all readers still read Chapter 1, "The Intranet Impact," at some point. Not only does it provide some good context setting and definitions, but it may prove useful to you in describing the benefits of intranets when you are talking to those who sign the checks at your company.

Chapter 3, "Taking the First Steps," helps you to answer critical questions—"Should we implement an intranet?" and "Do we need help?"—as well as to provide you with other pointers for getting started.

Chapter 4, "Organizational Issues," is an important chapter that addresses crucial, nontechnical issues. These issues include how the intranet can change—and will change—the way people in the company interact and how you organize your information technology (IT) group. It also discusses a number of important legal issues with which you should be familiar.

Chapter 5, "Intranet Architectures," covers the basic layers of intranet architecture and explains how they can be combined in various common architectures, as well as how to select various components to complement your chosen architecture.

Chapter 6, "Object Request Brokers," deals with a very important trend in intranet development (and IT architecture in general)—the use of the intranet as a means for distributing objects and small applications (called applets) throughout the network. Although the technology is still in its early stages, there is a broad consensus that it will emerge as an extremely powerful way of building business applications.

Chapter 7, "Intranet Design," looks at the major factors that we always try to balance in designing any major system—cost, performance, ease of use, manageability, and flexibility. Overall, the decisions that you make based on the information in Chapters 5, 6, and 7 will absolutely shape your development effort, and ultimately, the level of success of your intranet.

Chapters 8 through 11 form the developmental heart of *Building the Corporate Intranet.* Chapter 8, "Intranet Development," hits the basics from differing types of development efforts to core steps such as prototyping and testing. Chapter 9, a real companion to Chapter 8, is a straightforward overview of "Intranet Tools" and our observations about them, which we thought would be helpful.

Chapter 10 on "The User Interface" is by no means a replacement for a page design style guide or one of the many build-your-own-Web-site books you can find at the bookstore. Instead, its purpose is to provide guidance and clarity to the important decisions you need to consider for what appears on the desktop screen—in almost all cases, the most visible part of your corporate intranet. Conversely, Chapter 11 on "Back-End Applications" covers some of the least visible parts (at least, to the end user) of your corporate intranet. However, these applications provide the crucial glue that holds the system together.

Chapters 12 and 13 finish the process of building the intranet, by covering the subjects of putting your intranet into production ("Implementing an Intranet") and then making sure it stays up-and-running ("Managing the Intranet").

And finally, Chapter 14's "Tips, Tricks, and Gotchas" is our pragmatic acknowledgment to the twin truths that there's (1) an exception to every rule and (2) a bug in every program. Think of this chapter as a first installment on our lessons learned, which we intend to keep evergreen on our Web site. Not surprisingly, you'll find a great number of the "gotchas" are not technical at all.

That's it, except for the appendixes and other backmatter, like the glossary. Of course, we have no doubt that by the time you read this sentence, we'll have discovered all kinds of tips and techniques that we wish we had included in the book! However, that's the beauty of intranets and the Internet upon which they are founded—you can simply drop us a line and we'll discuss it in real time!

CHAPTER ONE

THE INTRANET IMPACT

- ◆ Overview
- ◆ What Is an Intranet?
- ◆ Why Build an Intranet?
- ◆ A Word About Intranet Costs
- ◆ Is it Time to Start Building an Intranet?

Overview

If ever there was a technology megatrend, it's internet computing. And the *intranet*—the term that has stuck for the internal corporate application of internet computing—seems to be an overnight sensation. But unlike a "one-hit wonder," the intranet is the kind of overnight sensation that results from years of activity and many related technology breakthroughs. It is actually the product of decades of research, development, and applications that have all contributed to a market momentum that seems unstoppable.

One of the first real public uses of the term *intranet* was in a delightful column by William Safire published in *The New York Times* in early 1994. The column—as so often occurs with high-tech terms that eventually become part of the common vocabulary—introduces the term as part of a set of new information age technologies that will deliver information at our beck and call "some day soon." Far from being a futuristic, dream technology, however, internet/intranet technology has mundane, practical roots that contribute to its great success today.

In many respects, one might say that the history leading to the current adoption of intranets was inevitable—only a matter of time. The widespread public and private acceptance of the Internet and its underlying technologies paved the way for intranets.

Companies from A(T&T) to Z(eneca) are installing and using intranets to their advantage today. These and other companies have found that the advantages of the ease of use of the technology, the flexibility of the desktop software, the lower cost of the software and hardware, and the ability to centralize management of the intranet are particularly compelling—making intranet implementation nearly irresistible. In this introductory chapter, we'll discuss the basics of the technology, the business forces that drive it, and the specific applications of intranets that you may want to consider for your company.

What Is an Intranet?

While it is nearly impossible to give a precise Webster's-like definition of an intranet, the following definition suits our purposes:

> *An intranet is a corporate network and the business applications that run on it that shares the "DNA" of internet computing technologies (e.g., Internet Protocol, browsers, Web servers) and exists behind the corporate security "firewall."*

In other words, an intranet is a secure, internal, single-company implementation of the Internet. All of the technology originally developed for the Internet—Internet Protocol (IP), the World Wide Web, and browsers—are being applied inside the security of a company's firewall.

A *firewall* is a collection of computers, software, routers, and services that together enable the connection of the network while maintaining its security and integrity with other networks. Taken to the extreme, the firewall for some companies' intranets is literally an "airwall," with no connection to other, external networks. In a purist sense, this approach provides optimal protection from external security breaches, but there is always the potential for an internal breach if someone gains access to your premises and your network.

Based on the above definition, Corporate America has shown that it believes in intranets. As shown in Figure 1.1, fully two-thirds of Global 2000 companies either have an intranet installed or are actively considering installation of one.

It is becoming increasingly apparent that intranets offer the most innovative, cost-effective way of freeing corporate information from the inaccessibility of expensive-to-maintain legacy systems, which account for 95 percent of the installed worldwide information systems (IS), as indicated in Figure 1.2.

It is difficult, of course, to talk about intranets without also discussing their close relations—the Internet and the World Wide Web. However, because this is primarily a how-to book intended for readers with some familiarity with the Internet, we'll stick to a quick, refresher definition.

Ed Krol, in *The Whole Internet*, defines the Internet as the world-wide network of networks that are connected to each other, using the IP protocol and other similar protocols. The Internet provides file transfer, remote login, electronic mail, news, and other services.

Before we go on, for the sake of clarity, we need to state how we'll use the terms Internet, intranet, and internet computing, throughout the remainder of the book. The *Internet* is the world-

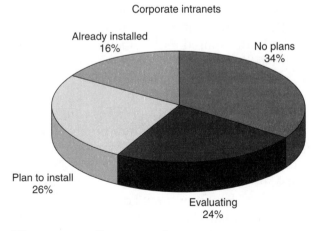

Figure 1.1   Corporate intranets.

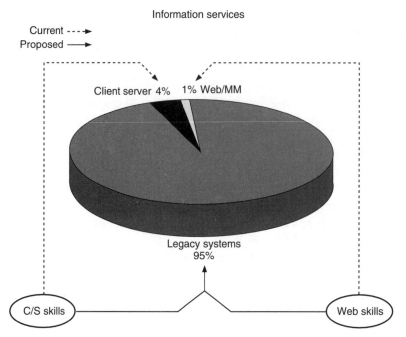

Figure 1.2   Installed information systems—worldwide.

wide, public network of networks. An *intranet,* as we mentioned earlier, is defined as a single company's internal implementation of an IP network and the applications on it, sharing the technological "DNA" of the Internet. *Internet computing,* is the term that we'll use to refer to the shared technology of the Internet and intranets. We'll use this term, for instance, when we're speaking about trends, products, advantages, and so forth that apply to both the Internet and intranets.

Referring back to Krol's definition, the first among the "other services of internet computing is the hypertext information flow made possible through the World Wide Web—or simply the Web, as we have all come to know and love it. The Web is a global collection of pages and hypertext "hyperlinks." Because the information that comprises a document may come from any number of sources, a single document can appear to stretch—weblike— throughout the world. Web is also an accurate reflection of the interconnected nature of the Internet. When a user accesses any given location on the Web, the request is passed from computer to computer until it reaches its destination.

Client/Server Roots

Internet computing is generally recognized as having its roots in "client/server computing." Client/server, which has for the past decade come to stand for the popular model of PC and network-based distributed computing in corporate America, is really the fundamental enabling architecture that provides the framework for plugging in internet computing technologies. During the late 1970s, the old paradigm of host-centric, time-shared computing gave way to the client/server approach, which is message-based and modular. In fact, most new computing technologies can be viewed as different implementation strategies using the client/server foundation.

In a simple, narrow definition, client/server computing is nothing more than a user program (i.e., "client") calling on the services of a separate "server" program, such as data retrieval, printing, or other processing. While this definition is not wrong, a broader definition must include mention of protocols, conventions, and even expectations regarding the use of client/server technology, including for example, the rapid development expectations characterized by statements such as "if an application ain't developed in 90 days, it ain't client/server." So, client/server computing also elicits expectations for a graphical user interface (GUI), personal computer or other intelligent desktop computer (as opposed to a "dumb terminal"), distributed relational or object-oriented databases, and local or wide area networks.

Intranet Building Blocks

Like client/server computing, a proper description of intranets includes protocols, standards, software and hardware, other internet computing technologies, and even expectations.

PROTOCOLS

Protocols are the building blocks of an intranet—the foundation that the technology is based upon. The "building block" protocols include IP (Internet Protocol), which is the most important protocol in internet computing, and its kissing cousin TCP (Transmission Control Protocol).

IP is the specification (or rules) for allowing packets of data from a source computer to traverse multiple networks to a destination computer. IP specifies things such as the size of the packet of data to be delivered, the composition of internet addresses, and other basic rules.

TCP is a connection-oriented protocol for ensuring the reliability of the IP-transmitted data. In addition to providing rules for ensuring the reliability of transmission, TCP also breaks the data you want to send into smaller chunks and assigns some identification for the chunks before they are encapsulated in an IP packet. This makes it easier to quickly and accurately reassemble the data at the receiving end.

Another well-known internet protocol, HTTP (Hypertext Transfer Protocol), is used to link hypertext data across an intranet or the Internet. HTTP server software resides on a separate, dedicated computer, usually referred to as the Web server. The software's job is to "listen" for the hyperlinks being transmitted over the intranet and ensure that the link is made to the appropriate information, or is forwarded to the computer where the information resides.

STANDARDS

Internet computing standards are the agreed upon means for companies to develop their Internet and intranet software and hardware products to facilitate interoperability (i.e., to let them work together without special "middleware" or other "translation layers" of products). Internet computing involves numerous important standards, but we'll discuss two particularly critical standards here: the domain name system (DNS) standard and the hypertext markup language (HTML) standard.

DNS is the system that allows English-language names to be translated into IP addresses to facilitate convenient identification. On its own, the IP protocol only specifies an address consisting of four numbers (with each number less than 256). Thus, an IP address might look like:

```
182.121.63.7 or 129.147.6.5
```

DNS is a method of allowing different groups to administer names that correspond to these IP numbers. DNS makes it far easier to remember and use the addresses for internet computing resources.

HTML is the standard language for writing World Wide Web documents. The beginning of a Web document, written in HTML might look like:

```
<HTML>
<HEAD>
<TITLE>Welcome to BSG!</TITLE>
<META NAME="AUTHOR" CONTENT="Steve Guengerich">
</HEAD>
<BODY bgcolor="#00E5EE" background="gifs/starbk1.gif">
```

The words enclosed in the left and right angle brackets are known as "tags." Tags notify an HTML interpreter (commonly known as a "browser") of the various actions it should perform. In the example above, the HTML is indicating some initial actions associated with identifying the web document and displaying a predefined background color and image on the screen. We'll cover HTML and various design issues related to building your corporate intranet in far more detail in Chapter 5 (Intranet Architectures) and Chapter 7 (Intranet Design).

SOFTWARE AND HARDWARE

The *browser* is probably the best known intranet software component. Browser is the generic name for a program that is typically used to explore the servers on an intranet (or the Internet). Browsers are, almost by definition, "Web browsers"—meaning that they can view hypertext documents—although they do not have to be. The browser runs on a client computer, typically an IBM-compatible PC, an Apple Macintosh, a UNIX workstation, or some other desktop device. Netscape's Navigator is currently the most popular browser and the market leader, but Microsoft's Internet Explorer is gaining ground with release 3.0.

The HTTP server, also known as the Web server, is the other well-known intranet software component. This software is essentially the piece that "glues" the World Wide Web together.

Finally, the firewall software is another key component of intranet architecture. The firewall software runs on a server that is generally connected to a router, which is, in turn, connected to an external network. The firewall software protects the intranet by stopping network transmissions (or "traffic") that you don't want to reach your intranet. We'll discuss this in more detail in Chapters 7 and 12 (Implementing an Intranet).

In terms of hardware, most of the key intranet components were originally developed for local and wide area networks (i.e., LANs and WANs). Clients, routers, and servers, as well as the networking "plumbing" (e.g., network interface cards, cabling, etc.) comprise the major pieces of the intranet hardware. Many of the intranet-specific hardware components that are marketed today are really general-purpose components that are specifically tuned, prepackaged, and priced for an intranet implementation. In reality, much of the hardware is equally applicable to Internet connectivity.

OTHER INTERNET COMPUTING TECHNOLOGY

Internet computing technology also includes a host of new software products—primarily languages and development tools—intended to facilitate application development for intranets, as well as the Internet. These new products, which are literally flooding the market, include Web page authoring tools, applet development tools (e.g., Sun's Java and Hot Java Browser), and rafts of middleware that provide network services.

In addition, there are a number of new hardware devices designed specifically for the internet computing age. These products include the cable modem, which is intended to provide higher speed/lower cost connectivity for home-based Internet users, and Oracle's famed $500 internet computing terminal. It's really too soon to predict if these devices and other, comparable internet computing technologies will achieve substantial market share as intranet components, but we can be certain that many more products will appear during the next few years, targeted specifically at the intranet market.

Intranet Applications

Applications on the intranet are still widely believed to be in the "Model T" stage of complexity. Like Ford's Model T, designed one way for the masses, the majority of business applications on the intranet deliver one type of functionality—information sharing. Sure, it's delivered with many different looks, but the vast majority of current intranet applications fall into the "pretty page," Web-based category, as shown in Figure 1.3.

Far more application functionality is possible, however, with the products that are emerging on an almost daily basis. The industry is moving beyond the "pretty page" stage to a fuller internet computing model of applications, as shown in Figure 1.4.

In the enhanced intranet application, there is an exchange of active, intelligent multimedia information being composed and delivered on demand. Forrester Research calls this "transactive content." We call it the next obvious step in application richness for intranets. However, there is huge complexity in creating such applications for an enterprise, which we discuss in more detail later in the book.

For now, we'll focus on some of the more notable examples of intranet applications that exist. Intranet applications can be used by any type of organization, from management consultants to manufacturers. As one might expect, some of the earliest and best-known examples of companies with intranets are those in defense and aerospace (e.g., McDonnell-Douglas, Boeing), pharmaceuticals research (e.g., Genetech, Eli Lilly), telecommunications (e.g., US West and Northern Telecom) and of course, major

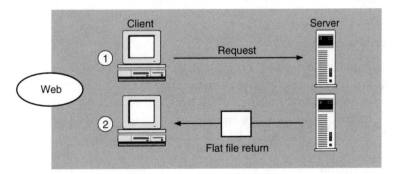

Figure 1.3   Basic Internet computing—the "pretty page" phase.

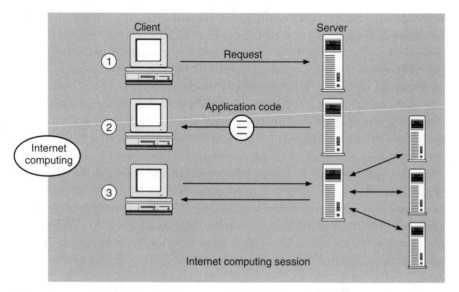

Figure 1.4   Enhanced Internet computing application example.

internet vendors (e.g., Silicon Graphics and Sun Microsystems), to name just a few.

Most of these companies initially used their intranets as a bulletin board system for information sharing. But they are rapidly enabling database interfaces, related networking services, and additional transactional functions, which we will discuss later. The scope of the applications themselves spans the corporate spectrum.

CORPORATE MANAGEMENT

Companies are targeting a wide range of applications with their intranet development. For example, one manufacturing company uses its intranet to provide upper-level management with the necessary information to make important business decisions on a timely basis. This intranet-based executive information system (EIS) enables executives to share information with managers throughout the globally distributed manufacturing environment. The low costs involved in securely transmitting data over the intranet make the system cost-effective as well as efficient.

General Electric Co. uses its intranet, the GE Information Network (or GEIN) to give its employees desktop access to more and better information and to provide them with convenient access to corporate and financial information. For example, GEIN contains the company's annual report and other financial and business information that enables GE stock–owning employees to manage their own investments. Plans call for eventually linking all 220,000 GE employees worldwide via the intranet. In addition, the company uses GEIN to provide employees with online access to its travel center, enabling them to help schedule their own business trips.

Booz-Allen Hamilton uses its intranet as an electronic repository for the company's knowledge base. The firm's analysts use the Knowledge On Line intranet to search databases for topics such as best practices in banking or software reengineering in the transportation business. Users can also obtain a list of every project any Booz analyst has worked on, every person an analyst has ever worked with, and an analyst's specialty in the firm.

Silicon Graphics' intranet serves 7,200 employees with 144,000 Web pages stored on 800 internal Web sites. SGI's intranet, dubbed Silicon Junction, makes more than two dozen corporate databases available to employees and regularly sends video and audio feeds to employees around the world. Similarly, Eli Lilly & Co. links 16,000 of its 26,000 employees via intranets, using the Web as a gateway to its corporate, legacy databases.

SALES, MARKETING, AND PRODUCT DEVELOPMENT

The sales and marketing departments in many companies can take credit for pushing their firms toward connection with the Internet. Now, after two or more years of Internet-campaigning, many sales and marketing departments use the information on their Web servers as storehouses for sales and marketing literature—ensuring easy access for in-house personnel as well as external customers. For example, at Home Box Office, the cable TV programming firm, the sales and marketing group manages its own Web site, while the finance department creates pages to provide top management with up-to-the-minute strategic information about the state of the company.

Taking the marketing function a step further into the product development arena, the technology leaders in the Dreamworks SKG animation division are developing a state-of-the-art, intranet-based production-management system to coordinate the many facets of the studio's first animated feature film. The system is used to check the daily status of projects, track animation objects, and coordinate scenes. Eventually, the intranet will be used throughout the company to aid in the production of live-action films, music, TV shows, and new media being developed at Dreamworks Interactive.

ACCOUNTING, FINANCE, AND HUMAN RESOURCES

Numerous third-party software development companies recognize potential in the expanded client/server model created by the network-centric view of intranets. The applications here are largely enhancements to core accounting and financial systems that take advantage of intranet functionality.

Dun & Bradstreet Software, for example, has committed to build the SmartStream Web Series, a set of Java-based enterprise applications specifically designed for use on intranets. An initial application will allow local and remote users to download, fill out, and file purchase requisitions for a manager's approval. The company intends to follow this application with a series of human resources (HR) applets (i.e., miniapplications) that will allow employees to check their benefits, change exemptions, and adjust 401(k) plans—all through the intranet. A number of other enterprise application vendors, including Peoplesoft, SAP, and Baan are reputed to have similar products under development.

Many companies are not waiting for the third-party software developers to provide answers to their intranet software applications, however. For example, Compaq Computer Corporation is one of many companies that currently uses an intranet to provide access to employee-directed 401(k) pension programs. The Compaq intranet, which includes freestanding intranet stations for assembly-line workers or other employees with nondesk jobs, permits workers to review their program status and/or investment options at their leisure.

ENGINEERING AND MANUFACTURING

Engineers and designers in the Space Systems division of Rockwell Aerospace use an intranet for online access to schematics of components of the space shuttle, for which Rockwell is the principal contractor. The intranet eliminates their reliance on other, less efficient means of transporting and viewing the drawings.

In another example, Chiron Corporation, a pharmaceutical manufacturer, uses an intranet to distribute a database of graphical images of molecular structures for company-created chemicals, thereby ensuring that the information is accessible to everyone in the company, regardless of the desktop computing environment (i.e., PC, Macintosh, or UNIX workstation). The intranet greatly facilitates collaboration in a company like Chiron, which has more than doubled in size through mergers and acquisitions in recent years.

For payback, few intranets can rival the one being developed by aerospace vendor Northrup Grumman for use by U.S. Air Force personnel. The Federal government estimates that the intranet—Contractor's Integrated Technology Information Service—supported, in part, by Northrup's corporate intranet, will save the Air Force more than $800 billion during the 20 years it is expected to be in use. Air Force personnel access Northrup's intranet via a Web browser running on IBM RS/6000 workstations to view and manipulate a variety of information, including technical data, engineering drawings, and component specifications involving the B-2 bomber. Intranet access allows the Air Force to reengineer components originally created by Northrup for the B-2, then place the redesigned components out for competitive bid, resulting in the projected savings.

CUSTOMER SERVICE AND MANAGEMENT

Most people think of customer service applications as a means of giving customers direct access through the Internet to the resources of the company. Customer service and management, however, are also excellent application areas for intranets. For example, *Visa* International developed portions of VisaInfo, the company's intranet, specifically to enhance customer service.

VisaInfo currently contains such information as a listing of Visa's 19,000 member banks. Visa plans to begin connecting member banks to the intranet during the summer of 1996 with the goal of drastically reducing, if not eliminating, the two million paper documents that the banks collectively transmit to Visa on a daily basis. VisaInfo will also incorporate tools to help detect fraud, track questionable transactions, complete business forms, and provide access to Visa's files.

In another example of customer management, Hollings Cancer Center's intranet helps researchers recruit patients (i.e., their health care "customers") for its clinical trials. Clinical trials often take years to complete, partly because of the nature of the testing, but also because of the difficulty in recruiting patients. Recruiting difficulties are largely due to community physicians' lack of awareness of trials in progress and their difficulty in pinpointing a contact person within hospitals. The Hollings Cancer Center intranet, however, allows community physicians to dial into the Web, determine what clinical trials are in progress, then fill out a short form to refer a patient to the trial. The log-on process is fully automated and, once the physicians are online, they view predominantly text-based material that loads quickly. The latter feature is particularly important for physicians using dial-up access because they (like nearly all users) don't like to wait for pages to load.

INFORMATION SYSTEMS SUPPORT

As one might expect, applications that enhance information systems (IS) development and management are prime candidates for an intranet. At MCI, for example, more than 12,000 IS professionals use the Washington telecommunications company's intranet to follow its motto "Collaborate, don't duplicate." The employees have online access to a "developer's store" that contains kernels of software code. The MCI Director of Strategy and Technology has commented that the intranet lets MCI personnel walk around the company and collaborate electronically.

Cap Gemini, an international professional services firm, uses its intranet, called Knowledge Galaxy, for a wide variety of IS support functions. The intranet serves as a storehouse of software objects (i.e., prefabricated chunks of software code) that the company has developed to help consultants avoid reinventing the wheel. In addition, the intranet has areas for electronic chats and bulletin boards, a database of current projects with links to the employees working on them, and hundreds of Web pages aimed at keeping the 17,000-person global workforce up-to-date on technological developments. The intranet even has an "Internet Cafe" at its Paris headquarters so that employees can access the Internet and "surf" while they are on break.

Finally, Pacific Gas & Electric Company gives us a noteworthy example of an old-time intranet used in support of IS activities. PG&E is one of California's oldest and largest companies, providing electrical service to 4.5 million customers. More than half of the 1,200 employees in the company's Computer and Technology Services (C&TS) division have been using an intranet since 1994. The division uses the intranet for approximately 70 to 80 relatively small applications, including a forms-based application that permits a user to send a message to another employee's alphanumeric pager. Another intranet application publishes a Lotus Notes database to the Web (without using Lotus's own InterNotes Web Publisher).

Why Build an Intranet?

The promise of the intranet is significant. Almost every leading technology company has announced that internet computing is its primary strategic focus for the future. But, what makes intranets so important?

Intranets are important because of technological requirements imposed on our business and personal lives by the impetus for faster, better, and cheaper information. The need for information—particularly interconnected information—has become a major driving force in our economy. Thus, the requirements for efficient communications, collaboration across space and time, and effective knowledge management are driving the development of intranets.

It may be helpful to review these requirements to illustrate how organizations are responding to these requirements and adjusting to the changing economy and, how intranets fit into their strategic information technology (IT) infrastructure.

Communications

Economic forces are steadily driving organizations toward decentralization. Heightened competitive pressures obligate organizations to lower overhead costs and to increase their agility in order to respond to ever-decreasing windows of opportunity. Reducing layers of middle management can help accomplish both objectives; but efficient communication becomes crucial as companies reduce their reliance on middle managers as information conduits and push decision-making out to frontline employees. To compete in the "nanosecond nineties" and to meet increasingly diverse customer demands, employees must have the right information, in the right form, when and where they need it.

Organizations—from high-tech software developers to low-tech process chemicals manufacturers (and everyone in between)—are on their way to becoming "virtual enterprises"—organizationally decentralized and geographically distributed. To succeed in today's competitive environment, however, the individual components of the virtual enterprise must be much more tightly coordinated than the comparable parts of older, hierarchical organizations ever were. Individuals, teams, and business units must function autonomously and be able to respond rapidly to market opportunities (and threats!). But, optimizing responses to ensure maximum benefit to the organization demands tight coordination—coordination achieved through the improved flow of information rather than restrictive policies and hierarchy.

Integration in a decentralized organization depends on open standards and interoperable communications. This is particularly true in today's business economy, where many companies expand through acquisitions and mergers, and rely on outsourcing for many critical functions. Even if a company is able to enforce a single internal standard, that standard is subject to change at any time—with the next merger, for example.

Efficient communications must also be developed and properly staged for outside organizations. In a knowledge-based economy, market success is directly proportional to the information an organization can bring to bear, which, in turn, is largely a function of the reach of the enterprise's network. That network comprises both insiders and outsiders, as tightly linked *webs* of partners, customers, and suppliers replace vertical integration as a source of market power. Communication is the glue that holds the network together.

Collaboration

The virtual enterprise lives or dies by its ability to bring dispersed assets—particularly knowledge and expertise—to bear on a specific project or opportunity. Problems, opportunities, and the environments in which they appear continuously grow more complex. To manage such complexity effectively, enterprises must bring experts with specialized knowledge together to *collaborate* in creating solutions that are beyond individual contributions. Simple communication—transmitting information—is not sufficient. Michael Schrage in his book *No More Teams! Mastering the Art of Creative Collaboration* asserts that:

> *In society, academe, the sciences and business, the age of complexity confronts the era of specialization. The new reality is that it will take the collaborative efforts of people with different skills to create innovative solutions and innovative products.*

Schrage goes on to point out that the quality and quantity of meaningful collaboration often depend upon the tools used to foster it. In a very real sense, the tools we use define who we are and how we act. Tools transform our perception of the world: Leeuwenhoek's microscope transformed biology just as surely as the telescope forever changed our view of the earth and its position in the larger cosmos. Tools define how business is done: A telephone on the desk invites communication in a way that a pay phone down the hall does not; phone mail provides a substitute for having a constant presence; and E-mail allows instant communication independent of space and time constraints. Schrage asks:

"Is it unreasonable to believe that tools designed to encourage collaborative work could similarly motivate people?"

It is unlikely that anyone would pay to see a symphony orchestra perform without its instruments, and it would be incredibly stupid to provide blueprints and materials for a new house, but deny construction workers the tools with which to build it. Tools are important because they directly create and enhance value; indeed, those are the only tools worth having. Similarly, technology that fosters collaboration must provide a medium for creating productive environments.

Tools designed to support collaboration, however, will look qualitatively different from tools designed to support individuals. Computers have transformed the way in which we process information, but the personal computer is just that—*personal.* In fact, there is nothing in a typical office to support collaboration. Desks are intended for personal use, as are telephones. Printers and photocopiers merely support individually generated memos and reports. Schrage points out that: "The issue isn't automating collaboration, it's using technology to enhance the collaborative relationship."

Collaborative tools create shared space. They add a new dimension to exchanging information (communicating)—a dimension that embraces symbolic representation, manipulation, and memory. Those shared spaces should invoke the senses as well as the mind, so collaborators can experience what they are doing while they think about it. Effective collaborative tools should work in real time, they should be highly interactive, and they should readily accept new types of information—adapting to the collaborators' needs. Shared spaces should transcend space and time, allowing collaboration by groups separated by geography and schedules. Finally, collaborative environments require room for curiosity and serendipity.

Internet technologies have the potential to evoke the power of shared space. In a computerized environment, ideas are both external and manipulatable—prerequisites for sharing. Web technology adds a new hybrid of text, image, sound, video, and computation that provides the framework for collaboration. Groupware products (e.g., Lotus Notes) will interface with intranets to support human interaction, rather than merely manipulating data. The explosion of the Internet is the best demonstration of how compelling technology can be as a medium of community.

THE INTRANET VERSUS NOTES QUESTION

While we are on the subject of Lotus Notes, let's quickly address it, given that it has been a source of confusion for many companies migrating to an intranet. Realizing the inherent benefits of information sharing, many companies adopted groupware products such as Lotus Notes. At this point in development, however, many of the companies using Notes (and comparable products) find themselves involved in a passionate, long-standing debate concerning a potential switch to the intranet. An Andersen Consulting partner, for example, has been quoted as saying that Andersen would currently be using Web technology as its groupware if it were possible to go back in time before they committed to 25,000 seats of Lotus Notes.

The real answer to the question "Notes or Intranet?" depends on a number of factors. As Figure 1.5 indicates, on a purely cost basis, Notes is economically a better option than an intranet—up to a point.

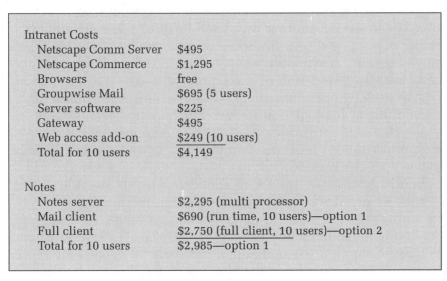

Intranet Costs
    Netscape Comm Server $495
    Netscape Commerce $1,295
    Browsers   free
    Groupwise Mail $695 (5 users)
    Server software $225
    Gateway $495
    Web access add-on $249 (10 users)
    Total for 10 users $4,149

Notes
    Notes server $2,295 (multi processor)
    Mail client $690 (run time, 10 users)—option 1
    Full client $2,750 (full client, 10 users)—option 2
    Total for 10 users $2,985—option 1

Figure 1.5   Cost comparison table: Intranet versus Notes.

But regardless of the Notes/intranet decision, the integration of an intranet as a communications, information, and project management tool across the organization is a key indicator of a successful Internet computing strategy.

If, however, the collaboration system is not well integrated—available only to a limited number of people, for example—it's not going to have the impact that it should. But, a lack of integration is sometimes the result of a lack of corporate commitment rather than unavailability of integration facilities. The adoption of strong corporate policies that support and encourage collaboration is necessary for a successful intranet implementation. In truth, the specific application areas are of less concern than the existence of the policy itself, along with a corporate-wide understanding of how it applies, and a demonstrable commitment from the company's leaders.

Knowledge Management

When collaboration occurs, two or more individuals with complementary skills interact to create a new, shared understanding. In fact, Schrage defines collaboration as the process of sharing creation. Expressed in another way, team learning takes place. This ability of teams and organizations to learn may be considered the only long-term, sustainable competitive advantage. Implementing new technology does not, in itself, provide a sustainable advantage; eventually our competitors will have the same time-saving, cost-cutting technology that we have. Peter Senge persuasively argues that as the world becomes more interconnected and complex, organizations must develop the capacity to learn at all levels if they are to truly excel.

Pundits from Peter Drucker to Tom Peters to Alvin Toffler assert that the knowledge derived from continuous learning is rapidly becoming the source of all economic value. A long-term study by the International Monetary Fund provides a convincing statistic to support this notion: The amount of raw material needed for a given unit of production in the world economy has been dropping at a compounded rate of 1.25 percent per year since 1900. In other words, *knowledge* is substituting for the material cost of what we produce, and that shift is accelerating. Nearly every company can (or should be able to) trace virtually everything that it successfully produces back to a knowledge asset.

The goal of knowledge management then is to leverage knowledge assets from one problem domain to another, and from one user to another. For example, the solution one programmer develops to a difficult, but generalizable software problem is instantly retrieved when another programmer encounters a similar problem. Knowledge management attempts to make knowledge a recyclable, accessible, and expanding resource.

Technology alone is clearly not the answer to effective knowledge management. Instead, it requires an architecture and infrastructure—although not a ponderous expert-staff bureaucracy. For many companies, intranets represent the first step toward investing in that architecture. Bob Buckman, chair of Buckman Labs, describes the characteristics of an ideal knowledge management technology in Tom Peter's book, *Liberation Management:*

> *. . . the system should have the following characteristics: 1) it should reduce the number of transmissions of knowledge between individuals to one, to achieve the least distortion of that knowledge; 2) everyone should have access to the knowledge base of the company; 3) each individual should be able to enter knowledge into the system; 4) the system should function across time and space with the knowledge base available 24 hours a day, seven days a week . . . ; 5) it should be easy to use for those who aren't computer experts . . . ; 6) as questions are asked of the knowledge base by the users, and answers given, it should be updated automatically—the accumulation of technical questions and answers would generate our knowledge bases for the future.*

Buckman wrote this in 1991, well before the popularization of the World Wide Web. Yet, the ideal knowledge management technology that he espoused sounds uncannily like a description of the Web.

Intranet Benefits

Given the many intranet applications that we've discussed, one might suspect that information systems professionals view intranets as the second coming of client/server. Driven by stealth purchases of PCs and departmental LANs, client/server snuck up on many companies, wreaking havoc on IS control of information technology. Rather than fearing intranets, however, many IS professionals realize the benefits they can derive from intranet technology in the areas of communications and systems management. Through intranets, low-cost "virtual private networks" are a valid alternative to public leased-line networks, offering significant savings in data communications costs.

According to a 1995 *Information Week* survey, cost was cited most often as the reason why client/server computing had transformed only a few percent of the legacy market prior to the inception of internet computing technology. Similarly, cost was the major hesitation in adopting an enterprise-wide groupware solution such as Notes. With intranets, the cost barrier is significantly lowered.

Dataquest predicts that half of all corporate IT budgets will either remain unchanged or decrease in this era of increasing need. This major challenge for IT leadership is likely to encourage them to employ more creative, innovative ways of stretching those IT dollars. Turning to intranets—to gain either lower-cost alternatives to private networks or access to lower cost products and information on the "net"—is one of the ways in which IT leaders are being more creative.

More important than the pure technology costs, however, are the people costs. The universal interface of internet/intranet computing presents a very simple metaphor—point-and-click—that involves almost no training. Further, Internet standards such as HTML (hypertext markup language) and CGI (common gateway interface) are relatively straightforward, compared to C++ routines or object modeling. Thus, it takes relatively little time to educate users in the basics required to effectively use an intranet.

Of course, adopting a new technology like an intranet frequently introduces new, often unforeseen, costs. One of these is the potential cost of having your information system invaded and/or damaged by outsiders. Fortunately, there is no need to actually connect to the Internet, as the protocols work just as effectively over existing networks and point-to-point long distance connections. An adequate security system generally provides the necessary level of protection for networks using public long-distance service.

The next step for intranet vendors is to enhance the technology with full network services, such as directory, E-mail, file, print, and network management. When this occurs, the lives of IS professionals will improve in a number of ways. For example, they will no longer be hostage to a single network operating system vendor, such as Novell or Microsoft, and they will be able to simplify complex, redundant processes like directory maintenance. (Many companies currently maintain three directories—one each in E-mail, corporate scheduling, and a groupware package, such as Lotus Notes.)

QUO VADIS—WHITHER THE WEB

The Latin *quo vadis* for "whither thou goest, it does not matter," is a wonderful way of expressing the freedom of Internet computing and describing how it can be employed via intranets. The Web, which is the foundational technology concept for intranets, offers users unprecedented freedom in obtaining information in the corporate data stores. It allows people to work in the manner that best corresponds to their personality, style, and work habits. In addition, however, the web offers other attractions that make it irresistible for intranet application development.

It is easy.   Most people can learn to use the web front end in only a few days, as compared with weeks or months for many existing tools.

It is consistent.   Multiple applications can be easily built—ranging from database, to document retrieval, to bulletin boards, to OLE-assisted CAD/CAM, to E-mail—all using the same browser interface! This ability can significantly reduce the time it takes to train new users.

It is sophisticated.   Through extensions such as Sun Microsystems Java/Hot Java environment, it is possible to have client/server "on demand." In other words, Java applets (in the form of small applications intended primarily for viewing) can be automatically downloaded on demand.

It is cross platform.   The client (i.e., the browser) can run on any platform with a consistent interface.

It is secure.   Additional levels of security can be incorporated, including an application firewall, certificate authority, and/or encryption. Discretionary access controls can also be made available, for example, building menus "on the fly" based on the user profile. Few of the recent, well-publicized security breaches could penetrate the security systems that are readily available to companies today.

It is standardized.   TCP/IP, and the architectures based on it, has become a de facto standard, with approximately 30 million users throughout the world. It is also a de jure standard, endorsed by the IETF (Internet Engineering Task Force) standards committee, among others.

It has a bright future.   Given the large consumer base, internet computing standards are likely to survive for quite some time—to some extent, they might be considered universal. Even if the Internet as we know it ceases to exist, many of the standards upon which it is based are likely to continue to survive, given their ability to operate within virtually any communications infrastructure, including point-to-point.

It is very harvestable.   Given the standardized, modular, semi-object-oriented nature of these applications and the basic similarity of the underlying architecture, Web-based intranet applications are very harvestable (i.e., able to be taken, improved, and used by others). The HTML source code of almost any Web site can, for example, be copied carte blanche (assuming, of course, that you abide by copyright and trade/service-mark rights of others), and used in any other Web site. Such harvesting of material includes not only the text and HTML coding, but also the figures themselves—all through a few simple clicks of the mouse. Such easy access to the de facto image and text standards on the Web, along with access to the best practices of various Web providers, has helped to propel the development of intranets.

It is not expensive. This is probably the most compelling reason for the continued growth of intranets. The vast majority of Corporate America (95 percent) is still using legacy systems. These companies are already facing the need to upgrade and/or modify the existing systems to correspond with recent technological advances, as well as to compete effectively in an increasingly global economy. Intranets offer the most efficient and cost-effective methods available for achieving the necessary changes.

It is noninvasive. It does not require the replacement of any part of the existing IT infrastructure. Instead, it is a parallel infrastructure that sits "on top" of any existing network and can be deployed on whatever timetable is deemed appropriate.

It is scalable. It is hugely scalable with many intranet sites handling tens of thousands of users and transactions a day.

It can be modularized. We can identify discrete steps or modules, the first of which are relatively inexpensive and do not irreversibly commit the company to a course of action. This makes the decision to proceed much easier.

A Word about Intranet Costs

So, how much does an intranet cost? By now you can probably guess that the answer to that question is highly dependent on the scope of the applications to be used. To date, marketing has paid most of the tab for internet computing technology. With an intranet, the time has come for IS to step up and pay for it as a part of the corporate infrastructure.

Figure 1.6 shows a preliminary budget for a very basic intranet platform. The system specifications in this example can (theoretically) accommodate a company of 5,000 users across multiple locations and multiple platforms (i.e., various desktop operating systems ranging from Apple Macintosh to versions of Windows to flavors of UNIX).

In addition to these costs, other often-overlooked costs include ongoing communication charges, server maintenance, and internal marketing costs, the latter necessary to promote and ensure active participation and use of the intranet.

In addition, it may be useful to note some of the opportunity costs of *not* harnessing internet computing via a corporate intranet. Indeed, these may prove more costly in the long run than the acquisition and installation costs of establishing an intranet. A number of opportunity costs loom, including:

SW/HW Costs:	Quantity	Price per Unit	Cost
Development			$7,000.00
Web/database server	1	$25,000.00	
CGI developer workstation	1	$10,000.00	
HTML developer workstation	1	$ 8,000.00	
Developer admin workstation	1	$ 3,000.00	
Deployment			
Server software	1	$7,000.00	
Server hardware	1	$9,000.00	$9,000.00
Application firewall	1	$5,000.00	$19,000.00
Additional hard disk space	4	$2,500.00	$1,000.00
Back-up drive and media	1	$2,000.00	$2,000.00
Communications router	1		$1,500.00
Network services (3rd party)	quality of service??	~$1,000.00/mo	
Web clients—software only	up to 5,000	~$40/client	$10,000.00
Admin clients—software only	up to sev. hundred	~$1,000/client	$18,000.00
Totals (not including labor costs for development)			$67,500.00

Figure 1.6 BSG Web development system budget.

◆ *Legacy maintenance.*   Software upgrade and communications costs for legacy systems are significantly more
expensive than intranet alternatives. In this context,
legacy includes relatively young (i.e., installed within
the past three years) production client/server systems, as
well as older traditional systems.

◆ *Public perception.*   A company, particularly one with
more than 1,000 employees, that isn't considering or
using an intranet is likely to be seen as falling behind by
both its external public (i.e., customers, investors, etc.)
and internal public (i.e., staff and management). With the
wide availability of routers and standards such as TCP/IP
and HTTP, an IS group that does not include a corporate
intranet on the IS work list may be perceived as not keeping pace with technology and/or failing to take a leadership role—not an enviable position for any group.

Is it Time to Start Building an Intranet?

The answer to the question "when?" depends on your particular
company and its current state of development.

While "faster, better, cheaper" tends to be the mantra of new
technology use by the mainstream, it is seldom so for the *early*
innovation and adoption of new technologies. Rather, the real catalyst for acceptance at the beginning stages of a new technology
like intranet computing is the potential for unique competitive
advantage.

One way to assess the readiness of your company to develop an
intranet is to determine where it is on the technology adoption
curve. The technology adoption curve, shown in Figure 1.7, is a
useful illustration of the changing dynamics of a new technology's
audience over time. (One of the best discussions of the curve and
its implications for high-tech marketers is *Crossing the Chasm,* by
Geoff Moore.)

The idea behind the technology adoption curve is simple: Every
new technology goes through an acceptance cycle that is bell-
shaped over time, with its smallest audiences at the beginning and

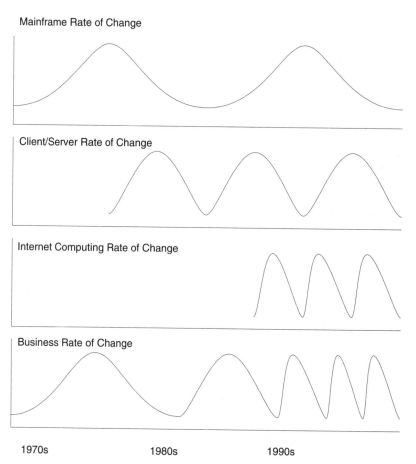

Figure 1.7   Technology adoption curve.

end of its life cycle, and its largest audience at the midpoint of mainstream acceptance. Not only does the size of the audience change, but its characteristics change as well, with the profile of early buyers differing vastly from the profile of mainstream buyers.

Early Adopters

Early adopters buy new technology because they see some inherent strategic advantage that the technology may offer. They are not economic buyers in the traditional sense of cost/benefit and return-on-investment (ROI) analysis. Often, they are found in industries that regularly experience dramatic change or that are known to make competitive use of new technologies.

Publishing and entertainment companies are good examples of early adopters for internet computing technology. Because they were typically early developers of public Web sites, they were also among the first to tie in their internal, "back-end" systems via intranets, to accommodate functions like online ordering.

Mainstream Buyers

Mainstream buyers are the "sweet spot" for new technologies. They comprise the majority of buyers and typically buy as a "herd," all tending to convert to a new technology within a 18-month to three-year window. Unlike early adopters, however, mainstream buyers are not strategically motivated. Instead, they are motivated by operational advantages, such as lower cost, higher productivity, greater dependability, and so forth. And, unlike early adopters, mainstream buyers are primarily influenced by others within their industry peer group that they can reference. In fact, peer group references are the single most important buying criterion for mainstream buyers.

If your company falls into the mainstream category, this is an extremely important issue to understand. If you, as an IT or cyber-professional, are convinced of the benefits of a new element of an intranet for your company—let's say three-dimensional, VRML Web pages—but there are absolutely no referenceable examples of the technology being used by other companies in your industry, you must either seek out a project champion who exhibits an early adopter profile, or bide your time until the technology matures and references begin to appear.

Late Adopters

Late adopters, as the name implies, are the last to use a new technology. They are typically found in industries where there is less competitive pressure—for example, conservative business services such as the legal profession or industrial concerns with fewer manufacturers, such as paper milling. Almost by definition, late adopters do not buy *new* technology, and may do so only when customers or regulators demand it. Late adopters are likely to avoid or otherwise defer implementation of intranets, at least for the time being.

Generalizing across all industries, it's safe to say that intranets are in a mainstream market right now. The cost/benefits and reference points are established and it is clear that all but late adopters are either planning or in the process of migrating some portion of their applications to an intranet. In the next chapter we'll review the steps involved in the intranet planning process and discuss some of the issues you'll face in beginning your implementation project.

CHAPTER TWO

THE 12-STEP PROGRAM

- ◆ Overview
- ◆ The Major Steps Decision Tree
- ◆ Summary of Steps
- ◆ If All Else Fails

Overview

By now, you've probably guessed that building a corporate intranet—especially one that meets your users' needs and satisfies your budget and organizational constraints—is likely to be a time-consuming, complicated, and occasionally frustrating experience. Don't give up hope, however, or try to pass the project off to another department. We've been through the experience innumerable times and—through a bit of trial and error—we've learned that the intranet implementation process can be broken down into a series of logical, manageable steps. And, these steps can be tailored to fit nearly any corporate environment.

Indeed, the BSG 12-Step Program is much more than a catchy name. It is a logical process that can help you to break down the component parts of an intranet implementation project, analyze those parts with regard to your own environment, and derive solutions that are appropriate for your specific technological and organizational requirements.

In this chapter, we'll describe all 12 steps within the framework of the entire intranet implementation process. Then, we'll expand on the specifics of each step in subsequent chapters. We'll also show you how to use the BSG Intranet Toolkit—a set of matrices, checklists, flowcharts, and other useful decision-making tools— that can take some of the guesswork out of your intranet implementation project. These tools, which have evolved from our experience in helping other organizations with their intranet projects, help to focus on the right issues at the right time.

Try to keep an open mind as you begin this 12-Step Program. Be as objective as possible in your answers to the various questionnaires and avoid making assumptions. There is, after all, no such thing as a "magic bullet"—and that includes intranet projects.

Most of the tools that we describe in this and subsequent chapters are included in this book, and they are also all available on the BSG Web site (http://www.bsginc.com). Although none of these tools are *required* for the intranet building process, we think that you'll find them to be helpful supplemental materials.

The Major Steps Decision Tree

Figure 2.1 illustrates the overall process of planning, implementing, and managing an intranet. As you can see, the process is broken down into a series of discrete, interrelated steps. To be sure, each of the steps involves several (sometimes many) activities and decisions, but taken one-by-one, they add up to an implementation plan that you can address in a logical, linear fashion.

The Tools to Support Decision-Making

Where appropriate throughout the 12 major steps, we've indicated a tool that can help you reach a decision—and move to the next step. The tools may be further decision trees, questionnaires, matrices, facilitated sessions, or workplans:

- *Decision Trees.* Remember the old decision trees? They're coming back into popularity as a way of managing the fluid, ever changing intranet environment. They provide an easy means of navigating the complex web of decisions that you'll need to make in planning an intranet.

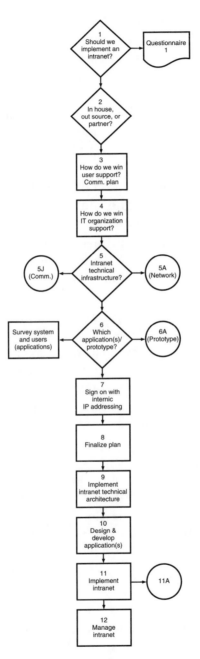

Figure 2.1 Major steps decision tree.

- *Questionnaires.*   We recommend that you use the questionnaires both quantitatively (i.e., scoring your responses to produce a ballpark answer) and qualitatively (i.e., making sure you are considering the key issues).

- *Matrices.*   A matrix generally provides the easiest means of determining rank among a number of factors, each with a different weight, in the decision-making process.

- *Checklists.*   In some cases, a plain old checklist is the best medium for listing the component tasks in a function, and for ensuring that you complete all of the tasks.

- *Facilitated Sessions.*   At times, the best way to reach a decision is to work with a knowledgeable source and review the various alternatives in a facilitated discussion.

- *Workplans.*   Workplans provide a useful checklist of issues and activities. Also, many IS professionals are comfortable using workplans. But, remember that many of the items in traditional methodologies simply don't apply in the intranet environment.

- *Action Items.*   Where appropriate, we identify specific actions for you to take.

- *Other Tools.*   In later chapters, we discuss a number of project management tools such as Microsoft Project, and several Internet-based project management tools (e.g., Major Domo and Sidekick), as well as an intranet-modified LBMS workplan (i.e., a popular methodology for developing applications in a client/server environment).

Summary of Steps

Now that you know a little more about the implementation process and the tools that we'll be using, let's start by summarizing each of the various steps in the 12-Step Program:

Step 1: Should We Implement?

This really is the fundamental question that you must deal with before moving on to the planning process. Take nothing for granted; your company may not benefit from intranet implementation at this time.

Essentially, there are three major components in this decision step:

- Defining your business goals and values to ensure that an intranet implementation is consistent with your corporate and/or IT objectives.
- Assessing your information needs to determine if an intranet can meet those needs.
- Identifying the business-enabling technology environments that support your core business values.

Any technology effort, intranet or otherwise, should meet your organization's goals for the future as well as its current needs. You must be able to clearly identify both the current needs and the future objectives to determine if your organization can benefit by implementing an intranet at this time. If your organization doesn't already have a clearly defined set of goals and objectives (i.e., a mission statement), this is a good time to develop one. Chapter 3 offers some ideas to help you prepare a mission statement (even if you choose to call it something else) and explains how the intranet project should fit into the goals of the organization as a whole, as well as the specific goals of the IT department. Ideally, at any point during a technology implementation project, you should be able to clearly identify how the project contributes value to the organization.

After you've defined (and documented) your organization's objectives, you're ready to begin the actual intranet evaluation process. The *Should We Implement?* questionnaire (shown in Figure 3.1) in Chapter 3 can help you with this determination process. Remember, there are no absolute answers! The outcome of this exercise should be a starting point for your overall intranet plan—if you do decide to implement.

If you decide *not* to implement an intranet at this time, we recommend that you revisit the issue in six to eight months. Communications technology is changing at an incredibly rapid pace, as
are many of the traditional methods for conducting business in
our increasingly global economy. In six or eight months, you may
find that your needs have changed sufficiently to warrant an
intranet, or that the necessary technology has decreased in price
to a level that makes an intranet cost-effective for your organization. If you decide that your organization can benefit from an
intranet implementation at this time, you should start to assess
your specific information needs and begin planning the type of
intranet you want to implement. (We discuss more about the various types of intranets in Chapter 7, Intranet Design.)

Information needs assessment is, by definition, a complex process, and one that is likely to require considerable time and
energy. Don't underestimate the cost involved in this process.
Short-changing your information needs assessment is almost certain to have a negative affect on the quality of your results. For
this reason, many organizations choose to hire outside help to
assist them in this phase of an implementation project. But,
whether you decide to perform your needs assessment with in-
house personnel or hire outside help, you're going to need a base
set of information about your organization, users, and existing
information systems. Chapter 3 describes the information that
you'll need and offers some suggestions for gathering it.

The actual process of determining how business and technology
values translate into tangible technology sets can be confusing.
You'll need to evaluate a range of factors including (but not limited
to) data access requirements—including speed and frequency of
retrievals, the integrity of your information base, and the age of
your existing information system and database. Also, consider how
your data should be structured or organized for consumption.

Fortunately, there are some good sources to help you with your
information needs assessment and to ensure that your technology
goals are consistent with your business goals. For example, BSG's
Technology Infrastructure Planning Service (TIPS) is an intensive,
facilitated process that guides you through a complete analysis of
your business and IT structure, then helps you to formulate a flex-

ible technology strategy for the future. We'll tell you more about I-TIPS (for Intranet-TIPS), which is the inter/intranet-specific version of TIPS in Chapter 3, but the important thing to remember here is that help is available from a variety of sources. Don't hesitate to seek it out—correctly defining your information needs and matching those needs with a feasible technology strategy are the first steps in building your intranet foundation.

Step 2: Do We Need Help?

If you've decided to proceed with your intranet implementation project, your next step is finding the "people power" to get the job done. You've probably heard how easy the HTML authoring language is to work with (and it is), but implementing an intranet involves numerous tasks in addition to HTML authoring, many of which are quite complex. The overall process—from these early planning stages through implementation—requires a variety of skills and experience levels. Few organizations initially have all of the resources they need to complete the process.

Of course, your existing staff is the first place to look for the resources that you'll need for your intranet implementation team. Begin by reviewing their capabilities and experience with respect to your implementation project requirements. Then, determine what additional resources you're likely to need and make plans to acquire them. Essentially, you have a choice of providing additional training for your in-house staff, hiring new staff members that already have experience in inter/intranet computing, outsourcing the project to a vendor, or partnering with an expert. Each option has its merits—and drawbacks—and may be a viable solution for your organization. The *Do We Need Outside Help?* questionnaire (Figure 3.3) in Chapter 3 is intended to help you identify some of the key issues to consider in deciding if you do need outside help.

USING AN OUTSIDE RESOURCE

If you do decide to look outside of your organization for the skillsets you need, you still must decide what kind of help you need and to what degree. Your options range from using an independent contractor for a single facet of the project (e.g., to implement the security system) to outsourcing the entire project to a consulting firm that specializes in inter/intranet technology. *Partnering,* an arrangement that combines some of the advantages of outsourcing with the advantages of in-house development, is another alternative you can consider.

The beauty of outsourcing is that it allows you to pass the burden—all those complex considerations and decisions—off to someone else and let them figure out how to satisfy your organization's needs. The arrangement is not without its drawbacks, however. Outsourcing is typically the most expensive type of outside help, it does little to increase your internal staff's knowledge and experience, and the success of your intranet relies almost entirely on an outside organization. Thus, your choice of an outsourcing firm is crucial to the success of your project. Chapter 3 includes a checklist (Figure 3.4) to help you select an outsourcing firm— never an easy decision.

Partnering offers an excellent compromise for organizations that are wary of outsourcing (and many are) and do not have sufficient in-house experience to successfully implement an intranet. In a partnering arrangement, you share the responsibilities and benefits of an IT project with an expert provider.

If you decide to try a partnering arrangement for your intranet project, find a company with experience in intranet implementation and have them work *with* (rather than for) your organization. This type of arrangement has two distinct advantages: The partnering company brings the skills and experience that you need for the project and works closely with your staff to build their skill level and ensure that your organization's needs are adequately addressed.

CONTINUE BUILDING YOUR PLAN

Incorporate your decisions from Step 2 into your intranet plan. By this time, you should be able to document your goals for the intranet and your strategy for implementing it (Step 1) as well as your plans for acquiring the necessary experience and skills to build it (Step 2). Now that you have a firm understanding of what you want to do, it's time to start enlisting assistance from outside of IT.

Step 3: Enlist User Support

Don't ever underestimate the value of your user community's support. Your project may be doomed from the start if the users don't support it. While this may sound overly dramatic, anyone who has been through technology migration can tell you how true it is. And, the need for user support is ongoing through all phases of your intranet implementation plan and through all segments of the organization.

First, you'll need to get *executive-level* support for the project. This support is important for two reasons: The executives are "steering the ship" and it is your responsibility—as one of the main "engines"—to let them know if there is sufficient power to reach the corporate goals. And, because the executives are ultimately responsible for paying the bills, they need to clearly understand that the intranet is a high-value proposition. We'll discuss a number of methods for gaining such support in chapter 3, but using a prototype (as we mention in Step 6) is one particularly effective method.

After you've enlisted the backing of the executives, try to identify the *grassroots* decision makers in your organization and gain their support as well. These grassroots leaders exist in all organizations, and they're not necessarily the individuals with titles. They are, however, usually individuals with considerable experience and responsibility, and their support for your intranet project can be nearly as valuable as that of the executives. Chapter 3 offers some ideas on winning this type of support and making these key individuals advocates for your project.

When your intranet plan is complete, be sure to communicate it to the rest of the organization, or at a minimum, share it with your user base. Use whatever information distribution resources are available within your organization (i.e., electronic discussion forums, newsletters, or bulletin boards) to let people know about the intranet project—what benefits it offers to the organization as a whole and how it may affect them as individuals.

Depending on the magnitude of change that the intranet represents in your organization, you may want to consider using more sophisticated methods to communicate the who/what/why/

when/how of the intranet project. Remember, change is frightening to many people and your project is much more likely to be successful if you address those fears at the beginning, rather than the end, of the project. Chapters 3 and 4 discuss these issues in greater detail.

COMMUNICATE VALUE

A demonstration of intranet capabilities is, unquestionably, the best way to convince users of the value of the technology. While nearly everyone knows about the existence of the Internet, surprisingly few have actually seen or used it (although this is changing rapidly). Even individuals that are familiar with cyberspace don't fully comprehend how the medium translates to *real* business. A good demonstration can help to clarify the issues and communicate the value of an intranet.

Above all, be honest and realistic with your future users (and everyone else in the organization, of course). You definitely don't want to encourage unrealistic expectations! If anything, be conservative and let the users be pleasantly surprised that the intranet is everything they expected—and a little more.

Because you'll need to maintain user support throughout the intranet project (and beyond), we recommend that you include in the intranet plan specific mechanisms for communicating with users and soliciting feedback. Typically, you'll want to devote from 5 to 10 percent of your intranet management effort to this type of ongoing communication, but we discuss the need for ongoing support more fully in Chapter 13.

Step 4: Address Organizational Issues

The intranet is a new breed of information technology. Much like the IT culture that conceived it, the intranet is a fast-paced, evolving medium that changes with ever increasing speed. So, how do you reconcile this type of technology with the existing corporate IT structure—especially an IT structure that is rigidly defined or resistant to change?

NEW TIMES, NEW ORGANIZATION

The answer—and it isn't always easy—is based on making corresponding changes in the IT structure. Where there were rules and rigidity, now there must be openness and agility. "Just-in-Time" implementations of "best-of-breed" technologies are requisite to the new, dynamic IT organization. In today's fast-track IT environment, it is no longer possible to spend months or years making plans and decisions; now, there are only weeks or months to debate issues, reach decisions, and implement changes. Fortunately, the entire industry seems to be moving in the same direction; users, vendors, programmers, and support people are all adjusting to the new pace of technology—albeit at different rates and with varying levels of resistance.

MANAGING THE INTRANET CULTURE

Effectively managing the new IT organization is a challenging task. The opportunities are great, but there are also lots of opportunities for chaos—and few organizations can survive chaos, let alone remain profitable. Chapter 4 discusses the potential effects of the intranet culture on organizations and suggests some ways to manage the necessary changes.

With some planning and organization, intranets do tend to be very manageable. But, as we discuss in Chapter 7, you'll need to consider manageability in your intranet design, at the same time understanding that there are some trade-offs with the other major design criteria.

Step 5: Determine Technical Architecture

One of the most fundamental decisions that you'll make with regard to your intranet is the technical architecture. There are essentially five basic intranet architectures (which we examine in detail in Chapter 5), each of which satisfies a specific set of needs. Chapter 5 also describes all of the basic components of intranet architecture and explains how these components fit into the intranet infrastructure—layer by layer.

The architectural components are the heart and soul of your intranet. Be sure to thoroughly research all of the available options, then seek information and bids from as many providers as you reasonably can. And, don't forget to document your decisions in the intranet implementation plan at each step along the way.

Finally, your selection of an appropriate communications technology is key to your intranet's performance. The comprehensive checklists in this book (particularly in Chapters 3 and 5) are intended to help you determine which type of service best fits your needs, and which provider offers the most cost-effective solution.

Step 6: Decide on Applications and Prototype

The next step in building your intranet is to decide which applications you're going to implement in the short- (3–6 months), medium- (6–12 months), and long-term (12–18 months). Obviously, you can't implement all of the selected applications at the same time, but the application prioritization matrix (figure 8.6 in Chapter 8) can help you prioritize your applications and determine an appropriate implementation sequence.

Be warned that this process can be rather intensive, depending on the size and complexity of the applications that you're considering moving to the intranet. On the other hand, try not to let your team get bogged down in details; this is not the design phase for the applications, merely the research and prioritization.

CHOOSE A PROTOTYPE

If you have not already done so, now is the time to pick a high-value, quick turnaround prototype that you can show to all levels of your support base. There are four basic types of prototypes: the "Overview," the "Strawman," the "Trojan Horse," and the "Glitz," all of which are intended to serve a specific purpose. Refer to Chapter 8 for a complete description of each of these prototypes.

After you've prioritized your applications and determined their implementation sequence, be sure to document those decisions and the corresponding implementation schedule in your intranet plan. If possible, begin to develop your prototype application immediately—even while you're still hammering out details of your plan. If you choose an appropriate prototype, and have a talented staff to implement it, the prototype may well be finished before your final plan.

Step 7: Complete Registration and IP Addressing

As soon as you decide to implement an intranet, be sure to register your Internet domain name and IP address with the InterNIC (the Internet Network Information Center)—domain names are disappearing rapidly. (Refer to Chapter 3 for the details on IP registration and reserving domain names.) Even if your intranet is going to be completely isolated from the outside world and you don't anticipate any need for Internet connectivity, you may well change your mind in the future. (Remember, the Internet is going to be a multibillion dollar transaction medium for consumers and businesses alike.)

Some companies are opting to reserve domain names now—even if they don't need them yet. Registering a domain name is still remarkably inexpensive, and having a good, easily identifiable name can be extremely valuable to your organization in the future. Depending on the outcome of your technical evaluation (in Step 1), you may want to reserve several domain names at once to accommodate your future needs.

Step 8: Finalize the Plan

At this stage, your intranet plan should really be taking shape; now is a good time to consider some longer-range issues for the intranet project. While you won't be dealing with the issues of migration, maintenance, and support for weeks or months yet, you should begin planning for them now and include your decisions in your intranet plan. Of course, as you get closer to the actual production environment, you may change some of your decisions, but at least you will have a structure for the entire planning and implementation process. We address each of these issues in detail in Chapters 11 and 12.

As you wrap up the plan, don't forget to build in management time for ongoing user interaction and communication. A relatively minimal investment in time at this stage can really pay off later in a satisfied user community. Also, put the finishing touches on the skills procurement plan you began in Step 2, adding whatever resources you think you may need.

ESTIMATE TIME AND COSTS

Now is also the time to assemble all of your plan details and generate time and cost estimates. The sample workplan available in Appendix B (Intranet Project Workplan) is intended to help you with this task. It is, unfortunately, nearly impossible to accurately estimate the cost of the hardware and software that you'll need for your intranet since prices fluctuate so wildly and vendors are "bundling" more and more items in their intranet-specific products. Do, however, try to list all of the various components that you know you'll need. You should be able to generate some type of ballpark cost estimate from this list; then, when you're nearing the start of actual implementation, obtain bids from as many suppliers as is feasible.

PLAN APPROVAL/SIGN-OFF

Depending on your organization's internal procedures, you may need to have your intranet plan reviewed and approved by multiple departments and/or levels of management. It is advisable to begin this approval/sign-off procedure as soon as possible after you finalize your plan, since it is often a lengthy process and you don't want to delay the intranet implementation.

The "deliverable" from this step is a working intranet implementation plan. Use this plan as a "living" document, modifying it as necessary throughout the build process. You—and your successors—will need the valuable information that you've collected during the planning stages to complete the implementation effort.

Step 9: Implement the Architecture

Now you're executing the plan! Your top priority now is to get the ball rolling on your communications infrastructure. Communications providers are notoriously slow and bureaucratic, so be sure to give yourself plenty of lead time. In fact, if you identify your communications requirements before you finish your implementation plan (and, if you don't need prior approval of the entire plan), begin soliciting bids from the communications companies as early in the planning process as possible.

Building your intranet architectural infrastructure is relatively straightforward—if you chose well during the planning phases. Now is the time to solicit bids from suppliers to acquire the hardware and software you're going to need. Remember to consider essential factors like ongoing support and upgradability, along with price, when you select the necessary vendors and components. Finally, you—or the suppliers—will need to configure the various components to fit your particular intranet infrastructure. Chapters 5 and 12, respectively, address the issues involved with intranet architecture and implementation.

Step 10: Develop the Applications

After you've successfully implemented your architecture, you can begin to design your intranet applications, using the implementation priority plan that you developed in Step 6. Of course, because intranet implementation is a dynamic process, you may have already started to design your applications, beginning, of course, with your prototype. And, by this stage, your prototype may be up-and-running, having (hopefully) gained an enthusiastic user base—all clamoring for additional intranet applications.

The functional design process for an intranet is much like that for any other system. Once you understand the business processes (which, of course, you should before you lock yourself into a toolset), you can apply the appropriate technology to solve the issue at hand. Designing for the intranet does, however, differ from traditional development efforts in a number of ways. The development timeframe, for example, is typically much shorter than that of traditional applications, and users are much more involved in the entire development effort—from defining application requirements through testing. And, intranet applications must be designed to function within the Web environment, taking advantage of the versatility and graphics capabilities of inter/intranet computing while maintaining compatibility with an ever-increasing number of specialized tools and interfaces, as well as the numerous legacy systems that maintain huge bases of information. Finally, testing is also somewhat different in an intranet environment. Rather than a set amount of time at the end of a development project, testing in an intranet environment is a ongoing (almost constant) process in which the users and developers share responsibility for the applications. The frequent iterations of an intranet application necessarily involve regular communication between the users and the developers. In fact, it's not rare for the users in an intranet environment to do much of their own HTML coding—the current Web authoring tools are that easy to use!

We address all of these various issues in detail in later chapters of this book: Chapter 7 focuses on intranet design considerations; Chapter 8 provides practical advice on the actual development effort—with special attention to the rapid, iterative nature of inter/intranet applications; Chapter 9 gives some guidelines for selecting tool sets and reviews the major tools categories; Chapter 10 focuses on the importance of designing for a browser interface; Chapter 11 describes the back-end applications that you may want to implement; and Chapter 12 discusses issues related to application migration and testing, as well as the policies and procedures you'll want to establish to maintain control over your intranet and the information that appears on it.

Step 11: Implement Intranet Policies and Procedures

Once your intranet infrastructure is in place and you are implementing applications, you'll need to establish some type of information dissemination policy. Whether your IT department maintains centralized control of the information that is published on the intranet, or the users have authoring tools at their disposal, you must be able to control the information that goes onto the intranet. If you don't establish policies to deal with who can (and can't) publish and to determine how information is to be linked and indexed, as well as updated and/or deleted, your intranet is likely to become a totally unorganized tangle of largely unusable information. And, don't fail to consider the liability issues involved in publishing information on your intranet—especially if your intranet is available to external users (i.e., linked to the Internet). Chapter 4 addresses several of these organizational issues—including the legal considerations—and Chapters 12 and 13 offer some suggestions for structuring and managing content. We've also included some sample guidelines and policies that you can use as templates for your site.

Remember, you're likely to be swamped with requests for additional applications as soon as your intranet goes into production—especially if you've garnered user support throughout the planning process and your prototype is an unmitigated success. You can make your life a bit simpler at this stage if you plan ahead and establish some mechanisms (even if it's only your E-mail box) for receiving suggestions, then categorizing and prioritizing them in your working intranet plan.

CONVERSION AND IMPLEMENTATION ISSUES

As with any production environment, you'll need to address conversion and implementation issues for your intranet project. We discuss many of these issues—as they relate to the intranet implementation—in Chapter 12. Our assumption here is that you've taken a product "live" before, so we focus on intranet-specific issues that are likely to come into play as you implement the system.

It is important to track your progress throughout the intranet implementation process (as it is with any development effort) both for reporting purposes and for future reference. When you embark on your next intranet development cycle, taking into account the time and effort that you've expended in this, be aware that your initial implementation effort will be invaluable—so don't rely on memory alone. Be sure to document each step of the way, focusing especially on your initial expectations and decisions.

Step 12: Managing the Intranet

You're there! The intranet is up and running. Now, all you have to deal with are the usual issues related to operating, supporting, and maintaining the environment. As with any other IS environment, you'll need a management structure that is stable, yet flexible, and dedicated to customer service.

Commitment and speed are the two essential components of managing an intranet operation. Expanding on the themes in Chapters 4 and 12, Chapter 13 (Managing the Intranet) discusses managing your intranet in our fast-paced business environment.

As technology delivers advances in data access and systems performance, user expectations rise at a corresponding rate, making it more and more difficult for the IT community to satisfy those expectations. Chapter 13 offers some guidelines for creating the type framework you'll need to manage your intranet (and the related information systems) and describes some of the tools that are available to help you automate the intranet management functions. It is possible to ensure a "service culture" in your organization, but you'll need to ensure that your user community's expectations are in tune with the intranet's capabilities. Perhaps most important, you'll need to establish an intranet management team that understands user requirements and can respond in a logical, reliable manner.

If All Else Fails

No one we know has ever completed a technology implementation project without encountering some unpredictable problems. That's just as true with intranet projects as with any other type of technology. Following the BSG 12-Step Program can help to avoid many such problems, but no two organizations are alike, nor are their intranet implementation requirements or the problems they encounter. Sometimes though, it's useful to know what procedures have been effective for other organizations during their implementation projects, or to learn where they've gone astray. Building on other organizations' experiences may help you to develop creative solutions to unusual problems or to avoid needless stress during the course of the intranet project. So, we include some "war stories" at the end of our 12-Step Program—case studies of intranet implementation projects that encountered those unpredictable problem situations. Of course, we also relate how the difficulties were resolved, from changes in intranet design or structure to modifications in the user expectations. And, we include some positive cases, situations in which even we were pleasantly surprised with the new intranet culture versus traditional client/server or legacy models.

CHAPTER THREE

TAKING THE FIRST STEPS

- ◆ Overview
- ◆ Making the Decisions
- ◆ Step 1: Should We Implement an Intranet?
- ◆ Step 2: Do We Need Help?
- ◆ Step 3: Enlist User Support
- ◆ The Registration Process

Overview

Although intranet architecture is often considered simpler than traditional client/server architecture, it does involve multiple tiers and a host of ever changing decision points that can seem quite bewildering. In Chapter 2 we reviewed the entire 12-Step Program from the initial "Shall we . . ." through production and support. Now we're going to get into the details and specifics of the process.

Before we get started, understand that although this book is sufficient to address the major issues and activities involved in implementing a modest, non-mission-critical intranet, it is not intended to replace the advice of experienced professionals—whether they are members of your IS group or from outside the company—who understand your particular organization and its intranet requirements. This book can, however, help you in conversations with them. It also provides invaluable checklists that ensure that you and your implementation team deal effectively with all of the planning and implementation issues involved in a successful intranet project.

Making the Decisions

In this chapter, we'll guide you through each of the early steps in the intranet planning process to help you reach the appropriate decisions—or at least prepare you for a facilitated session—for your particular environment and user requirements.

The questionnaires that accompany this and some of the later chapters are intended to be used in two ways:

1. *As a very simple way to reach an initial decision based on "ballpark" scoring.* Please note that we urge caution in using this approach for an enterprise-wide system or for one that is strategically critical or which potentially could expand into a very large system. Although developed to help you make a decision, it does not replace common sense or other impartial, knowledgeable advice.

2. *As a topic list for issues that you'll need to consider during the intranet planning process.* We strongly recommend that you consult with an experienced intranet professional when reaching these decisions. An intranet professional typically offers the benefit of past experience and objectivity, along with a broad technical knowledge. It is advisable to use one who is experienced in several implementation strategies; in general, avoid those with only a single solution.

Step 1: Should We Implement an Intranet?

In Chapter 2, we cautioned against making assumptions. The first assumption that you should avoid is that an intranet is right for your organization, or, that now is the right time to implement an intranet in your organization. An intranet may, indeed, be very beneficial for your organization and now may be the best time to begin the project. But you still want to ask yourself a series of questions about your business objectives and thoroughly assess your needs—then document the entire analysis—before proceeding further into the intranet implementation project.

Define Your Business Values

Of course, you should evaluate any new technology project in terms of its costs and benefits to the organization. An intranet is no different—its intrinsic value must be high enough to justify the time and expense required for its implementation. And, the objective of the intranet must be clearly defined and aligned with your overall business objectives. Finally, your choice of the actual technologies with which to implement an intranet project will largely depend on your organization's current position in the market and its goals for the short- and long-term future.

Remember that technology alone, no matter how wonderful it may seem, is completely meaningless in a business context unless it supports your overall goals. If you have a company mission statement, that is a good place to begin reviewing your goals with regard to the intranet. If you have an IT mission statement, that may be an even better place to begin. Use these documents as the starting point for all of your decisions about the intranet, and keep them in mind throughout the planning process. Your decisions should always relate directly back into your values.

If your organizational values aren't well-defined, you might want to search through some of the excellent books cramming the shelves at your local library or bookstores. They can help you immeasurably in this process (and, it's a useful process regardless of your decisions on an intranet project). But, if you're skeptical about the value of "mission"-type statements (and, you're not alone in that), try to keep in mind that such statements represent an excellent way for the people steering the ship to communicate the course to be traveled with the people doing the rowing. Granted, a mission statement has real value only if management knows where it wants the organization to go, and that the mission—once defined—is clearly and consistently communicated to everyone else. A mission statement and its corresponding objectives also provide a single, common reference point from which consensual decisions can be made—and this alone is often a real time-saver.

Similarly, if you have an IT department, it too should have a statement of goals and objectives—and those goals and objectives should be clearly communicated throughout the organization as well as in the department itself.

If, after defining or reviewing your business goals and values, you determine that an intranet is consistent with your objectives, you're ready to move on to the next phase in this decision process—determining if an intranet will meet your current and future needs. Should you consider implementing an intranet? If so, is this the right time for it? Obviously, you'll need to consider a wide range of factors here, but the questionnaire in Figure 3.1 should serve as a good starting point for most organizations.

Assuming that you now feel reasonably certain that an intranet is worth pursuing and that it is relevant to your business goals, your next step is to gather the materials you need to start your planning.

Information Needs Assessment

Depending on the size of your organization and the scope of your intranet considerations, your information needs assessment can be a massive process. In fact, as we mentioned in Chapter 2, many organizations choose to have an independent consultancy review their existing data structures and determine information requirements. If your information needs are large and/or complex, you (or your designated agent) will need to spend considerable time assessing the situation.

Whether you decide to perform the assessment yourself or hire an outside consultancy, you'll want to have the following information available for reference:

- ◆ *Background information* (i.e., history, reputation, perception, etc.) about the organization and the IS department (or equivalent), including a complete description of the company's physical and logical organization for people, processes, and decisions. Be sure to consider the company's tendency for change (i.e., how constant is the model? what kind of change is expected?).

- ◆ *Functional information* about the organization and its business structure (i.e., how does the business function

1. Do we have a need to communicate beyond a small, defined group? (Consider vendors and customers as well as staff.)
2. Do we acknowledge that the intranet phenomenon will have an enormous impact on the industries in which we compete?
3. Do we have more than 10 employees?
4. Are we in a service business?
5. Is our business related to or dependent upon technology?
6. Do we have more than one location?
7. Do we contact clients electronically?
8. Does our business address more than a very local market area (such as a convenience store)?
9. Does our current telcom bill represent a significant portion of our ongoing business expense?
10. Do we have a heterogeneous information technology environment (many differing systems and interfaces)?

Scoring

- If you answered "No" to nine or ten of these questions, you probably don't need an intranet at this time. You should probably defer implementation now and revisit the issue in six months (that's 2–3 years in "Web" time).

- If you answered "Yes" to between two and six questions, you may gain a competitive advantage from implementing an intranet at this time.

- If you answered "Yes" to seven or more questions, you definitely can gain a competitive advantage from an intranet.

Figure 3.1 *Should We Implement?* questionnaire.

now? what problems currently exist? what changes are anticipated?). A high-level functional flowchart of the business units and their interaction with internal and external entities is excellent for illustrating the business structure. If such a chart currently exists, be sure that it accurately reflects the business organization. If a functional flowchart doesn't currently exist, you may want to create one; it is invaluable for helping a consultant (or new members of your IT organization) to understand the flow of information within the organization. Finally, be sure to consider any identified needs that the ITs department can help to satisfy (e.g., E-mail systems or discussion mediums).

◆ *Systems information* about the organization's existing legacy systems. You'll need to know what functions the current systems perform and the users' level of satisfaction with them (i.e., what problems currently exist? are there identified needs that are not being met?). Then, review the IT standards for your industry, as well as the effort (i.e., in both time and cost) that would be required to satisfy identified needs and/or to gain competitive advantage. Finally, determine if there are plans (or expectations) to build new systems or expand existing ones. If such plans exist, what functional purpose are they intended to serve?

◆ *Scheduling information* (i.e., time constraints) that may affect your decision to implement an intranet or help you determine what kind of intranet you're going to implement. This information is closely related to the systems information and, to a slightly lesser degree, the functional information, and may be key to gaining user and management support for the intranet project. In other words, if the intranet can address identified needs within an acceptable timeframe, both users and management are likely to support it—but they may also impose unacceptable time constraints on the project.

> **T**IP *Identify and prioritize information needs: Use this basic set of information to systematically identify and prioritize the information needs in your organization, noting the "best-case" timing for each. Remember, you're identifying and prioritizing at this stage, not planning systems! The platform is irrelevant at this point.*

Begin now to evaluate your technology options, considering both your overall approach to information management as well as your general technical direction for specific functions. Given the enormous number of options available—in traditional information management systems as well as intranet computing technology—the evaluation alone can be an overwhelming task.

I-TIPS

At this point, you may want to use a tool like I-TIPS to ensure that your technological goals (i.e., implementing an intranet) are consistent with your corporate business goals. The TIPS (Technology Infrastructure Planning Service) process was developed by consultants at BSG and Object Space specifically to help organizations to develop a solid foundation for strategic technology investments. A structured, business-driven process, TIPS (and I-TIPS, the intranet-specific version of the process) is intended to complement traditional, technology-driven planning methodologies.

I-TIPS can help your organization identify the business-enabling technology environments that are consistent with your core business values. It entails a series of intensive, facilitated sessions that bring together your organization's internal business and IS partners with expert consultants who provide industry, technology, and organizational perspectives, as well as process facilitation.

I-TIPS uses a structured approach to relate each technology alternative back to a specific business value, making the value the dominant driver in your decisions. The process, which normally requires three to five days of intensive, facilitated sessions, can deliver a solid technology plan that is tailored to an organization's specific needs. If your organization doesn't currently have a strategic technology plan, you should consider developing one. It could be the single best investment you make toward ongoing IT success.

Once you decide to proceed with an intranet, be sure to document all of the information that you've gathered in Step 1 and incorporate it into your overall plan for intranet implementation. Your future decisions about the intranet will need to adhere to this framework.

Step 2: Do We Need Help?

Your next major step after you've decided to proceed with an intranet implementation project is to begin identifying and acquiring the resources you'll need to do the job. As we mentioned in Chapter 2, implementing an intranet requires a range of skills and experience—as well as flexibility and a willingness to continually learn new skills and adopt new technologies.

Remember, the quality of your intranet implementation team is key to the success of your project. (We'll talk more about assembling your intranet team in Chapter 4.) The team—collectively—should be familiar with all aspects of the underlying intranet technology. Only the intelligent application of that technology—in a constantly changing environment—can assure the success of your intranet. We've all heard too many horror stories of perfectly good technology misapplied by well-intentioned, but underinformed teams.

Regardless of how much—or how little—experience your implementation team has, keeping current with the ever widening array of Web technology options is likely to be one of its biggest challenges. The team members will need to make a conscious, continuing effort to read, explore, and use emerging toolsets. Fortunately, books and magazine articles abound, but the Internet itself is still the best source of all for practical, hard-core information about Web technologies—and it's free.

Don't hesitate to enlist knowledgeable assistance for any or all phases of your intranet project. Some phases of the project will, of course, require greater skill and knowledge than others (basic HTML authoring, for instance, is *very* low-tech) but for many organizations, this type of implementation project represents uncharted territory.

Skills Assessment

Begin your skills assessment by reviewing your current staff's skills and experience. Determine not only what skills they are likely to bring to the intranet project, but also their level of availability. Some staff members will, of course, have to maintain the existing information systems and respond to user requests during the implementation project. (The systems information that you gathered in Step 1 can help you to estimate staff availability here.)

If you're not sure what skills your existing staff can contribute to the intranet project, ask them to complete a skills matrix. This type of skills review can help you—and the employees—determine where their strengths lie and what they can best contribute to the implementation project. The BSG Skills Matrix, explained on our Web site, is one good source of ideas. It is a self-evaluation tool that can help your staff to assess their skills. Then, we recommend that you individually review the completed matrix with each staff member to target the individuals that can bring needed skills to your intranet project.

Remember, you're trying to assemble a team, and skills and experience don't necessarily indicate that an individual is well-suited to be a team member. You're also looking for versatility, flexibility, and a willingness to learn. The net-based skills interview presented in Figure 3.2 offers some additional suggestions for interviewing existing staff members or potential new hires for your intranet implementation team.

A note of caution, if you're not thoroughly familiar with inter/intranet technology and tools, you should probably skip ahead and read some of the later chapters in this book before you conduct this type of an interview. We suggest, at a minimum, reading Chapter 5 (Intranet Architectures), Chapter 9 (Intranet Tools), and Chapter 10 (The User Interface) to give you a better idea of the skills and experience that you're looking for.

1. Ask to see examples of the individual's HTML work. For example, does the individual have a "home page" on the Internet? If not, what other examples of HTML work can he or she show? (If the individual can't show you any samples of HTML authorship, it may well indicate that he or she doesn't have HTML authoring experience. Web developers are notoriously willing to show off their work, so reticence or an inability to demonstrate a completed project should raise a red flag.)

2. Look for good design in the screens—visual aesthetics as well as a logical flow of information. All of the screens (i.e., pages) should be linked and logically organized.

3. Ask about the use of advanced techniques (i.e., animated GIFs) in their pages. Are they using Netscape plug-ins? JavaScripting? or CGI scripting? Do the pages incorporate any custom HTML tags? It's a good idea to have the individual explain each of the pages to you, including their objectives for the sample work and their use of the technology. Also, try to assess their vision of the future—their own and that of the technology; their answers may indicate their willingness to learn and/or adapt as the technology (and your project) evolves.

4. Ask the individual to show you some of the code they have developed and discuss how the pages might be modified or improved. Try to determine the *depth* of their understanding and experience. Remember that linear time is nearly irrelevant to good Web developers; some very talented people can demonstrate incredible results in only six months,

Figure 3.2 Net-based skills interview.

especially if they have prior technical experience and are eager to expand their knowledge base.

5. Ask if they have any referenceable object experience? Again, their answers may indicate their level of involvement with the technology and their willingness to learn.

Figure 3.2 *(Continued).*

Acquiring Skills

As we mentioned in Chapter 2, few (if any) organizations begin an intranet implementation process with all of the resources they need readily available. So, if your organization is like most, you have three major options for acquiring the inter/intranet skill sets that you need—training your existing staff, hiring new staff members, or hiring outside help.

TRAINING

Depending on your company's attitude toward staff development and the availability of existing staff to move into the new technology area, you may wish to entertain training as an option. It does offer a number of advantages and the decision can easily be rationalized:

- Many elements of internet computing are relatively quick and easy to learn, especially for individuals who already understand information systems basics.
- Using in-house IS staff for your intranet implementation allows you to leverage the existing IT experience, business knowledge, and traditional skills (like networking).

Because intranet computing—and the underlying Web technologies—are a major focus for many companies, many business and community colleges, technical schools, and universities are offering a variety of training courses. So, you should have lots of options available if you decide to invest in training for existing staff members. Don't, however, confuse classroom hours with hands-on experience. Classroom training can provide a good foundation in the basic technologies, but there is no substitute for experience. For that reason, many Web developers express disdain for classroom training sessions. A "certificate of completion" is not necessarily indicative of Web expertise.

If you do decide that training is a viable option for acquiring the skills you need for the intranet project, you should be aware that it is a "seller's market" for inter/intranet skills. You'll need to seriously consider how you can retain the newly knowledgeable staff members, given the competitive environment for "Webmasters." Remember, you're likely to be competing for intranet skillsets with many other early-stage companies in a wide range of businesses. Many of your competitors are willing (and able) to offer attractive incentives, including flexible work environments, lucrative salaries, and substantial stock options.

HIRING

If you decide that you need to hire new, Web-specific talents for your organization, you'll come face to face with the competitive environment for "Webmasters." Not long ago, individuals with inter/intranet experience were in good supply and commanded average salaries. But things change quickly in the world of Web technology. Table 3.1 reports the results of a 1995 survey of New York–based "Webmasters." As you can see, "Webmaster" salaries have increased rapidly in a remarkably short period of time.

It is, of course, possible to hire "Webmasters" for less than $100K per year, but as the table illustrates, salary scales are climbing rapidly and gaining momentum. This trend is unlikely to change—at least during the foreseeable future.

TABLE 3.1   Webmaster Salary Survey Results

Average annual salary for a Webmaster (1995)	
June	$35,000
July	$45,000
November	$110,000

If you decide to hire, use the same skills assessment guidelines as you applied in your internal staff assessment. A skills matrix can give you a good idea of the individual's overall systems knowledge (i.e., do the skills extend beyond making "pretty" pages?) and an interview that focuses on the net-based skills issues (see Figure 3.2) should also indicate the individual's command of the available toolsets.

INDEPENDENT CONTRACTORS

If you determine that your organization—through in-house experience, training, and/or hiring—can successfully implement most facets of the intranet, but needs to acquire a specific skillset to assist with the implementation of a particular piece of your intranet (e.g., security), you might do well to hire an experienced independent contractor. A word of caution here, however: Many of the most highly skilled Web technical consultants are the embodiment of "counterculture." It's not unusual for technical "superstars" to have pierced body parts, tattoos, and unconventional coiffures. In fact, some seem to believe that an unusual appearance is a prerequisite for talent.

And, the Web superstars can be difficult to deal with; some are absolutely arrogant while others merely seem tactless. In any case, they don't always interact well with the traditional denizens of Corporate America or, at best, they make such interaction very challenging. We've found, however, that most independent Web technical contractors are well worth their idiosyncrasies, so try not to overlook their talents or potential contribution to your project because of their appearance or initial attitude. There are, of course, inter/intranet technology superstars that are relatively conformist, but the selection is fairly limited.

Outside Resources

Seeking help from outside your organization is the obvious alternative to training your existing staff or hiring new staff members, but here again you face a range of options. How much help do you need and what kind?

Up to this point we've really been discussing your options for bringing inter/intranet talents in-house. Although the in-house approach gives you a lot of control and leverages your experience for the future, it also puts the responsibility for implementation squarely on your IS team. Using an outside resource allows you to share that responsibility, and leaves your staff available to continue supporting the existing legacy system during the implementation process.

Whether you need help to implement your intranet depends on a range of factors, principally the size and complexity of the intranet you need, and the experience (and availability) of your in-house staff. In reality, there is no substitute for experience; if the intranet is a major strategic initiative for your organization or if it involves complex security issues, you should probably be hesitant about relying solely on in-house expertise.

The questionnaire in Figure 3.3 is designed to help you determine if you need outside help with your implementation project and, if so, what level of help. Like all other questionnaires and matrices in this book, it is intended for general-purpose, "vanilla" intranet projects. If your organization has special requirements, be sure to factor those into your decision.

There are a number of important issues to consider when selecting and managing an outside resource. Many of the old rules that applied to using professional service firms for help with main-

◆ How quickly do we need to develop the intranet and have it in production?

◆ How complex are the applications that we'll be using on the intranet?

◆ Are the application development skills readily available?

◆ How essential is the intranet and its applications to the company's business expectations?

◆ What is the organization's philosophy and experience regarding the use of outside help?

Figure 3.3 *Do We Need Outside Help?* questionnaire.

frame or client/server applications don't make sense for selecting an intranet help provider. For example, creativity and an innovative approach to the intranet application are just as valuable to inter/intranet architectures as a sophisticated development "methodology" and a deep bench of technical and industry luminaries who understand your business.

Also, intranet technology project timeframes are significantly different from those of traditional architectures; be sure that your help vendor is attuned to these differences. For example, the contract for an intranet help provider should not typically extend beyond one year, as compared to the traditional 1- to 10-year contract with a professional service firm. The rate of change in the inter/intranet market is much too fast for you to commit to a particular technology or vendor for more than a year or two at the most.

Partnering Versus Outsourcing

So, if you decide that you need help, you must still determine what kind of help is most appropriate for your organization. Again, there are no easy answers. You may find that the initial expense for partnering is a bit higher than just outsourcing the project, but partnering is an effective means for training your staff and may facilitate bringing the intranet implementation and management functions entirely in-house at some point. Also, partnering typically offers the most relevant and cost-effective training for your staff (although the knowledge transfer does take some time).

OUTSOURCING

Outsourcing offers a number of very tangible potential benefits: Your organization is essentially a "customer" contracting for service and, because your IS staff is largely absolved of the day-to-day tasks involved in the intranet implementation, they are free to maintain the legacy systems and respond to user requirements in the near-term. Outsourcing may also be the fastest and most efficient means for implementing an intranet; this is especially important if you have severe time constraints or are implementing an intranet for mission-critical applications. If you choose wisely, an outsourcing firm can bring all of the skillsets and experience that are necessary to plan and implement an intranet tailored to fit your organization's particular requirements.

Obviously, there are also some disadvantages to outsourcing. Because you are "buying" technical skills and experience, outsourcing is often the most expensive option for an implementation project. And, choosing someone to outsource to is a major decision in itself—one that can easily determine the fate of your project.

Be sure to thoroughly review the skills and resources of the outsourcing firms you consider working with, including their implementation staff members. You may want to use some of the same skills evaluation questions as you used to review your in-house staff. And, regardless of the outsourcing firm that you select, be sure that you have a contract that defines both your expectations and the outsourcer's, as well as a detailed service-level agreement that covers all possible contingencies (or, at least all of the contingencies that you can think of).

If you decide that outsourcing is a viable option for your organization, use the checklist in Figure 3.4 to help you choose an outsourcing firm:

PARTNERING

Partnering combines many of the merits of in-house development with the strengths of outside expertise. After all, no one knows your business as well as you do, and systems integrators make it their business to know technology and how to apply it. In this respect, partnering can form an unbeatable team for your implementation project. And, because a partnering company works *with,* rather than for, your IS department, your staff members have the opportunity to gain hands-on experience in the underlying web technologies. This experience can be invaluable for managing the intranet in the future and for any future implementation projects.

Partnering goes beyond the traditional concept of consulting, however, in that it is based on the notion of truly sharing risks and rewards. The goal of a good partnering arrangement is to provide mutual benefit, unlike the generic fee-for-service exchange in an outsourcing arrangement.

If you decide to try a partnering arrangement, your first step is to find a partner company that can bring the technical expertise that you need to the project. Your choice here, much like choosing an outsourcing firm, is key to the success of your entire project. Use the same selection guidelines (Figure 3.4) to select a company with good partnering potential. Then, jointly determine what level of partnering is best for both partners. You can use a partnering arrangement at any (or all) of three levels of involvement: preliminary information and planning, development and implementation, or ongoing service. Your choice of a partnering level depends on the type of technical assistance and

◆ Is the firm large enough to comfortably manage a project of your size?

◆ Has the firm had prior experience with intranet implementation for companies of your type?

◆ Does the firm have experience in developing major intranet systems of the type you're contemplating? (Remember that intranet applications involve a far broader set of skills than just developing a pretty Web site.)

◆ Is the firm experienced with several approaches to intranet implementation or is the company just selling one vendor's solution?

◆ Is the firm recognized by industry analysts as being a leader in this field?

◆ Does the firm have a system (or methodology) appropriate for intranets.

◆ Is the firm experienced in building secure systems? At the very least, you will need to seriously consider security issues; in all probability you will want to implement a secure system.

Figure 3.4 Choosing outside help.

expertise that you need and, of course, the technical expertise and experience that the partnering company can bring to the project.

A note of caution here: Once you've selected a partnering company and determined the appropriate level of involvement, be sure to thoroughly document your expectations for the project and for the partnering arrangement. And, don't forget that the partnering arrangement necessarily involves mutual risks and rewards; both companies should understand the goals of the project and mutually share the responsibilities for the implementation.

Step 3: Enlist User Support

User support, or the lack of it, can literally make or break your intranet project. Like any new technology, the inception, implementation, and support of an intranet will need plenty of backing. Even the best solutions can be "hard sells" because much of the organization will feel either confused or threatened. Although an intranet is not a cure-all, it should be a relatively easy sell in terms of quick, demonstrable value. If you plan ahead, anticipate your users' needs and possible objections, and communicate the intranet message in a timely, consistent manner, you should be able to rally the support you need for project success.

Gaining Executive Support

If you are not on the executive board yourself, try to identify a "champion" for the project—an individual who understands that the organization can gain a competitive business advantage through an investment in technology. The project "champion" may be the executive to whom you directly report or an individual in another department; in fact, if you identify multiple "champions" in the same or different departments, so much the better. Sometimes, you find a "champion" in an unexpected place. For example, the VP of Human Resources championed a recent intranet implementation project in one large company that we know of. That individual more readily recognized the value of technology to benefit the company's competitive position than the CFO did, despite the fact that the IS department actually reported to the CFO.

Be sure to stay in regular contact with your project champion(s) during the course of the project to ensure (1) that you understand the executive board's objectives for the project and that you're meeting them, and (2) that the board acknowledges the IS department's efforts and contributions. Unfortunately, the IS department is often seen as expensive "overhead," so take the time to ensure that the board understands both the value of the department and the intranet project.

Some of the major points to focus on when dealing with the executive-level decision makers are the intranet's relatively low cost to implement, rapid development patterns, and improved access to timely information. It may also be helpful to identify board members' "hot topics"—those areas of special interest that nearly everyone has—and (if possible) explain what effect the intranet is likely to have in these areas. But, as we mentioned in Chapter 2, be somewhat conservative and don't raise unrealistic expectations. Ideally, the executive-level decision makers will recognize the intranet's inherent potential but not view it as the ultimate solution to all of the organization's communication and management problems.

An intranet can, however, provide many unexpected benefits. At one company we know, many of the executives and staff felt out-of-touch with their fast-moving CEO. He, in turn, was bewildered by a seeming lack of support for his constantly shifting priorities. In truth, he was moving at a different pace than the rest of the company and not adequately communicating his focus through the ranks of the organization. The intranet, however, provided an incredibly simple means for solving this problem. The IS department developed a discussion mechanism that the CEO can use to articulate his vision, and the other employees—from the executive level down through the ranks—can use to discuss the ideas and respond. In reality, the application is somewhat more sophisticated—with tiers of goals, objectives, and specific action items for the organization as a whole and by department—but it is a practical and somewhat creative application of intranet technology. It is also an effective way to show the value of an intranet.

If you're going to build a prototype to demonstrate the intranet's capabilities—and a prototype is one of the most effective means for gaining both executive and user support for the project—you should look for just this type of application. An ideal prototype addresses an identifiable problem and provides a practical, creative solution that is not easily available through traditional technology. But, don't go overboard in your choice of a prototype application; it must be "do-able" in a relatively short amount of time and it should be "fail-proof." We talk more about the various types of prototypes that you may want to consider in Chapter 7 and give some pointers for identifying an appropriate application.

Grassroots Support

In addition to enlisting executive-level support, you need to win the support of the user community at large—the individuals who will actually be using the intranet on a day-to-day basis. One of the most effective ways to gain this type of broad-based support is to cultivate the grassroots leaders in your organization. The grassroots leaders are not necessarily the individuals with titles (although they may, indeed, be group managers or supervisors). They are, however, typically individuals who understand and appreciate technology and have gained the respect of their peers. If you've been with your organization for more than six months, you can probably name at least a half-dozen grassroots leaders in a couple of minutes with minimal effort—assuming that you keep your eyes and ears open.

When you identify the grassroots leaders, take the time to explain the goals of the intranet and describe how it will fit within the organization's existing infrastructure (as opposed to replacing that infrastructure). Then, ask for their ideas and listen to their suggestions; these individuals can become valuable advocates for the intranet! Remember, you generally won't get meaningful input unless (or until) the individuals understand and support the project, and a low-key approach—asking rather than telling—is generally most effective in gathering support.

Once you've enlisted their support, you can work with the "advocates" on a formal or informal basis. If your organization is small enough, an informal basis is usually very effective; the information exchange process can be more personal and meaningful, and less bureaucratic. Unfortunately, an informal approach probably isn't feasible if your organization has more than 200 or 300 users.

If you need a more formal approach, consider creating an IT "advocates" group. You can, of course, still solicit their opinions on an individual basis during the course of the project or organize small, *brief* meetings to discuss ideas for applications or review design suggestions. Be prepared to give your advocates some "ownership" of the project—perhaps by making them part of a user input group (for development iterations, etc.)—in return for their early support of the initiative.

Figure 3.5 summarizes some things to look for in good advocates.

After you've identified and enlisted advocates for the project, be sure to communicate with them on a regular basis. Don't overwhelm them with information, but do send them periodic updates on the project and solicit their ideas or suggestions in areas that may affect their jobs or departments. We're not suggesting that you play favorites with the advocates, or their departments, but do make sure that they know they're appreciated.

User community communications. You'll also need to communicate regularly with the overall user community to make sure that they understand early in the project lifecycle what the intranet is and isn't (especially *not* the Internet). As soon as you have formal approval for the intranet project and a clear set of goals, spread the word! Members of your corporate community (i.e., the user community and the organization as a whole) like to know what's going on and to feel that they're involved. They also like to know management's views about the new technologies and—perhaps most important—how the new technology will affect them and their role in the organization.

There are lots of effective means for communicating with your corporate community and easing their apprehension about new technologies and changing methodologies. Essentially, you should use whatever medium is most effective at reaching the greatest number of people in your organization and presenting them with clear, timely information. Any of the following can work well:

◆ *Electronic newsletters.*   If your company has E-mail or some type of groupware medium, you may already have electronic newsletters. These are generally an excellent place to publish articles about the intranet project, its objectives, and the potential user benefits. Depending on

◆ Individuals who are interested in, or talented with, technology. You know the type—the people who frequently ask you about new software and/or know more cool keyboard tricks than you do.

◆ Individuals who have gained the respect of their peers and communicate well at all levels of the organization. Unfortunately, the shy, quiet individual—however talented and well-intentioned—can't be an effective advocate for your project, nor can the know-it-all that everyone tries to ignore.

◆ Individuals with a can-do attitude and a desire to help others. These people are usually willing to encourage their peers to try new systems, and to think of systems as tools rather than as confusing new obstacles.

◆ Individuals who are continually busy, but not over-whelmed. You don't want to burden someone who is already buried under work, but people who like to stay busy and who enjoy new challenges some-how seem to make the time they need to explore new ideas and systems. Your advocates should be busy, efficient people who know how to use tech-nology to make themselves more productive.

Figure 3.5   Selecting project advocates.

your corporate culture, you may find it most effective to regularly publish brief articles—perhaps one per week—about the project to reinforce your message, expanding and changing the information a little bit each time. If you already have a name for your intranet, start using it now to generate name recognition.

◆ *Electronic posters.*   If you have electronic discussion or bulletin boards, use them to post information about the intranet project. Use the same type of information as an electronic newsletter, but focus more on graphics than text. If possible, use some creative graphic designs and a Web-type layout.

◆ *Brochures.*   With some creative artwork and a good, *brief* message, a brochure can be an excellent medium to communicate a new IT initiative. This medium is gener- ally most effective for organizations that don't have a corporate E-mail system or when used to express a major shift in IT strategy. (In other words, a small intranet ini- tiative probably doesn't need this kind of "sell.") If they're carefully planned, brochures can be surprisingly inexpensive. In many cases, you can design them in- house and incur only the printing expense.

◆ *Posters.*   Admittedly low-tech, printed posters can effectively communicate your message to virtually all employees in an organization. Nearly all companies have corporate bulletin boards that display the current policies, events, and so forth. Use this medium to present a brief, graphical description of the intranet proj- ect and focus on the benefits that it offers to the organi- zation as a whole. Posters are a relatively low-cost means of creating name recognition and familiarity with the intranet concept.

◆ *E-mail.*   If your organization doesn't have groupware or an electronic newsletter, use the E-mail system to "spread the word." Broadcast an E-mail bulletin to all of the system users. But, remember to keep your message short (one screen) and easy to read. If possible, include a return address or set up an intranet project E-mail address so that employees can pose questions and/or offer suggestions.

Your communication with the corporate community need not be long or complex. In fact, the most effective communications are as simple and concise as possible; many individuals resist reading lengthy articles, regardless of the format or medium. Like almost everything in corporate culture, communications should follow the tried-and-true K.I.S.S. (Keep It Simple Stupid) principle. Your goal is to keep people informed of the changes around them, not to burden them with meaningless trivia.

Do emphasize the potential benefits of the intranet throughout your communications; stress the intranet's potential for reducing paper and E-mail volume while improving the quality and timeliness of internal information. One company we know gradually weaned its employees away from the paper newsletter by publishing articles *about* the new electronic version that appear on the intranet instead of in their in-boxes. When the newsletter application was finally implemented on the intranet, the new format was an overwhelming success!

SOLICIT FEEDBACK

Your project champions and advocates can be helpful in many ways. They are often excellent sources for the information that you *don't* hear—the rumors and grumblings that many individuals (especially in a corporate community) are reluctant to discuss openly. Try to keep the informal lines of communication to tap into this user "underground." If the advocates and champions aren't comfortable bringing these issues to you, be sure to *ask* them what they hear from the "underground." Then, solicit their opinions on the issues and, wherever possible, be sure that the answers get back to the original grumblers.

HTML DEMONSTRATION

Finally, your users are much more likely to be supportive of the intranet project if they can actually see how it functions and understand first-hand how it will operate in the organization.

We've prepared a basic demonstration to help you illustrate the ease and versatility of intranet technology and to gauge your users' reactions.

Available on the BSG Web site, this document is designed to show valuable introductory features of I-Net technology. After customizing it for your own purposes, you may want to schedule a seminar for your users and encourage them to ask questions and/or voice their concerns about the intranet. This type of seminar is usually most advantageous if you have support from the entire IS staff and any outside resources that are assisting you with the implementation project.

Whatever you do, be sure that your users have realistic expectations for the intranet. Describe its benefits in both the long- and short-term, acknowledging any problem areas that you anticipate during the implementation phase. The real benefits of the intranet may not be apparent until the long-term—after a number of applications have been ported to the intranet and/or external Web access provided. Your users will feel more comfortable living through the transition phases if they know what long-term advantages to expect.

The Registration Process

Although you don't actually have to complete the registration process until much later in your intranet implementation project (Step 7), we're including it here because the time element of registration is critical. You may want to complete Steps 4 through 6 before you register a domain name and/or IP address, but we recommend that you begin the registration process as soon as possible after you have approval for the intranet project—even if you haven't yet decided if you're going to have an Internet link or need a domain name. In fact, it's generally wise to register several names—any that you think you may want to use since you can configure a single server to be accessed by any one of several names.

Registration for domain names is still remarkably inexpensive. As this book went to press, you could still reserve an Internet domain name for two years for only $100 (U.S.). Two years is, after all, quite a long time—especially in Web years—in which to decide if you're going to implement an intranet or link your intranet to the Internet. And names, particularly generic names like www.flowers.com, are disappearing rapidly. Even specific names such as your own company name may already be taken. If this is the case, don't despair! In 1996 the InterNIC adopted a policy of trying to re-allocate names to those holding the trademark. In any case, it's best to avoid potential domain name problems by registering as soon as possible.

Registering IP Addresses

IP address registration depends on the size of your organization. Small organizations typically need a Class C registration while large organizations need either a "contiguous block of Class C registrations" or a Class B registration.

Visit the InterNIC WWW site to apply for either type of registration. Be sure that you apply as *one* organization (as opposed to a department within a larger organization) because eventually if not immediately you need to establish an enterprise-wide IP addressing convention.

TIP   *Register your domain name and IP addresses: To register for a domain name, visit the InterNIC site at http://www.internic.net and complete the online registration form.*

ESTABLISH IP ADDRESSING CONVENTIONS

If your intranet is isolated from the Internet or you have a proxy firewall, you can—at least in theory—use any IP network number. You should, however, assume that at some point your intranet will be connected to the Internet. For this reason, you should have a unique set of IP addresses to ensure that your network number is globally unique. Connecting directly to the Internet without a unique network number can cause extensive problems—both for your own network and for other Internet users. Similarly, you'll need to allocate a set of unique IP addresses within your organization to avoid major problems with your own internal addresses.

The most common way of allocating internal IP addresses is to establish a series of logical subnets within the organization as a whole. (As we've mentioned, it's advisable to coordinate activities throughout your entire organization and develop a single enterprise-wide IP addressing convention.) You'll also want to establish enterprise-wide procedures to reallocate internal IP addresses to correspond with changes in your organization and/or staff. A more sophisticated approach to IP address allocation is to dynamically configure the IP devices within your network. In this way, an IP address is allocated for each session as a device logs onto the network.

The good news is that you can delay establishing the subnets until you are further along in the intranet planning process. Just being aware of the IP addressing conventions and need for enterprise-wide coordination is sufficient for now.

At this point, you have made solid progress in your intranet implementation. You have a plan for meeting your business needs, acquiring the skills you need to get the job done, and gaining support within the organization. In the next chapter, we discuss some of the organizational issues that you need to address in the early stages of your project.

CHAPTER FOUR

ORGANIZATIONAL ISSUES

- ◆ Overview
- ◆ Evolving Corporate Structure
- ◆ Cultural Issues
- ◆ Organizing the Intranet Implementation Project
- ◆ Integrating the Intranet with the IS Organizational Structure
- ◆ Legal Issues

Overview

Clearly, the process of planning and implementing an intranet is not an easy task! It involves multiple, interrelated steps in a fast-moving environment where yesterday's decisions may be superseded by today's information. Dealing with the organizational and cultural effects that an intranet can have on your organization, however, may be just as challenging a task as finding and implementing the appropriate technology. A number of cultural, structural, and procedural issues relate directly to the effects that intranets have on organizations. And, like all other aspects of planning for an intranet, it's advisable to be aware of these issues and prepare for them in the early stages of your intranet project.

In this chapter, we discuss the evolving corporate environment and review each of the major issues, then suggest ways in which you can optimize the impact of the intranet within your organization. Finally, we look at some of the legal issues that you should be aware of with regard to your intranet and offer some suggestions for dealing with them—along with some resources that can help you to avoid legal problems in implementing and managing your intranet.

Evolving Corporate Structure

The unprecedented rate of growth of inter/intranet technology requires corporations to implement a new type of agile, responsive, organizational structure. Several large corporations, including Sony, AT&T, US West, Intel, and IBM among others, are addressing this need by establishing intranet development teams that function as small, fairly autonomous groups with cost center or other expense responsibility. Beyond attending to this responsibility, the groups operate essentially independently—sometimes even competing in application areas with the existing IS application development groups.

For the most part, these corporations chose this type of organizational structure for their intranet groups because they believe that a competitive, creative environment lets the groups demonstrate how they can contribute maximum value to the organization. Before implementing this type of structure, however, most of the corporations had to ask (and answer) a number of basic questions. You too, should consider these questions with regard to intranet planning and your current organizational structure:

◆ Are we prepared to accept the changes that may be necessary in our existing IS organization and infrastructure?

◆ Are we prepared to commit the necessary resources to gain the skills to build or migrate to intranet-based applications systems?

◆ Are we prepared to provide incentives for the talent we need to acquire and develop and, more important, retain?

◆ Do we want to open our intranet(s) and become involved in the Internet marketplace (or can we afford not to)?

In addition to providing honest answers to these questions, you must be willing to commit to the necessary changes in your organizational structures and methodologies to ensure that your organization realizes the maximum benefits of intranet development.

Like so many issues that are change-driven, however, this commitment must extend beyond new policies and reporting relationships. You must be committed to recognizing and addressing the cultural effects that an intranet will have on your organization.

Cultural Issues

The "cultural" nuances of the intranet may differ considerably from the traditional culture of the organization. The intranet, with its emphasis on open communications, collaboration, and knowledge management, tends to break down traditional organizational structure. In addition, it introduces attention to graphical design and begs for improved writing skills—traditional "soft skills" that have, in many companies, taken a back seat to the so-called "hard skills" such as programming or accounting. In today's competitive environment, however, as more companies realize the benefits of their intranets to the corporate information flow, the cultural playing field between "soft" and "hard" skills is leveling, with equal emphasis being placed on both.

An intranet also introduces a pronounced awareness of the pace of change within the organization. Already, the rate of change brought about by the wave of internet computing technologies is quite unprecedented, even in industries accustomed to rapid change. Coping with this rate of change has led many organizations into a different culture—one that is less formal, less planned, and which leans toward rapid prototyping and short development cycles. These rapid product cycles, often expressed in terms of "Web years," can make even fruit flies seem leisurely. The new corporate culture also emphasizes the rapid assimilation of information, and entails a heightened awareness of visual cues and user interface considerations. Finally, the evolving culture brings with it a tendency toward humor and playfulness—concepts not often noted in large corporate settings, but refreshing in an era of ever increasing competitiveness.

A number of other major cultural issues related to internet computing and intranet development may also have a profound effect on the organization.

Agility

Companies are developing and bringing new intranet tools to market at a phenomenal rate. The new tools are coming primarily from two directions: existing vendors rushing to produce intranet-savvy versions of their existing products, and new companies, often funded by anxious venture capitalists, rushing to create intranet-based applications. The vendors' fascination with the evolving intranet market is justifiable. As an example of the rapid market development, Netscape officials have observed that as many as 7 out of 10 browser licenses for their Navigator product are for intranets.

In addition to new software products, more and more hardware manufacturers are repackaging existing products as "Intranet Servers." While the repackaging sometimes involves optimizing the hardware to function as a Web server, in other cases, it simply involves bundling some server software along with the hardware. In any case, the increased competition is driving the price of hardware and software down—all the while driving the vendor companies' stock up. Major players in this arena include Sun Microsystems, Digital Equipment, Compaq, Dell, Silicon Graphics, and Apple.

Given the downward price trend, it's probably a good idea to wait as long as possible before ordering new server hardware for your intranet—even if it means building the prototype on an existing machine and using that hardware through the early phases of the project. In general, try not to buy new hardware until the performance on the existing system is so poor it begins to affect productivity.

In the traditional, pre-Web corporate culture, companies the size of Sun, Digital, Apple, and the others, would have taken months to develop new products or repackage existing ones to address a new market. But, in the new "Web years" culture, even the very large vendor organizations realize that they must be agile, or form an agile unit within their lumbering infrastructures, in order to compete effectively in the fast moving intranet market.

In response, your organization must also become more agile to deal efficiently with these companies. For example, you'll probably want to rethink some of your decision-making procedures regarding purchasing to be able to take advantage of fast-moving technological developments and new vendor offerings. Similarly, as your intranet develops, you may want to rethink the ways in which you deploy the technology.

Just-In-Time Culture

The ever accelerating growth of inter/intranet technology, coupled with the need for rapid product development, has led to a resurgence of the just-in-time philosophy, particularly for companies that are involved in internet computing. The just-in-time philosophy is just what its name implies: It advocates deferring certain decisions until the last possible moment to ensure the most favorable pricing, most current information, most developed technology, and/or the maximum number of choices.

Internet computing, with its vast stores of readily accessible information, perfectly complements the just-in-time philosophy. Sophisticated search tools enable companies to derive specific information from the Internet and receive regular updates about technological developments or new product introductions in their area of interest.

Openness versus Security

While the culture of the intranet is generally very open (due largely to its roots in the Internet), business needs often dictate a high level of security. So, in the business environment, the open culture of the intranet must coexist with the corporate requirement for secure information. Fortunately, there are a number of ways to secure the information on your intranet. Dynamic menus, for example, which recognize specific users and their assigned level of security access, can display everything that is accessible to a user "on the fly," thus avoiding the need to deny access to areas beyond the user's assigned security level.

If you plan to offer external Web access for your intranet users, you must decide if users should be able to access the entire Internet or only portions of it. There are several issues to consider in this decision:

◆ *Productivity.* All too often, users enter a "time warp" when they begin to browse the World Wide Web—hot linking endlessly from one site to the next through an endless succession of fascinating, but not always relevant, associative links. While this "time warp" can have a very real, very negative effect on the user's productivity, the behavior is most common during the initial stages of Internet use and tends to decline as the "newness" wears off and the Web becomes merely another tool.

◆ *Liability.* If users are allowed to access newsgroups, there may be an issue of potential corporate liability if they post comments that are considered libelous. Although this issue is still awaiting clarification from the courts, you may want to institute some ground rules for user postings if you allow this type of access.

◆ *Censorship.* A small percentage of material on the Internet is sexually oriented or politically offensive. You may want to restrict user access to some or all of this material. One large company that didn't restrict access, reports that its access log showed thirty hits on the *Playboy* site within one day of a trial implementation for twenty IS users!

Managing Change

All of the aforementioned cultural factors are likely to have an effect on your organization. Ignoring them can mean the difference between deriving maximum value from intranet technology or being constantly frustrated by it. Marginal results in an intranet project may be due to many factors: People in your organization may not understand the goals of the intranet, may not know how to access it, or may feel that there is no incentive to use it. In some cases, they may also feel that the intranet is "pirating" a system which they have a vested interest in saving. Be sure that you understand (rather than ignore) these sensitivities within your organization and use effective change management to deal with them.

While it is beyond the scope of this book to provide an in-depth discussion of change management, Appendix A (Determining Change Magnitude) offers some background on the nature of change and change management techniques, along with a survey that can help you to assess the magnitude of intranet change on your organization.

In addition, you may want to refer to some other resources to learn more about change and the need for applying change techniques in your organization. A classic reference is *Managing at the Speed of Change* by Daryl Conner, of the ODR Inc. change consultancy in Atlanta, Georgia. By using ODR techniques, or those of other change consultants, you may realize a more effective introduction of the intranet into your organization.

The Role of Intranet Policies

Whatever your corporate culture, you will need a clearly stated intranet policy. The policy—and the training, communications, and enforcement to go with it—will help you to manage many of the cultural issues associated with the intranet implementation. While there may be multiple inputs to the policy, your CIO or other senior IS executive should take the lead in formulating it. Typically, the development of an intranet policy involves two major steps.

First, draft a concise, unambiguous statement of "Intranet/Internet Usage Policy." Ask your company's senior management and legal counsel to review it, then communicate it to the organization as a whole. Be sure to include the following issues in the draft policy:

- ◆ Define what constitutes "business-related usage" and what does not.
- ◆ Define "acceptable" non-business-related usage and specify what is strictly prohibited (e.g., reading *The Wall Street Journal* site as opposed to visiting the *Playboy* site).
- ◆ Specify times (if any) when acceptable non-business-related usage is permitted (e.g., before or after regular business hours).

Figure 4.1 presents a sample Intranet Use Policy that you can modify for your specific needs. Remember to ask your legal department to review and approve it before you publish it, then be sure that it's easily accessible to your users. You may want to link it to your intranet's opening menu page to continually remind users of the policy.

In addition to a use policy, you may want to consider using technology to control access to the Internet. The range of available options includes:

◆ Completely open access with no logging
◆ Open access with logging (you are obliged to tell users if they are to be logged)
◆ Restrict access at the client
◆ Restrict access at the server
◆ Restrict access at the firewall

If you decide to restrict access, there are again a number of options to consider:

◆ List the sites that can be accessed; users can generally request access to additional sites that have business relevance
◆ List only those sites that are specifically excluded
◆ Exclude only certain protocols (e.g., FTP)

There are, of course, both client (i.e., desktop) and server options for the intranet security software. Server offerings are generally the better choice since they are network-based and sit behind the corporate firewall. With client-only products, users are sometimes tempted to modify or dismantle portions of the application, thus creating the potential for a security breach.

Blocking non-business related sites ensures that employees do not spend their time (or your budget) browsing interesting but irrelevant sites. Restricting usage to a limited number of approved sites is, however, counter to the open culture of the intranet. And, it can vastly reduce the intranet's inherent value—access to a

With technology comes both opportunity and responsibility. Use of the Company intranet, including the software, hardware, and information that compose it, constitutes your agreement to adhere to the following.

1. The Intranet is solely for Company information dissemination and use.

2. Intranet components including browser software and modems are for Company business use only. They are not to be used for Internet/World Wide Web access, Online Service Providers (e.g., Compu-Serve, America Online), or access to noncompany entities.

3. If you require external access, contact the IS department for information and follow the External Access Policy.

4. If you do access external entities of any kind, you are responsible for performing virus scans as appropriate and taking other reasonable precautions to protect the Company from external agents and security breaches. Refer to the External Access Policy for more information.

5. Viewing, distributing, and/or downloading of material of any kind and in any medium that is in conflict with Company values is strictly prohibited. This includes anything that can be construed as libelous or offensive. Refer to other Company policies on Equal Opportunity, Nondiscrimination, Sexual Harassment, Conduct, and Gaming/Gambling for more information.

6. Failure to adhere to this policy constitutes grounds for termination.

Figure 4.1   Intranet Use Policy.

huge, rapidly expanding store of information with innumerable, often undefined links to related storage areas.

Organizing the Intranet Implementation Project

No doubt about it—the intranet has a profound effect on both the people and the processes of your organization in many ways. One of the areas that is most directly affected is, of course, your information systems (IS) organization. Fortunately, the intranet phenomenon may face slightly less resistance than the client/server revolution encountered a decade and a half ago. There are two basic reasons for the lower resistance:

1. The shockwaves of change that the client/server revolution brought to IS are now understood to be conditions of doing business. In general, today's IS organizations are a bit more resilient than they once were.

2. The intranet technology uses a familiar environment; essentially, it places the central control at servers and lesser control and power at the desktops. Some industry analysts are already speculating that mainframes will eventually "host" most Web services. Powerful intermediate-level machines from Hewlett-Packard, Sun Microsystems, Digital Equipment, and IBM, among others, are currently being used as Web servers.

Nonetheless, the changes brought about by intranets are very real and your intranet project stands a better chance of success if you understand and plan for these changes before implementing the technology rather than playing "catch up" after the project is complete. Some of the issues you'll need to consider are discussed in more detail in the following sections.

Intranet Resources and Development Differences

The resources required to implement intranet technology (i.e., the skills, the type of team organization, the sponsorship commitment, etc.) are broad and varied; they are also brand new to many companies. The following paragraphs summarize some of the areas in which intranet development differs from traditional application development projects.

SIZE OF PROJECTS

Understandably, many companies are cautious about making an initial, enterprise-wide commitment to intranet architecture. The typical scenario is one of a small, pilot project being deployed to gain acceptance. Once the infrastructure is in place, however, companies are compelled to move applications toward the intranet platform—resulting in larger and larger applications and an ever expanding intranet. As we discuss in Chapter 5, intranet architecture should be both modular and flexible, capable of accommodating larger and larger applications in a constantly changing environment.

LEVERAGE

Leverage is the concept of having fewer highly skilled managers supervising a greater number of less-experienced coders, developers, designers, and so forth. With an intranet, leverage differs from the traditional model in two ways:

- *Harvesting leverage.* The infrastructure of an intranet is basically the same from site to site, with variations in server platform and software having minimal impact because of the loosely coupled nature of the intranet and the availability of tools linking databases and Web servers. Thus, reapplying the knowledge to subsequent sites and/or promoting junior resources on one project to more senior positions on the next is much easier than in a traditional environment. This enables IS groups to rapidly increase their knowledge, while also improving the career path of their employees. The harvesting process of Learn-Master-Lead-Train is collapsed into a much shorter time frame.
- *Information leverage.* Entry-level trainees collect data and, in the process, learn. More-experienced managers

add value to the data by organizing it and structuring it, thus converting it to information that is leveraged throughout the organization as expert advice.

USER PARTICIPATION

Prior to the introduction of client/server computing, user participation was typically solicited when the system requirements were being written, and then again on delivery of the final application. In client/server computing, however, users typically participate in the process all the way through a series of rapid prototypes. With intranets, this participation goes a step further—users often actually build their own presentation level. With the new types of authoring tools, HTML is *that* simple!

CONTROL

One company found that it had a large number of Web sites (approximately 200!) that had "grown up" within departments without the knowledge of the IS department. Once discovered, the company pondered the question of banning user-developed sites. When intranets arise out of a genuine need for disseminating information, the IS department's need for control can conflict dramatically with end users' business needs.

Fortunately, there are some options for managing such potential conflicts. The IS department can, for example, license one of the search engines to "crawl" the local Web and index all of the sites, thereby providing a sponsored overview of all sites. A number of public domain Web crawlers are available on the Internet. There are also numerous books available to guide you through the development or enhancement of Web crawlers, including, for example, *Internet Agents: Spiders, Wanderers, Brokers, and Bots,* by Fah-Chun Cheong (New Rider's Publishing, Indianapolis, IN 1996).

In any case, you should realize that evolving to an intranet can significantly challenge the control of an IS organization. IS control options range from a "laissez-faire" minimum of advice and guidelines to a strict, totalitarian maximum of intranet regulation.

It is generally preferable to adopt a nontotalitarian approach as far as possible, since a totalitarian approach frequently encourages people to find ways around it. Such avoidance can result in an even greater loss of control and potentially serious security breaches. A less-structured approach is also much more in keeping with the general corporate trend away from centralized planning and with the open nature of the Internet itself. Further, it puts you in the role of a favored consultant rather than an IS enforcer.

So, the shorter the list of rules, the better. If you maintain a short list of simple rules and a more comprehensive list of recommendations, users are likely to view IS as an internal consulting group—and be more willing to cooperate with the intranet controls. Rules should be clear, concise, and relevant:

◆ Notify IS of *any* external connections other than those already provided by IS.
◆ Request IP addresses from IS.
◆ Check IS recommendations prior to purchasing hardware or software and, if you wish, check to see if there is a recommended vendor.

Position IS as a conduit to information organization that can benefit everyone. For organizations with fairly autonomous departments or regions, we suggest you take the following approach:

◆ Explain the need for organization so that everyone can benefit from the resources.
◆ Give the department or region control explicitly for maintaining and managing their own information.
◆ Offer structure assistance and advice only; give them the directories they need and show them how to use central "start" or "home" pages to link the material in a usable manner.
◆ Assist with public versus private access security.
◆ Link their public information back to the company-wide menu pages.

Managing the Implementation Project

Hopefully, it is now clear that implementing an intranet requires some new ways of assembling and managing information and personnel resources. However, the fact that you're employing some new techniques doesn't mean that you can abandon fundamental management principles. Solid project management is an example of such a fundamental.

A 1995 study by the Standish Group revealed that more than half of all systems-integration projects are completed late and exceed their budgets. In addition, the study showed that companies that consistently paid close attention to rapid development, strong-scope management, and detailed project management fundamentals experienced a higher degree of success in on-time, on-budget delivery.

Good project management is as much an art as it is a science. And, every project manager has a set of preferred metrics and automated tools. Figure 4.2 indicates the project initiation phase of a project workplan that we've created for a simple intranet development project. (Appendix B contains the complete project workplan.)

As you can see, the intranet implementation project involves much more than just selecting an appropriate authoring tool and writing code. While these steps are obviously necessary, you must also perform a host of other tasks such as scoping the project, establishing schedules and budgets, and defining control reporting structures. In fact, a good project management tool is invaluable for helping to identify the early stage administrative setup for a project, particularly if you are going to use an external IT service firm or contractor. Some of the issues that you must consider in the early-phase setup (e.g., facilities planning, network access, and acquisition of development hardware) can literally take weeks to complete.

Additionally, as Figure 4.2 indicates, to fully comprehend the overall effort and cost of the project, you must consider and manage the numerous resource teams that may be involved. Figure 4.2 shows four teams, but you may have more or less, depending on the complexity of the project.

Task #	Task	TOTAL	X-check	Team 1	Team 2	Team 3	Team 4	Deliverable
PI	**Project Initiation**	0	0	0	0	0	0	**0 Project Initiation Report**
PSU	**Project Start Up**		0	0	0	0	0	**0 Project Organization, Schedule,**
10	Recruit Project Sponsor							Project Organization
20	Recruit Project Initiation Stage Manager							Project Organization
30	Review Related Project Studies							Project Reference Documents
40	Prepare Project Initiation Stage Schedule							Schedule
50	Review Project Start Up							Project Reference Documents, Review Checklist, Schedule
PSPM	**Project Scope - PM**		0	0	0	0	0	**0 Project Scope**
10	Establish Project Business Objectives							Problem/Requirement List
20	Confirm Scope of Investigation							High Level DFD
30	Confirm Outline Solution							DFD Diagram, Outline Solution, Problem/Requirement List
40	Document Project Scope							Project Scope
PSB	**Project Schedule and Budgeting**		0	0	0	0	0	**0 Project Budget, Schedule,**
10	Determine Project Approach							Project Template
20	Re-estimate Effort							Effort Estimate
30	Revise Project Schedule							Schedule
40	Revise Project Budget							Project Budget
50	Document Project Process Success Criteria							Success Criteria
PO	**Project Organization**		0	0	0	0	0	**0 Project Organization, Training Requirements,**
10	Define the Project Organization							Project Organization Chart
20	Determine Training Requirements							Training Requirements (if any)
PCP	**Project Control Procedures**		0	0	0	0	0	**0 Project Control Procedures**
10	Establish Quality Standards							Quality Standards
20	Establish Quality Control Procedure							Quality Control Procedure
30	Establish Progress and Process Control Procedures							Process Control Procedures, Progress Control Procedure,
40	Establish Tolerance Parameters							Tolerance Parameters
50	Establish Change Control Procedures							Change Control Procedure
60	Establish Issue Resolution Procedure							Issue Resolution Procedure
BC	**Determine Project Reporting**		0	0	0	0	0	**0 Business Case**
10	Confirm Project Costs							Cost/Benefit Analysis
20	Quantify Benefits							Cost/Benefit Analysis
30	Analyze Risk							Risk Analysis
40	Define Critical Success Criteria							Business Success Criteria
50	Document Business Case							Business Case
SETUP	**Setup Administrative Environment**	0	0	0	0	0	0	Set up administrative facilities
10	Facilities - Office Space, Telephones, Fax, Parking, Security Pass, etc.							
20	Network Access - Cabling, Logon Id's, e-mail Access							
30	Development Hardware - Software Loaded and configured, printers							
40	Necessary Software purchased							
50	Back up and recovery procedures established							
60	Invoicing requirements documented							
PISA	**Project Initiation Stage Assessment**	0	0	0	0	0	0	**0 Project Initiation Report**
10	Stage End QA							Project Initiation Report

Figure 4.2 Project initiation phase—intranet project workplan.

Integrating the Intranet with the IS Organizational Structure

The distributed structure of the intranet complements the trend toward decentralized, virtual IS organizations. Managing distributed systems, however, presents IS with some interesting challenges. Culturally, decentralization requires moving away from command and control management toward an approach of enabling independent decisions and actions.

One of the biggest potential payoffs of decentralization is the increased initiative and innovation that is encouraged at all levels of the organization. Realizing the payoff, however, entails a delicate balancing act. Without some standards, organizations lose their ability to communicate effectively and collaborate on projects. Without a support infrastructure, knowledge workers spend too much time in low-level maintenance activities—often at the expense of high-level functions that require their expertise and typically offer the most benefit to the enterprise.

The challenge is to meet the organization's needs for coordination and efficiency without destroying the independent decision-making and individual initiative that businesses need to remain competitive in today's climate.

In most companies, intranet usage originates with technical experts that employ the technology for specific projects or business units. There is typically little coordination among groups developing internal Web sites or intranet projects. Because they do not have an overall framework for managing Web technology, these projects generally remain separate from the mainstream business.

To realize the true benefits of an intranet project, however, you must incorporate the technology in your business and IS infrastructure where it has the most potential to transform your existing methods of communicating and collaborating. Because Web technology is still evolving, and companies are building management frameworks "on the fly," you should have mechanisms in place to learn from each project.

The Web Information Framework

In a Web information framework, as described in *The IntraNet Methodology: Concepts and Rationale* (Amdahl Corporation,

1995), roles differ from positions in that the same individuals are likely to play more than one role during a project. The framework encompasses four primary roles:

USERS

Users access and view information on the Web. They also determine the value of Web content and dictate the ultimate requirements. If the difficulty of accessing information exceeds that information's value to users, they will either not use the Web or will find an alternative method of obtaining the information (e.g., calling the content provider on the telephone).

AUTHORS

Authors create the content on the Web. The Web changes the structure of content and, therefore, the processes and functions of authoring. In traditional media, the information access paths are primarily linear, with all related information bound together and delivered together. If users require a different access path or a different combination of information, it is usually more efficient to build a new document, replicating the common information, than to try to tie together pieces of different documents.

Because hyperlinks allow users to dictate how, and in what order, they access information, the structure of authoring differs from that of traditional media. While the author still needs to provide structure, the primary function of that structure is to help users determine which information is important for their current needs. Authors no longer need to attempt to determine the users' needs.

Web technology encourages information reuse. When authors need to reference or recombine information, they can hyperlink the original instead of copying it. With Web technology, authors focus on building reusable information modules (much like object-oriented programming) rather than creating specific linear structures.

INFORMATION BROKERS

Brokers help users find information. While Web technology allows prolific, independent creation of information and offers easy access to huge stores of data, it also involves certain inefficiencies for users trying to find specific information. Information brokers address this problem by providing information access paths for constituencies, rather than repackaged content. With traditional media, an information broker's deliverable might be a 100-page bound document. In creating this document, the broker spends considerable time cutting, pasting, and editing information from other documents. On the Web, the deliverable for the same project might be a single page of hypertext links. As a result, the broker's role shifts to understanding users' decision processes and structuring access paths to support their information needs.

PUBLISHERS

Publishers put authors' content on the Web. Even more important, publishers provide predictable and efficient mechanisms for managing, coordinating, and communicating information content. To efficiently manage the information content for which they are responsible, publishers and managers need a structure with a distinctly different kind of "page." The publisher's "home page" is a management map; it links to map pages that are structured according to rules determined by the organization. The map pages typically provide an overview of Web content, explain how the content is structured, and offer relevant details such as author, validation requirements (if any), and expiration date.

As illustrated in Figure 4.3, the Web information framework focuses on business goals. Brokering, publishing, and content approval form three pillars supporting the business goals. The technical infrastructure, which provides the foundation for the pillars, consists of the hardware, software, networks, and protocols as well as the standards required to build a Web structure.

Intranet Organizational Structure

The intranet organizational structure, illustrated in Figure 4.4, is intended to provide the following functions:

- ◆ Expedite efficient deployment of Web technology
- ◆ Promote Web technology as a cost-effective tool for communication, collaboration, and knowledge management in the decentralized organization
- ◆ Facilitate access to the Web for users and authors alike

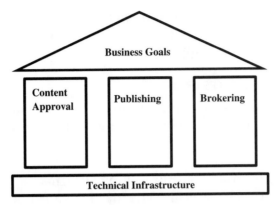

Figure 4.3   Web technical infrastructure.

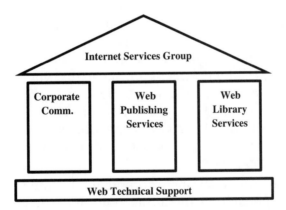

Figure 4.4   Web organizational structure.

What the Web organizational structure must not do in any case, is become an obstacle to the efficient use of the technology. At times, the goals of easy access and distributed content development conflict with organizational needs for coordination and efficiency. The challenge for management is to strike an appropriate balance as such conflicts arise.

There are five Web support functions that an organization can begin to implement with the adoption of an intranet. Initially, a relatively small, overlapping group of individuals may perform all of these functions, but as Web usage grows, each function is likely to require specialized support.

INTRANET/INTERNET SERVICES GROUP

The Intranet/Internet Services Group (or ISG) provides overall coordination of intra/internet technology. This group has several responsibilities:

◆ Promote specific Web applications designed to meet identified business goals. The idea is to nurture the corporate intranet strategy in a kind of "petri dish," where you can examine the vigor of selected approaches to communication, collaboration, and knowledge management. With a rapidly growing and evolving technology like intranet computing, you need to learn from all possible experiences. One way to do this is to undertake a series of highly targeted pilot projects using intranet technologies, then extract knowledge that you can apply to other projects and situations. By focusing on bringing intranet technology and content to specific business situations, you limit the risk of expending significant resources on ineffective projects, while maximizing your learning opportunity.

◆ Establish and disseminate corporate intra/internet policies and procedures including, but not limited to, acceptable use policies, data security standards, content approval and implementation processes, and external access privileges.

◆ Coordinate intra/internet activities across the company. The relative ease with which intranet technology can be implemented invites ad hoc projects, particularly in companies that have decentralized IS organizations, strong end-user discretionary authority over IS spending, or autonomous business units with P&L responsibility for acquiring resources to help them meet their time-critical targets. The role of the ISG is not to discourage such projects, but to assist project leaders in implementing projects in the most efficient and effective manner possible. ISG can, for example, direct project leaders to appropriate resources and serve as a clearinghouse for intranet projects and technology initiatives.

To effectively carry out its responsibilities, the ISG should include representatives from all of the major business units, as well as from the other Web support functions. The group's first pilot project often establishes a collaborative environment for discharging its responsibilities—even if its members are geographically dispersed.

WEB LIBRARY SERVICES

Traditional reference library tasks focus primarily on brokering information. It is the librarian's job, for example, to listen to (and often interpret) a client's information needs, and then apply the appropriate resources to obtain the information. Web library services provide many of the same functions.

- ◆ Act in a consulting role, assisting users with specific information needs.
- ◆ Train users (and create related, web-oriented training materials) in a range of subjects—from browser usage to hyperlinking.
- ◆ Administer and disseminate tools for information management, such as comprehensive directory services, search engines, and help sites.
- ◆ Interface with the other Web support functions to help authors design and implement effective, informative, and accessible Web pages.

WEB PUBLISHING SERVICES

The Webmasters in Web publishing services assist authors and information brokers to design and implement effective pages or, for a chargeback fee, construct pages for users. Typically, the group's responsibilities include:

♦ Defining and publishing corporate standards, guidelines, and templates for Web page layout and design
♦ Training authors in designing effective Web pages
♦ Evaluating and recommending authoring tools

In addition, the Web publishing services group usually maintains the corporate Web site(s) and assists business units with their individual Web sites. It also helps the company to stay abreast of technological developments and to evaluate new intranet tools and business applications (e.g., security and authentication software). This latter role is crucial, given the rapid proliferation of intra/internet technologies, products, and standards; companies must be able to recognize and deploy only those tools and applications that serve a genuine business purpose.

CORPORATE COMMUNICATIONS

The primary responsibility of the corporate communications group is to judge the content and design of *external* Web pages (i.e., those that extend beyond the corporate firewalls) before the pages are implemented. Pages on an external Web site must accurately represent the desired corporate image. Investors, business partners, and clients form much of their impression of an organization's management, culture, and technological capabilities from the Web site. Because the content on external Web sites may also have significant legal, financial, and business ramifications, you will probably want to establish a procedure to ensure approval.

The corporate communications group is also typically responsible for responding to concerns about inappropriate, misleading, or offensive content on *internal* Web pages. The group should not, however, be expected to routinely screen internal pages before they are implemented. Instead, you should rely primarily on the organization's policies and guidelines and, most of all, foster a sense of personal responsibility among your employees to ensure that high standards are maintained on your intranet pages.

Corporate communications should include, at a minimum, representatives of the legal, marketing, and investor relations departments, as well as the Internet publishing services group, and senior executives from the IS organization. Senior executive involvement is essential for reviewing and approving *external* Web content.

WEB TECHNICAL SUPPORT

The Web technical support group implements and maintains the technical infrastructure required to support intranet/Web services, including hardware, software, and network connectivity. The group also serves as the interface between users and other information technology services. If, for example, the sales department wants to use a browser to access legacy databases, the Web technical support group works with them and the appropriate IS group to determine the feasibility and cost of the project.

Legal Issues

The following discussion is intended merely to alert you to some of the legal issues that may be involved with an intranet implementation. While some of these issues apply primarily to intranets that are linked to the Internet, others apply to the internal management of an intranet. In any case, *this information is not intended to be legal advice.* In fact, we strongly recommend that you seek expert counsel from your organization's legal department or, better yet, from a law firm that specializes in "cyberlaw." We've included a partial listing of such organizations; your local library or regional bar association is likely to have a more complete list of cyberlawyers in your area (i.e., Martindale-Hubble directory). And, word of mouth can also be an effective means of locating a cyberlawyer. Ask your colleagues for their recommendations.

Note that we focus on intranet-specific legal issues in this section. If your organization is implementing a virtual private Internet or an external Web site, or is providing access via the Internet, you will need to consider a range of Internet-related legal issues as well.

Information Access and Publishing Policies

In any case, one of the most important steps that you can take to protect the information on your intranet from misuse is to develop a comprehensive set of access publishing policies for your organization.

Fortunately, as we discuss in Chapter 7, there are a number of ways to protect your intranet from security breaches, but you also need to protect the information on your intranet—yours, as well as your partners' and customers'—from misuse or unauthorized use. Such protection is particularly critical if you keep confidential information such as medical records, credit data, or credit card information on any of your intranet servers.

The "black bulletin" boards that are used to trade stolen credit cards, telephone card numbers, or proprietary information do not typically reside in a hackers' home computer. Instead, most hackers access a corporate computer and use it as the server—usually without the "host" organization knowing anything about the illicit use. There are some interesting potential liability issues here for the "host" organization.

It is usually advisable to configure your corporate firewall to exclude anonymous IP addresses or known anonymous remailers. This helps to avoid the risk of employees receiving and/or distributing information without accountability. For example, two sites that you may want to consider excluding are:

- http://online.offshore.com (out of Anguilla)
- info@penet.fi (out of Finland)

E-Mail

Some type of groupware or E-mail is usually the first application that is implemented on an intranet. Remember that E-mail is, in general, discoverable and with efficient back-up practices can far outlast its paper equivalent. A good rule of thumb for E-mail communication is not to write or send anything that you wouldn't feel comfortable seeing blown up on a three-foot by five-foot courtroom exhibit.

E-mail also raises some concern because of its potential as a medium for harassment. Be sure that your intranet publishing policy clearly states the organizational policies on harassment and emphasize that the rules on harassment extend to the E-mail system.

Intellectual Property

There are two major areas of concern with regard to intellectual property: protecting your own intellectual property and protecting the rights of others.

If your intranet allows broad external access, be sure to register and protect your intellectual property internationally as well as in your own country. Even international registration may not, however, protect your intellectual property rights in all countries throughout the world. If that is the case, you may want to take steps to block access from the regions that do not offer protection or use different trademarks for those territories. You can do this by blocking IP addresses originating from those countries (or directing traffic from those countries to a different directory). While the legal validity of this approach has yet to be tested, it would certainly seem to provide a basis for arguing that reasonable steps were taken to protect the rights. CompuServe's early 1996 blocking of Germany in response to that country's strict obscenity laws (which hold the information provider responsible for content) is an example of this approach.

Domain Names

If your domain name suffix is a two letter country identifier (such as .fi for Finland), all you have to do to protect your domain name is make sure that you have a Federal trademark registration and are not infringing anyone's trademark. If, however, your domain has a three-letter suffix (such as .com), you face the risk of potentially losing your right to use the domain name. If another organization (i.e., the holder of a Federal trademark registration with an identical name) challenges your right to use the domain name, you may indeed lose that right. Be aware that such a challenge may be held valid even if the holder of the Federal trademark has a later registration date than yours. Often, a letter from the Internic is your first notice of domain name challenge. The standard Internic letter asks you to sign an indemnification agreement and/or post a bond. The alternative is the loss of your domain name.

To avoid problems with domain name challenges or lack of a suitable domain name—companies are reserving many of the desirable, generic names—you may want to consider registering in another country. In this type of arrangement, performance may suffer a bit while the server looks for the domain name, but the server can be located in your own country. Alternatively, you may want to register for a trademark in another country if you do not have or cannot get one in the United States; trademarks are readily available in some other countries. Again, we recommend that you seek expert legal counsel on any of these approaches. Also, be sure to check the current Internic policy with regard to domain names; we've included the appropriate URLs at the end of this chapter.

Trademarks

In general, you can use trademarks internally on an intranet without problem (although you should follow your organization's publishing policy guidelines). Once you publish information outside of your organization, however, you must ensure that you do not in any way inadvertently jeopardize the protection of your trademarks. Also be sure that employees are aware of the need for permission before downloading and using trademarks belonging to other corporations. Your publishing policy should clearly state what is and isn't permissible with regard to trademarks.

Copyright

Publishing information on the Inter/intranet raises some new concerns about protecting that information. While all new work is automatically protected by common-law copyright, as documents achieve a much wider distribution, registering for copyright protection becomes more important than ever before. But, there is understandable hesitancy about registering proprietary information since everything that is filed for protection under copyright law is filed in the public domain. One way to avoid placing valuable proprietary information into the public domain is to file a partial copy. If, for example, you are registering program code, you can print out the information, then cut the hard copy in half and file for protection on only one half of the information. When combined with your own half, the "registered" half is sufficient to prove that you did indeed create the information.

Trade Secrets

Trade secrets (both yours and others) gain new importance with the advent of your intranet. If you are storing trade secrets on your Web server (or anywhere on the LAN that is connected to your server), you should understand that these secrets are in jeopardy of unauthorized access. Also remember that the HTML code associated with any of the pages on your intranet cannot be protected from view by the users; you can, however, protect the back-end scripts.

Protecting Physical Assets and Intellectual Property

When a user or customer (i.e., internal or external client) provides you with material to be published on an intranet server, be sure to have them agree to waive your liability in the event of the subsequent loss or misuse of that information. If the information is valuable (e.g., an original photograph), they should make a copy of the original and provide you with the copy. All too often, the loss of a seemingly unimportant 35mm slide can result in a replacement fee of thousands of dollars.

Also be sure to have a disclaimer for any breach of intellectual property rights for any material provided to you for use on an intranet server.

General Reference Information

Obviously, we've only touched on some of the legal issues that you'll need to consider in implementing and managing your intranet. There are many others, including encryption restrictions (which we touch on in Chapter 7), contracts, and privacy issues that you may also need to consider. It's always advisable to work closely with your organization's legal department or counsel during the planning and implementation phases of an intranet project. You may even want to include a representative of the legal department in your implementation team, particularly if you have extensive dealings with customers or agents outside of the United States and/or intend to link your intranet to the Internet.

In some cases, you may find the need to consult with a "cyber-lawyer." The following list is, by no means, comprehensive; your own legal department or general counsel may be able to suggest an experienced "cyberlaw" firm in your area or you may want to ask your local bar association. *We provide the following organizations only as a general reference.*

> **Electronic Privacy Information Center:** epic@cpsr.org
>
> **Encryption Policy Resource Page:** http://www.crypto.com
>
> **FCC Law Journal:** http://www.law.indiana.edu/fclj/fclj.html
>
> **Georgetown University Domain Name Information:**
>   http://www.law.georgetown.edu/lc/internic/
>   domain1.htmlHigh
>
> **Internic Domain Name Information:**
>   http://rs.internic.net/domain-info/internic-domain-4.html
>
> **Legal Information Institute:**
>   http://www.law.cornell.edu/~jolt/
>
> **The Journal of Online Law:**
>   http://www.law.cornell.edu/jol/jol.table.html
>
> **The Legal Domain Network:**
>   http://www.kentlaw.edu/lawnet/lawnet.html
>
> **Technology Law Journal:**
>   http://www.server.berkeley.edu/HTLJ
>
> **Villanova Center for Information Law and Policy:**
>   http://ming.law.vill.edu/vcilp.html
>
> **The Electronic Frontier Foundation:** ask@eff.org

Now that we've looked at some of the organizational issues that you're likely to face during the intranet implementation project (and some resources to help you resolve them), we're ready to move to the next chapter to tackle the specific technology issues involved in designing your intranet architecture.

CHAPTER FIVE

INTRANET ARCHITECTURES

- ◆ Overview
- ◆ Elements of a Web-Based System
- ◆ Web Framework
- ◆ Broad Architectures
- ◆ Architecture Selection
- ◆ Component Selection
- ◆ Basic Server Components
- ◆ Logical Server Arrangements
- ◆ Mainframe Integration

Overview

In this chapter, we'll consider the various "layers" of a Web-based system and illustrate how they are interrelated. Then, we'll talk about how you can combine the layers into the various broad categories of intranet architectures and help you choose the appropriate architecture(s) for your intranet. We use a matrix to summarize the attributes of each architecture, thereby facilitating the selection process.

Once you've determined the best architecture for your intranet, you're ready to consider the technological alternatives with which to implement each of the underlying "layers." We'll define some of the components and protocols that you'll encounter, and discuss alternatives for configuring the server. Then, we'll make some recommendations to help you match the intranet technologies to your particular environment and requirements.

Of course, given the volatility of the market and the ongoing, rapid introduction of new products, it's nearly impossible to choose specific technologies or products in advance of your actual installation. So, we'll focus on the techniques that you can use for technology selection—abstracting the interface between the browser and the server as well as the connectivity alternatives between the application layer and the legacy systems, particularly mainframes.

Elements of a Web-Based System

The following Web system elements serve as the basis for our discussion throughout this chapter:

1. *Presentation layer.* This layer presents the artifacts that are manipulated by the users, appearing as the "application" from the user's perspective.

2. *Client browser.* This is essentially the "container" for the presentation layer components and through which the user manipulates the components (e.g., Netscape Navigator or Microsoft Internet Explorer).

3. *Network communications services.* This layer contains all of the hardware, software, and underlying services that enable the browser to communicate with the Web server. This layer involves numerous alternatives, depending on client and server location, bandwidth requirements, cost constraints, and so forth. The International Standards Organization (ISO) has a standard model called the open service interconnect (OSI) for decomposing this layer into its constituent components.

4. *Web server.* A server that supports HTTP for the exchange of information with a client (e.g., Netscape, Microsoft, or Apache).

5. *Server application interface layer.* This layer provides the actualization methods for the application layer. While your choice of application invocation mechanism

at this layer is important, the level of abstraction that it provides to the underlying application is even more important because abstraction provides the basis for system scalability and flexibility over time. The various mechanisms also differ in performance and development capabilities. There are three primary interface protocols for this layer:

- ◆ CGI, Common Gateway Interface (Note that CGI scripts are typically implemented in C or PERL and suffer from a lack of performance and scalability, especially in the Windows NT environment).
- ◆ NSAPI, Netscape Application Programming Interface
- ◆ IISAPI, Internet Information Server Application Programming Interface

Your choice of an API depends on your choice of a server. But, by using a tool like the BSG Web Framework (which we'll describe shortly), you can insulate your application from the various APIs—thereby increasing the portability of your applications.

6. *Application layer.*   This layer contains the business processing services, which automatically apply context to the raw data. The sophistication and modularity of this layer are critical to supporting rapidly evolving business requirements. To a certain extent, this layer can be simplified by applying libraries (like those that we describe in the Web Framework section).

7. *Service interface layer.*   This layer abstracts an underlying data repository, transaction system, or other "service" from the actual application. Abstraction at this level provides a basis for hiding the nature of the underlying system from the user. It also serves as a basis for continual technical evolution with minimal impact on the application. Because this layer "wraps" the native invocation mechanism of the service and manipulates returned data into a consistent, non-service-specific context, a programmer can use the business services layer

without understanding the nature of the underlying service itself.

8. *Service layer.*   This layer incorporates the underlying services (e.g., DBMS, document manager, imaging, engine, text engine, TP monitor, RPC, messaging, E-mail, and 3270 streams) that provide the process and data manifest in the Web presentation layer. These services represent both new and legacy system components.

9. *Operating system services.*   This layer incorporates the file, print, and program execution services, and extends across all of the computers throughout the system.

10. *Hardware.*   This layer incorporates all of the various client and server (and possibly services) components. Like the operating system services layer, it extends across all computers in the system.

While the well-established inter/intranet protocols supply the link between the client(s) and the server(s), you have a number of options for establishing the links between the server and the application(s) and between the application(s) and the various services. These links can be:

- ◆ Custom-developed (i.e., written in a low-level language such as C++ or PERL).

- ◆ Selected from value-added libraries, which are available in the public domain or from vendors. An increasing number of these libraries are available online through the Web.

- ◆ Purchased commercially "off the shelf" as complete applications. Many such links are currently available (e.g., dbWeb or Cold Fusion). Refer to Chapter 9 (Intranet Tools) for more information on these products.

Figure 5.1 illustrates the function of each of the elements of a Web-based system; component numbers represent items 1 through 10 in our description of the Web elements.

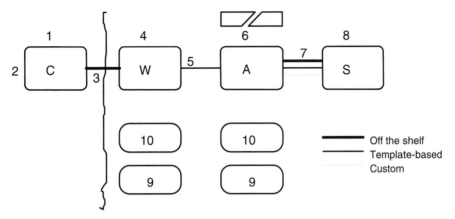

Figure 5.1   Elements in a Web-based system.

Abstraction

You've probably noticed that we refer to the concept of abstraction in several of the element descriptions and you may wonder what we mean by the term. Essentially, *abstraction* refers to the separation of data, business logic, and presentation across technical components. We'll refer to abstraction frequently in this chapter since a number of the architectural layers are designed to provide the service. Since the early days of data processing in the 1960s, system designers have historically created logical designs that reflect a high level of abstraction, but the corresponding physical implementations have typically employed less, since abstraction tends to reduce performance (in that every level of indirection costs CPU cycles to resolve). The discrepancy between our logical designs and physical implementations, however, is shifting in response to the need for rapid change in the information industry.

The need (and increasing ability) to support change presents a whole new set of challenges for the IS department as the various elements of an architecture now change at disconcertingly different rates.

- ◆ *Data.*   While this continues to be the most stable component of any architecture, we are storing more of it and are combining/analyzing it in many different ways to extract the inherent "knowledge." And, the new types of data (e.g., video, audio, and animated graphics) require massive storage facilities and new indexing mechanisms.

◆ *Hardware.*   According to some experts, processor capacity is doubling about every 24 months (Moore's Law), and costs are falling precipitously. The cost associated with inefficient programming is steadily declining as the trade-off between labor and capital equipment shifts to reflect the new realities of a service economy.

◆ *Software.*   This is literally changing on a daily (if not hourly) basis. As technology becomes a part of everyday life for nearly all segments of the population, it has caused massive shifts in software development styles. New development techniques (e.g., object-oriented development) offer new ways in which to shield the intricacy of software elements from one another, and to provide new means for rapid recombination. User interfaces have progressed through at least three major cycles in the past ten years—from terminal to early GUI to WEB, and now are moving rapidly into metaphor extension designs.

◆ *Communications.*   Only five years ago, data communications was arcane, throughput was mediocre, alternatives were limited, and costs were relatively high on a $/Kb basis. Today, millions of homes in the United States use the Internet on a daily basis and costs have dropped dramatically—and continue to decline. For example, an analog line that delivered 9600 bps transmission capability in 1990 cost about $30/month. Today, the same $30 buys 28.8K bps (or higher). Advances in cable modems, ISDN, ADSL and similar services are continually driving throughput higher and costs lower.

◆ *Business processes.*   As the world continues to change, we can either leverage chaos for business advantage or become its victim. Essentially, this means that the processes that support business must be able to change rapidly, with minimal interruption to users or the existing technology investment.

As a fundamental architectural principal, abstraction brings a rationalizing capacity into this maelstrom of change. *By requiring the insulation of components, it allows for the independent evolution of each.* This provides the ability to selectively change system components based on the differing cost/benefit ratios at each level. The concept of component interdependence versus absolute integration provides new opportunities for business and new challenges for system architects and programmers.

In general, tightly coupled (i.e., nonabstracted) systems that mix data, logic, and presentation at all layers lack the ability to support a rapidly evolving business/technical environment. They do, however, offer some benefits. They can be developed and brought to market in a relatively short time and are quite easy to implement since they require less technical skill and precision engineering. While these systems often provide good point solutions, they are not well suited as the *basis* for enterprise IT solutions. We refer to the architectural approach of building flexible systems with the needs of the future in mind as *flexi-tecture.* Flexi-tecture is more than just a phrase to capture the concept of an architecture that can evolve over time—it also expresses the explicit need to evolve *all* aspects over time—people, process, and technology.

Abstraction is a fundamental concept within flexi-tecture. The real value of abstraction lies in its ability to decouple components and to evolve them separately in response to the various external and internal pressures and constraints. Thus, it offers near term value with long-term potential.

Applying the principles of the Web Framework is one way in which you can use the concept of abstraction.

Web Framework

Large, complex intranet projects typically involve multiple Web servers, database products, product upgrades, and the like—all of which make the task of developing the system that much more complicated. There are, however, a number of options for designing a system for "the long term."

Template libraries are one way to shorten your development cycle when creating a platform-independent system. If you choose to invest in such an authoring environment, you can either build your own library or buy one. In either case, the library should:

- Provide a means of handling Web queries independent of platform, server, and/or database.
- Allow for easy modifications by making the system "loosely coupled."
- Allow for future growth (i.e., scalability).
- Support the major operating systems and servers for future portability.
- Reduce development time in large projects by leveraging experienced staff efforts across the full development group.

At BSG, we found the need for control over the development environment to be so important to our business that we chose to build our own called the BSG Web Framework. Specifically designed to meet all of the aforementioned objectives, the BSG Web Framework currently supports most major operating systems, including NT for Intel-based machines and NT for RISC (Reduced Instruction Set Computing) machines, as well as UNIX environments. It supports the Netscape, Apache, Microsoft, Tradewave, Oracle, and WebSite servers.

To satisfy the diverse needs of the ever changing customer and vendor environments, BSG's Web Framework was designed using C++ and the RogueWave Tools H++ Class Library. This ensures portability across UNIX, NT, Macintosh, and Windows operating systems. The BSG Web Framework supports SQL access to most major DBMS using native or ODBC drivers. It has also been used to "wrap" other service APIs, including imaging and document-management systems.

In the BSG Web Framework, the library scripts act on templates that are written in standard HTML.

The major benefit of a library-based development environment is its ability to reduce development time for complex projects. In large-scale efforts, this type of environment also allows for "leveraging" the highly skilled resources. Andy Roehr, a BSG technical director and one of the primary developers of the BSG Web Framework, refers to this leverage as the Producer/Consumer model. "Producers" are the experienced technicians who analyze the business logic and design, and develop the template libraries. "Consumers" are the remaining development staff members who, with a bit of training, can use the basic building blocks of the libraries to develop applications. In other words, the "Producers" hide the implementation complexity from the less experienced "Consumers." Figure 5.2 illustrates this model.

Broad Architectures

The following paragraphs describe the various ways in which the web system elements can be integrated into specific architectures. We are, however, only addressing the most common types of intranet architectures here since the Web elements can be combined in an almost limitless number of ways. In some cases, an architecture is associated with a particular application; we discuss applications (and their relationship to architecture) in Chapter 11.

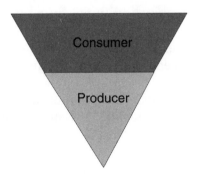

Figure 5.2 Web Framework Producer/Consumer model.

1. *Content Distribution (e.g., newsletters, forms, manuals).*
   This architecture serves as the basic infrastructure for all
   the other intranet architectures and is usually the first to
   be implemented. By way of example, this type of architecture is used by a major restaurant chain to cost-
   effectively distribute information on company
   procedures and training policies to all of the restaurants
   in the chain.

2. *DBMS Direct Integration (i.e., two-tier or tightly coupled
   client/server).* This traditional client/server architecture is used by a chemical company to provide its sales
   force with access to a database of sales leads and status.
   In this case, the Web provides easy access to a geographically dispersed sales force.

3. *Traditional Process Integration (i.e., OLTP client server).*
   This architecture is typically used by companies that
   handle a high volume of transactional traffic, such as
   reservation systems.

4. *Nontraditional Integration (i.e., nontraditional services).*
   This type of architecture is used by a major pharmaceutical company that uses the Web as a front end to its document management system.

5. *Collaborative Computing.* This type of system is often
   considered an alternative to Lotus Notes, but can actually incorporate many additional functions including
   real-time conferencing. (While such conferencing is initially limited to text, as bandwidth increases it will support audio and even video conferencing.)

Figure 5.3 illustrates the organization of the five common intranet
architectures. Of course, in reality, several architectures may coexist
in a single system.

Architecture Selection

As you begin to select your intranet architecture, you may find it
helpful to review the early steps in the intranet implementation

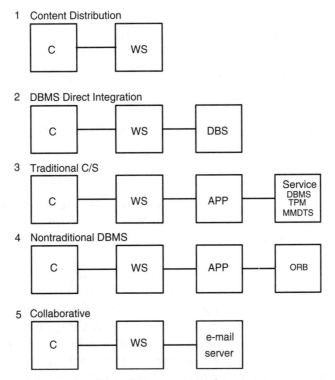

Figure 5.3 Broad intranet architectures.

process. Take a moment to review your decisions in Steps 2 and 3 and to consider the business problems that you're trying to address with the intranet, as well as the data that supports the resolution of those business problems.

For example, consider the nature of your data:

♦ How much is there?
♦ Where does it reside?
♦ What is its nature (i.e., is it text, numeric, complex video, audio, or image)?
♦ If the data is complex, will it be streamed?
♦ How volatile is it?
♦ Does all of it change or is it just supplemented?

- How important is context?
- How much business value does it have?

Then, consider your clients:

- How many are there?
- Are they internal (company-controlled) or external (customers, etc.)?
- How sophisticated are they?

You will also need to know what resources you have at your disposal, including your internal staff, independent contractors, and other outside help. If you have not yet determined what resources you have available or planned how you're going to add the skillsets that you need, we suggest that you go back to Chapter 3 and complete the process of defining your resource requirements and review your options for acquiring those resources.

Be sure to consider the applications that you're going to implement on your intranet in order to determine which architecture is most appropriate. This is a decision that you will almost certainly want to make with expert counsel, possibly in a facilitated session. The matrix in Table 5.1 can, however, help you with your architectural decision.

Component Selection

Once you've selected an architecture, you can begin to consider what components to use for the various layers within the architecture. Many of these components, such as the underlying hardware and operating system for your clients and legacy systems, may already be in place. Wherever possible we encourage you to reuse these facilities in your initial intranet implementation, thereby limiting the scope of technical risk and cost.

You will, however, still need to make some decisions about the browser (see Chapter 9, Intranet Tools), hardware, operating system, and Web server. You'll also need to decide how to connect

TABLE 5.1 Intranet Architecture Comparison Matrix

ARCHITECTURE

Parameter	1	2	3	4	5
Cost	Low	Med	Med-Hi	Hi	Varies
Info content	Low	Low	Med	Hi	Hi
Bus value	Hi	Med	Hi	Hi	Hi
Context	Hi	Low	Med	Hi	Hi
Volatility	Hi	Low	Low	Med	Hi
Data content	Low	Hi	Hi	Hi	Low
Infra impact	Low	Med	Hi	Hi	Med
Scalability	Hi	Hi	Hi	Med-Hi	Hi
Time to implem.	Quick Hit	Rapid	Med	Med-Hi	Med
Resistance	Low	Med	Hi	Med-Hi	Hi
Generated by	Human	Computer	Computer	Computer	Human

Key to Architectures:
1. Content Distribution (also the Basic Architecture)
2. DBMS Direct Integration (Traditional Client/Server)
3. Traditional Process Integration (OLTP Client/Server)
4. Non-Traditional Integration
5. Collaborative Computing

your server to the back-end applications and how to link the back-end applications to the services or legacy system.

Presentation Layer

The only decisions you need to make with regard to the presentation layer (i.e., the "application" from the user's perspective) concern the look and feel of the interface. We discuss the factors that go into these decisions in some detail in Chapter 10, The User Interface.

Client Browser

Your major choices for the browser (i.e., the "container" for the presentation layer components) are Netscape Navigator and Microsoft Internet Explorer. While we discuss browser selection in much greater detail in Chapter 9, you should be aware that

Netscape (with more than 70 percent of the market at publication time) is currently the clear leader but that Microsoft (with less than 20 percent) is rapidly gaining market share.

In some circumstances, you may want to choose a browser other than Netscape or Microsoft. In a very closed architecture, for example, you might want to choose one of the lesser-known browser vendors, license the source code, and modify it to access only the URLs that you designate. In some situations—such as integrating with mainframe applications—you may want to consider a text-only browser such as Linux.

Network Communications Services

Presumably, the decisions for this layer have already been made. If not, it's beyond the scope of this book to review the numerous possibilities to consider for this layer. We suggest that you refer to one of the many books that are available (such as *LAN Management* by Gil Held, published by John Wiley & Sons, New York, 1995).

This "layer" communicates among computers. The appropriate choice depends on many factors, including location, bandwidth requirements, cost constraints, and so forth. Your major options here are:

TCP/IP

TPC/IP is the lingua franca of the Internet, and the basis for Web communication services. TCP/IP relies on every machine in the network having a unique ID—generally expressed as ###.###. ###.###. Because addresses are becoming scarce (due to the rapid growth of the Internet) a new TCP/IP definition provides an extended numbering scheme.

The major issue with IP on the intranet is address management, since every device must have a unique identification (ID), and those IDs may need to be changed as the intranet topology or device location changes. There are two major options for reducing this operations load—dynamic host configuration protocol (DHCP), which Microsoft uses with its Windows NT and Windows 95 operating systems, and Bootp, a common implementation that has its basis in UNIX. While both protocols have their merits, Microsoft-focused shops should probably use DHCP (unless it cannot meet some requirements). Both provide facilities that are logically similar to "LU Pooling" in the SNA gateway environment, where a device-emulating 3×74 controller or similar device controls a pool of logical units (LUs), assigning them as requested (e.g., Microsoft SNA Server or Novell Netware SAA). This arrangement had a significant impact on the maintenance of PU/LU mapping within VTAM, and DHCP/Bootp provide similar operational relief in the TCP/IP arena.

While most inter/intranet applications are based on the TCP/IP protocol, nearly all systems management functions and a few applications use universal datagram protocol over IP (UDP/IP). UDP is a compatible, connectionless, datagram protocol that is generally faster than TCP/IP, is compatible with all major TCP/IP drivers, and supports DHCP, BootP, audio, and video. However, UDP doesn't guarantee delivery. Consequently, it is most commonly used when speed is very important and a lost "frame" is acceptable.

WEBDCE

The distributed computing environment (DCE) is a set of services (remote procedure call, time, security, distributed file, naming) that are implemented across multiple vendors and platforms. Thus, DCE guarantees interoperability of services within a heterogeneous distributed architecture. While DCE does provide some superior technologies and services, it has not caught on as rapidly as once hoped, primarily due to the complexity of implementing its naming and security services. Although DCE was originally designed for distributed client/server architectures, the Open Systems Foundation (OSF) has championed the development of a set of technologies called "WebDCE" which provide the high security advantages of DCE in a Web environment. Remember, HTTP, the fundamental protocol of Web communications, is a TCP/IP protocol. WebDCE implements the Web services on top of DCE, permitting standard browsers and other devices to use the service. WebDCE is essentially a work in progress. It does not enjoy anything like the broad acceptance of conventional Web technologies, however, it is quickly gaining acceptance because of its security capabilities. For the most part, it is used only in organizations that have a strategic commitment to implementing DCE protocols throughout. (For additional information, refer to http://www.osf.org.)

Web Server

The server is the heart of any intranet; it supports HTTP for the exchange of information with a client. The server also typically provides the environment for all of the intranet software, including security, data processing, and database connectivity. With all of these responsibilities, servers must be fairly powerful machines running robust server software.

Web servers are also called HTTP servers because their primary purpose is to serve data using the HTTP protocol. Server software runs primarily in two operating system environments: UNIX and Microsoft NT. There are some other platforms that Web servers can run on, but UNIX and NT are—by far—the primary Web server environments. Your choice of a server environment depends on many variables, including the type of security that you need, the number of users, the type of database that you'll be running, your budget, and so forth. You'll need to consider all of these elements during the architecture and planning phases of your intranet implementation project.

And, as is true with most tools, there are free servers and commercial servers available. Commercial servers have been developed to meet users' needs for a more feature-rich server environment. The added features in these servers include security (e.g., authentication and encryption), logging facilities, and integration with other products.

It is possible, however, that a free server can meet all of your needs; this is largely determined by the size of your intranet and the applications that you'll be implementing. The good news is that there is support available for many of the free servers. Some of the free Web servers have a very loyal following, and are widely supported on the Internet, as well as in trade magazines and newsgroups. The following Web servers are currently the most popular:

♦ *Apache Server.*   One of the most popular public domain servers in the world, Apache runs on UNIX and

OS/2 systems and is actually supported by people who run Web servers for a living. For more information on Apache, refer to its Web site: www.apache.org.

- *Netscape Enterprise Server.*   A high performance, secure web platform for managing, distributing, and creating information, the Netscape Enterprise Server supports multiprocessor servers and secure client-side certificates, as well as Java and other tools for content creation. For more information, refer to www.netscape.com.

- *Microsoft Internet Information Server (IIS).*   A Windows NT server that is extremely easy to set up, IIS is tightly coupled with the rest of Microsoft's back-office suite including the SQL Server database. For this reason, IIS is a good platform for application development. Refer to www.microsoft.com/infoserv for more information.

- *WebSite O'Reilly & Associates.*   A complete environment for creating, editing, and managing Web documents on an NT server, WebSite comes with many useful tools, including HotDog, a popular HTML editor. Two versions are currently available—WebSite and WebSite Professional. WebSite is free and can be downloaded from the O'Reilly Web site. For more information on WebSite and WebSite Professional, refer to www.website.ora.com.

For additional information on Web servers and browsers, refer to www.webcompare.com. This site contains a complete, updated comparison listing of all browsers and servers that are currently available on the market.

Server Application Interface Layer

This layer provides the actualization methods for the application layer itself. It is also key to providing abstraction within the system and for integrating mainframe-resident services with the intranet. For more information on this layer, refer to the section on Mainframe Integration later in this chapter.

Application Layer

Because this layer contains the business processing services (which apply context to the raw data), its sophistication and modularity are crucial for supporting rapidly evolving business needs. Increasingly, this layer is being implemented using object models to handle the complexity.

Some type of database generally resides on the server; the type of database is largely dependent on the applications that run on the intranet. A database may not be required, however, if your information is simply HTML pages (e.g., company phone lists or policies). But, you are likely to need a robust relational or object-oriented database if your intranet applications consist of financial services, inventory processing, or multimedia presentations with video. Remember, the larger and more complex your applications, the more important it is to consult with as many experienced sources as possible—vendors, analysts, outside integrators and so forth. And, if your organization already has a datastore, drawing on multiple sources can help you reach the best decision regarding the numerous tools that are available to bridge the gap between your existing database and the intranet server. These tools are particularly useful because they enable you to retain your current database architecture. Whenever possible, buy solutions and integrate rather than develop your own tools.

Service Interface Layer

This layer abstracts an underlying data repository, transaction system, or other "service" from the actual application. Abstraction at this level provides a basis for hiding the nature of the underlying system from the user. It also provides the basis for continual technical evolution with minimal impact on the application. This layer "wraps" the native invocation mechanism of the service, and manipulates returned data into consistent, non-service-specific context, enabling a programmer to use the business services layer without understanding the nature of the underlying service itself.

Service Layer

This layer incorporates the underlying services (e.g., DBMS, imaging, document managing, messaging, etc.) that provide the process and data manifest in the Web presentation layer. These services represent both new and legacy system components.

Operating System Services

This layer incorporates the file, print, and program execution services. The three most viable choices for your operating system are UNIX, Microsoft NT, and Novell Netware.

MICROSOFT NT

Although Microsoft NT was regarded as a smaller, weaker operating system than UNIX, a new generation of Intel processors (the most common hardware platform for NT), coupled with the release of NT 4.0, is making NT into a serious contender—even for the high-volume transaction processing environments that have traditionally been a UNIX domain. Some analysts do, however, question Microsoft's commitment to NT on non-Intel hardware (e.g., DEC Alpha), and doubts still linger about NT's scalability on machines configured with more than four or six processors.

In spite of those doubts and questions, however, NT is definitely suitable as a Web server in a multiserver environment, and the recent addition of DNS server capabilities has made it a minimally qualified stand-alone platform as well. DHCP Services help to manage the IP addresses of Windows-based client computers by allowing address pooling and, as an added attraction to NT, the remote access server (RAS) program offers PPP dial-up access with security log-in for remote Windows client machines.

While NT does support anonymous FTP, the current release is not a very robust implementation. And, while NT does not currently support a number of other important, optional services such as WAIS, SMTP Mail, News, and Gopher, there are "user-supported" versions freely available on the Internet as well as from companies like Netmanage. As we write this, Microsoft is releasing NT version 4.x; we do not, however, know what additional capabilities it will contain.

UNIX

UNIX is still the platform of choice for truly large-scale systems. It has a well-deserved, solid reputation for power and scalability on numerous platforms. And, UNIX is particularly well-suited for Web servers because it is the environment where FTP, Telnet, and TCP/IP were nurtured.

Netscape's commerce/commercial server is presently the major Web server for the UNIX environment; versions are currently available for a wide range of hardware platforms. Additionally, HTTP daemon programs are available in source code for those hardware platforms that do not support a commercial version. A number of Web server vendors offer good-quality HTTP server packages for specific platforms or for platforms with unique security features. Again, we recommend that you use the Internet to research products for the UNIX environment and determine which product(s) are most suitable for your environment and requirements.

Most of the standard and optional services, such as News, Mail, FTP, PPP, and WAIS are included with the base UNIX operating system or available as low cost add-on products from the operating system vendor. Third-party vendors also offer enhanced versions of many of these tools and adventuresome folks can find a source-code version of these services that, with a little effort, can be compiled on most UNIX-like operating systems.

NETWARE

Long a favorite in the network operating system area, Novell is presently positioning Netware as a Web server. The Novell server is pretty much functionally complete, but Netware as an OS is not yet well suited to play this role on an enterprise basis. However, Netware is probably a good choice for "departmental intranets" or for small companies with a Netware investment that they want to leverage in their intranet solution to support "content" class systems.

SELECTING YOUR OPERATING SYSTEM

Your choice of an operating system for your intranet environment is largely determined by what you're going to do with the system. Consider the following questions and refer to the vendor's specification sheets to see where you can get the best fit:

- ◆ Are you using the intranet strictly for document management?
- ◆ What type(s) of transaction processing do you expect the intranet to handle?
- ◆ What volume and complexity of data is it serving?
- ◆ What strength of machine do you need to get the *speed* you require for the data you're pushing?
- ◆ Cost? Remember to calculate long-term value and support along with the initial purchase price.

And, don't forget to consider your database requirements. Depending on the size and complexity of your data types, and your particular data access requirements, you may necessarily be driven away from the less expensive SQL Server (which is ideal for NT) and back to a more platform-independent, traditional DBMS like Oracle, Sybase, or Informix. In this case, UNIX may be your best choice by default. Of course Oracle does work on NT (as Microsoft will tell you), but the same reasons that led you to a heavyweight DBMS will probably also lead you to a heavyweight platform on which to run it.

Hardware

While hardware actually refers to all of the various client and server components in the intranet layers, your major decision in this area is the Web server.

In choosing your Web server, consider the current level of usage as well as the potential (i.e., near term) usage levels. Because the intranet architecture is loosely coupled, it is relatively easy to upgrade. Thus, you do not have to purchase hardware to meet your long-term future needs. It is more cost-effective, especially with continually decreasing hardware costs, to gradually expand your hardware platform as your requirements (and technology) change. Be aware, however, that many intranets are victims of their own success; they are so successful that they rapidly outgrow their initial deployment platforms. While this situation is certainly preferable to nondelivery, it can lead to user dissatisfaction.

Scalability and initial commitment are the basis for your hardware decision. While we do not differentiate greatly between an

Intel solution or a UNIX solution for today's requirements, UNIX systems can potentially scale to larger implementations through symmetric multiprocessing (SMP) or clustering. However, recent Pentium Pro benchmarks indicate that the Intel systems are narrowing the performance gap. Ultimately, your hardware decision involves trade-offs of operational complexity, retraining, and existing investment. Only you can determine your priorities with regard to these factors and select a Web server that best suits your needs.

Although we don't know of any organizations (other than IBM) that have chosen to use a mainframe for their Web server, we do see enormous utility for mainframes as near term DBMS or process servers in the distributed Web architecture. This is largely because mainframes are currently the repositories for much of what we consider "mission critical" process and data. For the most part, however, unless your organization has a mainframe that it is not using and can't "get off of the books," it's difficult to make a case for using a mainframe as the host for the Web server engine.

Your primary alternatives for Web server platform are:

- *Intel.*   A familiar environment, generally easy to maintain, and relatively inexpensive.
- *Proprietary RISC.*   This architecture is used by a number of the popular workstations, including models from Hewlett-Packard, Sun Microsystems, Silicon Graphics, IBM, and Digital Equipment.
- *Outsourcing.*   You can outsource an intranet, or at least some components of it. Outsourcing may be a good solution if you need to get a server up and running in a short timeframe and are waiting for communications, or if you are still beta testing and want to wait for the test results before committing to a hardware expenditure.

Figure 5.4 illustrates the breakdown of Web servers by platform.

Basic Server Components

Obviously, server hardware and software can vary significantly, depending on your specific systems environment and the com-

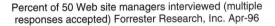

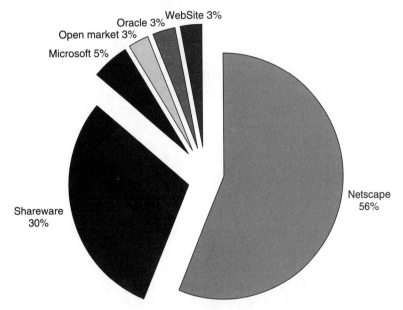

Figure 5.4   Web servers by platform.

plexity of the inter/intranet infrastructure and resident applications. But, all servers require a basic set of hardware and software components to perform their functions. The following sections describe these basic functions and explain how they interact with one another.

Universal Resource Locator (URL)

A universal resource locator (URL) uniquely identifies each document on the Internet, using a *service-host-directory-document-document type* identification scheme. A URL is associated with each hypertext link in an Internet document—regardless of document type. The URL, which is usually transparent to the user, works in conjunction with sophisticated browsers such as Netscape, Mosaic, or Microsoft's Internet Explorer to hide the complexity of the Internet from the users. Because URLs contain very complete information, browsers use the same point and click hypertext/graphical interface with any service or system—regardless of the system's location, protocol, or agent capability—users need not deal with the complexities involved with logging in and out of each protocol. This versatility minimizes training requirements and allows users to move from service to service and host to host without consciously choosing the protocol, service, or host.

In the following URL grammar specification, { } indicates a substitution keyword and [ ] indicates optional.

```
[{protocol}://]{host name}[:{socket
number}]/[{directory}/]{filename}[.{mime extension}][{arguments}]
```

The URL itself looks something like the following:

```
http://www.bsginc.com/pub/xyz/d1234/index.html
```

The following paragraphs describe the various parts of the URL grammar specification:

◆ *Protocol.*   This tiny text string is the key to everything; it determines which protocol the browser and server will use for communication as well as which service will be used (on a system with more than one type of service). The protocol can be any type of TCP/IP socket request that the browser (or one of its helper applications) is capable of supporting. If a protocol specification is missing from the URL, the browser defaults to "HTTP."

The protocol in this example is HTTP, meaning that the browser will connect to the WWW hypertext service at the standard socket interface for that service (i.e., 80) unless the socket number string specifies a different number. Other common protocols include: FTP, telnet, Gopher, WAIS, Finger, and local file system (on the client computer itself).

◆ *Host name.*   The host name is usually a character string containing the DNS standard name for the system that will service the request. While DNS is the usual Internet method of resolving a systems IP address, the URL may use a server's numeric IP address instead of the DNS. In that case, the host name string looks like 192.0.0.1—four numbers from 0 to 255 separated by periods.

- *Socket number.*   This optional string overrides the protocol's default socket number. This field is used fairly often, for example, to run two instances of the same service with different properties (i.e., one secured and one unsecured).

- *Directory.*   The directory string is usually a UNIX-style directory tree entry, but it can be interpreted by most Web servers to kick off a CGI (or API) call to provide extended functions. It can, for example, instruct the server to run a local shell script and return the results as a hypertext document that incorporates other "embedded" document components including sounds and graphics. This method is used to invoke database interfaces such as those for Sybase and Oracle, and to make full-text searches available.

- *File name.*   The file name text string is usually pretty straightforward. Often a "virtual" filename used as a CGI or API call when a server agent handles a "special request," html form, or other WWW extension.

- *MIME.*   The MIME-compatible file extension string determines which part of the browser will interpret the file or if a helper application is needed to display the file. Browsers are configured to save, display, pass on, or ignore any MIME extension. For more information on Multipurpose Internet Mail Extensions (MIMEs), refer to Appendix D.

Server Software Components

An operating system, file system, and network system are the standard software components of each server; they, in turn, support all the other functions. Almost all servers use a multitasking operating system. The file system is usually based on a hierarchical directory structure that, at a minimum, supports the standard DOS naming convention. Depending on the specific operating system, however, the file system may also support other enhancements such as long file names.

You'll probably want to consider using some other, optional server software components in your intranet environment:

INETD

The network connection monitor. In UNIX terminology, this is the inetd daemon. It works with the operating system to handle new processes, multitasking, and multithreading. In PC technology, the process that is going to service the task must be running, have the port captured, and deal with multitasking and multithreading within the application.

FTPD

The file transfer protocol (FTP) daemon. FTP is commonly used as a dedicated secure connection by other client programs. In UNIX, the FTPD is started by INETD when an FTP socket request is received. Most FTP services accept the use of "anonymous" as the user ID and virtually all browsers take advantage of this capability. UNIX password-level security is enforced for any nonanonymous connections. If you implement FTP on your site, be sure to perform a complete security audit.

FTP and its lightweight version—TFTP—were the primary file transfer protocols universally supported on the pre-1995 Internet. For additional information on FTP, refer to RFC-1780 (Appendix D—Request for Comment Listings—contains brief descriptions of RFC 1780 and other relevant RFCs).

HTTPD

The Hypertext Transfer Protocol (HTTP) daemon. HTTPD is the original program that converted network UNIX systems into Web servers; the National Computer Security Association (NCSA) describes HTTP as "a protocol with the lightness and speed necessary for a distributed collaborative hypermedia information system." In UNIX systems, HTTP requests may spawn many HTTPD processes to satisfy multiple requests. HTTP is sessionless and synchronous. An HTTP request does not require a log-in or the session overhead associated with its predecessor (FTP).

In Windows NT and many UNIX servers, the Web server program replaces the function of INETD/HTTPD by *listening* to the designated socket number(s). Although 80 is the default socket connection number for HTTP, any socket number can be used for HTTP if an application requires it. Be aware, however, that some socket numbers are "well known" or unofficially reserved for certain applications. Using these socket numbers for other applications may cause conflicts among services.

GOPHER SERVERS

Gopher is a distributed document search and retrieval system that is supported by most Internet server architectures. It offers both content browsing (i.e., searching for and retrieving documents by content across multiple servers) and full-text searches. Veronica is a Gopher service that offers additional functionality.

DNS

Domain name server allows IP numbers to be abstracted into host names or domain/host name translations. With this capability, we can use names rather than numbers to locate host systems.

ARCHIE SERVERS

Archie is a mangled anagram for "Internet Archive Server Listing Service." It allows you to query a database of freely available software and information residing on Internet-connected hosts. Most of the hosts are accessible by anonymous FTP. Archie's primary functions have, to some extent, been usurped by the preeminence of the World Wide Web and the rapid explosion in the number of servers.

WAIS

Wide area information server (WAIS) is a noteworthy implementation of the Z39.50 protocol maintained by the Library of Congress. It is a search-based document retrieval system that was developed by KPMG Peat Marwick in conjunction with Thinking Machines and Dow Jones, and placed in the public domain.

IP AND SIPP

Internet protocol (IP) is the underlying protocol that is the basis of the Internet. The current version (4) is often represented as IPv4. In theory, every IP-capable device in the universe has a unique IP address. In reality, because of the overwhelming success of the Internet and the current scheme for IP address sets (or subnets), we're likely to run out of practical IP addresses in the near future.

SIPP is the current working specification for IPv4's successor, sometimes designated IPv6. SIPP will use a 64-bit address field (rather than the 32-bit field in IPv4) and address some additional issues such as security and authentication. Developers aim to provide user-transparent interoperation between Ipv4 and SIPP.

PPP AND SLIP

Point-to-point protocol (PPP) and serial line Internet protocol (SLIP) are implementations of LAN protocols over a serial dial-up line. PPP can implement other protocols, but is primarily used to connect to IP networks. SLIP, which predates PPP by several years, only supports IP. Although the two are functionally equivalent, PPP is becoming the de facto standard for new installations because it is more robust in performance and reliability. Refer to RFC-1055 for additional information on SLIP or RFC-1134 for information on PPP.

SENDMAIL, SMTP, AND POP3

Sendmail, simple mail transport protocol (SMTP), and post office protocol version 3 (POP3) are Internet mail services that have become Internet standards. All three provide different functions; together they make up the backbone of UNIX-based mail. Use a general search facility on the Internet to retrieve additional information on their functionality or refer to RFC-821, RFC-1081, or RFC-1082.

NNTPD

The network news transfer protocol (NNTP) daemon supports both NNTP clients and other NNTP servers. NNTP is the basis of the worldwide Internet discussion groups (i.e., *news groups*). NNTP (or News, as it is commonly known) predates much of the Internet; it was formerly fed server-to-server in a loose confederation using dial-up modems and the UUCP protocol. It is still the most widely used group-enabling software on the Internet. See RFC-977 for additional information on NNTP.

SNMP

Simple network management protocol (SNMP) supports the transmission of nearly any type of metrics over an IP network. The current release (2) is expressed as SNMP2. SNMP data is sent and stored according to the management information base (MIB) or MIBII Standards. Most network management systems are based on SNMP. Refer to RFC-1157 for additional information on SNMP.

Logical Server Arrangements

By now, you realize that the server can provide a wide range of services and that the client requires considerable configuration. In the next several years, intranet architectures are likely to evolve to contain many—possibly all—of the services we've described, along with many new ones. While today's "minimalist" intranet need not include all of the currently available protocols and services, its architecture should be compatible with future technological developments.

In an ideal situation, you would have an unlimited amount of time in which to become familiar with the inter/intranet computing components and to design an intranet that suits your current environment and applications. Unfortunately, this is seldom the case in today's highly competitive business environment. You should, however, take the time to consider all of the intranet logical arrangements so that you can design and implement an intranet capable of meeting both your current needs as well as your future, as yet undefined, requirements.

Figure 5.5 illustrates the components in a current internet application. The bottom cloud represents a UNIX system's intermittent processes that come alive to receive a request, service it, and return a response. After they return a response, the services "die" on UNIX systems. On a Windows NT system, however, these same services must be persistent and run as processes continually monitoring their respective port, while waiting for something to do. The figure does not illustrate Sendmail or DNS since these types

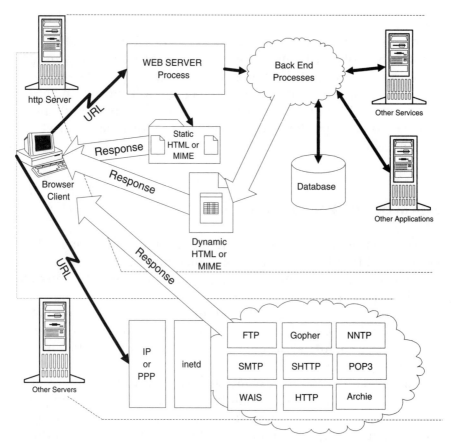

Figure 5.5   Web application extended conceptual structure.

of services are not directly responsible for returning a response from a URL request.

Stand-Alone Systems

Web applications invariably follow a client/server architecture and, therefore, typically require multiple platforms. You can, however, load both the client and the server on the same machine for some limited applications. For example, in rare cases where simple HTML is being manipulated, you can eliminate the HTTP server component and let the native file system provide a limited structure. This type of system is, however, only useful for one user at a time and does not use the network. The internal file system serves as the object repository.

Stand-alone systems are useful for demonstrations and presentations where a network connection is inconvenient. To some extent, they can also be used to build and test new concepts. However, because applications invariably perform differently on multiplatform systems, stand-alone systems should not be used in development except by very knowledgeable developers who fully understand the nuances and issues of porting the application(s) to a production environment.

STAND-ALONE SYSTEM CONFIGURATIONS

A typical stand-alone intranet system is based on a desktop PC, laptop, or workstation equipped with a display screen, keyboard, mouse, and network device. (Although a network device is usually necessary to install the TCP/IP driver software, it need not be connected to a network in most configurations.) Software for a stand-alone system typically includes the operating system, TCP/IP driver, browser, helper applications, and HTTP server.

We recommend the following configuration (illustrated in Figure 5.6) for a stand-alone intranet system:

◆ A laptop or desktop PC equipped with an Intel Pentium processor with 16M to 32M bytes of RAM, a 500M+ byte hard disk, and super-VGA display

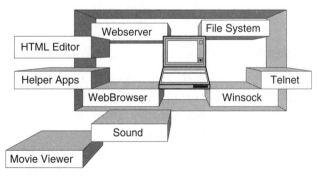

Figure 5.6   Sample stand-alone Web system.

- The Microsoft Windows NT or Windows 95 (latest version) operating system, which includes a TCP/IP Winsock interface configured for TCP/IP dial-up networking on a serial port and/or a TCP/IP on the Network interface card
- A Netscape Navigator Gold (latest version) and/or Microsoft Internet Explorer (latest version) browser
- Website by O'Reilly and Associates for Windows 95, or Microsoft IIS for Windows NT or Netscape's server for Windows 95

There are, however, a host of possibilities for comparable hardware and software configurations; we recommend that you search for them on the Internet using your favorite search engine or check out www.webcompare.com.

Single-Server Systems

A single-server system like the one illustrated in Figure 5.7 is generally an ideal configuration for first-time intranet development projects. The single server can be a desktop, Intel-based PC running one of the supported operating systems such as Microsoft Windows NT or a commercially supported UNIX-like system (e.g., BSDI). Alternatively, one of the "user-supported" UNIX-like operating systems may be suitable for adventuresome souls who enjoy problem solving. As shown in Figure 5.7, a more mainstream alternative is to use a dedicated or shared production-grade minicomputer as the server, running some variant of UNIX.

Multiserver Systems

As with any other architecture, bottlenecks often occur as capacity increases on the single-server intranet system. In this case, however, the bottlenecks may result from network or server overload, and you'll need to identify the source before you can effectively address the problem. Network bottlenecks are actually quite rare and should be verified by a network expert. Server bottle-

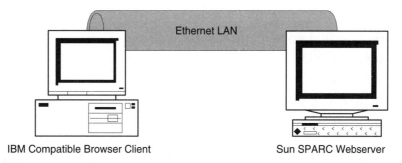

Ethernet LAN

IBM Compatible Browser Client   Sun SPARC Webserver

Figure 5.7   Sample single-server Web system.

necks, on the other hand, are very common but can often be avoided with some advance planning.

If you do experience a server bottleneck, you can usually remedy the problem by replacing the existing server with a larger one. While this solution has some merit, a more flexible approach is to divide the processing load among multiple servers. Initially, you can simply clone the server and switch some users over to the new server. This approach is costly, but particularly effective in situations where server requirements include a very low mean time to recover from a server failure. Another, more common approach is to break up the services onto two or more separate servers, with each server providing a set of unique services. As processing loads continue to increase, you can continue to add servers and divide services—to the point that each server provides a single, unique service (i.e., one for FTP, one for DNS, one for HTTP, one for Mail, one for News, etc.).

Sessionless services such as HTTP can also run transparently on multiple servers. URLs make it easy to point at different servers and to the different files they contain—all without confusing the user.

DIVIDING SERVICES AMONG MULTIPLE SERVERS

As you can see, there are many strategies for separating services or dividing processing loads among servers. You might, for example, want to consider the relative merits of dividing services by any of the following criteria:

◆ By application
◆ By function within application
◆ By transaction
◆ By service
◆ By data accessed
◆ By local LAN segment

There are, of course, advantages and disadvantages associated with each approach, but you can use any combination of strategies to suit your particular requirements, environment, and available resources. Because the browser consolidates applications on the desktop, users are not aware of any multiserver division. However, we encourage the use of network and device management software to gather real data about performance rather than "guessing."

By application. Dividing servers by application is a relatively simple, straightforward strategy. A single server contains all of the services necessary to support one particular application. The next server contains the services for the next application, and so on. However, this strategy does nothing to standardize the services on the servers and, without good documentation and procedures, can lead to maintenance problems.

By function within application. This approach further divides the application into the constituent services or functions that it supports. This strategy, which typically assigns one server per service and only services one application, may be accomplished through a specialized service like a geographic information system (GIS).

By transaction. This approach advocates a further division, with each server supporting a specific transaction (or type of transaction) within a service. For example, one server may handle all CGI database transactions while another server handles all nondatabase transactions, with yet a third server handling static HTML.

By service. The most common method for dividing the processing load among multiple servers, this approach uses a separate server for each "service" (i.e., HTTP, Secure HTTP, FTP, NNTP,

Mail, etc.). Any application that uses these services shares the server with the other applications.

By data accessed.   This strategy is similar to dividing the processing load by service or by application, except that the same data can be accessed by multiple applications, or even by multiple services. In this approach, all services that use the same data (i.e., database) and all applications that use the same data, share the same server. This strategy often requires adding a Web server to the existing database server. In this case, some of the applications using the data may be traditional online, client/server, or batch applications, rather than Web applications.

By local LAN segment.   This is a practical strategy if performance problems can be attributed to the network, such as WAN bandwidth limitations. While one local server can generally support the needs of a medium-size office, you may need to divide the load among multiple servers to support a larger office. Small offices can usually be serviced remotely over a relatively limited WAN connection.

Distributed Systems

From a system standpoint, geographically isolated areas are much closer now than they were before WANs became commonplace. All locations are not, however, created equal on a WAN. Some locations have limited bandwidth-access; this is especially true of networks that use a spoked-hub configuration with remote locations all connected to a central site. This type of network is generally designed according to the number of users at each remote location and their need to access WAN resources. Problems arise if remote users establish a server and grant access to users at other locations. The limited WAN bandwidth can easily be overwhelmed if there is heavy usage from other sites. This situation can, however, be remedied by moving high-use Web sites to a central location or increasing bandwidth to the remote sites. The increased availability of digital services like ISDN, as well as new communications technologies like ASDL and cable modems, provide new opportunities on a daily basis.

Mainframe Integration

In our description of layer 7 of a Web-based system, we mentioned the specific instance of the application-server interface that relates to interfacing with a mainframe. This layer is a major consideration if you're going to integrate your intranet with a mainframe. And, because more than 90 percent of U.S. data classed by CIOs as "mission critical" currently resides on mainframe systems, such integration is a common occurrence. As you can imagine, mainframe integration is a complex process that requires experience and skills beyond Internet or Web site implementation. If you decide to seek outside help, be sure to look for an organization that can demonstrate specific experience in the mainframe integration arena!

You may want to consider one or more of the following approaches to integrate your Web server with a mainframe.

3270 Data Streams (Screen Scraping)

In this approach, the client computer appears as a terminal while the current application and infrastructure are largely undisturbed. This type of integration effort may save some initial expense, but can become a maintenance headache in the future since changes to the 3270 application require changes to the process interface. Figure 5.8 illustrates a 3270 data streams implementation.

RPC Architecture

This approach involves a process-process design, and requires that both the client and the server be simultaneously available. RPC architecture supports most multiplatform standards (e.g., DCE, TCP/IP sockets, APPC, and DBMS) and maintains the programmers' current programming context (i.e., function call). However, its low level of technical abstraction makes it poorly suited for consumer use. Figure 5.9 illustrates mainframe integration via RPC architecture.

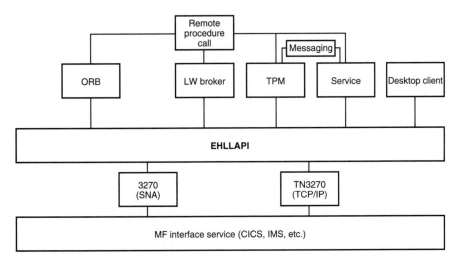

Figure 5.8   Mainframe integration via 3270 data streams.

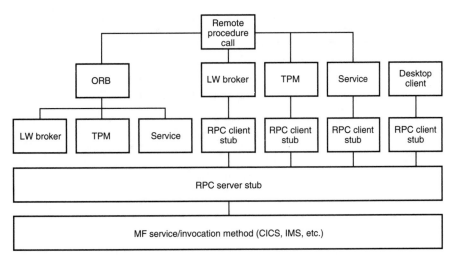

Figure 5.9   Mainframe integration via RPC architecture.

Message Architecture

This approach involves a queue-queue design, so that either the client or the server can be disconnected but transaction delivery is guaranteed. There are, however, no standards for interoperability. A message can act like an RPC (guaranteed delivery) but an RPC cannot act like a message (deferred interaction with transaction persistence). Figure 5.10 illustrates this approach.

TP Monitor (Transaction Processing Monitor)

TP monitors (e.g., IBM CICS or Novell Tuxedo) generally contain a procedural language for data manipulation and transaction handling. They are usually RPC-activated and provide transaction management across heterogeneous systems, including systems that do not have inherent TP facilities. The transaction-based interface is a programmatic interface rather than a consumer interface.

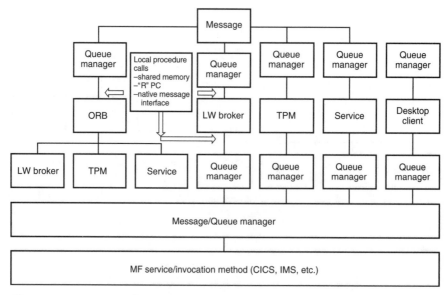

Figure 5.10   Mainframe integration via message architecture.

TP monitors are also interoperable via native calls or via the X/A standard.

ORB (Object Request Broker)

ORBs, which we discuss in more detail in Chapter 6, typically use an object-oriented language to drive instantiation behavior (i.e., data and business logic). The Common Object Request Broker Architecture (CORBA) supports TCP/IP as its preferred interaction mechanism, but also supports DCE. However, object modeling is required to enable object implementations of the business process.

Publish and Subscribe Architecture

In this approach, subscribing systems apply specific business process and manipulation techniques to published data. Figure 5.11 illustrates a publish and subscribe model. New systems integrate wherever possible by subscribing to existing publica-

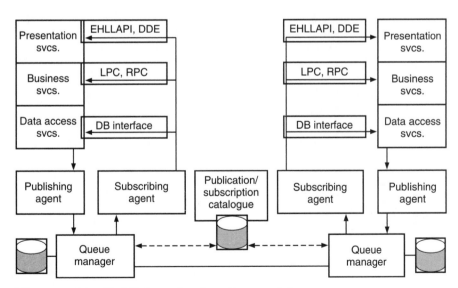

Figure 5.11   Publish and subscribe model.

tions. This architecture facilitates the evolution of the system by abstracting source from destination and allowing interface versioning.

Service Brokers

This approach abstracts the business process location and the data repository. The former can be achieved through a naming service, while the latter can be achieved through an access mechanism wrapper (i.e., RPC or messaging). OEC's Entera and Netwise's MS RPC are examples of this technology.

Now that you're familiar with the pieces that go into your intranet architecture and their relation to one another—and to your existing information systems—you can make the necessary decisions on intranet architecture and move on toward design and development.

CHAPTER SIX

OBJECT REQUEST BROKERS (ORBS)

- ◆ Overview
- ◆ What Is Object Technology?
- ◆ Definition of ORB
- ◆ Distributed Object Technology and the Web
- ◆ Issues Related to Distributed Object Technology and the Web
- ◆ Three Major Contenders
- ◆ Interoperability
- ◆ Making a Choice
- ◆ Future Trends

Overview

The combination of the Internet and multimedia produced the "killer app" of the World Wide Web. Now it seems that the combination of object technology and the Internet is about to produce a new "killer app"—or to be more accurate, many "killer apps." Object technology has long been viewed as an approach that made sense but suffered from problems related to initial cost, scalability, and performance. However, the concept of distributing objects through the Internet, and especially intranets, has generated an unprecedented level of excitement about languages and protocols such as Java, J++, and ActiveX that did not exist a year ago. And, we can see from the architectural models described in Chapter 5, that distributing objects over the Web has the effect of extending the application box in both directions throughout all of the layers.

What Is Object Technology?

Objects have characteristics that reflect the way in which individuals and organizations function, as well as the way in which we interact with them. This is analogous to the way in which an organization such as a bank offers services that define the way in which a customer can interact with it. Object-oriented technology (OOT) employs the principles of object-oriented (OO) software engineering. The most fundamental of these principles are the OO concepts of *inheritance, encapsulation,* and *polymorphism.* (Note: For those unfamiliar with the basics of object-oriented technology, Taylor's *Object-Oriented Technology: A Manager's Guide* [Addison-Wesley Publishing Co., Reading, MA, 1981] is an excellent "quick read" on the subject.) These basic concepts were not introduced by OOT; rather, OOT includes languages, tools, and techniques that provide specific support for the consistent application of these concepts. OOT also provides a framework in which to define and package collections of software components that may need to collaborate with other components. Software components implement useful functions and can be implemented for a variety of platforms (i.e., utilizing various operating system, programming language, and hardware platforms). The useful functions may be low-level, technical services such as networking or database access, or high-level services such as spell checking, stock quoting, or online shopping.

Definition of ORB

An *ORB,* or object request broker, is software that handles requests for objects in a distributed object system. The foundation for ORB technology lies in the concept of distributed object computing (DOC). This concept refers to objects that can communicate—seamlessly and openly—with other objects across a network. ORBs are essentially traffic cops, providing directions to applications looking for specific objects. This approach offers a number of advantages including enhanced performance because of scalability, reliable systems because of reuse and replication of objects, and cost-effective software development and information retrieval.

Although ORB technology is still maturing and is likely to continue to develop for many years to come. It is also likely to become an integral part of your corporate information system in the not-too-distant future. Netscape and Microsoft have already pushed object computing into a precocious adolescence by including ORB support in their net-based products. So, although ORB technology will certainly undergo some significant changes during the next several years, it is important to understand the concept today and realize its potential for the future so that you can manage its inclusion in your corporate intranet.

ORB Standards

The Object Management Group (OMG) of Framingham, Massachusetts, is a group of vendors that worked together to develop a standard means of interacting with distributed objects. The group, which began with only about 12 vendors (i.e., IBM, Hewlett-Packard, and Novell, among others) has grown to include more than 500 member companies, all of which support the specification known as the *Common Object Request Broker Architecture* (CORBA), now in its second release. A primary goal of CORBA is to facilitate the development of distributed applications by establishing and enforcing standards for interoperability and portability. The CORBA standard is currently used in many mainstream ORB products, including those developed by NeXT Computing, Sun Microsystems, IBM, Hewlett-Packard, and Digital Equipment. Not surprisingly, many of these products are being integrated with major intranet tools (as we discuss in Chapter 10).

Microsoft's participation with the OMG has been limited and it does not use CORBA within its products. Instead, Microsoft has created its own ORB system called the Component Object Model (COM), and has released a distributed implementation (DCOM) with NT 4.0. Microsoft has also submitted DCOM as an Internet draft and hopes to have it accepted as a true standard.

The OMG and Microsoft continue to work together to bridge the gap between CORBA and COM/DCOM. In April 1996, they announced the adoption of an interface between the two ORB systems based on the OMG's object management architecture (OMA). The solution will be implemented in two parts: A and B. Part A deals with COM/CORBA integration while part B deals with DCOM/CORBA integration. Refer to the OMG Web site (document reference orb-96-01-05) for a copy of the specification.

CORBA

The OMG was founded specifically to address the issue of distributed object-oriented application development using open standards. It is endorsed by a number of open system–compliant hardware vendors, and a number of companies presently market products that provide ORB functionality in a manner that is compliant to the CORBA specification. The CORBA specifications allow objects that are developed using OO languages (e.g., C++, Smalltalk) to be turned into distributable sets of processing functionality that can be integrated into a distributed object environment. The distributed objects can then be used by client applications and services through the use of locator services. The locator services are provided through an ORB, which is responsible for setting up a connection between a client and the requested object. CORBA also defines how issues of hardware incompatibilities and marshaling (i.e., the ability to get typed data to and from a distributed object and its client) are to be resolved.

Historically, CORBA had a number of problems that kept it out of mainstream use. Its lack of interoperability was, for example, so significant that an ORB from Digital Equipment could not communicate with an ORB from IBM. The lack of transactional services in early CORBA definitions was yet another stumbling block. This flaw was serious enough to exclude CORBA from true enterprise-class solutions.

The introduction of CORBA 2.0 has, however, done much to resolve these problems and increase the technology's usability. Release 2.0 significantly expands CORBA interoperability—making CORBA a realistic alternative for large enterprises with platforms and applications from multiple vendors. Release 2.0 also incorporates ORB transaction service—providing critical functionality options. Although many companies still opt for a better-known (i.e., comfortable) solution like TP monitoring because of its established success, a number of more progressive companies are beginning to implement CORBA projects. You should, however, understand that CORBA transaction services are *not* for the faint of heart, and we continue to recommend the use of TP monitors like Encina and Tuxedo under the ORB to provide these services.

CORBA also defines the Interface Definition Language (IDL), which is the interface that enables each object to interact with the rest of the world by communicating with the object's methods and procedures through the ORB. IDL is considered a major component of CORBA and plays a crucial role in its goal of interoperability.

CORBA works by using an asynchronous remote procedure call (RPC) to a target object on the network. (Although TCP/IP is currently the primary solution, DCE is also supported.) The ORB finds the object using its naming service, issues the RPC, ensures that the method executes, and reports back to the sender. Because the RPC is asynchronous, the originating machine can continue processing until the requested object completes its work or the ORB detects an error condition and notifies the sender.

Returned data streams are often interpreted at the client computer by local run-time modules. This approach translates nicely to the use of a browser that supports "component." In fact, in mid-1996 Netscape and Sun both announced support for this type of arrangement.

COM/DCOM

Microsoft's Component Object Model (COM), which is intended as an alternative to the CORBA standard for object implementation, evolved from dynamic data exchange (DDE) and object linking and embedding (OLE). The evolutionary path ultimately led to the development of COM and ActiveX, an important but complex element of Microsoft's object/Web strategy.

While DCOM, the distributed version of COM, is inextricably linked to Microsoft there are currently attempts underway to support it in UNIX and Macintosh environments. Unlike CORBA, DCOM is based on a synchronous processing model and is sometimes considered slow, largely because of its high API count. In truth, DCOM's apparent slowness probably has more to do with the design of COM-based applications that, in the past, tended to be monolithic.

DCOM does, however, have a problem with its use of a synchronous processing ORB. In DCOM, the ORB issues a synchronous RPC to find OLE- or ActiveX-enabled programs, which are then executed. Like CORBA, the DCOM ORB then returns the information to the requester, which then applies the appropriate reader or application. The synchronous nature of this design raises some inherent performance issues because the calling processor or thread is unable to continue processing until the requested service returns control. This arrangement requires very elaborate thread management, making it very likely that Microsoft will ultimately need to support an asynchronous RPC approach.

ActiveX, Microsoft's evolved OLE, supports the DCOM approach of returned data being handled by viewers. ActiveX plays much the same role in Microsoft's object/Web strategy that OpenDoc does in the CORBA world. One advantage of Microsoft's COM approach is the large number of OLE components that can be supported by ActiveX. In addition, Microsoft has incorporated support for ActiveX into Visual Basic, Visual C++, and Visual J++. Because of the widespread support, many ISVs, consultants, contractors, and potential employees are likely to have some competence in the technology.

Slow Adoption

For the last several years, "object oriented" has served as a popular label in the IS market, much like "relational" was used in the early 1980s. While commercial software vendors and corporate IT shops have indeed begun to apply the principles of object-oriented software development, progress has been slow. There are several reasons for this:

1. The essential theoretical research that was required to address some of the more esoteric aspects of object technology (OT) has only recently matured. This research, which forms the foundation for serious software engineering, is required to develop software infrastructure tools such as database systems, compilers, and operating systems. OT is now reaching a level of maturity where

we can expect to witness a dramatic increase in the available number, variety, and sophistication of commercial, object-oriented software products.

2. Colleges and universities have lagged behind the commercial IT industry in incorporating object technology, theory, and practice into their core curriculum. It has taken time for higher education to produce a new generation of graduates that understand OT. The availability of technical skills is essential to achieving sufficient momentum for widespread adoption of OT.

3. Until recently, there has not been a "burning platform" (i.e., compelling situation) to highlight the compelling need for OT in the eyes of the general IT community.

4. Most IS professionals do not have the conceptual education required to effectively perform analysis and design, nor are they familiar with the methodologies needed to manage execution.

Current Popularity

In recent years, OT has gained momentum through the popularity of GUI-based applications and operating systems such as Apple Macintosh OS and Microsoft Windows. Because of their complex nature, GUI-based applications are generally developed with object-oriented tools. But it is the incredible rise in popularity of the World Wide Web and the Internet that has provided the burning platform for OT, at least in the eyes of the popular press. The vision of ubiquitous computing—the "democratization" of technology—highlights the need to address major technical issues for which OT is particularly well suited.

Distributed Object Technology and the Web

While understanding the concept of distributed object technology is essential to the OO software engineering process, it is equally important to realize how this concept positions OT to address the technical issues raised by the advent of the Internet and distributed computing. Why does object technology address the issue of distributed computing? The OO software engineering process has proven to be an effective mechanism for packaging software into appropriate bundles of functionality or components that can be used by other software application software as "black boxes." In turn, however, this has exacerbated the problems related to (1) version control, (2) application administration, and (3) application performance. Distributed computing, particularly distributed object technology, is now starting to address these issues in a number of ways.

For example, centralizing specific business processing functionality at known processing locations (i.e., servers) and allowing all users to call this functionality when required, facilitates better application administration, security, and version control. This approach is far more effective than distributing the business processing functionality to all user workstations.

Similarly, in the event that business processing functionality does not meet user performance requirements, you have the option of replacing the processing platform (i.e., the server) with faster hardware without affecting the user workstations.

Just as standard applications have benefited from the use of object technology—and will continue to reap benefits from the use of distributed object technology for many years to come—so too can applications designed and developed for the World Wide Web. In fact, World Wide Web–based applications stand to see the most benefit from object technology; implementing distributed processing for the World Wide Web requires the same set of techniques for locating services and components as OT, and can therefore take immediate advantage of existing distributed processing research, techniques, and technologies.

Ultimately, the value of object technology is the underlying premise that complexity can be best dealt with through abstraction. Today's business environment *craves* this flexibility.

Issues Related to Distributed Object Technology and the Web

There are a number of technical issues related to the use of distributed object technology with Web-based applications. Many of these issues underscore the need for tools and techniques that can support software development in an integrated, global environment where an application can interact with a variety of platforms, some of which may be remotely located to the requester of the service.

Some of the major technical issues include:

- Platform interoperability (programming language, operating system, hardware)
- Software version management and distribution
- Customization and integration
- Component-based software
- Distributed computing
- Name resolution (i.e., the ability to find a distributed object based upon its URL, or Uniform Resource Locator)
- Type of network connection (i.e., high speed/low speed)

Three Major Contenders

There are three major approaches that enable intranets to distribute applications across the Internet:

- *Plug-ins.* Although the first approach cannot really be classified as object-oriented, it does allow applications to be run on a client machine—even if the application is not available locally. Netscape developed plug-ins as an extension to the browser; the concept was then adopted by a number of third-party vendors, including Macromedia (with its Shockwave) and Adobe (with Amber for pdf documents). Netscape has also announced support for CORBA-based objects in its browser.
- *Java.* Sun Microsystems' Java (which has now also been spun into SunSoft), was the first true object-oriented language for Web objects in that it incorporates inheritance as well as aggregation. Never before has a

language been adopted quite as rapidly as Java. Even before its official release, books on the subject were selling out as fast as they were printed and Java seminars were consistently sold out. Java already has phenomenal mindshare and is very likely to capture significant market share in the near future.

Java's advantages include the fact that it is interpreted, enabling it to produce applications that can run unmodified on many operating systems. This is accomplished through the use of a Java "virtual machine," which abstracts the calling interface from the underlying operating system. Additionally, Java is designed to constrain the OS services that an applet can access, providing a way of insulating local system data from "rogue" applications or viruses.

For Java to be completely successful, however, it needs an integrated development environment (IDE) to facilitate the process of building applications for developers. IDEs typically provide a good editor (for source code), a capability for browsing within the code, and facilities for application resource editing, as well as compilers and debuggers.

Several such IDEs are already available. Sunsoft provides JDK, the Java Developers Kit, free on its Web site (http://www.javasoft.com). Others include Symantec Café from Symantec (http://cafe.symantec.com/), Visual J++ from Microsoft (http://www.microsoft.com), Jfactory from Rogue Wave (http://www.roguewave.com), Borland C++, which includes Java tools (http://www.borland.com), NetBuild of Foster City, and SourceCraft (http://www.sourcecraft.com).

◆ *ActiveX.*   With the explosion of the Internet and Microsoft's epiphany came the realization that OLE, which was originally developed for use in high-performance shared-memory LANs, was too "big" for use in limited bandwidth WWW environments. Thus, ActiveX was born out of necessity. While it is not strictly an object-oriented approach, ActiveX does represent an update of OLE technology. Its OLE foundation gives it two distinct advantages: the availability of a large library of OLE controls, and the ability to run them in containers such as a Visual Basic application as well as in a browser. Microsoft seems to be moving toward an approach in which the operating system is the browser, with the browser itself being an ActiveX component. Microsoft has also developed an ActiveX library for Java, allowing Java applets to use COM/DCOM services.

Interoperability

As users and developers, we seem to be moving toward an ideal environment—two large, well-funded competing vendors (i.e., Microsoft and Netscape) developing interoperable solutions. Hopefully, they will both survive and thrive and keep each other honest. It is still too early to assess the full picture on interoperability, but the following table summarizes the current situation.

In addition, there are a number of tools being introduced to bridge the gap between the rival standards of OMG's CORBA and Microsoft's COM. Iona Software's Iona Form is an example of one such tool. It is also important to remember that CORBA has a variety of flavors, including IBM's SOM, Digital Equipment's COM (which has no relation to Microsoft's COM), and Sun's DOE (Distributed Objects Everywhere). Confused? That's not surprising—so is everyone else.

TABLE 6.1   Interoperability between Microsoft and Netscape Browsers and Web Object Approaches

	Netscape	Internet Explorer
Java	Yes	Yes
ActiveX	With a plug-in	Yes

Making a Choice

While these competing methods of using ORBs may well ultimately become totally interoperable, such interoperability is by
no means certain. You'll still need to make a decision now about
which to use. Fortunately, the decision may be easier than you
think. The decision tree in Figure 6.1 enumerates the various

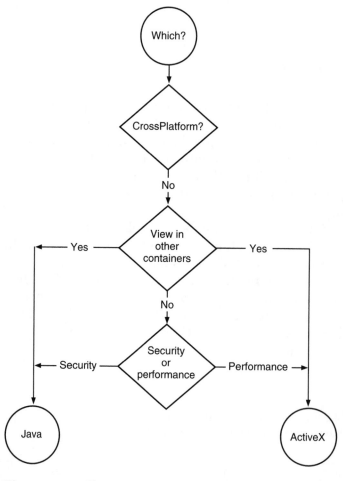

Figure 6.1   Choosing an OT approach.

steps in the selection process. And, it may also be useful to compare OMG's CORBA and the Java language and Microsoft's COM and ActiveX using the variables that we describe in Chapter 7 (Intranet Design). In this comparison, you'll see that each solution scores very differently on each variable. Thus, if you can prioritize the following variables the answer falls out.

- Platform independence
- Environment
- Performance
- Local system access
- Security

Future Trends

Clearly, we can expect to see a great deal of activity in the area of development environments, utilities, and tools for building applications from distributed objects over the Web. Java and ActiveX are likely to remain the two major approaches, but we can also expect to see significant activity from object databases such as Illustra (which is being combined with Informix as the Universal Server), Object Store, GemStone, Poet, Object Design, Versant, and Objectivity.

CHAPTER SEVEN

Intranet Design

- ◆ Overview
- ◆ Type of Intranet
- ◆ Performance
- ◆ Cost
- ◆ Security
- ◆ Manageability
- ◆ Usability
- ◆ Trade-Offs

Overview

Now that you've completed your intranet implementation plan and determined the components that you'll need, you're ready to address some of the finer points of intranet design. These design considerations will help you to optimize such factors as cost, performance, security, manageability, and usability. However, because these factors are all interdependent, you'll first need to determine your priorities.

Usability and security should be high on your list of priorities. After all, you lose the benefits of an intranet if your users don't use it and, while some types of information are more attractive to hackers and competitors than other types, all of your information is important and deserves to be protected from external (as well as internal) security breaches. Cost is often a priority as well, but be sure to focus on your ongoing intranet costs rather than the initial implementation costs, which are typically amortized.

Although we address all of these considerations in fairly general terms in this chapter (i.e., as they relate to the initial intranet *design*), we address many of them in more detail in Chapter 5 (Intranet Architectures).

Type of Intranet

Before you go much further in considering the design of your intranet, you should decide just what kind of an intranet you're building. There are several major categories of intranets and considerable overlap among the categories.

The Communications Intranet

This type of intranet is intended primarily as a means of linking the various sites of a large, geographically dispersed organization and, in so doing, reducing the cost of numerous point-to-point communication lines and (hopefully) the voice telephony bill as well. Organizations with a large number of salespeople or agents in the field frequently employ this type of intranet, as do large franchises. Often, cost reduction or increased efficiency is the prime motivation for implementing a communications intranet. If you determine that you are implementing this type of intranet, be sure to pay particular attention to performance issues, standardization, and manageability.

The Integrating Intranet

In today's fast-paced corporate environment, it's not unusual for companies to be frustrated by a complex mix of in-house communications and processing systems—often using different interfaces and commonly lacking any means of interconnection. For this reason, many companies view an integrating intranet as a means of establishing a common interface (i.e., the browser) for the diverse systems and a way to link the information through hypertext links. In addition, these companies often gain the benefit of moving from one or more tightly coupled systems to a loosely coupled system, which makes it much easier to implement future changes. Again, standardization is paramount in an integrating intranet, as is an integrated tool set that can help departments to migrate their existing systems. Some of the architectures that we discuss in Chapter 5 in conjunction with the layers of abstraction further enable the intranet to integrate heterogeneous environments.

The Catalog Intranet

This type of intranet is typically implemented by companies that want to provide wide access to a large catalog of information, particularly a multimedia catalog. If you are implementing this type of intranet, be especially careful in your selection of the server database since it must be capable of efficiently handling large volumes of data and complex data types. Also pay close attention to the underlying data model and be sure that it can accommodate all of the various product types that will be included.

The Single Sign-On Intranet

This type of intranet has been something of a holy grail for IT professionals for quite a while. After many years of relying on passwords and user IDs to safeguard security throughout an organization, client authentication finally eliminates the need for those hard-to-remember words and phrases, using instead a single sign-on for all users and letting each system look-up the appropriate access privileges for each user. This type of intranet security arrangement works just as efficiently over a wide area through the Internet as it does on a local level. If you are implementing a single sign-on intranet, security is of paramount importance.

Performance

There are many factors that affect performance, but you should pay particular attention to the following during the intranet design phase:

- *Servers.*   To optimize performance, use servers with fast processors (or multiple processors, as in SMP machines) and large amounts of memory. Good multi-tasking and multi-threading ability is also crucial for most Web applications.

- *Clients.*   Sufficient memory and disk capacity at the client can also help to improve performance since they increase caching. Similarly, server-based scripts that anticipate future requests (i.e., any links from the current page) and cache them to the client can also improve performance.

- *Content.*   Limiting complex data types such as large image files may also improve performance, but be cautious with this factor since it may also reduce usability to some extent.

- *Architecture.*   A number of vendors are introducing products, such as the Proxy Server from Netscape, specifically intended to improve performance through sophisticated caching. Be sure to research the latest product offerings to determine which may be useful for your particular environment and applications.

- *Database.*   Because many applications are built on top of a database, the database itself can have a significant effect on performance. Replicating the database rather than running queries against an existing legacy system may provide a significant improvement in performance.

Cost

In any large network (i.e., one with many users), reducing the cost of the client is one of the most effective ways to minimize the overall cost of the network. There are a number of ways in which to do this; in a large network, you can use a powerful server and configure it to support most of the business logic. Other alternatives are to minimize the use of large, complex data types and/or minimize client-side processing. Keep in mind however, that hard disk capacity is relatively inexpensive and does contribute to satisfactory performance, particularly when the information being accessed is repetitive and not very volatile.

Your primary cost-saving option is generally related to wide-area network (WAN) bandwidth. Because bandwidth is an ongoing cost (which is typically expensed), even minimal savings here can represent a very significant savings over the life of the network. If you can make do with a relatively low bandwidth (or dial-up access if your access sessions are infrequent and not long in duration), you can realize considerable savings and be able to sustain reasonable performance if you are transmitting ASCII data rather than images, sound, and/or video. You may be able to realize further savings by using a less expensive internet service provider (ISP). Be aware, however, that you may sacrifice some degree of reliability. You may need to spend more initially from the capital budget to, for example, install caching servers at large, remote offices, to gain greater savings in the on-going expense budget.

The cost estimation table in Figure 7.1 is intended to help you generate a very rough estimate of the capital and ongoing expense likely to be incurred by your intranet project. A regularly updated version of this information is available in spreadsheet format on the BSG Web site.

Security

Security is, of course, a very crucial topic in its own right and something that you need to consider very early in the intranet design phase. You should continue to keep security foremost in your intranet project throughout the development, testing, and maintenance phases. While the cost of the intranet may be a major factor in your design, security is *not* the area in which to cut corners! Saving a few dollars in the intranet security design can cost your organization its credibility (at best) and its very viability (at worst). This thought is well summarized by Alex Sharpe, security expert at Rapid System Solutions, Inc., when he says, "Intranet security is enabling technology that allows industry to make use of internet computing technology without the Internet making use of them."

Intranet Cost Estimator	No./No. of seats		
Type of Architecture			
1. Basic/Content	200		
2. RDBMS Connectivity	100		
3. Traditional Process Integration			
4. Non-Traditional Integration			
5. Collabaritive Computing			
a. E-mail	200		
b. Discussion database	140		
Security			
High	150		
Medium			
Low			
None	150		
Total Unduplicated Seats			
Communications			
Point to Point	1		
Virtual Private Internet	3		
No of sites	4		
Content			Electronic Y/N
Images	150		No
Text (Pages)	600		Yes
Sound (seconds)	140		No
Movies (seconds)	90		No
PDF's (pages)	30		n/a
Streamed Audio (seconds)	90		
Streamed Video (seconds)	15		
Applications			
New		Complexity	
4GL	1	2	
3GL			
ORB's	1	3	
Porting		Complexity	
from Client/Server	3	3	
from Mainframe	2	7	
Approx Estimated Cost	$xxx,000		
Ongoing Cost/Year	$xxx,000		

Figure 7.1   Cost estimation table.

A recent survey by the Computer Security Institute indicates that 4 out of every 10 companies in the United States have been victimized by cybercrime in the past year. Some organizations are victimized more than others—the Pentagon reported 250,000 intrusions in 1995 alone! More than half of the companies surveyed attributed the intrusions to external competitors. The severity of attacks varied from casual hackers to determined attacks by knowledgeable intruders with strong financial (or other) incentives to penetrate even well-designed security systems.

Unfortunately, serious intruders can apply considerable time and resources to breaching your security system. Their motives, which are as varied as their capabilities and methods, may include obtaining proprietary information for business competitors, seeking high-value information such as credit card–and/or telephone numbers for resale, or making false trades on a trading system. While electronic funds transfer (EFT) is always a prime target for intruders, most of this activity is still based on point-to-point connections.

One of the most important aspects of security relates to the people using the intranet. While chapter 4 tackles some of the "people" aspects of security, the technological issues cannot, of course, be entirely separated from the organizational concerns. In general, there are five major issues related to intranet security:

1. Unauthorized access
2. Authorized users performing unauthorized functions
3. Unauthorized modification or deletion (i.e., failure to maintain the integrity of the intranet)
4. Confirmation that a transaction has occurred (and the ability to make it legally binding), referred to as nonrepudiation
5. Denial of service attacks (or availability), which refers to the ability to provide acceptable level of service to users

The Major Threats

The following pages summarize some of the major security breaches that you should consider (and guard against) in your intranet design. Obviously, this list is not all-inclusive; as you read this book and design your intranet, you can be certain that hackers are thinking up new and devious ways to penetrate network security systems—and some of them are likely to target your system.

UNAUTHORIZED ACCESS TO YOUR CORPORATE LAN

If your external web server is connected to your corporate LAN, 40 million people have (at least theoretically) potential access to the LAN. Your major concern in this case is not merely securing confidential data from a few hundred employees, but preventing access by those 40 million potential intruders. The problem can also extend to unauthorized disclosures from your corporate LAN.

Solution: *A firewall.* A firewall is probably the first thing that most people think of when designing an intranet security system. Indeed, you should probably consider a firewall as a necessity, but remember that a firewall alone may not be sufficient to safeguard your intranet. In fact a third of all penetrations occur after a firewall has been installed. There are two major types of firewalls: router-based firewalls that simply filter IP address and application/proxy servers, which present a proxy IP address to the Internet and pass messages to and from the internal IP addresses that are not visible to the Internet. (Refer to Chapter 12 for a more detailed description of both types of firewalls.)

If your server provides public information to the Internet, you may want to configure the routers to prohibit any device on the Web server segment from communicating with the firewall segment or with any internal address. And, conversely, configure the firewall to prevent internal addresses from communicating with addresses on the Web server segment. This type of arrangement does, however involve a couple of disadvantages: it prevents internal LAN addresses from directly viewing the Web site and complicates the process of transferring data from the internal LAN (often the location of much of the production activity) to the external Web server.

The highest possible level of security involves an "air wall" between the external Web server and the internal LAN (i.e., no physical connection between the two). It is not positions. Server spoofing is commonly used to collect credit card and telephone card numbers for resale on bulletin boards.

Solution: *Server authentication* assures the client that the server it is communicating with is, indeed, the server that it means to communicate with. To accomplish this, the company providing the server gets a certificate from a trusted, third-party—referred to as the certificate authority (CA). To receive the certificate, an officer of the corporation must provide the CA with company documentation (including a certificate of incorporation) via traditional mail. In this way, the CA certifies that the company hosting a particular server is indeed that company; users do not have to rely solely on the representations of the company. In addition to acting as a source for certificates, the CAs maintain the name space and keep updated lists of access controls (i.e., to tell which users are allowed what access) and to track user revocations.

For example, Netscape users select "Document Info" from the view menu to verify the server they're talking to. The system then tells them which server they're communicating with, establishing the identity of the server beyond doubt. With server authentication, the client is challenged for a password and a secure session is opened only after the password has been provided and verified. When a secure session is established with a Netscape client, the broken key in the lower-left of the browser window changes to a solid key.

PACKET SNIFFING

In this type of security breach, intruders actually remove IP packets from the Internet and extract useful information from them. Unencrypted packets containing credit card information or passwords are a typical target, raising some very legitimate concerns about the security of electronic commerce and prompting VISA and MasterCard to agree on SET (Secure Electronic Transactions) for encrypting credit card information that is transmitted over the Web. This agreement, although something of a proprietary solution, is still a relief as the companies had previously been pursuing different proprietary solutions.

If the clients on your LAN have access to the external Web, your network may be vulnerable to a particular kind of "sniffer" observation (i.e., the process of observing IP packets from the net) that uses information about the sites that are visited to gain insight into corporate activity. For example, if you suspected that an investment banking company was working on a merger, you might be able to confirm your suspicions by observing frequent visits to the sites of the companies involved.

Solution: Using any of the major cryptographic algorithms— Public Key, Private Key, or DES—can solve the problem of packet sniffing (and also password interception). The strength of the ciphers (i.e., the encryption algorithms) is, however, important in determining the level of protection. Even a 40-bit key, which is currently the strongest cryptography that the U.S. government allows to be exported, has been broken. Admittedly, the solution required massive resources in terms of MIPS (millions of instruction per second) and manpower, but it does indicate that organizations with access to supercomputing resources can eventually break this level of cryptography (although there are certainly doubts about the cost/benefit justification). There is currently substantial debate about the feasibility of the U.S. government restricting the use of cryptography by U.S. companies doing business overseas. Indeed, some U.S. companies use foreign companies (e.g., Finnish in once instance) to provide the cryptographic part of their security services. Companies that communicate regularly with wholly owned subsidiaries overseas are probably exempt from the Munitions Export Act (which restricts cryptography export), but it is certainly advisable to check with a lawyer qualified in this area rather than risk a violation.

ABUSE OF ACCESS

In this type of threat, employees exceed their assigned system security levels to access information or areas for which they are not authorized. There are a number of ways in which employees can exceed their security levels, including watching other employees log on to a system and memorizing their passwords, accessing the system administrator's files, recording passwords as they are transmitted through the system and replaying them, or running password guessing programs like Crack (developed by Alec Muffett at the University College of Wales and available from ftp://info.cert.org/pub/tools/crack/).

Solution: Several software vendors, including Northern Telecom, X-Cert in Vancouver, and RSA, offer products that integrate the process of identifying the user with the access security incorporated in most major applications (e.g., database programs). For example, Northern Telecom's Entrust product and RSA's BSAFE both enable systems administrators to link the initial challenge for a new user with the APIs of other applications for which the user does have access privileges. In addition, both Windows and UNIX permit some of these access controls to be implemented on a more basic level.

This type of security challenge is largely transparent to the user; in a large, complex environment, for example, users only need to enter their password or physical token once in the course of a session or longer, at the discretion of the system administrator. Thus, users can access a system's public area with no challenge. They will, however, be challenged at their first attempt to enter a secure area. If they respond appropriately and have the appropriate access privileges, they can move freely between the secure areas and public areas of the intranet (and the Internet) without further challenge. The administrator can select any length of time between challenges—up to 24 hours, the maximum allowable time under the X509 standard. Conversely, the administrator can set a much shorter duration between challenges—as little as a few minutes.

DENIAL OF SERVICE

With this type of threat, computers are programmed to make repeated access calls to your site. The purpose of this kind of attack is not to gain access to your site but rather to prevent others from doing so. An example of this kind of attack is the one against the alt.religion.scientology newsgroup.

Solution: Denial of service attacks are probably the most difficult security breaches to prevent. One solution is to determine the source of the attack and turn it off at a routing node upstream. You may also be able to program your firewall to exclude the IP address from which the attacks are coming.

OTHER POTENTIAL THREATS

You should also be aware that your communications infrastructure may harbor a number of other areas that are prone to security breaches. Modems on the network and terminal servers represent two such areas, as do the CGI scripts or database connectivity applications behind the server. Additionally, metacharacters can easily be used to penetrate servers. If you are unfamiliar with these concepts or need assistance in establishing security systems to address these areas, consult with a knowledgeable security consultant.

Finally, although Java has some built-in mechanisms to protect the security of your network, some questions still remain. Among them is Sunsoft's lobbying of Congress to allow more rigorous security in the export versions. This heightened security is necessary for Java to become a fully secure international, distributed environment.

The Major Needs

Unlike security threats, security *needs* describe essential controls that you should consider implementing in your intranet security system. The number of controls that you actually require depends on the type of intranet that you're implementing and the vulnerability of your company, as well as the nature of the information you're transmitting.

REVOCATION

Revoking security access from ex-employees or from employees who, for one reason or another, are no longer entitled to their previous level of security is a significant problem in many companies. The problem of revocation applies to passwords, physical tokens, and certificates.

Solution: A combination of certificate authority (CA) and public key encryption can remedy this type of security breach. Public key encryption, as its name implies, requires publishing the public key and its associated access privileges. The information is generally published by certificate authorities, organizations that hold unlimited-use licenses for the key. (RSA, the developer of public key encryption, issued a limited number of such licenses six years ago.) Once the CA has received documentation to verify the company's identity and is satisfied as to its authenticity, the CA generates a pair of encrypted keys. In the case of public key encryption, one of the keys is kept private while the other is published on a public server that is available on the Internet—usually 24 hours a day, 7 days a week. The CA provides not only a formal verification of the identity of each party, but also maintains a list of user access rights. The CA can immediately revoke employee access privileges if an individual leaves an organization or changes responsibilities and no longer requires security access. The CA issues a certificate which conforms to international standards and "binds" the name of the company with its key, then adds its own signature key. Figure 7.2 illustrates the admittedly complex process involved in public key encryption.

ROYALTY COLLECTION

The Web poses a real dilemma for information publishers. While the Web is an incredibly attractive medium for distributing information to a worldwide audience, it is also difficult to control distribution to ensure payment or to prevent redistribution.

Solution: *Encrypted envelopes.* Fortunately, there are a number of control mechanisms available. IBM's use of the Cryptolope is one such method. This service "wraps" the publishers' content in a secure envelope and sends billing information to the publisher each time a user "opens" the wrapper. An added advantage of the service is the ability to search all "wrapped" documents with a single search engine. A California-based company is taking a similar approach, but makes the envelope software available to the publishers to let them "wrap" their own information. If some of your information is going to be available on a "premium" (i.e., for a charge) basis, it is very important to separate that information in the directory structures. Additionally, you may need to keep royalty-based

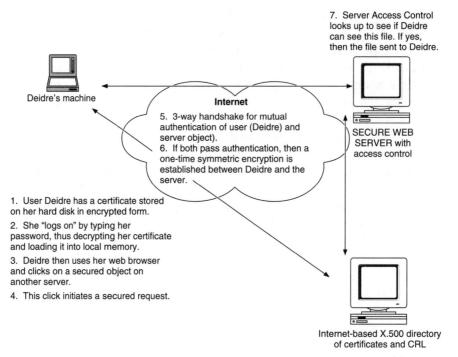

7. Server Access Control looks up to see if Deidre can see this file. If yes, then the file sent to Deidre.

Deidre's machine

Internet

5. 3-way handshake for mutual authentication of user (Deidre) and server object).
6. If both pass authentication, then a one-time symmetric encryption is established between Deidre and the server.

SECURE WEB SERVER with access control

1. User Deidre has a certificate stored on her hard disk in encrypted form.

2. She "logs on" by typing her password, thus decrypting her certificate and loading it into local memory.

3. Deidre then uses her web browser and clicks on a secured object on another server.

4. This click initiates a secured request.

Internet-based X.500 directory of certificates and CRL

Figure 7.2   Public key encryption process.

information separate from non-royalty-based information and/or to differentiate several levels of royalty-based information.

Security Protocols

The heightened interest in security is causing a corresponding interest in security protocols, along with the development of new products capable of taking advantage of the evolving protocols. The following paragraphs describe the major security protocols that you should consider during the design phase of your intranet security system.

Note that the early security protocols, SSL and S-HTTP, which initially competed with one another, have since been combined in the interests of standardization.

◆ SSL (Secure Sockets Layer) was originally a Netscape standard; it is now widely supported. It provides link encryption at the transport layer.

◆ S-HTTP (Secure Hypertext Transfer Protocol) protects all information over secure transport sessions. While S-HTTP, like SSL, is beginning to gain widespread support as a result of standardization, there are presently few actual implementations of S-HTTP. Many of the existing implementations support only a subset of application protocols.

◆ RSA (Rivest-Shamir-Adleman, named for its developers) is a secure private-key encryption method originally introduced by RSA Data Security, Inc. It uses key pairs for each user: One key is retained by the user and the other is released to the public. With RSA, data is encrypted using the recipient's public key, and can only be decrypted by the recipient's private key. Because RSA is computation-intensive, it is often used to create an "RSA digital envelope," which holds an RSA-encrypted DES key and DES-encrypted data. RSA is also used for authentication. You can, for example, verify your identity with a digital signature by encrypting it with your private key and letting others decrypt your message with your public key. This requires the sender to compute a hash value of the message being sent, which is encrypted along with the message. The recipient then decrypts the hash value and computes the hash value from the message using the same algorithm. The signature is authenticated if they match. This approach also ensures data integrity because any changes to the content invalidate the hash value.

◆ Kerberos, the encryption standard for DCE (Distributed Computer Environment), was originally designed as a private-private key system. It was modified in its latest release (mid-1996), however, to function as a public-private key system.

◆ SET (Secure Electronic Transaction) is the standard adopted by VISA and MasterCard to resolve their two separate standards for safely transmitting credit card information over the Internet. SET is based on RSA technology.

◆ PGP (Pretty Good Privacy), modestly named by its developer (Philip Zimmerman), is actually very good encryption system for most applications. In fact, the U.S. government threatened Zimmerman with prosecution under the prohibitions on munitions exports when he put the DES algorithm into the public domain via the Internet. PGP is based on a combination of public and private key encryption methods, combining the advantages of the former with the speed of the latter. It is primarily used for encrypting E-mail messages; the Massachusetts Institute for Technology (MIT) maintains a server for the public keys. Alternatively, you can post the public keys on the Internet.

◆ X509 refers to the ITU (International Telecom Union) standard for data formats used in key management. In theory, products that comply with this standard are interchangeable or, at least, interoperable. As is often the case with "standards," however, there are several different interpretations of X509, which significantly reduces its theoretical interoperability. These differences are likely to be resolved in the near future, however, through a revision in the standard or as a result of the certificate authorities designing systems to recognize all of the major interpretations of X509.

Security Trends

Most major corporations seem to be moving toward fully mutual (i.e., using server and client) authentication services. Although they may initially establish a fairly open network, as that network expands, there is an increased need to grant differing access rights to different classes of users in order to secure transactions on the network. The corporate (i.e., private) sector typically uses the RSA encryption method to ensure network security while the public sector is attempting to finalize NSA's Fortezza recommendation. The government is, however, meeting with resistance because of the expense involved in the Fortezza method and faces increasing pressure to adopt RSA.

There is also a movement toward incorporating fees for maintaining certificate pairs into the ISP charges, thereby producing one charge for an open connection and a slightly higher charge for a secure connection. As large companies with deep pockets enter the CA field, however, and develop long-term strategies to capture market share, the price differential for maintaining client certificates is likely to narrow significantly.

Manageability

As you can probably anticipate, managing an intranet site differs somewhat from managing a traditional IS group. For example, the intranet typically involves new skills to learn and teach, new processes for sharing information, and new expectations and incentives; all of these factors can have a major impact on the intranet's ongoing costs. We discuss these considerations again in chapter 13, but you can mitigate some of the intranet management concern through careful planning now, in the design phase of your project. Some of the issues that you should address now to optimize the manageability of your intranet include:

Naming Conventions

Establishing (and enforcing) some naming conventions will facilitate managing the files on your Web server, as well as associating those files with a specific product line or department within your organization. Because users do not need to see the file names, you can adopt a naming convention that uses long but descriptive names, such as HR_whatsnew_final.gif.

One company that did not impose a naming convention discovered, much to its dismay, that its designers all used their own naming conventions. As a result, literally hundreds of images, movies, and sounds were stored on multiple disk drives with no clear means of identification. System administrators had no recourse but to open and view all of the files—a particularly tedious process since some were very large (e.g., 17MB) images—to identify and name them. The situation was further aggravated by the departure of one of the designers who had been using an especially cryptic naming convention. In his absence, and without the use of a supercomputer, it was impossible to attribute any logic to the naming convention.

Defined Roles

Similarly, if you establish clear roles for the individuals involved in maintaining the intranet site during the project design phase, you will ensure a much smoother start-up operation. You can, of course, modify any of the user roles and access levels as you move further into the implementation process, but it is advisable to establish your management "skeleton" now to ensure that someone "owns" each of the important tasks.

In one company that neglected to establish such roles, numerous individuals prepared designs for the Web site. As a result, the company's Web site was much too busy and lacked a consistent "look." Further, because no one was assigned to refresh the site on a regular basis, it was soon outdated.

Standards

As we mentioned in chapter 4, establishing and enforcing standards within your organization requires a delicate balancing act—recommending products and/or services and encouraging your users to follow the recommendations without setting strict guidelines that users are likely to ignore. Establishing standards (and achieving user support for those standards) can significantly facilitate managing the intranet and is also likely to help control intranet operating expense. For example, it is much easier to design pages for internal use if you know that everyone is using the same browser to view the pages and that the browsers are set for the same font. Netscape includes a provision to establish standard settings on all of its browsers. Overall, a lack of standards can significantly increase your intranet costs and may lead to compatibility problems with your business partners.

Procedures

Like standards, effective procedures are crucial to managing an intranet site. Essentially, they ensure that everyone knows what is supposed to be done, and who is responsible for doing it—greatly reducing the chances of things falling through the cracks. The design phase is a good place to begin establishing and documenting procedures, even if you have to modify them later in the implementation project. At this stage of intranet design, you need only a rough outline of procedures (e.g., a tasks and responsibilities list); you can fill in the necessary details and expand task definitions as the project progresses.

One Fortune 100 company failed to document its procedures. When the person responsible for developing and enforcing those procedures left the company, subordinates were left to try to figure out the necessary procedures to keep their internal site active.

Documentation

You'll save considerable time and heartache if you take the time, during the design and implementation phases of your intranet project, to document the procedures, file naming conventions, locations of original "assets," and so forth. The old three-ring loose-leaf binder is no longer an effective means of documenting—if, indeed, it ever was! That old standby (which was generally hidden away when you most needed it, anyway) has, at long last, been replaced by interactive, Web-based help systems. Documentation prepared in HTML and distributed via your intranet has a number of very tangible advantages; information is easily accessible to users and can easily be updated when necessary.

Style Guides

Style guides are another valuable tool for managing the intranet. They can help to ensure satisfactory performance and control the ongoing expenses. A well-designed style guide, as shown in Figure 7.3, should define acceptable file types, specify file formats, and limit the use of complex files types such as images and sound.

STYLE GUIDELINES

TEXT

Use any word processor to prepare text, but be sure to use a single font and limit yourself to two or three levels of headings. Remember that you cannot be sure of where lines will break. Bullets and tables are supported. If a particular word is to be linked to another page, underline the word and indicate the page to which it is to be linked in square brackets.

If a large amount of consistent data is required about a large number of items ensure that it is "fielded". One of the best ways of doing this is to place it in a table. If it already exists in a database just provide us with the database file.

File Name	Comments
Copy ID	Comments (Beginning and ending text, title etc.)

PHOTOGRAPHS

If you are shooting new film for your site, it is more economical to use 35 mm formats rather than professional "plate size" formats. Once you have shot the film, keep it on the roll and send to BSG undeveloped. We will return developed film and prints to you (it is less expensive to scan film in the roll than flat). The level of resolution does not justify large format film. To capture the full amount of data on a 400 ASA slide would require 94 meg.

If you are photographing a large number of objects (e.g., for a catalog) it would help if a number is visible in the shot and a text file provided with information for each number. This can also avoid embarassing or expensive mistakes.

Figure 7.3   Sample style guide.

Photograph	Comments (Format etc..)

IMAGES

If you are providing images, the preferences are as follows:

MEDIA

Any of the following:

◆ **Floppy disks PC format** for a small number of images

◆ **Syquest, Macintosh format,** 44M or 88M for larger number of images

◆ **Photo CD**

◆ **DAT** may be acceptable

The following can all be read, but may incur additional costs:

◆ **9 track tape**

Output from a Scitex or Compugraphic or Linotype-Hell (in this situation check with us first and we can talk to your color separator and discuss preferred sub-sampling.

If color accuracy is important you can include a standard color bar in each photograph. Use appropriate film, although if circumstances prevent this we can correct if you tell us.

IMAGE FORMAT

We can convert from any format, but we prefer **GIF89** images at **72 dpi** and **system palette** to minimize costs and lead times. **JPEG, BMP, PICT, TIFF** are also acceptable, but let us know which flavor to expect.

If image quality is very important, save the images as 24- or 32-bit images and we will create adaptive palettes. You can also scan at higher resolutions and we will sub-sample as the last step. You may sharpen the images yourselves or we can discuss with you the optimum amount and type of sharpening or unsharp masking to apply.

Figure 7.3   *(Continued).*

REFLECTIVE COPY

Provide with desired cropping indicated (preferably on an overlay) and well protected.

IMAGES SUBMITTAL FORM

Fill out one section per image. Make copies of this form as necessary.

Image (Description or file name)	Medium (From list)	Format (JPEG, BMP, PICT, TIFF)	Resolution

Image Size i.e. 100 × 150 (In pixels)		Bits (24 or 32)	

Comments	

Figure 7.3   *(Continued).*

Site Management Tools

Many tools that are currently available, or under development, are intended to facilitate the task of managing the intranet. While we cover these tools in more detail in chapter 9, you should be aware of the wide variety of tools that are available. Microsoft's Front-Page, for example, checks links between pages and allows you to view the site as a whole in diagrammatic form and Sequel's Net Access Manager helps to manage and report intranet usage. Similarly, Web analyzers count pages and provide you with many useful statistics. Products are also available to facilitate managing a site remotely.

Centralized Data

Centralizing your data significantly facilitates site management, but may have an adverse effect on performance. You may also want to consider replicating or caching data to help control ongoing costs by reducing bandwidth requirements. If data is not centralized in this fashion, it is significantly more difficult to manage and tends to be duplicated, often in slightly different versions at multiple locations.

Multimedia Production

Multimedia can cause nightmares for any intranet manager, but it is especially problematic if you are add substantial content to the intranet on an ongoing basis. Managing the intranet editorial process is challenging in any case, but the use of complex data types compounds the usual difficulties. For example, images may have to go through multiple production stages for capture—scanning, cropping, sharpening, unsharp masking, tone correction, gamma curve correction (the relationship between the input and output values for each component color), resampling color depth and resolution, and palette adjustments. Remember, some 120 different file formats are used for multimedia image production.

While sounds are not quite as complex as images, they too involve multiple formats (approximately 12) and can be sampled at varying bit depths and frequencies. Videos add further complications, not just because of the format complexities (primarily AVI and Quicktime), but also because of considerations of the time code, palette, multiple compression algorithms, and window size.

If, however, you design your intranet to incorporate organizational elements (e.g., a combination of workflow products and object-oriented databases), it can actually help you to effectively manage the complex data types in all of their various versions and formats. We discuss a number of tools designed to facilitate working with complex data types in chapter 11 (Back-End Applications), along with some of the object-oriented database products that you can use to build a production management system.

Usability

All of the following elements contribute, to some degree, to the usability of your intranet. We cover each of these elements in more detail in chapter 10, but you should be aware of these factors during the intranet design phase and assess their impact on your specific intranet environment. Some of these considerations do not incur any additional costs, but you may need to plan ahead to include them in the initial intranet implementation.

◆ *Images.*   Using small images and/or image maps generally makes a site more intuitive for users to navigate. Remember, however, that images affect performance.

◆ *Consistency.*   Be sure to use the same look and feel throughout your site. Consistent use of the look and navigational elements makes the system much easier for the users.

◆ *Forgiveness.*   Always be sure that any step can be reversed. Often this involves being sure that users understand the "back" command. (Refer to chapter 10 for an explanation of the "back" command.)

◆ *Repeatability.*   The same operation should always cause the same result.

◆ *Standard UI (User Interface) and Platforms.*   As we discussed earlier in the section on Standards, by imposing standards, you can greatly facilitate users' ability to learn the system and learn from other users.

◆ *Bookmarks.*   Preset bookmarks facilitate user access to popular sites within your intranet or, optionally, to sites on the Internet. Bookmarks are a standard feature in Netscape Navigator.

◆ *Hot Links.*   If you provide access to the external Web, you may want to provide a "jumping-off" page with a list of hot links to useful sites. Alternatively (or in addition), you may want to provide preset bookmarks.

◆ *Cookies.*   Cookies, made popular with Netscape's Navigator, are a way to track user activity in Netscape by downloading information from the server into a file on the client. The cookies file appears as a text file called cookies.txt; it can be opened with any text editor. Typically, cookies are used to identify a particular client by downloading a serial number, preferences (e.g., use of frames), customer profiles (e.g., clothing sizes), and common usage patterns (e.g., favorite pages)—all of which make a specific site easier to use.

Originally developed to help Netscape track use of its browsers, cookies achieved widespread popularity and was published as an API (Application Programming Interface) when users recognized its potential. You can, for example, use cookies files to determine which parts of your intranet users visit most often. Then, use that information to plan and optimize your network accordingly.

Some sites hesitate to use cookies because of concerns over privacy issues. There are, however, some limits on the amount of data that you can download and you can date the information for automatic deletion after a specified time period.

Trade-Offs

So, what is the best way to balance all of these considerations and minimize the necessary trade-offs? We recommend a general-purpose design that we believe is appropriate for most intranets sites, then we look at specific areas in which you may deviate from the general rule, and describe the potential effect of changing any of the five major design considerations (i.e., performance, cost, security, manageability, and usability). Of course, this discussion does involve a necessary level of simplification; many complex issues are at play here, and no two intranet sites are (or should be) exactly the same. Hopefully though, this discussion can serve as a starting point for most organizations. For any mission-critical applications, we certainly recommend reviewing your decisions with your IT team—the internal staff, and outside consultants.

In general, we recommend that you choose a fast server with lots of RAM, a fast communications connection to the server, and the least expensive connection to remote clients that you can get away with (e.g., a dial-up ISDN for occasional use). Also, try to minimize

TABLE 7.1   Intranet Design Trade-offs

	Initial Cost	Ongoing Cost	Performance	Security	Manageability	Usability
Performance						
Faster server	↑↑	↔	↑↑	↔	↑	↑↑
More server RAM	↑	↔	↑	↔	↑	↑↑
More client RAM	↑↑	↔	↑↑	↔	↑↑	↑↑↑
Faster client	↑↑↑	↔	↑	↔	↑	↑↑
More client disk capacity	↑	↔	↑↑	↔	↑	↑
Anticipatory scripts	↑	↔	↑↑	↔	↔	↔
Content—limit complex data	↓	↓	↑↑	↔	↑	↓
Caching servers	↑↑	↔	↑↑	↓	↓	↑
Replicate database	↑	↔	↑	↑	↓	↑
Cost						
Thin Clients	↓↓↓	↔	↓	↑	↑	↔
Low bandwidth to clients	↓	↓↓↓	↓↓	↔	↔	↓
Low bandwidth to server	↓↓	↓↓	↓↓↓	↔	↓↓	↓↓
Security						
Router-based firewall	↑	↔	↔	↑	↑	↔
Application-level firewall	↑↑	↔	↓	↑↑	↑↑	↔
Server authentication	↑	↔	↔	↑	↔	↔
Mutual authentication	↑↑	↑	↔	↑↑↑	↑↑↑	↑↑↑
RSA encryption	↑	↑	↓↓	↑↑	↔	↔
DES encryption	↔	↔	↓	↑	↔	↔
Certificate authority	↑↑	↑	↔	↑↑↑	↑↑↑	↑↑↑
Security integration	↑	↑↑	↔	↑↑↑	↑↑↑	↑↑↑
Encrypted envelopes	↑	↑	↔	↑↑	↑↑	↔
Livepayment	↑	↔	↔	↔	↑	↑
Manageability						
Naming conventions	↑	↔	↔	↔	↑	↔
Define roles/ responsibilities	↑	↔	↔	↔	↑	↔
Standardization	↓	↓↓	↑	↑	↑↑↑	↓
Procedures	↓	↔	↔	↑	↑↑	↑
Site management tools	↑	↔	↑	↔	↑↑	↔
Centralized data	↔	↔	↓	↑	↑	↔
Multimedia Prod. System	↑↑	↓↓	↑	↔	↑↑↑	↑

TABLE 7.1 *(Continued).*

	Initial Cost	Ongoing Cost	Performance	Security	Manageability	Usability
Usability						
Images/image maps	↔	↔	↓	↔	↔	↑
UI standards	↔	↔	↔	↔	↔	↑
Hot links	↔	↔	↔	↔	↔	↑
Cookies	↔	↔	↑	↑	↑	↑

Key:

↔	Not much effect
↑	Positive effect (more arrows indicate more effect)
↓	Negative effect (more arrows indicate more effect)

the use of images and other complex data types, or encourage users to select text-only options. For your all-important security system, use mutual authentication and install an application-level firewall if you have a T1 or slower communications connection. If you have a T2 or higher speed connection, be aware that you're likely to see a drop in performance with application-level security. You'll want to consider this security vs. performance trade-off very carefully. (Remember, security is not an area where you want to try to save money!) Finally, standardize as much as possible and establish procedures and tools to facilitate managing your intranet.

So, as we mentioned in the beginning of this chapter, all of the major design considerations—performance, cost, security, usability, and manageability—are interrelated. Table 7.1 is intended to help you understand these relationships and to determine the effect of a change in any one of these areas on the overall design. Of course, this table assumes a typical intranet implementation. If your requirements demand that you stray from the general model, do your best to find a similar reference point to your requirements in the hope of identifying the specific relationships and impacts in your situation.

It may seem that we've presented you with an endless set of options in this chapter, but by balancing these options and their effects, you should be able to work toward an intranet design that is, as close as possible, the ideal—better, faster, safer, and cheaper!

CHAPTER EIGHT

INTRANET DEVELOPMENT

- ◆ Overview
- ◆ Differences from Traditional Development Efforts
- ◆ Step 9: Implement the Architecture
- ◆ Step 10: Develop the Applications

Overview

Now that you've completed the first steps of your intranet project (Chapter 3), considered the fundamental organizational issues (Chapter 4), planned your architecture (Chapter 5), and analyzed the design issues surrounding intranet development (Chapter 7), it's time to really dig in and start building the intranet.

This chapter primarily covers Steps 9 and 10—Implement the Architecture and Develop the Applications, respectively. But, before you actually start developing, you should understand some of the differences between an intranet project and a traditional information systems project. For one thing, users are generally much more closely involved in an intranet project than they are in a traditional IS effort. And, the timing of an intranet effort is considerably different from a traditional systems implementation—the process is much the same, but the steps are condensed into a much shorter timeframe with more overlap between the various phases. We discuss the differences, as well as the similarities, and help you to streamline the intranet development process by using your prior experience with traditional information systems and some of the new tools that are available for the inter/intranet environment.

Implementing the intranet architecture (Step 9) is really just the manifestation of the work you did in Step 5. It's time to actually install the hardware and software components that you selected, then implement your communications infrastructure. We'll review your connection options, provide some resources and guidelines for selecting an ISP, and suggest ways to optimize your relationship with your communications supplier (i.e., order your facilities as early as possible).

In Step 10, you'll actually begin to build the applications that you planned back in Step 6. If you haven't already chosen a proto-type application, now is the time to do so. We'll give you some additional guidance on choosing and building the prototype, then prioritizing your other intranet applications and starting to build them—beginning with developing the functional specifications and writing your business case scenarios through the user-testing phases.

Of course, none of these steps occurs in a vacuum. Before you actually begin installing your intranet components or building the applications, you should be thoroughly familiar with Steps 6 through 11 in the 12-Step Program. We recommend that you read Chapters 8 through 12 in this book before you begin building the intranet to ensure that you fully understand the entire process and the issues that you're likely to face at each step along the way.

Differences from Traditional Development Efforts

Those of you who are familiar with system development in tradi-tional IS environments (i.e., mainframe and traditional client/server), might want to step back a moment to consider some of the differences in the intranet environment. As we've mentioned before, the intranet environment involves a number of significant differences, including (but not necessarily limited to) the following:

◆ Rapid, incremental iterations and early prototyping
◆ User involvement
◆ Location-independent development

You will also see many similarities with traditional development projects. We have attempted to take the best, streamline it as much as possible, and modify it as necessary for intranet-specific needs.

Rapid, Incremental Iterations and Prototyping

Unlike a traditional development environment that typically involves a lengthy, detailed specification document, many months—or even years—of implementation, and final system delivery often with few or no checkpoints in the interim, intranet development efforts are based on much shorter development cycles. These cycles generally consist of a series of rapid, incremental iterations, often starting with a simple prototype. The developer, working with the user, incorporates feedback from the first prototype to further refine the system requirements. The prototype is then incorporated into the actual project—typically as a first version of the client HTML code if the prototype is in HTML. This process continues throughout the intranet development cycle, typically moving back from the client to the server. Links to the server, as well as connectivity between the server and the base application (i.e., usually a database) are established after the user interface is complete (using prototypes that are not actually linked to real data).

User Involvement

Another difference in the intranet environment relates to the degree and type of user involvement in the system's development. The basic types of user involvement are:

- Project sponsors (the primary sponsor(s) for introducing an intranet)
- Application sponsors (often different from overall intranet sponsorship)
- Advisors
- Authors

SPONSORS AND ADVISORS

When you enlist a project sponsor for intranet development—as with any IT project—you need to find someone who is willing to *actively* participate in the process. Sponsorship in an intranet project requires a level of commitment to actively participate in the design and continuing evolution of the system—including the communications infrastructure, technical architecture requirements, and application development. The ideal candidate for sponsorship is someone with relatively high influence and an interest in technology, but preferably from *outside* the IT department. The head of the department developing the proto-type and/or using the application, for example, is an excellent candidate.

For a large intranet project, you may want to find individual sponsors for each of the major intranet applications, along with a senior sponsor for the entire project. In some large intranet projects, it is helpful to form a sponsorship committee composed of representatives from each application area, along with the overall project sponsor and representatives from the corporate communications and legal departments. This type of committee can effectively address issues that are common throughout the user community and help to establish standards that are acceptable to all user groups, but they can also be ponderous and remarkably slow moving. If you have time constraints, you'll probably want to deal individually with the project sponsor and various application sponsors.

One committee that is particularly valuable in an implementation project is the user advisory committee. Composed of the functional experts that help you to decide on the intranet applications and to determine their actual operation, these committees play a major role in the development process. Often, the grassroots leaders that provided initial support for your intranet initiative are excellent candidates for your user advisory committee. These leaders are interested, knowledgeable users who—because of their early involvement—already have an investment in the success of the project. Be sure to warn your project sponsors and advisors (and their supervisors) in advance that the intranet project will require a regular commitment of time—probably a few hours per week—and effort. The best way to sell this commitment, of course, is as an *investment,* which ensures that the system, once in place, will meet its objectives and satisfy the needs of the user community.

AUTHORS

In the past, systems were typically built either by the in-house IT staff or by an outside systems integrator. With intranet technology, however, users have a chance to get in on the act. *Authoring,* the concept of putting meaningful content onto the intranet, does not require programming skills—just access to a computer equipped with a graphical user interface and an interest in the process.

Document storage is typically one of the first applications that an organization implements on an intranet. But, developing and maintaining quality content can quickly become an issue. Many organizations address this issue by permitting most users to become authors. With simple tools such as Microsoft's Internet Assistant for Word, which hides even the minimal complexity of HTML, document development is easy. And, users remain active and involved in the intranet.

A word of caution here, though. You'll need to plan in advance how the information on the intranet will be managed and updated before you allow nearly everyone in the organization to become authors.

Location-Independence

Another major way in which the intranet environment differs from traditional IS development is its decreased dependence on physical location. Developers no longer have to be physically located in the same geographic vicinity to work together. The location-independence of intranet development can be attributed primarily to faster, less expensive communications mechanisms such as Remote Access Service (dial-in remote network nodes), WANs, and the Internet itself. Outside developers can now work just as effectively in their own office or home as at your facility.

COLLABORATIVE TOOLS

The challenge in working with remote developers is ensuring that they have both a clear understanding of your needs and ready access to the resources they may require (e.g., development tools, data, technical support, and user feedback). A variety of new collaborative tools are, however, making this a relatively easy hurdle to cross. Specifically, a number of tools on the Internet, including various public-domain MUDs (multiuser dialogs) and MOOs (multiobject-oriented) environments, enable remote developers to exchange information and ideas almost as easily as if they were in the same room. We discuss MUDs and their progenies in Chapter 9, but they are essentially very similar to the online chat rooms that have become so popular on the Internet.

SETTING EXPECTATIONS

A service-level agreement with your remote developers can help you to ensure that they have a clear understanding of your needs and expectations. In fact, a service-level agreement should document their expectations as well as yours. You'll need to work with the developer to jointly plan how to handle design specifications, code standards, development and version control, code reviews, testing and debugging, change control, and scope management. Just be sure to document all of the expectations and decisions— then sign an agreement *before* the work progresses too far. You don't want to have a nebulous commitment that can confuse the issue and/or cause delays.

COST SAVINGS

As an added benefit for some of your staff—and a potentially significant cost savings in overhead for you—intranet technology can help you move toward telecommuting. If you decide to use a partnership approach to systems development (as we discussed in Chapter 3), you may find a significant cost savings in travel and expenses (the dreaded accoutrements of consulting experts) by allowing technical staff to work from their own offices or homes. Figure 8.1 illustrates a typical intranet working arrangement.

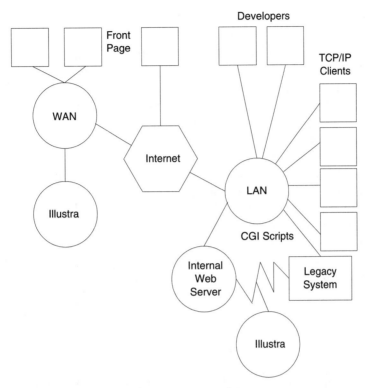

Figure 8.1   Typical intranet working arrangement.

Methodologies

Although we've stressed the differences between traditional and intranet development efforts, we don't mean to imply that all of the old methods have outlived their usefulness. Indeed, experience in managing large projects on an enterprise-wide basis is invaluable and many of the lessons learned from this type of experience are applicable to the intranet project. Such methods include managing resources and using project management tools such as Microsoft's Project and Applied Business Technology Corporation's Project Workbench, and MicroManager's Microplanner. Also, project management methodologies such as LBMS (i.e., Learmonth and Burchette Management System, which provides application development management/CASE products) are potentially useful, but you'll need to take care in this area since many of the details do not readily translate to the intranet environment, and may just slow the development process. Appendix B presents an LBMS work plan example for managing a large-scale intranet project—in this case an application for the electrical power industry. Remember to exercise caution with any tool or methodology that ties you to one particular vendor or integrator.

A flowchart, like the Major Steps Decision Tree that we introduced in Chapter 2, can help you with nearly any type of implementation process and can be useful whether you're developing a system in-house or working with a systems integrator. In fact, if you are working with an outside contractor, this type of flowchart—with its accompanying checklist and matrices—can help to minimize your expenses because it serves as a guide for gathering the necessary information for the planning and development process outside of billable hours.

Step 9: Implement the Architecture

After you've made some of the basic intranet implementation decisions, you're ready to get into the heart of the system development process—implementing your communications and architectural infrastructures. This implementation step picks up from the planning process that we described in Chapters 2 and 3.

Communications Infrastructure

Be sure to contact potential communications vendors—Internet service providers (ISPs) and/or regional Bell operating companies (RBOCs)—and give them the necessary information to begin the bidding process as soon as you complete your intranet implementation plan and determine the optimal communications infrastructure. If product or technology offerings change before the actual implementation of your intranet, you may need to ask for revised bids, but at least you'll have established your project requirements and prepared a preliminary budget.

If you have not yet determined all of the sites that are going to be included in your intranet, ask the vendors to prepare bids for the ones that you have finalized. Just be sure that you give the same implementation requirements to all of the vendors so that you can compare the bids on an "apples-to-apples" basis. (Be aware, however, that the price comparison is still somewhat fuzzy since the vendors all use different pricing algorithms.)

It's important to start laying the communications infrastructure *early* in the implementation process. Once you receive the bids and select a vendor, initiate the installation of the local link(s) for any broadband lines you need connected to your premises. This type of installation is a notoriously slow process and often fraught with frustration. To minimize the hassle, you may want to have your ISP handle much of the installation if they offer such a service. You can expect to wait a couple of months for connectivity to be complete; on rare occasions the installation is completed much more quickly but, all too often, it takes much longer.

Ordering ISDN (integrated services digital network) can be just as frustrating. If time is critical, you may want to consider initiating an ISDN order before your final decision, then sacrifice the small deposit that is usually required with the order if your plans change.

FINDING AN INTERNET SERVICE PROVIDER

If you decide to use an Internet Service Provider (ISP) for your intranet project, you'll need to do some research and analysis to find the right firm and the right level of service for your requirements. Unfortunately, finding an experienced ISP to help you with the implementation can be something of a project in its own right. Although the Yankee Group predicts a large increase in the ISP business over the next three years—expanding from less than $500 million in 1995 to more than $2 billion by 1998, they also predict a dramatic drop in the number of ISP firms—from several thousand in 1995 to about a hundred by 1998.

The implication of this trend is clear. Unless you want to face the prospect of changing your ISP in the near future, you'll need to choose carefully. Be sure that the firm you choose is likely to survive the market shake-out. There are about 3,000 ISPs in the United States alone, so be sure to give yourself ample time to sift through them. Remember, the biggest ISP is not always the best—and certainly not the most economical for your business.

A dial-up serial line interface protocol (SLIP) or point-to-point protocol (PPP) service account is adequate for most end users, but the issues become more complex if you're going to connect your intranet to the Internet. You'll need to master a core of Internet connectivity basics—or find a knowledgeable source to advise you—in order to make the right service choice.

ISP research sources. *Word of mouth* is still one of the best ways to locate information about an ISP. Colleagues who have already found a provider they're comfortable with can give you an excellent starting place for your search by letting you review their service agreements. If their connectivity requirements and expectations are similar to yours, and they're satisfied with the service they receive, you may very well be able to end your search there.

Another source, somewhat paradoxically, for finding ISPs is through the Internet. There are a few major ISP lists on the Internet that can speed you along your search:

- *http://www.thelist.com*   The List is a directory of ISP providers broken down for the United States, Canada, and the world, with an option to select by telephone area code or country code.

- *http://www.vni.net/thedirectory*   The Directory, which is provided by Rocklin Associates, features 25,000 listings of ISPs and bulletin board services (BBSs), including more than 10,000 links to 2,800 ISPs in the United States, Canada, and the Caribbean.

- *http://www.yahoo.com/Business_and_Economy/ Companies/Internet_Services/Internet_Access_Providers* This list is provided by Yahoo, one of the best-known search engines on the Web. It offers access to lists of ISPs (including itself) with breakdowns of international and domestic providers by country, region, and (in the United States) state.

◆ *Info-deli-server@netcom.com*   A list of access providers is also available via the PDIAL list. To obtain this list, send an E-mail message with the subject line, "send pdial" to info-deli-server@netcom.com.

◆ *http://www.tagsys.com/Provider/ListOfLists.html#World* This list provides a guide to some of the other lists of ISPs.

◆ *http://www.isoc.org/^bgreene/nsp-index.html*   This useful list is maintained by the Internet Society.

◆ *http://www.best.be/iap.html*   A world wide access list of ISPs.

THE ISP SELECTION CHECK LIST

The questions in Figure 8.2 are intended to help you with the ISP selection process; they should serve as a starting point for selecting an ISP and determining the type of service you need. (Note that these questions are intentionally generic. If you have special requirements, be sure to take them into consideration in your selection of an ISP.)

CONNECTIVITY CHOICES

In addition to choosing an ISP, you'll need to determine the most efficient means of connecting to your ISP. We summarize the various options in Decision Tree 7, which is illustrated in Figure 8.3. You may chose a different type of link at each site, depending on whether you're connecting one or more major servers or merely an individual client (or a few clients) at a small branch office or store.

Dial-up service specifics.   If price is a consideration, use is low, and you're connecting to a relatively small site (i.e., only a few clients), you may want to consider a dial-up option. Your solution may be as simple as a modem or you may choose an ISDN link that makes the connection on an as-needed basis—thereby gaining the advantage of the higher bandwidth. (Note that some RBOCs also offer a permanent connection pricing option for ISDN.)

◆ Be sure that your account includes SLIP or PPP.

1. Does the ISP have a Web site? If not, this probably
    indicates that it is not a professional ISP—you
    would do well to avoid it!

2. Are the Web pages on the ISP home page well orga-
    nized and complete? How many pages are marked
    "under construction"? Consider these points as an
    indication of the firm's professionalism.

3. Do the Web pages provide you with sufficient infor-
    mation about the ISP? How long has the firm been
    in business? What is the ISP address? How many
    customers does the firm have? Which area code(s)
    do they service?

4. Is there a one-time sign up fee? If so, what do you
    get for that fee? (Do not sign up for any deal on a
    prepaid basis! You should consider using a prepaid
    option *only* after you use the provider for a while
    and decide that you like the level of service.)

5. Is the ISP willing to provide you with written infor-
    mation to resolve all of your questions? If not, you
    should probably look elsewhere for your service!

6. Does your account include any disk space for you
    to put up your own Web page? Ideally, the ISP
    should provide you with at least 5MB of disk space
    for free, with the option to rent more if you need it.

Figure 8.2   The ISP selection process.

◆ Ask what the ISP's ratio of users-to-modems is. Generally, a ratio of about 7 users per modem indicates good
   service. A ratio of 10 to 12 users per modem is definitely
   high, and you should probably look for a different ISP. If
   the ISP cannot or will not provide this type of information, you can probably assume that the ratio is higher
   than 12 users to one modem, so it is best to avoid them
   completely.

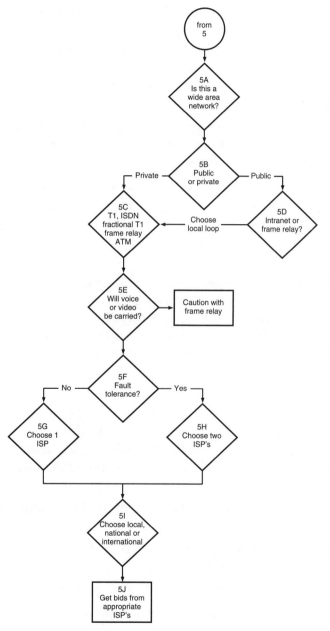

Figure 8.3 Decision Tree—Choosing your communications links.

- Quick test: Try to call the ISP modem line a few times to check for busy signals.
- Call the technical support line and time your stay on hold. Repeat the test several times at different times of the day and week to determine the ISPs commitment to service.
- Check how many newsgroups the ISP is carrying out of the more than 30,000 that are available. Be sure that they carry the ones that you want or need.
- Determine if there are any limitations on E-mail.
- Does the ISP provide you with 800/888 phone number for long distance calls? Be sure to check the cost of this service before you use it.

Dedicated service line specifics.   If you anticipate a large number of users or frequent use and are more concerned with performance than price, you will probably want to consider a dedicated line. A T1 connection is the most common, but there are a number of viable alternatives. But, be sure to consider the following factors:

- What is the ISP backbone speed?
- Check the ISP's bandwidth outbound-inbound ratio. A use ratio of 70 to 75 percent is pretty good; higher than 90 percent indicates that the provider is oversaturated and you will not be able to use your line to the full bandwidth.
- Be sure that the ISP has enough bandwidth to support an upgrade (if/when you need it).
- Determine how many permanent IP addresses the ISP will provide you with.
- Be sure that the ISP will provide you with Newsfeed.
- Check the availability of technical support—days and times.
- Check if the ISP will/can monitor your line for diagnostic purposes.

- Determine if the ISP offers a domain registration and, if so, what the charge is for this service.
- Check the ISP's escalation procedures for handling operational system problems.
- If the ISP will assign a point-of-contact technician, check his/her knowledge level.
- Does the ISP have a fault-tolerant redundancy on its backbone?
- Determine how many points of presence (POP) the firm has, and how many POPs you need to cross before connecting to a national/international backbone.
- Check if the ISP can offer redundancy to your location.
- Ask the ISP to provide you with press releases and news articles from local or professional magazines about its service.
- Call some of the ISP's direct competitors and try to get some information from them about the provider. Be sure that you can realistically filter any information that you get from the competitors.

COMMUNICATIONS SERVICE TYPES

The following paragraphs describe the types of communications that are readily available (as of this printing). Of course, we all know that things change rapidly in the world of communications! Examine your data volume and access requirements, then evaluate what size "pipe" you need:

Fractional T1.   Any data transmission rate between 56 Kbps and 1.5 Mbps (the regular T1 rate). A fractional T1 is simply a digital line that's not as fast as a full T1; it is typically provided on four-wire (two-pair) copper circuits.

ISDN.   ISDN uses both circuit-switched bearer channels (B channels) to carry voice and data and a separate data channel (D channel) for control signals via a packet-switched network. Flavors of ISDN are:

- ISDN basic rate interface, or BRI, provides a total bandwidth of 144 Kbps.

◆ The ISDN primary rate interface, or PRI, in the United States provides the equivalent bandwidth of a T1 line. In Europe, PRI is equivalent to European E1.

◆ Broadband ISDN, or BISDN, is a second-generation ISDN standard. It uses fiber-optic cables for speeds of 155 Mbps and higher.

T1.   Delivers a bandwidth of 1.5 Mbps on a line composed of 24 channels at 64 Kbps each, and an 8-Kbps channel for signal and control. T1, which is sponsored by the Alliance for Telecommunications Industry Solutions (ATIS), needs a DSU/CSU and a router.

T3.   Also known as "a T1 on steroids," T3 delivers a bandwidth of 45 Mbps on a line equivalent to 30 T1 lines. T3 requires fiber-optic cable, but can handle 672 voice or data channels at 64 Kbps.

Table 8.1 summarizes the basic communications options.

FUTURE TECHNOLOGY

You'll also want to keep an eye on the new, and continuously evolving communication technologies like the following two options:

1. *ADSL (asymmetrical digital subscriber lines).*   A communications technology that transmits digital data over telephone wires. It is expected to transmit up to 6 Mbps, and is likely to be used primarily for video-on-demand services. ADSL uses adaptive digital filtering to overcome noise and other problems on the line.

2. *Cable modem.*   A modem used to connect a computer to a cable TV system that offers online services. Although cable modems are being used at a few test sites, the technology is not yet commercially available.

Architectural Infrastructure

Presumably, you've already decided the major issues relating to your intranet architecture (Step 5). But, if you haven't yet

TABLE 8.1 Communication Facilities Comparison Chart

Access Technology	Capacity Speed	Initial Fee/ Monthly Fee	Pros	Cons
Dial-in modem	14 Kbps to 28 Kbps	$0/$30	Available everywhere.	Extremely slow.
ISDN	56 Kbps to 128 Kbps	$400/$150	Widely available. Years of experience.	Hard to configure, distance limitation of 18,000 feet to telephone switching center. Not all digital switches compatible.
Satellite	400 Kbps	$1,100/$50	Fast downloads. Good for multimedia broadcasts to remote offices.	A one-way medium, requires a dial-in modem for uploads. Difficult to install and adjust.
Switched 56	56 Kbps	$1,200/ $600	Dedicated version of the service is more cost-effective than ISDN. Mature products. Easy to install and configure.	No upgrade option. If you need more bandwidth, you will have to change your service and technology.
Frame relay	56 Kbps to 512 Kbps	$1,000/ $350	Easy to install, mature products. Good price/ performance ratio.	More expensive than ISDN. Not a dedicated line. Only a few ISPs support this technology.
Fractional T1	64 Kbps to 1,544 Kbps	$1,000/ $800	Gives the potential to grow to a full T1, without going to the expense of T1 initially.	More expensive than ISDN or Switched 56
T1	1,544 Kbps	$3,000/ $1,400	Well-established technology, supported by large ISP. Mature products and technology.	Somewhat expensive.
T3	45,000 Kbps	$50,000/ $8,000	The fastest affordable communication method available on the Internet.	Fairly expensive. Used mostly by ISPs.

acquired the hardware and software that you need for the intranet, now is a good time to research recent technological developments and to review the vendors' offerings. Be sure to check the vendors' Web sites to see if there are any last-minute product updates or bug fixes. The Web sites are also a valuable source of technical support information and usually much faster than traditional telephone support lines. In particular, review the current market shares for Netscape's and Microsoft's offerings, as well as the new developments in back-end databases for Web server architectures (we discuss these in more detail in Chapters 5 and 9).

Order the hardware and software products you need, then begin to install the servers and workstations. Remember, however, that simple installation configurations are usually most effective in an intranet environment because including extra utilities can cause potential weaknesses in the security system.

Proceed with the installation of Web server software and additional services (as determined in your plan), then install the back-end application(s)—typically a database. Be sure to check if your database requires any particular installation options for use with a Web server. Of course, retain all of the hardware and software manuals and installation diskettes, and keep them in a safe place. Be sure to register all of the various components so that you'll be able to access technical support when you need it. After you finish installing the software, you can connect (at a minimum) the local segments of your network and begin testing. (Refer to Chapters 11 and 12 for more information on testing.) Then, unless your RBOC is a bit speedier than most, you'll need to wait awhile for them to wire the connection to your ISP into your communication room or server site. Once that link is complete and connected with the appropriate hardware (routers and or CSU/DSU and/or firewall), your intranet architecture is in place. You're ready to start developing your intranet applications.

Step 10: Develop the Applications

Application development can begin as soon as your basic architectural and communications infrastructures are in place, tested, and operational. If you haven't yet developed your prototype application, now is the time to do so.

Your application project manager—whether you or someone else—should follow whatever development methodology your organization typically uses, adjusted for the intranet's differing nature. Although this chapter is in no way intended to be a substitute for the enormous body of literature that already exists on development planning, organization, and management, clearly you must go through some basic steps, which we have outlined in this section.

Note that just as the development process for intranet applications is iterative, so is the project management. Unlike mainframe management, it is *not* a science (yet). You will want to keep copious notes of your issues and their resolution, and keep your plan *flexible.* In fact, you should plan to use your initial project workplan—probably for your prototype—as a framework for future work. Consider it a living document and adjust it to reflect what you learn along the way so that you (or your successor) will have metrics and expectations tailored to your organization's needs.

Selecting the Prototype

Assuming that you are beginning with a prototype application, remember that simple is definitely best. If possible, choose one that has high value to the organization but is relatively low in complexity, so that there can be a short development cycle and quick delivery. Some of the advantages of using a prototype include:

- The opportunity to demonstrate applications to potential future users
- The opportunity to obtain constructive feedback from future users
- A vastly improved chance of succeeding in your first iteration of an application

You may choose an application that already exists in your current environment, thereby demonstrating the differences of the intranet. However, you may also look at completely new functional areas. One company that we know of chose to begin with an application that communicated organizational objectives and priorities—something that was definitely needed but had never existed before. This application was a discussion medium through which senior management could communicate the vision to the company on a daily basis (or whenever priorities shifted). It also provided a way for individual departments to respond to the company vision and to design their own priorities, which in turn supported the overall organizational goals.

This relatively simple application required only a browser interface (Microsoft Internet Explorer, Internet Server, SQL Server Database on NT) and some CGI scripting. From planning to completion, it took about six weeks to implement—including iterations for user input—and then was up-and-running, proving its value.

WHAT KIND OF PROTOTYPE?

There are four major types of prototypes that you may want to consider for your initial intranet project. Decision Tree 5 in Figure 8.4 can help you determine which type is appropriate for your organization.

- ◆ *The Overview.*   This kind of prototype is intended primarily to show the range of functionality that can be included in the intranet. It includes the headings (or icons), but does not link them to any underlying functionality.
- ◆ *The Glitz.*   This kind of prototype is intended to show the capability of an intranet. It might, for example, include animated images in gif format, a short audio or movie clip, or possibly a pdf file displayed in Amber (i.e., Adobe's applet for Web-based display). One word of caution with this type, however: Be sure to use an adequate machine to demonstrate it and take the time to test it thoroughly—with all of its bells and whistles—before demonstrating it to your potential users. You don't want to make

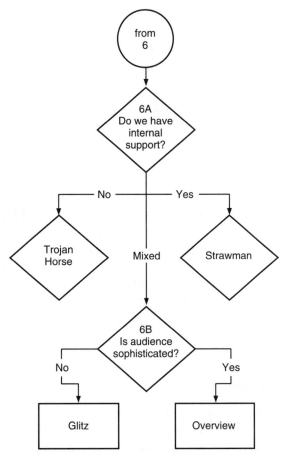

Figure 8.4 Decision Tree 5—Selecting a prototype.

it look overly complex or to experience a memory-related crash in the middle of the demonstration.

♦ *The Trojan Horse.* Use this kind of prototype to demonstrate how a specific application can benefit from intranet technology. Be sure to choose an application that is really useful and has high visibility among your users. This kind of prototype can help you win popular support for the intranet project.

◆ *The Straw Man.*   This kind of prototype is most useful
in a collaborative environment where support for the
intranet project is not an issue. You can use it to elicit
constructive feedback on one or more proposed applications by putting up a straw man to gather valuable feedback from your users, thereby accelerating the progress
of the project.

Application Scope

Like any program that you develop, begin by clearly defining your
applications' purpose and scope. Although you will later want to
incorporate your users' input (during the design and iteration
cycles), you also want to be able to adhere to a predefined list of
objectives that keep your time and work estimates attainable.
And, don't forget to obtain "sign-off" from your project sponsor(s).
The application prioritization matrix in Figure 8.5 is intended to
help you prioritize all of your various applications, beginning
with selecting the prototype.

Functional Specifications

Write a list of functional specifications for each of your target
applications, then go through the design process. If the data
already exists, where is it? How is it accessed? How will your
intranet application obtain it and keep it current? Will updates be
made/required? How will they be maintained? How many users
will be accessing the system at a given time? What are the requirements for availability/accessibility? What are acceptable performance criteria?

  Again, your local bookstore or library has lots of reference materials that can help you through these and many other issues. Your
systems integrator can also provide valuable assistance and
guidance.

  We strongly recommend that you write your business scenar-
ios/test cases or test scripts at this point in the development process, rather than at the end. Have your users and functional
experts jointly agree on exactly what the application is expected

Application Prioritizing Matrix	Weighting	E-Mail	Document Publishing	ESS/DSS	Web Access	Discussion Groups	Audio/Video Conferencing	E-Commerce	External Site	Application 1	Application 2	Application 3	Application 4
Factor		Score 1–10 with 10 being highest											
Urgency	0.6	8	7	5	8	5	8	5	8	6	5	7	6
Stage in Life Cycle	0.4	7	5	7	8	7	7	6	7	7	7	6	6
Visibility	0.6	9	6	5	7	6	9	8	9	4	8	5	9
Ease	0.7	7	6	6	6	8	7	4	5	7	4	4	7
User Cooperation	0.8	6	8	5	8	5	6	7	6	6	6	5	6
Existence of 'mature' product	0.7	7	4	6	8	8	7	5	7	6	8	7	7
Other Factor A													
Other Factor B													
Score		3.45	2.9	2.65	3.55	3.08	3.45	2.76	3.28	2.84	2.98	2.66	3.25
Rank		2	8	11	1	6	2	9	4	10	7	11	4

Figure 8.5 Application prioritization matrix.

to do and in what framework *before* you begin developing it. This will help to ensure a successful completion for the project—before you even begin.

> **TIP** *Write business scenarios/test cases:*
> ◆ *Determine logical units of work (LUWs) that naturally derive from your business process flow.*
> ◆ *Use LUWs as the building blocks of your application design.*
> ◆ *Drill your users on exceptions—don't let them give you just the "ought to be" scenario. You need a firm understanding of reality for application design to accommodate it.*

Resource Planning

Be sure that you have the resources you'll need to develop your applications and note them in the assumptions portion of your scope document. Your development plan should address all of the following resource issues:

- User input
- Functional/business process expertise
- Database access/administrative capability
- Advanced HTML and scripting expertise

Few things are more discouraging than getting well into the project, only to find that you lack the necessary resources to complete the job!

Timeline

When you have all the basic components of the project set (i.e., scope, functional specifications, and resources), establish a timeline for the development, including technical design, coding, iterations, and testing. This serves to set the expectations for both your users and your team, so be realistic. Because this project probably represents your first intranet development effort, be sure to gauge your expertise and build in any appropriate learning-curve time. Of course, if time is of the essence, you probably need to seek knowledgeable resources from the outset.

Standards

As with any program development initiative, you'll need to establish standards before you begin the process. If you're working with a consulting organization, ask their advice on these issues:

- Interface look and feel
- Coding standards
- Naming conventions
- Performance thresholds
- Documentation (code comments, design documents, and technical notes)

Remember, standards are often different on an intranet. Expectations, for better or worse, are usually set on the World Wide Web (and subject to constant change)—so be sure to find out what your developers think is feasible and what it will mean to your project. Chapter 10 can help you decide on some ideas for the UI design.

Be sure to document your standards and reference them as often as necessary—usually quite often! Also be sure to familiarize new programmers and developers with your standards documents; as your intranet grows in size and diversity, you'll appreciate the structure and continuity that your standards ensure.

TIP   *Be sure to review your standards on a regular basis and ensure that all segments in your organization are adhering to the same set of standards. At the same time, try not to go to the extreme and let standards dictate* everything *or stifle creativity.*

Iterations

We've talked a lot about the iterative nature of the intranet, but it bears repeating. More than any other medium, intranet applications are built with flexibility in mind—thus lending themselves to user input and changes. You may find, once development is solidly underway, that your core users will suggest updates on a weekly basis, and you'll respond with the necessary changes in that timeframe. Even very large scale, high-volume transaction systems lend themselves to this kind of development—a welcome change for the finicky user community.

Testing

Testing is a constant process in the world of the intranet. Unlike the traditional waterfall development methodology in which several weeks (at a minimum) are typically designated for unit, integration, and user-acceptance testing, intranet applications by their very nature are *always* in testing. Of course, as a project manager you'll want to be sure that the developers test individual pieces of the intranet before they show them to your users, but you'll want to encourage the users to "test-drive" the evolving application(s) as early in the development process as possible. The opportunity for users to evaluate the applications and provide feedback will ultimately give you an application that users really like to use. It also helps users to take some ownership of the project and pride in its development, all of which can be an invaluable asset when it comes time for deployment.

You cannot, of course, completely eliminate formalized testing, especially if the application is relatively complex. Database selects and updates, transaction processing, and all of the related functions require thorough, logical analysis and testing with the test scripts and scenarios that you developed in the application design phase. Also, this is a good time to make sure that you're meeting your baseline requirements for speed and operability.

Depending on the nature of your intranet and the application(s), you may also need to devise a security testing scheme. Again, develop test scripts—preferably in advance of your security system implementation—to test the effectiveness of your security once it is implemented. And, be sure to retest on a regular basis as elements of your intranet change and it expands in size and scope.

User Acceptance Testing

Although testing will be an integral part of your development cycle, it is also an important phase in its own right. Chapter 12 describes the common phases of intranet testing (i.e., unit, system, and integration testing) that you should build into your workplan prior to sign off and project completion. After you are satisfied that the application meets the requirements that you defined to ensure its functionality and reliability, you'll need to obtain approval from the functional design team and the project sponsor(s). Be sure that your sponsor(s) understands that sign off involves more than just passive acceptance, it also indicates a willingness to provide active support. When you are sure that such support is indeed forthcoming, you can confidently take your work to senior management in preparation for its release.

CHAPTER NINE

INTRANET TOOLS

- ◆ Overview
- ◆ Choosing Tools
- ◆ Browser and Server Software
- ◆ Major Tools Categories

Overview

Trying to choose appropriate, cost-effective tools for the intranet can be a difficult task. Many intranet managers are understandably hesitant to commit lest they acquire an inadequate or outdated toolset with which to support the enterprise. In this chapter, we discuss the various types of tools that are available and describe how they fit into the development model; then we give you some guidelines for choosing your intranet tools—without focusing on specific brands or products. We will, however, give you a quick overview of the capabilities of some of the better-known tools in each category. Then, by considering your operating environment, the skills of your developers, designers, users, and administrators, as well as your budget constraints, you can choose the best tool for the job.

Remember that the tool market changes, literally, on a daily basis. New products are continually introduced, with each new product and version delivering ever increasing levels of sophistication. When you're ready to purchase your intranet tools, we recommend that you thoroughly analyze the most widely used products available on the market (at that time), then choose the tools that best fit your specific needs. We've included some sources here to help you with that research when you're ready.

Choosing Tools

As with most other aspects of your intranet project, you'll need to consider both your current and short-term needs for tools during the evaluation process, as well as the long-term advantages that they may offer. And, your tool selections must correspond with your business goals and needs. Essentially, there are five values that you are most likely to look for in your toolset: performance, time-to-market, extensibility, portability, and scalability.

As we've mentioned in earlier chapters, intranet computing has its roots in client/server architecture and offers some of the advantages of that architecture, but it is not a panacea. You will still need to make tradeoffs as you build your intranet, determining your own priorities and aiming for a system that best fits your particular requirements. Tool selection is likely to be one of the areas in which you must make those tradeoffs—determining which of the five key values are the most important for your environment. And, of course, cost is a major selection factor for most organizations. It's true that today's development tools are faster and cheaper than ever before. But all too often, declining hardware costs help to mask the effects of cumbersome, inefficient code. As you consider price in your tool selection, remember that long-term, reusable, scalable, high-performance solutions are likely to require a substantial investment. Nothing worth having really comes cheaply, and that's as true of your intranet as it is of all other aspects in life. Fortunately, there are strategies to help you leverage your investment in the intranet toolset.

Performance is usually the top priority for most organizations. When we speak of performance, we're referring to the product's ability to provide the required response within an acceptable timeframe. Be sure to examine the composition of your intranet environment—for today and the future. Then, evaluate each tool that you consider, along with its underlying technology, to determine its performance in local and remote environments. Also, keep in mind that industry analysts predict that the line between intranet and Internet computing will blur in the near future as customers, vendors, and partners access each others' systems. Thus, your intranet is likely to evolve into a hybrid inter/intranet.

Time-to-market refers to your need to deliver useful applications to your users within a particular timeframe. This value is often the overriding factor in technology selection for a very understandable reason: It gets useful products to the consumers (i.e., your users) quickly, thus demonstrating its value. Time-to-market does, however, usually involve a penalty—higher price. High-level, rapid application development (RAD) environments that hide complexity can deliver speedy applications with minimal programming expertise, but they can also be slow, especially if they require large amounts of business logic. In addition, RAD environments tend to tightly couple (i.e., bind) the application layers (as we discussed in Chapter 5), making even minor changes difficult to handle. This type of coupling means that any modification to the code may have far-reaching implications, and that testing and debugging can become a source of continual headaches. These problems, in turn, make RAD technology score poorly in both extensibility and scalability.

By *extensibility* we mean the ability to adapt and persist over time. Proprietary languages, such as those used in RAD environments, are designed to interact in a certain, strictly defined manner, and can communicate only with the technologies that they were built to interact with. This means that if the surrounding technology changes, the program can't function without corresponding (often significant) changes, or without having additional code inserted to help it translate information to and from the new technology. On the other hand, tools that are based on a flexible, modular architecture can interface well with any type of technology, thereby providing the longevity that is so important in this era of constant change.

Portability refers to a technology's ability to operate on any platform. If you have a heterogeneous environment (i.e., one that comprises many types and combinations of hardware and software), your intranet "solution" must be able to function with the same degree of reliability and performance throughout all segments of the environment. Code that is specific to a particular vendor platform can be run only in the environment for which it was designed. Portability ensures that the solution can change platforms not only in your existing environment but also as your environment and the surrounding technologies evolve.

Scalability refers to a technology's ability to accommodate greater numbers and sizes of requests in an increasingly distributed environment. If your applications are going to have lasting value, they must be able to grow with the business. Scalability is generally derived from modular, open systems with low overhead (e.g., interpretated code) in which "pieces" can be moved and configured to provide efficient access to data and business logic.

Some IT managers choose to sacrifice extensibility and scalability in preference for quick time-to-market, knowing that some applications may be throwaways in a year or two. Although this is sometimes a legitimate strategy, it may be useful to remember that given the current climate of change, the needs you perceive to be two years out may only be six months away—making the "quick and dirty" application to address those needs a more expensive proposition than anticipated.

Skills Requirements for Tools

There are three primary categories for Web development tools by skill level. Reviewing tools in relation to these categories can help you design a solution that your programming team can deliver with confidence:

◆ *Rapid application development tools.*   Intended for use with client/server and client/server–style applications, the primary advantage of RAD tools is their quick development time. Many of these tools have been developed by client/server fourth-generation language (4GL) vendors to provide an HTML-compatible front-end for their proprietary code (e.g., PowerBuilder PowerScript, Visual Basic Script). In this respect, RAD tools can be beneficial for organizations that are seeking to stretch the useful lifecycle of their existing tightly coupled applications as they move toward an intranet environment. Such organizations tend to sacrifice performance and extensibility in favor of the quick development time and compatibility with existing applications.

♦ *Scripting tools.*   These tools can be used for common gateway interfacing (CGI) between application layers. They permit you to use many off-the-shelf products, with minimal coding required to link them to existing applications. Depending on the particular scripting tools that you choose, they can provide reasonable performance with moderate skill requirements.

♦ *Object-oriented tools for multitiered environments.* These tools function independently of the user-interface. Their modular nature provides a significant degree of flexibility, portability, and extensibility. We should note, however, that object-oriented programming requires a high level of skill on the part of the programmers and the object modelers. When it is undertaken by an experienced staff that understands the OO principles and knows how to maximize their value, object-oriented programming can be very rewarding. In the hands of inexperienced developers, however, it can be both unwieldy and expensive.

Evaluating the Technologies and Toolsets

We've found that it's generally useful to compose a matrix of tool types to help evaluate tool products and technologies. This matrix, which maps tool types against their ability to satisfy needs, should include all of the following aspects, in order of their importance:

1. Complexity of the task
2. Stability of the solution
3. Cost
4. Vendor

COMPLEXITY OF THE TASK

The sophistication of the tool that you need largely depends on the size and complexity of the tasks that you hope to perform with the tool. While there are numerous prepackaged tools available that can be very satisfactory for relatively simple applications, more complex tasks typically require somewhat more sophisticated tools to ensure that you can deliver the application quality that you desire within the specified timeframe. Of course, there are varying levels along the way and, once you determine your priorities for application development, you can select the tool that best suits your needs.

Simple document creation, storage, and retrieval applications typically require only a basic browser and the associated server software running on any of the popular operating systems, as well as authoring/editing tools. Applications that need to connect to a database management system, however, typically require some means of communicating the information. In this situation, your choices become somewhat more difficult.

A simple way to gauge the complexity of your task is to try to match your screens to database queries. If each of your screens involves only a single SQL query, you can consider tools like Microsoft's Internet Database Connector (IDC), Spider Technologies' Spider, or a comparable product. Even with these relatively simple queries however, you'll need to keep an eye on your business logic. If the screens incorporate a lot of business logic, you'll probably need a more advanced tool. The alternative is to code the logic in SQL.

If your screens require multiple queries, a simple tool is unlikely to deliver satisfactory performance. You'll probably want to look at some combination of custom code and prepackaged tools.

STABILITY OF THE SOLUTION

If you expect your solution to remain stable over time (i.e., the underlying business logic is unlikely to change), you may want to consider investing in a sophisticated toolset that is likely to meet your long-term needs. Be aware, however, that this option typically requires a staff that is skilled in both short-term development methods and long-term code modifications. Such modifications will eventually be required when one of the pieces *does* need to be changed.

If you need a "quick and dirty" application that is going to be accessible only to a limited number of users on a consistent platform, a RAD tool may be your best solution.

Many organizations report great success using Visual Basic and/or JavaScript as easy-to-learn programming tools. While these tools are not as fast or robust as some other solutions, they are generally very cost-effective in terms of programmer hours. Conversely, languages like Java and C++, which are very demanding in terms of programming skills, can be an effective solution for applications that require performance, portability, and stability.

COST

Calculating the real cost of your tools can be tricky because you need to consider much more than the sticker price. To evaluate the true cost of a tool, you'll need to consider all of the one-time and ongoing costs that are associated with a toolset. These costs typically include:

- *Cost per developer seat.*
- *Cost per server.*
- *Cost per user seat.*
- *Development time.* Many tools that use the traditional client/server 4GL model provide simple, visual development methods to produce applications with relatively little expertise. They may, however, also involve some long-term costs associated with scalability, extensibility, and performance. And, if quick time-to-market is one of your priorities, the traditional tools may not satisfy your needs. In that case, look to a RAD environment.
- *Deployment time.* Applications with high levels of abstraction and modularity can eliminate much (or all) of the problems associated with deployment since the software does not have to be distributed to client machines around the organization.

- *Maintenance time.*   Be sure to consider how well a toolset can accommodate changes in business logic, data access, and hardware/software configurations.
- *Performance.*   Users' time (and satisfaction) represents money to your organization. Conversely, lack of satisfaction (or lengthy struggles to use an application effectively) costs the organization in both time and dollars.
- *User training.*   While the intranet is generally a low-cost training environment, modularity can simplify requirements for user training by addressing only the specific needs for particular application within a given timeframe.
- *Developer training.*   This includes the costs associated with classroom courses as well as the hands-on trial-and-error learning that developers need to build their skill levels with a particular toolset or technology.

Vendor

Of course, you'll also need to consider information about the vendor when you evaluate tools for your intranet environment. Because much of the success of your intranet ultimately depends on the tools and technologies that you select as a foundation, you need to ensure—before selecting the tools or technologies—that you can depend on the vendor(s) to give you the support that you need when you need it! We recommend that you investigate all of the following factors:

- *Tool acceptance.*   Who is using this tool and for what? Get referrals from other organizations that are using the tool for tasks that are similar to yours on a scale similar to yours. This is especially important if your tasks are complex or "mission-critical." Also check the latest periodicals and newsgroups for information about the tool and or vendor (i.e., industry commentary, market share, stability, growth, and reliability).
- *Support.*   What is the vendor's reputation for service? Does the company offer varying levels of support? Can

you get the level of support that you need? What is the company's service-level commitment?

♦ *Web mindshare.*   What is the vendor's reputation in the IT industry? What percentage of Web developers like the tool? Do they believe that it is going to survive in the industry? Again, check the industry press (both electronic and print) for product evaluations and comparisons that can help you sift through the vendor hype.

Open versus Proprietary Tools

Because it is based on the TCP/IP protocol, the inherent nature of an intranet is like that of the Internet—platform-independent and scalable. This has given rise to a new generation of *open tools* that can function in any environment. Tools that use HTML or Java as their base language are good examples of open architecture; they can be created, modified, and used irrespective of their hardware/software platform. *Proprietary tools,* on the other hand, are pretty much vendor-specific. Because they use custom-code languages that do not communicate with other programs, they can be more difficult or cumbersome to integrate. And once created, the custom code can be interpreted and edited only by the vendor's toolset. Examples of proprietary tools include Powersoft's Power-Builder and Microsoft's Visual Basic.

Times are changing, however. As inter/intranet computing continues to gain popularity, many vendors of proprietary tools are gradually modifying their products to move into the new, sharable environment. Lotus Notes, a highly successful groupware product, is a good example of a proprietary tool that is adapting Web technology. With the proliferation of intranets, Lotus has changed its environment to be "intranet-enabled." Now, users can see a seamless integration of Notes and Web technology; in the intranet-enabled version of Notes, users don't know if they're searching a proprietary database or using a URL to find a Web page. Thus, rather than confront IT buyers with a Notes versus Web choice (as we discussed in Chapter 1), Lotus positioned Notes to be a desirable platform for intranet applications.

Public Domain versus Commercial

Public domain tools have contributed greatly to the popularity of the Internet and to its rapid growth. Many of the tools that are required to get a simple Web started are available in the public domain as *freeware*—meaning that there is no charge associated with downloading and using the program. While many IT managers cringe at the thought of using public-domain software because they perceive it as lacking quality or support, some of the best and most popular tools on the market are available from this source. Quality remains high for many of the giveaways because of their huge user bases, with many individuals and organizations providing continuous feedback and demanding improved versions. And, of course, many people use these products simply because they are free. With this type of development circle, many of the popular freeware tools continue to evolve to meet changing needs.

Of course, there are also many good commercial software tools available, many of which were originally part of the public domain. Commercial Web tools generally offer online support through the Internet, advanced security features (e.g., for electronic commerce), and bells and whistles to make them more usable and easier to support than freeware.

Some public-domain tools are also known as *shareware*. Shareware is a hybrid of free and commercial tools, distributed on a try-before-you-buy basis. This distribution method via the Internet offers some distinct advantages over conventional retail distribution because it lets you test a tool and become comfortable using it in your own environment and with your own data before making a purchase commitment.

Application Tools Models

It may help to refer to the intranet layer model that we introduced in Chapter 5 to understand how the various tools relate to one another in a Web solution involving a database. We've broken the model down for more detail in this discussion (see Figure 9.1), but it uses the same component solutions that we introduced in Chapter 5, Intranet Architectures.

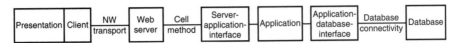

Figure 9.1   Web technology components model.

For this discussion, we're going to skip over the client computer configuration to focus on the Web server–database interaction. We'll consider several variations of this interaction, all derived in some fashion from the portion of our layered intranet model illustrated in Figure 9.2. (Note that we do not include the presentation, client, and network transport components in Figure 9.2.)

1. SINGLE-TOOL SOLUTIONS

In the never ending quest for simplicity, vendors offer some tools that they promote as complete solutions for your Web applications. While these "complete" solutions tend to be very easy to use and fast to deploy, as shown in Figure 9.3, they are proprietary and not always flexible or extensible. Oracle Web Server is the most comprehensive package available, providing Web server and DBMS all in one. Microsoft's Front Page is another broad-based solution.

2. COMMON GATEWAY INTERFACE

CGI scripting in C, C++, or PERL was the first method used to link HTML pages to database queries. As illustrated in Figure 9.4, data queries are encoded in a URL that is passed to the server like any other request; C code that has been placed in the CGI directory on the Web server then interprets the URL as a command to start a predefined or existing application, which then executes a database query. When the database returns the value, the application delivers it back to the HTML page for display.

One of the problems with this approach is the lack of state in HTML; the Web page itself cannot keep track of the fact that a

Figure 9.2   Web server-database interaction.

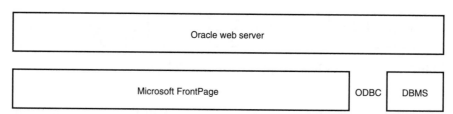

Figure 9.3   Single-tool solution.

transaction is being processed. To circumvent this problem, the programmer must insert some extra code to track state—by using the browser's cookies (informational text file) for example.

Although CGI is not proprietary, the overhead to track state and execute the database queries can slow performance and make scalability tricky.

3. APPLICATION PROGRAMMING INTERFACES

Another option for connecting the Web and application server is by accessing the Web server APIs. The Netscape Application Programming Interface (NSAPI) and Microsoft Internet Server Application Programming Interface (ISAPI) can be used with their respective Web servers to provide this collaboration.

Although similar to the CGI solution, the API method illustrated in Figure 9.5 substitutes the API extension DLL for the executable, speeding the process considerably and thus improving performance.

4. 4GLS

As shown in Figure 9.6, another model that resembles the CGI solution uses a fourth-generation language (4GL) in place of the executable. This "screen-scraping" type configuration for tightly coupled applications gives control to the 4GL. Tools that allow this type of configuration include PowerBuilder and Visual Basic.

Web server	CGI	EXE	Database

Figure 9.4   CGI interface-tool solution.

Figure 9.5   API interface-tool solution.

5. CGI RELAYS

Running a separate application server next to the Web server can help to alleviate the problems associated with regular CGI scripting. In this approach, the application server maintains persistent database connections (thus giving better response times) and can track state. Only a light CGI relay script (again in C or C++) is required to link the Web and application servers, thereby improving performance. This approach can also be applied to Netscape or Internet information server (IIS) to allow the application to run on a separate machine, again boosting performance.

In the first model in Figure 9.7, the CGI relay is completely custom-coded by a developer; the second and third models use the Netscape and IIS-based DLL with the custom scripting to link it together. An advantage of using the APIs however, is that they run faster when executed.

6. DATABASE CONNECTIVITY TOOLS

Another CGI/API call hybrid substitutes a database/Web package such as Microsoft Internet Database Connector or Spider Technologies' Spider, for the executable. This type of solution is illustrated in Figure 9.8.

7. OBJECT TOOL

Tools like NeXT WebObjects provide a great deal of flexibility, portability, and extensibility by using an object-oriented approach with predefined libraries of objects. They also use the relay model. Figure 9.9 illustrates this type of solution.

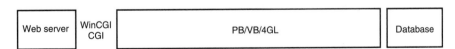

Figure 9.6   4GL-tool solution.

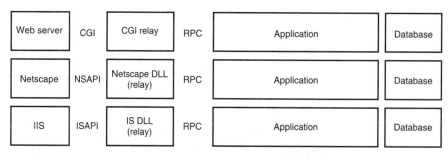

Figure 9.7   CGI relay alternative–tool solutions.

8. WEB FRAMEWORK

As shown in Figure 9.10, custom framework, such as the BSG Web Framework, can provide the desired levels of flexibility, extensibility, portability, and performance across a leveraged model with objects for CGI handling, HTML handling, database handling, and legacy application wrappers.

The mix-and-match components of Web tools offer a wide range of options to suit the needs of any intranet. Selecting the best strategy for your intranet requires evaluating each model according to its ability to meet your predefined objectives. Compare the tool criteria (i.e., complexity of task, stability of solution, cost, and vendor) with your values (i.e., performance, time-to-market, extensibility, portability, and scalability) to find the solution that best meets your needs.

Browser and Server Software

We discuss two main classes of software in this section: *products,* which we define as part of the intranet architecture, and *tools,*

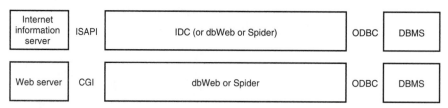

Figure 9.8   Database connectivity tools.

Figure 9.9   NeXT WebObjects object-tool solution.

which are the software utilities that help in developing or managing your intranet.

Browsers

Browsers are the most fundamental part of an intranet toolset and are largely responsible for the ease of use and scalability of our current information services. As we mentioned in Chapter 5, there are literally dozens of browsers to choose from on a range of platforms (e.g., UNIX, Windows, and Apple Macintosh). But, while there are numerous possibilities to choose from, two vendors stand out in any evaluation process: Netscape and Microsoft. Despite Netscape's overwhelming market share, these two browsers are battling to control the long-term market. In their attempt to win (and hold) market share, the two companies are continually offering new and improved features. This game of one-upmanship is certainly beneficial to users, but may make selecting your browser a bit more difficult.

Both companies typically make beta versions of their new browsers available during the development cycle. While these beta browsers are free to users, there is a catch involved—the software may have bugs! This is an important point. While beta versions are very useful to your development team, intranet managers need to be aware that users may try to bring in beta versions of the browsers (and other intranet-related software). You'll need to establish policies against this type of informal software testing since the beta versions—with bugs intact—can pose a very

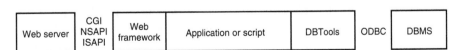

Figure 9.10   Web Framework solution.

real danger to your systems. Be sure that your development team tests all new software releases and version upgrades prior to releasing it for general use on the intranet.

CHOOSING A BROWSER

The following list reflects our general criteria for choosing a browser; you'll need to determine your own needs in each area, then rank the browsers you're evaluating according to your priorities:

- Performance
- Multimedia support (i.e., native sound/video, plug-ins)
- Language support (i.e., HTML, Java)
- Usability (i.e., user interface metaphor, online tools, help facilities)
- Vendor support

When you begin your search for a browser, you'll probably want to consider some (or all) of the popular "flavors" listed in Table 9.1.

THE NETSCAPE NAVIGATOR VERSUS MICROSOFT INTERNET EXPLORER DEBATE

Debate is probably too strong a word for comparing the latest version of Netscape Navigator with that of Microsoft's Internet Explorer because Netscape is currently the clear winner—in terms of market share and functionality. Microsoft is doing well playing catch-up though, accommodating most of the tricks and tags that were previously supported only by Netscape. But, Netscape still offers some distinct advantages with its plug-in technology that facilitates adding sound and video.

Both vendors and products are suitable for a closed intranet. And, Microsoft includes Internet Explorer without charge with Windows 95 (and offers the Web server software free with Windows NT). Netscape offers Navigator at a reasonable price, however, and gives it free to educational and nonprofit organizations. Also, Netscape has done an impressive job of continuing to push innovations in the browser market, retaining its number one position. Finally, consider the fact that Navigator also runs on UNIX

TABLE 9.1 Comparison of Major Browsers

Product	Company	URL (http://)	Comments
Netscape Navigator	Netscape	www.netscape.com	It owns 80–90% of the "primary" browser market. Highest ratings in each category. Charge for corporate use (for now).
Internet Explorer	Microsoft	www.microsoft.com	Supports all Netscape extensions. Slower than Navigator. Microsoft has promised its browser will always be free of cost.
NCSA Mosaic	NCSA	www.ncsa.uiuc.edu	The original Web browser.
Lynx	Univ. Kansas	www.ukans.edu	Nongraphical browser for UNIX and DOS systems (DOSLynx).
MacWeb	Trade Wave Corporation	www.einet.net:/ EINet/MacWeb/ MacWebHome.html	First browser developed for the Apple Mac environment; minimal memory requirements; lacks support for many Netscape extensions.
WinWeb	Trade Wave Corporation	andromeda.einet. net/EINet/WinWeb/ WinWebHome.html	Unremarkable browser; integrated news reader; runs on networked PCs without additional configuration.
Cello	Cornell Law School	fatty.law.cornell. edu/cello/cellotop. html	Free; available for Windows 3.1 platforms; lacks many features of newer browsers.
HotJava	Sun Microsystems	java.sun.com/ hotjava.html	Sun's browser to demonstrate Java applets. Not meant to compete with Netscape Navigator.

and Macintosh environments—something that Internet Explorer doesn't do (at least not at the moment) an important issue that your organization may have to consider.

Table 9.2 compares some of the notable differences between Navigator 2.02 and Internet Explorer 2.0. At this time, both companies have beta versions of their 3.0 releases, and both are likely to add new bells and whistles in that version. We recommend that you check their respective Web sites for the latest information and try out both of them for yourself.

Server Software

Server software provides the files (and services) that are requested by the various clients on the intranet and the Internet.

Table 9.3 presents a summary of the major Web servers.

Major Tools Categories

Development Tools

Fortunately, there are numerous tools available to help developers with the many and varied tasks involved in developing an intranet—from building a Web server to creating content on the intranet. Unfortunately, we can't address all of the tools that are available in this book—moreover, they change on a daily basis! This section describes just a handful of what is available, the tools that are currently most popular or those that are representative of a particular type. It is important to remember, however, that the skillset of the programmer (or programmers) will determine the ultimate success of your implementation project—not the tools that you choose to build it with. Development tools come and go, but a programmer's knowledge of design techniques and a solid understanding of application goals add the real value to any tool.

> *Microsoft IDC.*   The Internet Database Connector serves as a gateway between open database connectivity (ODBC) data sources and Microsoft Internet Information Server (IIS). Developers can use IDC to publish data from any ODBC source onto an intranet Web page, offering a powerful solu-

TABLE 9.2   Netscape Navigator versus Microsoft Internet Explorer 2.0

Selection Criteria	Netscape Navigator 2.02 www.netscape.com	Microsoft Internet Explorer 2.0 www.microsoft.com
Price	$49 for corporate use (can be negotiated down; free trial time)	Free
Platforms	Windows (3.1, 95, NT) Macintosh UNIX (AIX, BSDI, HP-UX, SUN OS, Solaris)	Windows (95, NT) Macintosh
Open API for plug-ins	Yes	No
Java compatible	Yes	No
Cache configuration	Yes	Yes
HTML extensions	Images, image maps, font colors, frames, type sizes, tables, sound	Images, image maps, font colors, marquee, type sizes, tables, table cell background color, sound
Plug-ins	Astound, Asymetrix, Live 3D, Shockwave, Vrealm, VR Scout, WIRL	Microsoft VRML Add-in
Audio, built-in	AU, AIFF	AU, AIFF, WAV
Audio, plug-in	CoolTalk, Crescendo Live, RealAudio, TrueSpeed, Xing Streamworks	None
Live Video plug-ins	CoolFusion, MovieStar, PreVU, Sizzler, Xing StreamWorks	None
E-mail	Yes	No
Usenet	Yes	Yes, but no view by thread, uuencode/decode binaries, or MIM capability

tion for organizations that are using ODBC-compliant databases. For more information, check the Microsoft Web site at www.microsoft.com.

Allaire Cold Fusion.   This is a second-generation tool that handles the low-level programming required to connect a Web server to a database. With Cold Fusion, developers need only be concerned with designing the Web pages, the queries to be run, and the query output. Cold Fusion handles all of the other details for the link. Cold Fusion runs on Microsoft Windows NT/95. For more information, check the Web site at http://www.allaire.com.

TABLE 9.3   Major Web Servers

Product	Company	URL (http://)	Comments
Netscape Communication Server	Netscape	home.netscape.com/ comprod/server central/index.html	Not much security.
Netscape Commerce Server	Netscape	home.netscape.com/ comprod/server central/index.html	Highly secure server.
Oracle Web Server	Oracle	www.oracle.com	New direction in the market because it's based on a database rather than as a file server for pre-formatted HTML files.
Apache	Apache	www.apache.org	Free for non-commercial use; fast & stable with many features; most popular browser on the Net
Website Professional 1.1	O'Reilly	www.ora.com	Industrial-strength server; fully customizable; available for Windows NT platform
IIS (Internet Information Server)	Microsoft	www.microsoft.com	Secure; first-rate server
NCSA (HTTPd)	National Center for Supercomputing Applications	hoohoo.ncsa.uiuc.edu	Free

Table 9.4 summarizes database connectivity tools.

Programming Languages

Although many development tool vendors would like to convince you that Web technology is ready for automation, it's not! Certainly, the underlying technologies associated with intranet development are changing and expanding at an incredibly rapid pace, but there is still a very definite need for the programming skillset.

Programming languages still serve as the bridges that link all of the intranet technologies and platforms—permitting the various entities to communicate with one another and to support the specialized solutions that are necessary for an intranet.

VIRTUAL REALITY MARKUP LANGUAGE (VRML)

Virtual Reality Markup Language (VRML), which was conceived in 1994 at the first World Wide Web convention, is a standardized language for real-time, interactive renderings of three dimensional worlds on a computer. It is very similar to HTML in that it is a description language rather than a traditional programming language. Commands in VRML describe an object and its relation to other three-dimensional objects with the goal of building a "seamless" cyberspace. The first version of VRML allows for the creation of "virtual worlds" with limited interaction; the second version is likely to include standards for animation and other features.

TABLE 9.4   Database Connectivity/Development Tools

Product	Company	URL (http://)	Comments
Spider Technologies	Spider	www.w3spider.com	Only works with UNIX-based systems. Provides connectivity between Web server and database without any CGI scripting.
Sapphire/Web	Bluestone	www.bluestone.com/ products/sapphire	Only works with UNIX-based systems. Power builder-like interface. It uses C, C++, SQL stored procedures, debug tools and project management tools.
Open Web	Open Software Associates	www.osa.com	Follows OpenUI standard. Potential to access mainframe-based applications through easy front-end HTML applications.
Oracle WebSystem	Oracle	www.oracle.com/ mainEvent/ webSystem	Only works with Oracle databases.

To date, VRML offers little practical application for business, but this situation will undoubtedly change in the future. IT pioneers are already dreaming of ways in which VRML can provide a competitive advantage. Visionaries see applications for VRML in marketing (Intel and Sony are already using it for this purpose) as well as geographic information systems, inventory control, project management, and more.

SCRIPTING LANGUAGES

Common gateway interface (CGI) scripting is the concept of programming software to move—and take actions on—data. Many languages can support scripting because the process crosses many hardware and software boundaries. Your choice of a scripting language depends primarily on your intranet design and architecture. Common scripting languages include C, C++, JavaScript, Microsoft VBScript, and PERL. Regardless of your choice of a programming language, however, remember that nothing can replace good design, skillset, and project management. For more information on CGI and public domain scripts, search for CGI on http://www.yahoo.com.

JavaScript   JavaScript is a scripting language that is not to be confused with the Java language from Sun Microsystems; JavaScript is used to bind HTML, applets, and other intranet components to each other. This scripting language lets even relatively inexperienced developers change images, play different sounds, and elicit responses from a multitude of events such as mouse clicks or screen entry. JavaScript can run on Java-enabled browsers as well as servers. In this respect, it offers another option to C++ or PERL for Web-server CGI programs.

VBScript (Visual Basic Scripting Addition)   Microsoft's VBScript language is similar to JavaScript in that it is designed to create active online content on Web sites. VBScript, which is a subset of Microsoft's Visual Basic programming language, is essentially Microsoft's response to the JavaScript language, but it adds the extra functionality of ActiveX controls (i.e., OLE objects/automation). Although VBScript was still in beta testing at the time this book was written, it offers a very valid solution because there are millions of programmers that already know Visual Basic. Microsoft is planning to tightly integrate VBScript with its browsers, backoffice products, operating systems, and applications. This tightly integrated environment is likely to be of interest to any intranet development team. For more information on VBScript, check the Web site at http://www.msn.com or http://www.microsoft.com.

PERL   PERL is a UNIX-derived language for scanning information and extracting data. It is an easy and efficient language that closely resembles C in context and runs on UNIX-based hardware. PERL is a great tool for CGI scripts because it has been widely used and shareware scripts are widely available. PERL may offer a good solution for your intranet if your developers have experience with UNIX. For more information on PERL, search http://www.yahoo.com.

Table 9.5 presents a summary of CGI scripting products.

TABLE 9.5   CGI Scripting Products

Product	Company	URL (http://)	Comments
JavaScript	Netscape	www.netscape.com	Netscape's Web scripting language. To be implemented within HTML scripts.
Visual Basic Script	Microsoft	www.msn.com	Microsoft's Web scripting language to compete with JavaScript. Based on the Visual Basic language. To be implemented within HTML scripts.
Visual Basic	Microsoft	www.msn.com	Good language for scripting and heavier programming. VB libraries for CGI scripting can be created.
PERL			Nice, concise language for CGI scripting. For UNIX-literate programmers.
C++			Excellent programming language; not usually preferred due to high cost of experienced programmers.

Note: Many tools mentioned in other sections of this document can automatically create CGI scripts. For example, Microsoft's IDC database connectivity tool and Front Page HTML editor both create CGI scripts.

JAVA

Java is as hot as it sounds and has captured a great deal of attention in a relatively short period of time. Developed by Sun Microsystems, Java is not a full-blown development environment (although a number of vendors are creating Java environments), but rather a programming language lucky enough to be in the right place at the right time. Similar in some respects to C++, Java is an object-oriented, multipurpose, multiplatform development language that can be compiled or interpreted. Its primary use is to create *applets* that can be included in Web applications. Applets are fully portable mini applications that are hardware- and operating system–independent—powerful tools in a heterogeneous intranet environment. Typical functions performed by applets include multimedia, general utilities, and financial reporting.

Some of the latest development environments include Java components such as compilers and debuggers within their frameworks. Certainly as the language and usage evolve, so will the tools. All of the mainstream development tool vendors are enthusiastically embracing the language, making it very likely that Java will, if it hasn't already, become an integral part of any intranet platform. To date, Java has been embraced by IBM, Apple, and Microsoft, all of which are integrating support for Java into their platforms.

But, don't let all the hype overcome your good judgment. Java isn't an instant answer to a successful intranet. It is only one of *many* options for developers to consider when designing and coding a Web-based application. Because Java is an object-oriented language, it is currently in vogue since object orientation is often viewed as the brass ring in code reusability. It is not necessarily the only key to success.

Using an object-oriented language effectively in a development project requires some experience (i.e., it is essentially an acquired skill). To successfully implement reusability, many key elements must be in place. If you're interested in learning more about object-oriented languages and their application to intranet development, we recommend that you read one or more of the excellent books that are available on the subject. Pay special attention to the discussions relating to the technical skills needed by programmers, training costs, change management issues, and code libraries. For more information, check Sun's Java Web site at http://java.sun.com.

Table 9.6 summarizes Java development environments.

Search Engines

A search engine can be a critical component of any intranet. A search engine provides the client computer with the ability to search and find information on the intranet—regardless of where

TABLE 9.6 Java Development Environments

Product	Company	URL (http://)	Comments
Liquid Motion and Liquid Reality	Dimension X	www.dnx.com	Drag-and-drop tools used to create animations in the Java language.
Java Cafe	Symantec	www.symantec.com	For Mac and Windows 95, includes graphical project manager, professional programmer's editor with syntax coloring, graphical debugger, and a native compiler. Drag-and-drop studio to create graphical interface.
Java Development Kit	Sun	java.sun.com	The creators of Java.
SuperCede	Asymetrix	www.asymetrix.com	Suite of applications for C++ and Java developments. "Flash Compiler" allows compilation as they download, which means developers will see immediate code changes in a running applet.
RadJa	Application Software Industries	radja.com	Point and click operation; no need to know Java.
Visual J++	Microsoft	www.microsoft.com/VisualJ	Java integrated developers' environment that includes Java (portable) and Active X (proprietary) flavors.

that information is located. Search engines run on the intranet server, and are available as both freeware and commercial software. If you're considering a freeware product, be sure to weigh the support issues that are involved with this type of product in relation to the cost of commercial software. Most search engines are available with a try/buy agreement. Some of the most widely used search engines include:

Excite for Web servers (EWS).   Architext Software offers its search engine for the intranet for free. Excite, which uses the same technology as the Excite Internet site, allows users to search for the exact item they want by name, as well as by a description of the item in their own words. Users also have the option of retrieving additional documents that are like the one that was just found. EWS is quick and easy to set up; it requires no programming and can be fully functional in less than an hour. For more information on EWS, visit the Web site at http://www.excite.com.

AltaVista.   Digital Equipment's AltaVista search software is undoubtedly the fastest on the market. AltaVista can retrieve a search item from the entire Internet in about two seconds. You can expect it to be even quicker on an intranet! Digital offers enterprise, workgroup, and personal editions of the product. For more information on AltaVista, visit the Web site at http//:www.altavista.digital.com.

Table 9.7 summarizes some public and commercial Net search engines.

Client Tools

PUBLISHER/AUTHORING TOOLS

Designing a Web page for an intranet is not a particularly difficult task. In fact, you can do it with any editor that you have at your disposal. All Web pages are written in HTML, a relatively simple language that describes how the rich content should be displayed on a Web page. The HTML development tools that are currently available make it as easy to create a Web page as it is to create a document using a word processor. Be aware, however, that regard-

TABLE 9.7   Public and Commercial Net Search Engines

Product	Company	URL (http://)	Comments
Lycos	Lycos, Inc.	www.lycos.com	Receives the highest ratings in speed and relevance.
Excite	Architext Software	www.excite.com	Another highly rated engine.
Web Crawler	America Online	www.webcrawler.com	Popular engine.
Yahoo	Yahoo! Corp.	www.yahoo.com	Not a complete listing of sites. Each site must be "approved" by Yahoo to be listed on this site.
NetOwl	SRA International	www.sra.com	HTML search-and-index system; visible index displays entries for a search term.
Intermezzo	SRA International	www.sra.com	Targeted for large organizations; users enter search terms to be found in a variety of databases.
WAIS (Wide Area Information System)	Public	www.ai.mrt.edu/the-net/wais.html	Searches directories of servers for name of source or by topic. Retrieval from databases via full text search.
Gopher	Public	go to Yahoo and enter Gopher	Text-based server that categorizes information in subject trees. Easily navigated via Veronica or Jughead.

less of which HTML editor you use to create a Web page, you'll also need to standardize design elements. Otherwise, your intranet is likely to appear very unorganized. The following paragraphs describe some of the HTML tools that are currently popular, but you can expect to see many new products and many new features for the existing products within the near future.

- ◆ *Microsoft Internet Assistant.*   Microsoft actually offers several Internet Assistants, which are add-ons to its Word, Excel, and PowerPoint applications. They allow users to easily create or convert documents to HTML code. These add-ons are available as freeware and can readily be downloaded from the Microsoft site (www.microsoft.com).

In addition to making it very simple to turn legacy documents to HTML code, the Internet Assistants eliminate the need to learn a new application since they work seamlessly with their respective applications, converting text, graphics, and tables to their HTML counterparts. There's almost nothing new to learn, and you also have the option of adding animated text and other Web formats (such as blinking text) that were not part of the original document. In addition, Microsoft includes a limited browser capability to facilitate embedding links and importing HTML.

◆ *SoftQuad Hot Metal Pro.*   Hot Metal Pro by SoftQuad is one of the most popular HTML authoring tools. It is a WYSIWYG HTML editor that features, among other things, a spell checker, dictionary, thesaurus, and full context-sensitive search and replace function. Although it's useful to have a working knowledge of HTML code when using Hot Metal, even novice users can achieve sophisticated results using it for the first time.

The latest version (3.0) boasts drag-and-drop capabilities that let you drag and drop text, links, and graphics anywhere on a page. It also includes numerous templates, a frames editor, and built-in graphics editing as well as a complete validation function that makes it virtually impossible to create an invalid Web page. Although the validation feature sounds good in theory, it can prove inconvenient if you're trying to create pages containing proprietary HTML code for use by some other server or application.

Hot Metal Pro is available for Windows 3.X and NT platforms and retails for $159. For more information, visit the SoftQuad site at www.sq.com.

◆ *Netscape Navigator Gold.*   Netscape Navigator Gold is revolutionary when it comes to HTML creation since it integrates an authoring tool *and* a browser! When properly configured, it allows a user to navigate to a Web page using buttons and controls that are identical to those in Netscape Navigator and other browsers. The similarity ends there, however, because once a page is up, users can go to edit mode and begin editing that document as if they were in a word processor. A simple click of the "publish" button uploads all of the newly edited information to the Web server without any further interaction on the user's part.

Netscape Navigator Gold is available for Windows and Windows NT. It is free of charge to students, charitable and nonprofit organizations, and can be used for a 90-day trial by commercial and government organizations. A $79 download license that can be purchased directly from Netscape allows you to receive technical support. A download license that includes an update subscription is available for $96. For more information and updated pricing information visit the Netscape site at www.netscape.com.

◆ *WebEdit (Ken Nesbitt).*   WebEdit is a very user friendly HTML authoring tool. It is a well-designed tool that lets users begin creating Web content in very short order. WebEdit also has a powerful HTML tag checker that validates the HTML code to ensure correctness, and a project support function that facilitates managing any number of documents as a group. WebEdit is currently available as shareware and can be downloaded from http://www.nesbitt.com.

◆ *Microsoft Front Page.*   Microsoft's Front Page (formerly distributed by Vermeer Software) facilitates the creation and management of large corporate Web sites. It allows for many people on a network to create, manage, and maintain Web pages and graphically view the layout of the site, ensuring that individuals can edit and update areas only for which they have permission.

Among the more interesting and useful features of Front Page is its WYSIWYG editing capabilities. This means that a user does not need to have any knowledge of HTML code in order to put together a quality Web page. With the use of "bots," users can also create more sophisticated Web features such as forms, search pages, and discussion pages, without any programming whatsoever. A tool like Front Page enables an entire company to participate in maintaining an intranet site; individuals or departments can be assigned to maintain specific pages or sections. And, because Front Page is easy to learn and use, even nontechnical users with little or no training can share in the maintenance tasks.

Front Page is available from retail outlets for $109 for current users of Microsoft Office or $149 for everyone else (through March of 1997). Microsoft offers the server extensions that are required to run Front Page with particular servers for free. For more information, visit the Microsoft Web site at www.microsoft.com.

Table 9.8 summarizes some other HTML Editors.

GRAPHICS/MULTIMEDIA

In addition to HTML editors, many Web page designers need tools to help them produce eye-catching graphics. Graphics can turn a mundane looking page of text into a creative, information-packed message. Almost any graphical drawing package that can save

TABLE 9.8   HTML Editors

Product	Company	URL (http://)	Comments
PageMill	Adobe	www.adobe.com/ prodindex/pagemill	Point-and-click building of front-end interfaces.
HTML Assistant	Howard Harawitz	cs.dal.ca/ftp/htmlasst	
HotDog	Sausage Software	www.sausage.com	Easy interface HTML Editor— one of the best; supports HTML 2.0, 3.0, and Netscape and Microsoft tags.
HTML Transit	InfoAccess	www.infoaccess.com	Creates HTML pages from native word processor formats, including tables, GIF/JPEG. Includes template control over appearances for consistent look (Windows platform only).

files in GIF or JPEG formats can be used. There are literally hundreds of these packages available, and some may already be in use at your organization. Some of the most widely used graphics programs include:

- *PaintShop Pro by JASC.* PaintShop Pro is one of the most easy to use and most powerful image editing, viewing, and converting programs available. It supports all graphics formats for Web publishing and includes many drawing and painting tools. It is available as shareware and the Pro version runs on Windows platforms. For more information visit the JASC Web site at http://www. jasc.com.
- *Adobe Photoshop.* Adobe Photoshop provides Web page developers with practically all of the tools they need to create stunning photo and graphic images. Photoshop supports all of the image types that can be published on Web pages and includes a variety of professional graphic tools such as special effects filters, retouch, and multiple layers. Photoshop software is available for Macintosh, Windows, and UNIX platforms. For more information visit the Adobe Web site at http://www.adobe.com.

Although not commonly used in intranet environments yet, audio enhancements are growing in popularity on the World Wide Web. Table 9.9 summarizes some of the most popular audio applications for intranets.

Management and Administrative Tools

Management tools are a vital part of any intranet implementation effort. These tools can help provide the framework for project management, software design, and quality assurance. Although intranet development doesn't follow the typical development framework, good management tools can help to keep the development effort organized. There are many management tools available in the market today, some of which do not need to run on an

TABLE 9.9   Audio Applications

Product	Company	URL (http://)	Comments
RealAudio	Progressive Networks	www.realaudio.com	Audio streaming. Gaining market share. Sound quality is not great. Works with 14.4 Kbps or greater.
StreamWorks	Xing Corporation	204.62.160.251	Audio streaming. Will compete with Real-Audio

intranet to be useful. Rather than describing specific management tools, we have categorized them by type. Your organization is probably using one or more of these tools now, and you can probably adapt it to your intranet effort with minimal effort.

PROJECT MANAGEMENT TOOLS

The project manager's job—scheduling, costing, and resourcing all development efforts—was a daunting one prior to the advent of project management software. Now, however, software tools handle many of the tedious details of project management—providing comprehensive project graphing (e.g., Gant and PERT charts), complex resourcing assignments, and graphical drop-and-drag scheduling for project components. Project management tools are available for all operating systems. Table 9.10 summarizes some of the popular project management tools, including the market leaders—Microsoft Project and Project Workbench by ABT Corporation.

COLLABORATION SOFTWARE

Collaboration software has really taken off since the Internet. The idea of groups of people working together from different locations is a very powerful concept. While some proprietary software used to support this capability, the proliferation of Internet-based systems has taken the concept to a new level. Collaboration is a very cost-effective way of coordinating schedules and meeting among remote locations. Some current products even permit users to participate in video conferences, enabling the users to see each other and work together via an electronic whiteboard. Most collaborative products are available for intranet as well nonintranet solutions.

TABLE 9.10   Project Management Tools

Product	Company	URL (http://)	Comments
Microsoft Project	Microsoft	www.microsoft.com	Works well for relatively small projects; inadequate as schedules grow.
Project Workbench	ABT Corp.	www.abtcorp.com	Offers industrial strength tools for management solutions; allows integration with Microsoft Project.
Artemis Views	Artemis Software	www.artemis-intl.com	Planning and control software product supports integration with Microsoft Project.
LBMS	LBMS Inc.	www.lbms.com	Well-structured, process-driven approach.
SureTrack Project Manager and Project Planner	Primavera Systems Inc.	www.primavera.com	Organizes tasks and resources clearly, but lacks strong facility for linking projects and updating master plans.

Table 9.11 summarizes some groupware/collaborative products.

MUDs and MOOs.   MUD, which is commonly interpreted as multi-user dialog but may also stand for multi-user dimension or multi-user domain, actually evolved from the computer games environment of the 1980s. MUDs have progressed far beyond their roots, however, and now offer some practical applications for business. Many MUDs, including those used in conjunction with object-oriented technology—known as MOOs—are geared specifically toward user interaction. Developer workshops are now using MOOs to provide their programmers with an easy, cost-effective means of communicating and collaborating. MOOs are

TABLE 9.11   Groupware Collaborative Products

Product	Company	URL (http://)	Comments
Odesta Livelink	Odesta Systems	www.odestasys.com	Fully integrated document management, workflow, and project collaboration.
FYI	Identitech	susan@identitech.com	Collaboration for teams,
Co-motion	Bittco Solutions	www.bittco.com	departments, task forces, and groups separated by distance and time.
Starfish	Philippe Kahn		A Net-savvy contact manager, calendar, and scheduler.
net.Thread	net.Genesis	www.netgen.com/ products/net.Thread/	Creates topic-sorted discussion areas on WWW sites.

ideal for meetings and discussions because they produce a record of the conversations for future reference.

Some sophisticated examples of MOO applications are now beginning to appear in the business and scientific communities. One example is *Jupiter,* a project at Parc Xerox designed to facilitate conferences with astronomers around the world; another is BioMOO, a cyber-community of biology researchers used for meetings and brainstorming sessions. A number of other environments have similar characteristics to MUDs and MOOs, with slight variations on the multi-user theme. Mostly used for entertainment at this time, these include MUSEs (multi-user simulation environments) and MUSHs (multi-user shared hallucination), a virtual reality "collective consciousness" world.

As a general concept, multi-user environments offer a very real potential for business collaboration. They provide an easy, inexpensive means for individuals or groups to communicate in real-time, without the costs involved with teleconferencing or videoconferencing technologies. For more information on MUDs and MOOs, see http://www.cis.upenn.edu/~lwl/mudinfo.html or http:www// mcmuse.mc.maricopa.edu/inetcourse/islands/muds.html.

ADMINISTRATIVE TOOLS

Many large intranet sites need to report status information on a regular basis. There are currently a number of tools that give the intranet manager a real-time look into the metrics of how the intranet is performing. Some tools offer counts of site visits (i.e., how many times a site has been contacted in a given time period) and indicate which locations within a site had the highest number of visits (i.e., the most *hits*). Hits are used to determine site traffic and the most popular sites. This type of information is invaluable for planning future content for the intranet as well as for fixing roadblocks, or making pages easier to use. For example, a developer can determine if the online employee phone book on your intranet is being used by counting the number of visits that the site gets each day. If the number of visits is low, it may indicate that the site is hard to find or not user-friendly.

Other tools such as site analyzers help to check each page, file, and link on an intranet site. An analyzer can trace broken links, missing images, and redundancies. Some packages can automatically generate a map of the site, and can even build a hypertext report that details its findings. This type of tool is not only useful for post-production intranet support, but also for testing the intranet before rolling it into production. One example of an analyzer is offered by Incontext. For further information on this product, visit the Web site at http://www.incontext.com.

Many administrative tools are available as shareware or freeware. Some are merely CGI scripts that can reside on your server; others are commercial products that can offer a wealth of administrative information to the intranet manager. Still others offer some degree of protection from external links or restrict access to (or from) some Internet sites. The following tools are examples of some types that are currently available:

- *Trend Micro's InterScan VirusWall.*   This package is designed to detect and stop viruses at the Internet gateway by scanning E-mail messages and attachments, and FTP traffic. It is available for Sun SPARC workstations using Solaris 2.4 and above. For more information, visit the Web site at www.trendmicro.com or www.antivirus.com.
- *SurfWatch.*   This package restricts access to sexually explicit sites and newsgroups on the Internet. Its cus-

tomizable database offers complete control of who sees what; a subscription service ensures that it stays up to date. SurfWatch is available for Windows 3.1 and 95, as well as Macintosh environments.

◆ *WebMapper by NetCarta.*   This administrative tool manages local and remote sites, integrates with authoring tools, and shows the structure of the site at a glance. It can also highlight broken links, track changes, and help to manage content. WebMapper is available for Windows 95 and NT environments. For more information, visit the Web site at www.netcarta.com.

Plug-ins

Internet technology was designed to view static data on HTML text pages. However, this plain-vanilla material is no longer robust enough for the corporate environment. Many organizations now offer applications to work with browsers so that users can view animation, listen to audio broadcasts, teleconference, and walk through three-dimensional worlds. All of these capabilities can be accomplished through the use of plug-ins.

Plug-ins are now available for most major browsers, with Netscape supporting most of the popular ones. There are literally dozens of plug-ins available and most of them are free. A note of caution here, though. Be sure to review any of the plug-ins that are going to be used on your intranet. Plug-ins often require data that needs an excessive amount of bandwidth, raising the potential for data traffic jams. Also, while the plug-in may be free, the server software needed to support the underlying technology can be quite expensive!

We've listed some of the most popular plug-ins, but new ones are introduced on a daily basis. For more information on plug-ins, visit the Web site at http://www.netscape.com.

◆ *Progressive Networks RealAudio.*   RealAudio allows an organization to deliver audio information—live and on-demand—to client computers throughout the enterprise. It is useful for presentations, training, and corporate communications and can be a cost-effective way to create an audio archive. RealAudio consists of plug-in software for browsers, encoder software to create RealAudio content, and server software to distribute the audio streams. The package works surprisingly well over low-bandwidth connects, but is actually geared for higher-speed architectures. RealAudio products are available for most operating environments. For more information, visit http://www.realaudio.com.

◆ *Macromedia Shockwave.* Macromedia's Director is the popular multimedia authoring tool currently used by thousands of developers for CD-ROM titles. Shockwave brings the same technology to the Web, and allows you to interact with Director animation files. Shockwave is a very impressive product and can certainly add spice to a site with its animation, audio, and video. The downside to Shockwave is that pages created with this technology take much longer to load than standard HTML pages. For more information, visit http://www.macromedia.com.

◆ *Adobe Acrobat Reader.* Acrobat Reader allows you to view, navigate, and print portable document format (PDF) files right in your browser window. PDF files are very useful in an intranet because they are platform-independent and easy to create. Acrobat Reader is available for all platforms and is particularly suitable for organizations that need to share files among different platforms. For more information, visit http://www.adobe.com.

◆ *Visual Components Formula One/NET.* Formula One/NET is an Excel-compatible spreadsheet with built-in Internet functionality. Formula One/NET spreadsheets can incorporate links to other intranet sites as well as formatted text and numbers, calculations, buttons, and controls. The package currently runs on Netscape browsers on the Windows platform. For more information, visit http://www.visualcomp.com.

Table 9.12 summarizes some other Netscape Plug-ins.

TABLE 9.12   Netscape Plug-ins

Product	Company	URL (http://)	Comments
Amber	Adobe	www.adobe.com	Allows for the reading of PDF file formats on the Web.
WebFX	Paper Software	www.paperinc.com	VRML plug-in.
Quicktime	Apple	www.apple.com	Not out yet. Incorporates video, sound, and VRML into Web pages.

Certainly there are hundreds of tools that we haven't discussed, and new ones are being developed every day. This is the beauty of having an intranet. Because the environment is open and millions of people are using intranets every day, the demand for high-quality, easy-to-use intranet tools is growing substantially.

CHAPTER TEN

THE USER INTERFACE

- ◆ Overview
- ◆ Understanding Your Design Environment and Goals
- ◆ User Interface Design Principles
- ◆ General Look and Feel
- ◆ Specific Page Elements
- ◆ Graphics Tips
- ◆ When and How to Set Standards

Overview

Planning and designing a user interface (UI) is just as important to the success of an intranet project as planning and developing your applications. The intranet's goal of providing easy access to information can be undermined if users have difficulty understanding and navigating the system. Conversely, a well-designed UI can provide meaning, consistency, and logical flow to an intranet of almost any complexity.

This chapter provides guidelines for designing a user interface including fundamental design principles, page elements and structure, and graphics considerations. We will also share some of the tips and tricks we've picked up in our development efforts, and guide you to other sources for design information.

Finally, we direct you to a number of Web sites that either serve as good reference sources or that we think are particularly good examples of effective user interface design. We chose these sites shortly before going to press, but things do change rapidly on the

Web! Hopefully, these Web sites won't change before you seek them out—but just in case they do, we've included at least one example of each.

Understanding Your Design Environment and Goals

As a preface to the rest of this discussion, it bears repeating that our goal is to assist the intranet—not Internet—designer. Although the two certainly share some of the same qualities and can benefit from some of the same advice (and some of the books on Internet design are excellent sources for ideas), they are indeed different roles. Fundamentally, the intranet designer is concerned with a relatively well-defined audience: the corporate information user. Depending on the organization and influence of your IT department, your intranet environment is probably fairly consistent. You know in advance how your users will access the intranet—what hardware they possess, what connection rates they have, and what software (especially browser) components they are likely to use.

Internet designers, on the other hand, never know what to expect. All flavors of browsers and all types of connection rates must factor into their design if they hope to attract and retain visitors—adding significantly to the complexity of their work. They tend to rely more on flash and "cool tricks" to insure application attractiveness and usage.

The intranet designer, on the other hand, has a captive audience. The applications are intended to help people work more productively, not provide hours of entertainment. And they are usually meant for intensive, *daily* use, not occasional visits (like Web sites).

Consequently, we will comment frequently that you *must* know your audience. If you have a small, single-location intranet for document storage and retrieval, you have different needs and options from someone who is designing for a multinational, massively distributed intranet running complex applications. If your intranet is supplemental to other IT systems and software, you will have different considerations from someone designing for an exclusively intranet platform. The bottom line is that common sense is often your best guide in finding a UI that satisfies your needs.

Note that much of our discussion about intranet design assumes that you are generally familiar with Internet basics including the browser interface and its functionality and general Web-style page presentation. If you are not, we strongly urge you begin by surfing the World Wide Web to understand the general nature of Web design. Watch how Web screens (aka "pages") are "painted" in your browser. Notice the tools that allow you to change pages, jump around a single page, and search for more information. And, of course, take note of those amazing graphics and consider how much they contribute to the overall value of the content.

Good places to start if you are a novice Web surfer include the infamous http://www.yahoo.com—a search engine and bulletin board of "cool" Web sites; http://home.netscape.com—for information from the world's leading browser developer; and http://www. microsoft.com—for a peek at Microsoft's latest ideas for taking over the computer industry. You'll be amazed at the infinite array of instant information, products, and service at your disposal!

User Interface Design Principles

Graphic designers often find that designing for the intranet is a frustrating task because HTML browsers are somewhat limited in their ability to display text and graphics. To compound the problem, users have the option of changing some browser display defaults, further lessening the designer's control over the end product. Even with these limitations, however, there are a number of basic design principles that help ensure a successful user interface design.

Consistency

"Foolish consistency is the hobgobblin of little minds."—
Ralph Waldo Emerson

While there is certainly an element of truth in Emerson's edict, it does not apply to user interface design. No amount of consistency is foolishly large in user interface design! Not only does consistency make the interface easy to use, it goes a long way toward creating a positive user perception of the system. Ideally, users should perceive the system as well designed, stable, and reliable—much of this perception is directly attributable to the user interface. A consistent user interface also creates the all-important first impression that can gain users' confidence.

Several design elements must be carefully planned for consistency throughout the system, but they must also be flexible enough to adapt to the needs of specific sections or pages within the system. These design elements include:

- Header graphics
- Text styles and formats
- Style and color palettes of graphics
- Background colors or patterns

We'll discuss specifics of each of these elements later in the chapter, but the key point to remember about consistency in the intranet user interface is that each page should have the same "look and feel."

Simplicity and Intuitiveness

Virtually all intranets are developed with the sole intent of gathering information and providing access to it—easily and efficiently—for a network of users. Intranets are not intended (except in rare cases) to entertain users or to wow them with hip graphics and Web authoring gimmicks. While hidden links and mystery pages may be suitable for MTV-type sites that aim to provide an interactive experience for users, the structure and elements of an intranet should be simple and intuitive. For example:

- Buttons should be obviously "clickable" objects; users should not have to "hunt the page" for hyperlinks. Graphics should be kept small and should directly explain or enhance content.

TIP   *The small graphics rule applies most strictly to large-scale, distributed intranets, especially those with remote users communicating via 28.8-Kbps modems or ISDN lines. If your intranet is accessible only in a high-speed LAN environment, you have more leeway in graphics size and complexity. Just don't go overboard!*

TIP   *If you have a WAN environment, you may still be able to use some large graphics if you use them on very stable (i.e., rarely updated) pages. A home (aka "start" in the Microsoft world) page that will be cached can use pictures without adversely affecting remote users. Just be sure to keep the subsequent content pages—which are regularly updated—simple.*

◆ Actions (e.g., what happens when a user clicks a button) should be intuitive and predictable.
◆ The user should feel like he or she is in control.

Simplicity, however, does not necessarily mean dull. Carefully applied design enhancements can yield an eye-catching site that users can navigate with ease.

Audience Awareness

A successful intranet interface must, of course, be designed to meet the users' needs and to correspond with their level of technical expertise. An intranet designed for a highly technical (i.e., "chip heads") audience should, for example, have a much different look and feel than one designed for sales people with little (or no) computer experience. While the technical audience is less likely to require navigational help and hand-holding, the nontechnical users are likely to need a considerable amount of guidance and a friendlier look and feel.

Thus, you should strive to speak the users' language. Tailor both the tone and content of the pages' text and instructions to your audiences' level of expertise. You might, for example, label a button in the technical users' intranet as "Parse Query," while describing the same function to the nontechnical audience as "Find the Answer."

Like any other intranet application development project, user input is critical to the success of your UI design. Solicit suggestions from representative users before you begin, then incorporate their input as you go through design and development iterations. Since you are, in essence, providing a service to the corporate community, you want user preferences and satisfaction to be built-in. Of course, you will discover that there are limits to what you can do given time and cost constraints, but a willingness to satisfy the users whenever possible goes a long way toward assuring the project's success.

Begin designing for your audience by determining who they are and what it is that they will be doing with the intranet. To determine their level of computer literacy, answer the following questions:

- Do your users currently have computers?
- If so, what kind (mainframe terminals, PCs, stand-alone, networked)?
- What operating system (Macintosh, MS Windows, DOS, other)?
- What else is standard to their physical work environment?
- What is unique?
- What is the expected education level of your user base? What is their propensity for learning and accepting change?

Next, you will need to understand what information the users will be dealing with:

- What type of information will they be accessing/using?
- What is the quality of the information?
- What quantity of information will they be expected to digest?

- How often will the information (i.e., nature or quantity) change?
- Will the users be updating the information?

Having completed your preliminary research, you're ready to talk directly to representative users. Be sure they understand what an intranet is—and isn't—and how the UI functions within a system. Then listen. Let them tell you who they think they are and what they think they need. Most users have very definite opinions on this so be prepared to take notes. If your users have used Web-style applications on the Internet, ask them which sites they like best and why. What parts of the Web do they find useful and/or easy to use?

As you progress in the UI development cycle, involve the users as much as possible, beginning with the very first page you design. While you, or your designer, may be able to anticipate most feedback, the users themselves are the best source of information. They may pick up on problems or issues that techies are immune to.

Aesthetic Integrity

User interface design necessarily requires a certain degree of artistic proficiency and general aesthetic intuitiveness. Aesthetic integrity is really a catch-all term for many things—the understanding and intelligent application of color, texture, shape, and space. Like all art, it is not quantitative but qualitative, and everyone has a very keen idea of what he or she likes. Unfortunately, its very nature makes aesthetics difficult to define (although philosophers continue to debate the issue as they have for centuries), so it's impossible to give "checklists" in the same fashion that we can elsewhere in this book. Aesthetic integrity is best achieved through an understanding of the principles and experience with the elements of UI.

If you are new to UI design, you need to log several intense sessions on the Internet. Fire up your browser and find out what designers are doing. Observe the use of space, as well as color and shape, and take notes of the sites that you particularly like—or dislike.

Whatever you do, don't assume that a one-size-fits-all template can solve your UI problems. For most intranet environments with complex needs, this solution is wholly insufficient. As a designer, it is your responsibility to understand and cater to your user base. Templates are wonderful mechanisms for creatively challenged users who assemble PowerPoint presentations, but they are inappropriate for meaningful interfaces.

One last word of caution: Don't go overboard! As you explore the Internet you will encounter many sites that are bogged down with graphics and overwhelming in their obnoxious use of color, graphics, and motion. As we said at the beginning of this chapter, simplicity is likely to be your best long-range investment in a design that really lasts.

General Look and Feel

Look and feel is the user's impression of a system's stability, functionality, navigability, and overall quality. It is determined by each individual design element, the way in which the elements function together, and how clearly function and meaning are conveyed on the screen. A few specific elements of page design contribute significantly to a successful look and feel, including choice of backgrounds, color palettes, interface metaphor, and overall intranet layout.

Backgrounds

Often not given the respect and consideration it deserves, the choice of a Web page background is crucial. It is one of the first elements of the page to load and acts as the cohesive force that brings together all of the other elements of the page.

All too often, the background image on a Web page interferes with the legibility of text. If users have to strain to read the text on a screen, they are likely to question the overall integrity of the site. Background images should be used to enhance the content of the page, or to provide additional information to the users. As a general rule, if you're having trouble deciding what to put in your site's background, *don't put anything.* A solid color background not only loads faster, it ensures that the text will be clearly readable, regardless of the display setup in use.

If you do choose to use a background image, you may need to edit its color content. Consider using an image manipulation application like Adobe PhotoShop to determine the RGB (red-green-blue) values of your colors, and then use an RGB-to-hexadecimal converter for manipulation. One converter that we like is offered by DesignSphere Online, a service of Cogent Software at http://www.dsphere.net/rgb2hex.html. This site also offers a hex-to-RGB converter that you may want to investigate.

Although it is rare to see a distinctive site that uses a solid white background, the example in Figure 10.1 shows that it *can* be done. The following pages on the WWW are good examples of the use of white as a background color.

- http://www.cnet.com
- http://www.word.com
- http://www.iworld.com

One clever use of background images is to design an image that, when tiled by the browser, creates a vertical "banner" that repeats itself along the length of the site, as illustrated in Figure 10.2. To increase its utility, this banner can contain navigational information to help users determine their location in the intranet.

On the BSG site, each main section has a banner of distinct color; this gives visual variety yet also provides consistency.

When creating background graphics, remember to make the elements at least 1,280 pixels in width. This prevents them from tiling horizontally on displays with high resolution. It's also advisable to keep the image's height to a minimum, and limit the number of colors.

To create a seamless image when tiled, start with an image that is either a solid color on its upper and lower edges, or one that is of a random, repetitive nature (e.g., clouds, a gravel-like texture, or the keyboard image used on the BSG site). Then, apply Adobe Photoshop's "Offset" filter, and duplicate parts of the image to cover the seam. For a more detailed tutorial, see "Making Seam-

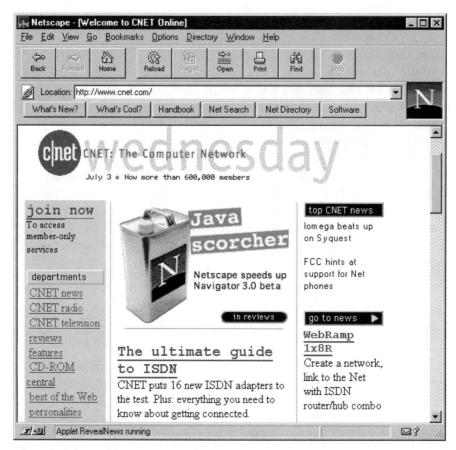

Figure 10.1   Effective use of white background (cnet.com).

less Backgrounds from any Graphic" on the Kai's Power Tips and Tricks site at: http://the-tech.mit.edu/KPT/Makeback/makeback. html.

The following Web sites offer ready-to-use patterns and textures:

- ◆ http://www.primenet.com/~robhood/pagebldr/ pagebldr.html
- ◆ http://www.netcreations.com/patternland

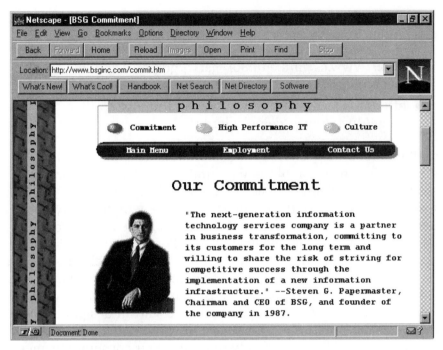

Figure 10.2   Example of a background banner.

♦ http://the-tech.mit.edu/KPT/bgs.html

Similarly, ImagiTek Network Graphic Design offers an HTML Background Color Selector on its site: http://www.imagitek.com/bcs.html.

The Selector allows you to enter various background, text, and link color combinations, then displays the results along with the HTML tags to include in your document. You can find a more complete list of shareware color-picker utilities at: http://www.primenet.com/~jlong/colors.htm.

Color Scheme

The color scheme (or palette) is another major consideration for the Web site graphic design. Essentially, color scheme refers to choosing colors that are harmonious, or that "go together." Color theory is beyond the scope of this book, but there are some very good, basic introductions to it on the WWW:

- http://www.cs.gmu.edu:80/~garyq/graphics_guide/color_theory
- http://www.contrib.andrew.cmu.edu/urs/tg2k/other_home/dw4e/www/color/color.html

While not always obvious to users, color scheme can subtly affect their perception of the Web site's integrity. A haphazardly selected color scheme (or lack of a selected color scheme) can result in a disjointed, thrown-together look—which clearly does not gain the users' confidence. The color scheme must also be appropriate in its psychological effects. For example, bright, cheerful, circuslike colors may be appropriate for a children's site, but not at all suitable for an executive information system.

We suggest you read one of the pages on color theory and try to select harmonious colors. A good place to start in designing your color scheme is with the colors used in your company's logo—and a good way to subtly, intangibly reinforce your corporate themes and values. Add in complementary colors as appropriate, attempting to keep the overall set rather discrete. Since understanding color theory can be tricky, you may want to consult a graphic designer for initial assistance.

Interface Metaphor

Be sure to consider your users' experience and background when choosing an interface metaphor for your intranet. If, for example, the intranet users are accustomed to using Microsoft Windows or Apple Macintoshes, try to use the same look and feel in your site design by incorporating a "desktop" metaphor where users can click on folders and files. If, on the other hand, your audience has little (or no) computer experience, you may want to use a "guide" metaphor where the users can take a "tour" through the site. Or, if you determine that your users have varied computer experience, but have all operated Automated Teller Machines, consider borrowing elements from a typical ATM interface.

Again, the choice of an appropriate interface metaphor reverts to the all-important basic interface design principle of knowing your audience and making them feel comfortable and confident.

Site Structure

Hypertext links are the elements that make intranet sites dynamic and useful. Unfortunately, poorly structured links can also make intranet sites extremely confusing. A well-conceived site structure can enhance the users' sense of control, while a weak structure can quickly frustrate even the most patient users. Because users see only one part of your site at a time, they build a mental picture or "roadmap" to help navigate. You may be in real trouble if their mental image resembles Figure 10.3.

Patrick J. Lynch of the Yale Center for Instructional Media publishes an excellent reference guide for publishing on the Web at: http://info.med.yale.edu/caim/StyleManual_Top.HTML. (*Note:* This URL is case-sensitive.)

In it, he emphasizes that users need *functional* continuity as well as graphic continuity. Notice how the carefully organized user interface elements illustrated in Figure 10.4 help the user construct a much more structured, intuitive picture of the site than those in the previous figure.

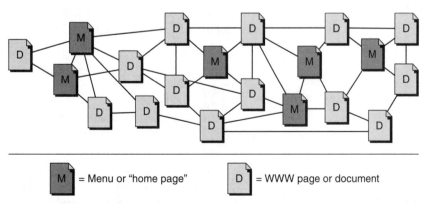

M = Menu or "home page"   D = WWW page or document

Figure 10.3   Poorly structured site.

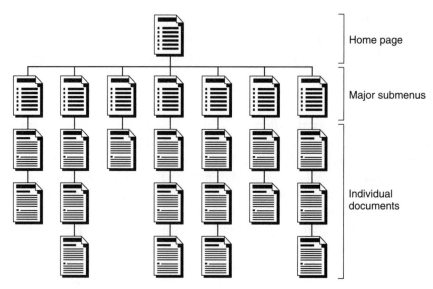

Figure 10.4   A well-structured site with graphic and functional continuity.

Lynch also warns of menu schemes that are too deep or too shallow. Structuring a Web site is a balancing act. Since the site will change constantly, you must try to strike a balance between menu pages and content pages. For example, Figure 10.5 illustrates the results of simply "tacking on" new content pages to the original menu system.

Menu systems can also hinder users' access to information by burying it too deeply within a series of menus. Figure 10.6 illustrates this problem.

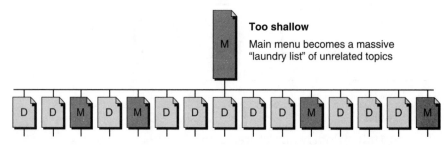

Figure 10.5   Example of a menu structure that is too shallow.

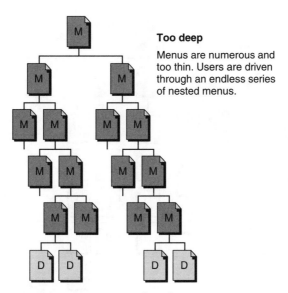

Too deep

Menus are numerous and too thin. Users are driven through an endless series of nested menus.

Figure 10.6   Example of a menu structure that is too deep.

As Lynch points out: "Complex document structures require deep menu hierarchies, but users should never be forced into page after page of menus if direct access is possible. The goal is to produce a well-balanced hierarchical tree that facilitates quick access to information and helps users understand how you have organized things." Figure 10.7 illustrates a well-balanced menu structure.

A good way to give your users direct access to any page on your site is to include a "site map" image map, that users can link to from any page. For example, users of the site depicted in Figure 10.8 can jump to the site map from the navigation bar at the bottom of any page, then click on the desired page in the site map to jump directly there. (We'll talk more about site maps later in this chapter.)

Specific Page Elements

Every single page of your intranet should incorporate specific elements that help users to navigate and lend visual consistency.

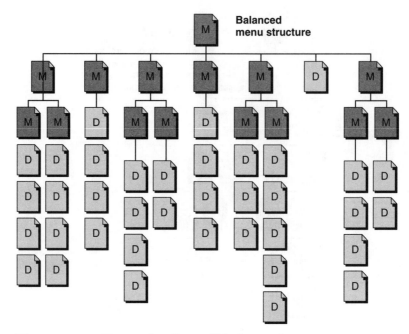

Figure 10.7   Example of a well-balanced menu structure.

These elements, as illustrated in Figure 10.9, include a graphic header, a body of text or information, a navigation interface, and an informational footer.

Graphic Header

The graphic header is particularly important for attaining a consistent interface, as well as for helping users to find their way around the intranet. Effective header graphics have several characteristics:

◆ *They contain the identity of the main application or geographic location of the intranet.*   If your intranet's applications have identifying bitmaps or splash screens, use them. Otherwise, you should provide some other location marker to help users ascertain their location, regardless of how they got there.

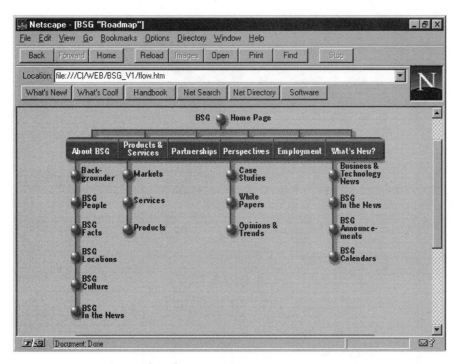

Figure 10.8   Example of a site map.

- *They contain the topic and subtopic (if there is one) of the page.*   Again, this helps users to develop a mental picture of the intranet's structure and prevents them from getting lost in the pages.

- *They are noninvasive.*   Since header graphics appear at the top of every page, they should be as small in height as practical. Users shouldn't, for example, ever have to scroll down to see the first line of text on the page. Similarly, users should never have to scroll horizontally to see the complete header graphic. To be on the safe side, design header graphics no wider than 500 pixels. Graphic headers should enhance the look of your pages, not dominate them.

- *They contain navigational links.*   Users generally find a link from the header graphic back to the main site very

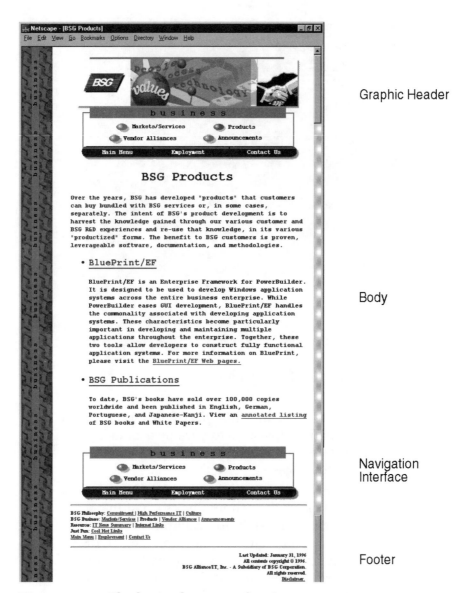

Figure 10.9 The basic elements of an intranet page.

useful. If, despite all of your best efforts, users do get lost
or if they directly access a page deep within the site's
structure, they can use the link to easily return to the
main site.

Links to other related pages may also be helpful. The header
graphic in Figure 10.10, for example, lets a user jump directly to
any of the other pages under the general topic, or main menu
item, of "Philosophy."

Also, the "dimmed" button in the header graphic lets users
know which page they are currently viewing. You must create
separate header graphics for each page in order to provide this
type of guide, but the extra work goes a long way toward making
your users feel at ease with the site.

Figure 10.10   Example of links within a graphic header.

Body

The body of an intranet page contains the text and graphic content. HTML allows limited control over graphic placement and the typographic appearance of a page, but there are still some important guidelines to remember when authoring well-designed pages.

GENERAL TYPOGRAPHIC PRINCIPLES

In printed materials, the appearance of text—bold, italics, font, etc.—is important for effective communications. Some of the same basic typographic principles apply to well-designed Web pages:

- *Use text emphasis sparingly.*   Too much bold text on a page tends to overwhelm the visual senses. If, for example, every fifth word is bold, *nothing* really stands out as emphasized. The same principal holds true for italics, underlining, the "dreaded" blinking text, and text in all caps. Especially in on-screen applications, users perceive all caps as shouting; NEVER USE ALL CAPS unless you really want to yell at the user.

- *Take advantage of visual contrast for emphasis and to help users make sense of the page.*   Contrast between larger type for headings and smaller type for text; between blocks of text and surrounding empty space; and between graphics, text, and empty space all help the user visually digest the page. A page with everything crammed together and no empty space is likely to overwhelm users, and often, discourage them from even trying to decipher the information.

- *Establish a clear visual pattern.*   Users typically first scan the overall layout of a page to establish patterns of organization to help them assimilate the information. Regular, repeating patterns increase the legibility of your pages and help users to predict where information will be when they go to unfamiliar pages. Compare the two pages in Figure 10.11; the one on the left exhibits poor visual contrast and organization, while the one on the right exhibits strong visual contrast and organization. Clearly, it is much easier to decipher the content of the page on the right.

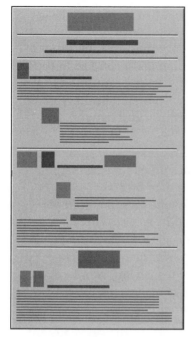

Figure 10.11 Sample pages illustrating differences in visual contrast and organization.

DIFFERENCES IN BROWSERS

HTML tags allow you to define basic physical styles of text, such as bold, italics, and underline, as well as logical styles based on the function of the text, such as emphasis, code, variable, and so forth. The browser then interprets these tags to display the text to the user. Unfortunately, different browsers interpret the tags differently. Fortunately, most intranet users are likely to use a company-standard browser, so you can design specifically for it. Even then, however, you may notice slight variations in the way the browser handles the same tags when you upgrade to new versions. There's not much you can do to resolve this problem; it's simply a way of life (and one of the more frustrating aspects of designing for the Web-style applications).

If your users do not have a single, standard browser, we recommend designing only for the characteristics common to most browsers. Don't, for example, go off and use the new Microsoft

HTML tags for fonts if many of your users browse with Netscape. Luckily, the current releases of Netscape Navigator and Microsoft Internet Explorer have done much to accommodate each other's tags (actually, Microsoft is the one who primarily gave in and used the Netscape extensions), so you shouldn't be too limited. However, if your intranet environment is very diverse, you may need to design with Mosaic and Lynx browsers in mind as well.

TIP   *Although proprietary HTML tags (like many Netscape and Microsoft extensions) cannot be read by other browsers, the browsers will simply* ignore *the tags they cannot interpret. For example, if you use one of the Netscape extensions that Microsoft Explorer doesn't recognize, it just won't be rendered on the page (no worries about error messages!). However, if the information contained in the tag is vital, you may choose to display it in another, commonly recognized format and put only the nonessentials in the proprietary tag.*

TIP   *Because many browsers are free to download off the Internet, you should consider occasionally viewing your pages with an assortment of brands to check for compatibility.*

It is possible to incorporate typographic elements beyond those supported by the browser by including them in graphics. You can, for example, create headings in an unusual font in Adobe Photo-Shop and include the GIF files on your page in place of the heading text. This approach can add visual appeal and contrast to your pages and ensure that the headings look the same on different browsers. Of course, you need to weigh the additional time it takes for these image files to load against the typographic advantage they provide.

TIP   *If you decide to put essential text in your graphics, remember that users who turn off graphics (or use non-graphical browsers) will be unable to see the message. To* *circumvent this problem, we recommend using alt-tags—HTML tags that allow you to substitute descriptive or meaningful text for nondisplayed graphics. For instance, behind a newsletter graphic that says "Happy Holidays" you would put this same text in the alt-tag.*

USING TABLES AS A LAYOUT TOOL

Simply letting your browser decide where type goes on the page usually results in text scrawling endlessly across the entire width of your browser window. By using the HTML 3 TABLE tag, however, you can increase the readability of text and enhance the visual contrast and unique look of your pages.

Recent versions of most popular browsers—including Microsoft and Netscape—support HTML tables. Tables have indeed become the interface designer's best friend with regard to page layout. The page in Figure 10.12 shows how tables can be used to set up a grid; page content is then laid out on the grid. (Note that the background image of this page includes the vertical bar separating the two sections of the screen; it does not use Netscape frames.)

Figure 10.13 depicts the same page, but with the BORDER tag activated, making the actual tables apparent.

The main table divides the page into columns: the first for the navigation buttons, and the second for the content of the page. Another table is then nested inside the content column to further organize the page. The HTML code used to generate this page is as follows:

```
<HTML><HEAD><TITLE>Kaleidoscope - Memorable Events</TITLE></HEAD>
<BODY background="gifs/back_prp.gif">
<CENTER><TABLE WIDTH=600>
<TD ALIGN=LEFT VALIGN=TOP WIDTH=125>
<A HREF="k_home.htm"><IMG SRC="gifs/home1.gif" BORDER=0></A><BR>
<A HREF="custom1.htm"><IMG SRC="gifs/custo_s1.gif"
BORDER=0></A><BR>
<A HREF="scene1.htm"><IMG SRC="gifs/scene_s1.gif" BORDER=0></A><BR>
<A HREF="events1.htm"><IMG SRC="gifs/event_s1.gif"
BORDER=0></A><BR>
<A HREF="people1.htm"><IMG SRC="gifs/peopl_s1.gif"
BORDER=0></A><BR>
<A HREF="stevep1.htm"><IMG SRC="gifs/steve_s1.gif"
BORDER=0></A><BR>
```

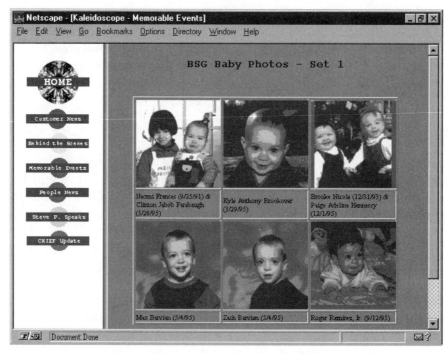

Figure 10.12   Example of a page structured with tables.

```
        <A HREF="chief1.htm"><IMG SRC="gifs/chief_s1.gif" BORDER=0></A><BR>
        </TD>
        <TD WIDTH=475><CENTER><H3><TT>BSG Baby Photos - Set
1</TT></H3></CENTER><BR>
        <CENTER><TABLE WIDTH=375 BORDER>
        <TD WIDTH=125><IMG SRC="gifs/babies/fara.gif"></TD>
        <TD WIDTH=125><IMG SRC="gifs/babies/brkover.gif"></TD>
        <TD WIDTH=125><IMG SRC="gifs/babies/hennes.gif"></TD>
        <TR>
        <TD><FONT SIZE=-2>Naomi Frances (9/25/91) & Clinton Jabob Farabaugh
(5/26/95)</FONT></TD>
        <TD><FONT SIZE=-2>Kyle Anthony Brookover (3/29/95)</FONT></TD>
        <TD><FONT SIZE=-2>Brooke Nicole (12/31/93) & Paige Adeline Hennessy
(12/1/95)</FONT></TD>
        <TR>
        <TD WIDTH=125><IMG SRC="gifs/babies/mbarv.gif"></TD>
        <TD WIDTH=125><IMG SRC="gifs/babies/zbarv.gif"></TD>
        <TD WIDTH=125><IMG SRC="gifs/babies/ramirez.gif"></TD>
        <TR>
        <TD><FONT SIZE=-2>Max Barvian (5/4/95)</FONT></TD>
```

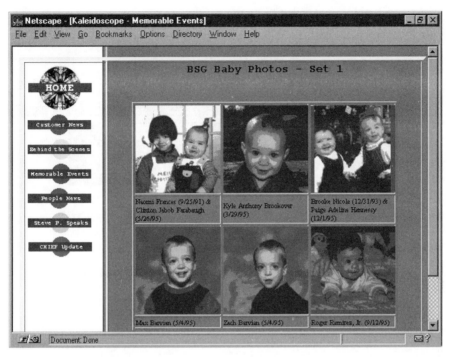

Figure 10.13 Example of a page structured with tables (borders activated for clarity).

```
<TD><FONT SIZE=-2>Zach Barvian (5/4/95)</FONT></TD>
<TD><FONT SIZE=-2>Roger Ramirez, Jr. (9/12/95)</FONT></TD>
</TABLE></CENTER>
<CENTER><H3><A HREF="events2b.htm">Baby Photos - Set
2</A></H3></CENTER>
</TD>
</TABLE></CENTER>
</BODY></HTML>
```

Figure 10.14 illustrates the effective use of tables. You may also want to take a look at the following WWW sites as examples of the effective use of tables as a layout tool:

- http://www.sun.com/styleguide
- http://www.tripod.com
- http://www.att.com

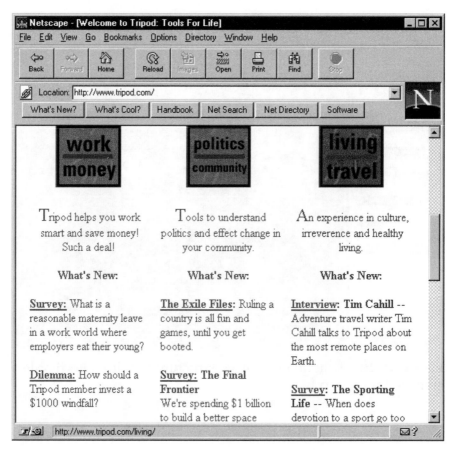

Figure 10.14   Effective use of tables (tripod.com).

PAGE LENGTH

There is no "ideal" length for a Web page. The amount of information that you put on a page depends on the type of information and the users' expectations. There are, however, some rules of thumb to help guide you.

◆ If the content of your site naturally breaks up into short, discrete sections of information, put those sections on different pages. When users read a seemingly self-contained section of information on the screen, they may not realize that there is additional information beyond the bottom edge of the browser window.

♦ If your content consists of information in the form of articles, essays, or analysis that should be read as a continuous logical whole, you may want to let the user scroll a few screens rather than linking to another page for the continuation. Following a link requires users to wait for the browser to load the next page, which may disrupt the logical sequence of the information. While scrolling generally allows the user to retain the context of the information, there is a limit to how much scrolling the user is likely to tolerate. According to Rick Levine in the *Guide to Web Style* (Sun Microsystems, Inc., Mountain View, CA, 1995, http://www.sun.com/styleguide), the limit seems to be about four screens of text.

♦ Restrict menus to a single window at the top of a page. This design allows users to navigate the site without requiring them to scroll down the page as they traverse your menuing system.

♦ And once again, know your audience. If the users require "quick hit" information, or if you want to make a high visual impact, limit the pages to a maximum of one to one-and-a-half screens. If the users need in-depth textual information, make it accessible without requiring them to follow link after link. Be sure get users feedback to assess their perceptions of the page lengths and information accessibility.

Navigation Interface

In some ways, the navigation interface is the most important element of a Web page. Without it, users cannot access the information they need; a poorly designed interface is likely to frustrate users to the point that they'll avoid the site at all costs.

As shown in Figure 10.15, navigation interface may be simply a series of text links, a series of icons or buttons that link to other pages, or an image map.

Figure 10.15   Example of text links, a series of images, and an image map.

For consistency, and to avoid leading users to "dead-end" pages, you should include your navigation interface on each and every page of your site. At a minimum, the navigation interface should include a link to your home page. If you have a site map, you should link to that from each page as well.

BUTTONS, IMAGES, OR TEXT?

Text links.   While text links are the easiest to maintain, they don't do much to enhance the visual appeal of your site. Text links may be your best choice for your navigation interface during development, however, or if your site structure changes regularly (e.g., daily or more frequently).

Be sure to take the time to provide your users with feedback as to their current location by "unhyperlinking" the current page in the navigation text. In Figure 10.16, for example, the user knows the current location because the Vendor Alliances page is not an active link option in the navigation text.

Buttons and icons. Adding graphic elements to your navigation system can greatly improve the visual appeal and consistency of your intranet. A common pitfall, however, is to create icons that have little or no apparent semantic relation to their function, as shown in the example in Figure 10.17. Users don't appreciate having to decipher cryptic icons to navigate your site. For example, the Photodisc site (http://www.photodisc.com) is graphically interesting, but has an almost indecipherable navigation system.

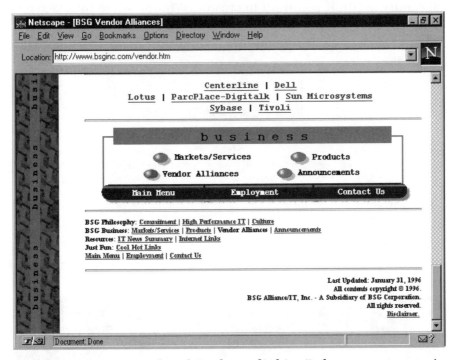

Figure 10.16 Example of "unhyperlinking" the current page in the navigation text.

Figure 10.17   Example of ambiguous icons.

Do your users a favor and incorporate text into your button graphics, as shown in the example in Figure 10.18. If you need to explain your icons, however, you probably shouldn't bother with them at all.

Much like common street signs ("Stop" and "Yield"), your navigational tools should be clear, consistent, and recognizable. Figure 10.19 illustrates the use of unambiguous icons and buttons that clearly communicate their function.

Fortunately, the HTML FORM tag offers an easy way to get nice looking, straightforward buttons for your site. This technique is especially useful if you want to create a Windows-like interface for your intranet. Figure 10.20 illustrates the use of FORMs buttons.

The HTML code to generate the screen in Figure 10.20 is as follows:

```
<HTML><HEAD><TITLE>BSG Weather Report</TITLE></HEAD>
<BODY bgcolor="#ffffff">
<CENTER><IMG SRC="gifs/wr_logo.gif"></CENTER>
<CENTER>
<FORM ACTION="wr_map1.htm"><INPUT TYPE="SUBMIT" VALUE="Weather
Map">
<ACTION="wr_loc1.htm"><INPUT TYPE="SUBMIT" VALUE="Local
Conditions">
<ACTION="wr_loc1.htm"><INPUT TYPE="SUBMIT" VALUE="Steve's
Forecast">
</FORM>
</CENTER>
</BODY></HTML>
```

Figure 10.18   Example of labeled icons in a navigational system.

Figure 10.19   Examples of unambiguous icons and buttons.

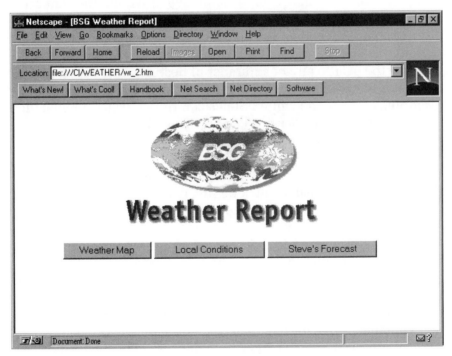

Figure 10.20   Example of the use of FORMs to create buttons.

Menu bars. A consistently available and easy-to-interpret *menu bar* will help your users travel through intranet pages with ease. Menu bars are exactly what their name implies—a row of consistently available navigational buttons provided on every page. Similar in principle to the button bars available in Microsoft applications, menu bars provide quick, reliable access to designated points in the intranet.

Bookmark tags. Another good navigational tool is the bookmark tag. Although they can be used in many ways, these tags allow a user to "jump" around a page—especially a long one with lots of content—without using tiresome scroll bars. Bookmark tags can also be used to separate information on a page. You can, for example, use a bookmark tag to take a user to various sections of a page to break the contents into logical units.

Image maps. An image map is an image in which different sections of a graphic act as links to other items or pages. Unlike an ordinary graphic link, which takes the user to the same destination no matter what part of the graphic is clicked, an image map can take the user to any of a number of destinations, depending on which predefined "hot spot" area on the graphic is clicked. For example, a map of the United States can link to pages for specific states or regions; the user need only click on a particular state to reveal information about that state.

Image maps are used in conjunction with "map files." While the image map is the actual image that the user sees (and clicks on), the map file is the associated code file, containing a description of the coordinates that define the hot spot boundaries and corresponding URLs.

Traditionally, a map file resides on the Web server, separate from the image map that is coded into the HTML page. Using this "server-side" map file requires a hit to the server in order to get the information needed to execute a map file link. Understandably, this extra server request can slow an application—perhaps to an unacceptable degree for remote users with modem connections.

Web browsers are being changed, however, to take advantage of map files embedded directly in the HTML code, much like the actual image map. These "client-side" map files do not require an additional server hit when the user clicks on the image, making the use of image maps much more attractive from a performance standpoint.

Using image maps in your navigation interface can heighten the visual impact of your intranet, but be warned that they can be time-consuming to maintain. As your intranet structure changes, you must update the coordinates in both the image file and the map file.

Modularity.   The most important consideration in planning your navigation interface is modularity. If you expect your site to continually change and grow (as most do), you don't want to have to redo the navigation system for each of the pages to accommodate those changes. Using text links, FORM buttons, or individual button images for each link (as opposed to an image map that includes all the buttons within a single image) allows you to add new buttons or remove existing buttons as your site changes.

Another way to achieve this modularity is to use a graphics tool such as Fractal Design Painter which allows you to create images with "floating" sections that can be turned into links. Floating sections *float* above the rest of the image and can be moved around, added, and deleted without changing (or replacing) the underlying image. Thus, you can update a complex image map simply by manipulating the floaters. Fractal Design Painter even goes one step farther and actually generates coordinates for the corresponding floaters, which you can then turn into client-side or server-side image map files.

If your site's structure is likely to remain fairly stable (or you have the resources to recreate navigation graphics and image maps fairly regularly), and the visual appeal and design integrity of your site are very important to you and your users, consider constructing your navigation interface with image maps.

If you choose any of the graphic methods though, always be sure to include text links along with the graphic links (as shown in Figure 10.16). Some users choose not to load images as they browse, and can easily become lost if no navigation interface is visible.

THE BEAST WITH TWO BACKS

Nearly all browsers provide a "Back" button to take the user back to the previously viewed URL. The concept isn't as clear as it might seem, however. If, for example, a user hyperlinks from section 1 of a document to section 3, and then wants to go logically "back" in the document to section 2, clicking the browser's "Back" button takes him to section 1.

If your intranet requires users to progress logically through a series of pages, the navigation interface should include a "Back to Previous Page" function to supplement the browser's "Back" function. Similarly, you might want to include a "Forward to Next Page" option in the interface, as illustrated in Figure 10.21.

WHERE TO PUT IT

Many sites duplicate the navigation interface at the top and bottom of each page. Although this may be useful if the pages are usually

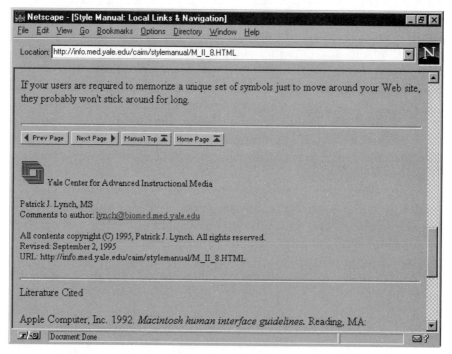

Figure 10.21 Example of "[back to] Previous Page" and "[forward to] Next Page" buttons.

longer than one and a half to two screens, it's not generally necessary if the pages are shorter than that, and just makes the users scroll that much more. If the navigation interface is at the bottom of each page, users quickly learn to scroll there to navigate.

Several sites use Netscape frames as a navigation aid, placing the navigation interface in a frame that is always visible. The examples shown in Figure 10.22 illustrate this technique very effectively. Unless you have a very extensive menu (i.e., longer than one screen's worth), however, the navigation frame just serves to reduce the amount of window space available for your content frame. Many users also find it difficult to navigate back and forth through frames. So, unless your users need constant access to a long list of links in order to jump around your site, it's advisable to place the navigation interface in the same window as the content. As long as the position is consistent (i.e., at the top, bottom, or top-and-bottom of each screen), the users can find it easily enough, and the interface will be significantly less cluttered.

Informational Footer

Depending on the size and nature of your intranet and its applications, you may choose to include an informational footer on your pages. This first example is for an intranet that is viewed only by internal users:

```
Human Resources Policies & Procedures
Please forward comments, questions, or updates to HumanResources.
Last Update: 8/31/96
```

If your intranet is accessible to outside users (i.e., vendors, partners, etc.), you may want something more formal:

```
© BSG Alliance/IT, Inc.
Comments or questions: webmaster@bsginc.com
Last revision: September 1996
```

The footer should provide the following types of information:

◆ *Who.*   Depending who your users are, you should provide the source of the information and, if necessary, copyrights or other legalese.

Figure 10.22   Example of using Netscape frames.

TIP   *To avoid having to change the footer on each page as the year or legal wording changes, create a separate page with the specifics. With this approach, you need only change a single page instead of numerous footers.*

- *Date of last revision.*   This is helpful to both you and your users. For you, it helps with version control. For your users, it lets them know how "fresh" the information is.
- *E-mail link.*   Unless you already have one in your standard navigation interface, always include an E-mail link in the footer. Users need to be able to contact someone involved in maintaining the information to report problems or send suggestions.

◆ *Application logo.*   The header graphic is undeniably the best place for your application logo, but if for some reason you can't include it there, put it in the footer.

Graphics Tips

Graphics are largely responsible for the popularity of Web-style applications. People like to look at pictures. Too much of a good thing, however, is likely to slow your site to a crawl and try your users' patience. Carefully planned and executed, *restrained* graphics are the key to a visually successful user interface.

Graphic File Formats

While the current Web browsers support both JPEG (Joint Photographic Experts Group) and GIF (graphic interchange format) graphic files, GIF is generally the format of choice for Web page design. GIF files allow you to create relatively small graphics files by limiting the number of colors in the image. In general, because of their compact format, GIF files download quickly—even over a modem connection. GIF also supports more popular graphics "tricks" for Web design than JPEG, including transparency, interlacing, and animation (the GIF file type known as GIF89a).

Transparency occurs when a particular color in a GIF file reveals a browser's background image or color. You can use transparency to enhance page layout or make images appear to be anything other than rectangular. Most of the recent graphics applications support the creation of transparent GIFs.

Interlaced GIFs appear as progressive bands as they download, giving the impression of a picture slowly and progressively coming into focus. This technique also gives the user an idea of what an image is before the download is complete, letting the user decide whether to finish the download or abort it.

Although animated GIFs have been around since 1989 (as the GIF89a format suggests), they have only recently become viewable through Web browsers. This feature allows a single GIF file to actually contain successive images or frames which are animated when downloaded. This produces effects that, until recently, were possible only through CGI, PERL, or Java scripts. The GIF89a format not only allows nonprogrammers to create animated graphics, but also provides images that are less taxing on Web servers. With GIF89a, as much of the animated sequence as possible is loaded into the client computer's RAM. It is then animated locally instead of being driven by the server. Browsers that don't take advantage of GIF89a animation capabilities simply display the first frame of the sequence.

Good places to get information and download GIF kits are:

◆ http://www.mindworkshop.com/alchemy/gifcon.html
The "GIF Construction Set for Windows," which is available in two flavors: one for Windows 3.1x and one for Windows 95.

◆ http://iawww.epfl.ch/Staff/Yves.Piguet/clip2gif-home/
GifBuilder.html   Provides details on GifBuilder for Macintosh.

Although GIF is the most popular graphics format for Web page design, the JPEG format is not without its virtues. Because JPEG was developed specifically to compress 24-bit graphics (unlike GIF, which is used primarily for 8-bit color graphics), it is able to render high-quality photographic images.

JPEG also produces excellent 24-bit color images and can compress large graphics files more effectively than GIF. So, if you're going to use photographic images, you may want to consider using JPEG to take advantage of its superior compression techniques and thereby minimize the time to download large graphics files from the server. Unfortunately, JPEG doesn't buy you anything in terms of representational quality unless your users have 24-bit color as well. (In fact, if your users have only 8-bit color, the JPEG images will look "dithered"—a subject that we address later in this chapter.) And, JPEG can't do many of the "tricks" that GIF can (e.g., animation).

JPEG is probably most useful for those organizations with remote intranet users (particularly those with modem access only), or for those that display lots of photographs. If you have a LAN-based intranet—or if the link between your remote sites is T1 quality or better—you'll probably want to stick with GIF images. If you have the luxury of a little time to experiment, however, you may want to compare and contrast image quality with end-file sizes to determine which format is most suitable for your needs.

Regardless of your decision to use GIF or JPEG for your graphics, we recommend that you first create images using a raster image format such as bitmap or tiff (tagged image file format). When the graphic is complete and "ready to go," convert it to either GIF or JPEG to ensure a crisp final image. If you need to change the image later on, edit the original bitmap or tiff file, then convert to GIF or JPEG again. Do *not* convert the GIF or JPEG files back and forth to bmp or tiff files; this conversion quickly erodes the quality of an image.

Graphic File Size

Graphic images should be kept as small as possible in file size. Although users like to look at pretty pictures, they don't want to wait several minutes (or even seconds) for pictures to download. Here's a checklist of things you can do to keep graphics from slowing down your site:

◆ *Reduce the number of colors in your color palette (i.e., use as few colors as possible).*   For example, try viewing your images as 4-bit (16 color) rather than 8-bit (256 color). In PhotoShop, convert your RGB image to Indexed color, specifying the minimum number of colors to achieve the effect you require.

◆ *Save at a resolution of 72 dots per inch (dpi).*   If you are scanning images, scan them at 72 dpi. If you are creating them, save them at 72 dpi. While some monitors have slightly higher resolutions, the difference is usually not noticeable, and every byte you can trim off the file size helps.

◆ *Keep large graphics off-line.*   If you must include a large (i.e., in terms of file size) graphic, provide a hypertext link to it rather than displaying it on the page. In this way, users have the option of viewing the graphic. Users also appreciate having the size of the linked file noted in the hypertext link so they can predict how long the image will take to download.

◆ *Use graphics sparingly!*   Remember, content should be the driving force in developing your intranet, not showing off your graphic designer's abilities. Each graphic should have an explicable purpose, and should be no larger than necessary to accomplish its purpose.

David Taylor, president of Intuitive Systems, holds that pages should load in no more than 30 seconds (*Guidelines for Web Page Design,* 1995, David Taylor, Intuitive Systems, http://www.intuitive. com/web-design.html). If some of your users connect via a 14.4-Kbps modem, that translates to about 45K bytes of data per page. A 10-Mbps connection, however, lets you include 235K bytes of data per page, thus giving you a lot more room for those great graphics.

Dithering

Dithering is generally the reason why a graphic looks great in your image editing application, but looks "dirty" or differently colored when viewed in the browser. More precisely, the browser uses a palette of its own to interpret and display the colors it encounters in graphic files. If the browser encounters a color that is not in its palette, it dithers the color, that is, it adds little gray pixels to the color to approximate the nonpalette color—often resulting in an ugly, muddy appearance.

You can avoid dithering by creating your image using the browser's palette. With this approach, the browser does not encounter any nonpalette colors and the image displays as intended. Browser palettes that you can download to use in your image editing application are available on the Web. These two WWW sites provide palettes as well as more detailed explanations of dithering:

◆ http://www.lynda.com
◆ http://www.onr.com/user/lights/netcol.html

When and How to Set Standards

The time to set user interface style guidelines and standards is before any coding begins. Logically enough, it's much easier to code properly the first time than it is to retrofit existing code to conform to the guidelines. Be certain, therefore, to include your graphic design or user interface team members in the very early stages of intranet development. They must also understand the needs and requirements of the users and sponsors of the site to design a successful user interface.

In many cases, the interface designers can develop prototypes, or templates, of typical pages that include basic layout and graphic elements. The content developers can then use the templates to generate the actual pages and the interface designers can tweak them as necessary in a final review phase.

In large intranet project implementations, many people may be responsible for developing pages for the various sections of the site. If this is the case, it may be helpful to appoint one or more people who have a solid understanding of interface design as "gatekeepers." Then, be sure that the gatekeepers review all pages for consistency and adherence to the graphic and user interface standards before linking them into the site.

Above all else, if you regularly solicit feedback from your users, listen to their suggestions. If you do this, and follow the general principles of graphic user interface design, your intranet user interface is positioned for success.

CHAPTER ELEVEN

BACK-END APPLICATIONS

- ◆ Overview
- ◆ External Access
- ◆ Groupware
- ◆ Data Retrieval
- ◆ Connecting to the Database
- ◆ Document Retrieval
- ◆ Business-to-Business Communication/Electronic Data Interchange (EDI)
- ◆ Business-to-Consumer Communication/Electronic Commerce
- ◆ Considering the Past and the Future

Overview

While we've focused on the intranet infrastructure in the preceding chapters, the real power of an intranet lies in the multitude of back-end applications that are accessible from its common interface. Not only does the intranet provide a common interface from which you can access a broad array of applications, but it also allows you to create links that jump from one application to another. This linking capability, which is fundamental to intra/Internet computing, was not possible with earlier forms of computer architectures and represents one of the major benefits of an intranet.

In this chapter we explore the wide array of data sources and services that live behind the Web browser, which in effect, provides the facade for more complex applications. We will, for example, describe database gateway systems that dynamically produce query results. We also address the concept of nonstructured data because much of the data and information that is accessible through an intranet is stored outside of traditional databases. We also cover the specific concerns involved with read-only and operational systems separately, and discuss the various techniques involved with searching for specific information. And, we describe some of the back-end applications that you may want to deploy on your intranet. We've organized these applications into broad categories and present them in the sequence in which they are often deployed.

External Access

While external access to the Internet is not actually an intranet application, it offers beneficial capabilities for any intranet but requires the same careful planning as other intranet applications. As we've mentioned in previous chapters, Internet firewalls and access restrictions can help you to ensure secure access to the Internet while, at the same time, allowing your users to gather information from the World Wide Web. You can, for example, limit access to specific Internet sites or protocols and/or install software that lets your corporate or IS administrators monitor user access to the Internet. If you do decide to monitor employees' access, however, be sure to inform the users of your policy prior to establishing the connectivity. While such notification may not be legally required, it is generally considered sound business policy and is ethically correct.

You can further enhance the utility of the external access by creating one or more pages of hot links to useful Internet sites, customizing the page(s) for different departments, if their needs or interests vary significantly. You may want to consider using an application like Pointcast (http://www.pointcast.com) to customize Internet news or stock updates. Some of the issues that you'll want to consider when planning for your intranet external link include the positive (and negative) effect on employee productivity and the potential legal issues related to posting items on the Web. (Refer to Chapter 4 for additional details on both of these issues, as well as other organizational concerns.)

Figure 11.1 illustrates the use of an Internet firewall with an add-on intranet infrastructure.

Groupware

Because intranets are perfectly suited for bridging the geographic and technological gaps of a widely dispersed, heterogeneous organization, groupware applications are typically among the first to be developed and/or deployed on an intranet. Groupware applications are usually quite easy to install and they provide high-value, high-visibility services. Groupware applications range from simple mail and news products to discussion forums, collaborative interaction, electronic bulletin boards, information repositories, and more.

Choosing a good groupware product or an appropriate group of products involves a balancing act—weighing the product's ability to fill your current needs against its ability to provide long-term extensibility. A sophisticated, highly developed, proprietary group-

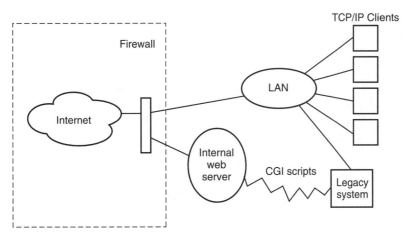

Figure 11.1   Internet access firewall.

ware product may suit your immediate needs, but it may also be overpriced and overpowered. And, buying a proprietary system may lock you into the choices that the vendor decides to provide instead of the flexibility of mix-and-match products. Keep in mind that such flexibility is likely to become even more important down the road as intranet architecture continues to gain ground.

Although different needs mandate different solutions, you should ask some basic questions about any type of groupware solution. Which tool(s) fit the current needs of the organization? Will the tool or tools adapt over time and allow change and growth? To this same end, are the products flexible and customizable? If you make changes in your technology platform(s), how difficult will conversion be?

There are currently two primary groupware solutions to consider: Lotus Notes and Web-based groupware. While either solution can be satisfactory (and we can report success—and occasional frustrations—with both), the following information may help you to determine which is most appropriate for your particular environment and requirements.

Notes-Based Groupware

There is no doubt that Lotus Notes has defined the groupware standard as we know it. When no one else could figure out what *groupware* really meant, Lotus created a sophisticated system of E-mail, forms routing and tracking, and customizable "databases" that have made knowledge-sharing and workflow a reality in the corporate environment.

Notes is a "complete" groupware package; everything is built in—and you pay for everything, whether you need it all or not. Notes also provides excellent replication facilities between servers and users, and the latest version (Notes 4.0) offers Internet access as well as advanced application development tools that give it even more power than before. The application development tools are built with LotusScript, a simple, proprietary programming language.

But Notes isn't right for everyone. It does have some downsides that you'll need to consider:

♦ It *is* expensive and it *is* proprietary.

♦ Connecting to database products such as Oracle, Sybase, and SQL Server requires a "pump" to get the data back and forth. And, the pump involves additional expense and complexity.

♦ It may be unwieldy for some organizations, particularly those seeking global communications solutions.

♦ Although many vendors offer add-ons for Notes, these products also tend to be expensive and proprietary.

Organizations that already have an investment in Notes may find a way to blend it with their intranet by using third-party products to bridge the two environments. Lotus' InterNotes Web Publisher helps convert Notes information to HTML for standard Web browsers while InterNotes News provides access to the Usenet News via NNTP (network news transfer protocol).

Other products that can help bridge Notes and intra/Internet environments include Tile (from the Walter Shelby Group) and Lotus Domino. Tile is similar to InterNotes in that it converts existing Notes applications into HTML documents for browsing, thereby minimizing the need for Notes clients to see the Notes-based data. Domino, which was released in beta version in June 1996, promises to integrate Notes and HTML servers. For additional information on Domino, visit the Web site at http://domino. lotus.com. Be aware, however, that Domino requires a Lotus Notes 4.x server. If you're trying to reconcile your intranet with a Notes environment, we recommend that you investigate both of these products, along with any others on the horizon.

DECISION-MAKING

If you're making an initial decision regarding groupware, Table 11.1 may help you to understand some of the fundamental advantages and disadvantages of Lotus Notes and Web-based products.

As you might guess, a Meta Group study that compared Web server users with Notes users revealed that most users favor the Web server approach because of its pricing, ease of use, and ease of deployment.

TABLE 11.1 Comparison of Web-Based Groupware and Lotus Notes

Areas of Difference	Notes	Web-Based
Initial costs	Expensive	Inexpensive
Administrative costs	High	Moderate (higher with security)
Scaling costs	High	Low
Scalability	Largest site 23,000 seats	Largest site 30 million seats (i.e., the Internet)
Security	Secure, but early gaps were found	Getting there but early gaps are being found
Extensibility	Moderate (via commercial packages like Watermark)	High (often via free products on the Internet)
Support	Fair	Virtual
Longevity	IBM/Lotus have a race to run between 4.0 and 5.0.	The base standard will remain, but susceptible to a plethora of proprietary extensions
E-mail	Feature-rich interoperation with SMTP	Universal SMTP and Sendmail
Workflow	Excellent but underused	Poor, needs to be developed
Databases	Good flat file database structures for use in specific applications like discussion databases	Good CGI and PERL links to most major databases. Better architecture.
Replication	A clear advantage. Replication allows users to work off-line and have changes resolved back into the master database automatically.	NNTP, basic replication at the document level. Enhancements proposed by several venders, but alternatives are still a ways off.
MIS involvement	High	Medium

OTHER GROUPWARE ALTERNATIVES

Believe it or not, Notes is not the only full-featured groupware product available. It is undeniably the best in today's market, but Microsoft's Exchange 4.0 is gaining sufficient functionality to warrant serious consideration. In fact, one company that we know reports great success with its blend of Exchange facilities (i.e., Mail, Schedule+, and discussion folders) and an intranet (for more complex database applications). Similarly, Novell's GroupWise 4.1 is a solid, easy-to-integrate (i.e., for organizations with Novell networks) product, but lacks much of the functionality of Notes.

Web-Based Groupware

Web-based groupware incorporates the same facilities as most of the full-feature groupware products like Notes, but offers some distinct advantages in some areas, as well as some weaknesses.

MAIL

Because most popular browsers support mail via SMTP or POP3 protocols, you can integrate mail into your Web applications. This capability facilitates routing comments and responses to the applications and also lets you embed HTML links within mail messages, providing a useful way to guide users to information on the intranet as well as the Internet, if appropriate.

NEWS

Netscape and Microsoft both support NNTP (news) as a URL protocol. Net News, or simply news as it is better known, is one of the oldest services supported on the Internet, as well as many intranets. Discussions, which are available on nearly any topic you can think of, are subdivided into groups. Groups are designated by the dot format, beginning with the general and leading to the specific. For example, some popular news groups are: comp.languages.pascal, comp.databases.sybase, and alt.rec. photography.

A local news NNTP server can let you add additional newsgroups, which may be available only to your intranet users, or to the Internet at large. You can also use these on your intranet as an internal threaded discussion database or to give your corporate users access to some of the more relevant news groups.

DISCUSSION/COLLABORATION

Collaboration tools supplement basic E-mail facilities with methods for shared information. Typically built as electronic "bulletin boards," these programs allow for threaded discussions and document posting and retrieval. Good examples of discussion/collaboration programs include Netscape's Collabra Share 2.1, FTP Software/HyperDesk's GroupWorks, and Trax Softwork's TeamTalk.

These tools are usually organized into separate forums by topic (e.g., Human Resources Q&A, Company General Info), and incorporate mechanisms to control what is actually posted by requiring approval from a "moderator."

For many organizations, the combination of E-mail and discussion forums is sufficient for disseminating and sharing information; this approach is significantly less expensive than a full-scale groupware solution and is flexible enough to keep pace with changes in requirements and technology. There are, however, a number of groupware products (e.g., GroupWorks) designed specifically to meet the needs of relatively small organizations.

Webboards, which are well suited for both internal and external Web discussions, are continually gaining popularity as the preferred medium for trading ideas and comments. O'Reilly & Associates' WebBoard is one of the better-known products in this category. It uses Microsoft Access 95 as its database and runs on any Web server that supports CGI. Much like Notes, WebBoard has public, private, and semiprivate discussions, including read-only databases that are ideal for document distribution (e.g., Policies and Procedures).

If you are considering a discussion tool, we recommend that you first try out the discussion medium at the vendor site. This lets you see other users' comments and questions as well as test the product. Then, download a demonstration copy of the tools and try it out in your IT department. Most vendors do offer "try before buying" arrangements. (Refer to Chapter 9 for some vendor URLs and details on product previews.)

WORKFLOW

Workflow, which involves organizing tasks in a particular sequence to optimize efficiency, is one of the fastest changing areas of Web application development. Workflow products are commonly used by businesses to manage projects via messaging (E-mail) and database technology. A workflow product typically incorporates some combination of the following capabilities, tailored to meet the needs of the particular environment:

- ◆ Tracking resources (i.e., people, technology, and processes)
- ◆ Initiating and routing requests and action items
- ◆ Tracking status
- ◆ Reaching consensus through polling
- ◆ Managing "to do" lists
- ◆ Managing contracts and the associated negotiations
- ◆ Building applications based on all of the above
- ◆ Managing documents (optional feature)

You can create a simple workflow system by integrating a combination of mail and Web pages. More complex workflow applications are available commercially to fill a variety of needs. Action Technologies' Metro is one example of a Web-based workflow product, providing workflow coordination services through a Web browser. Metro uses a paradigm that shifts the emphasis from what the business *has* (i.e., information) to what it *does* (i.e., action—hence their name). A very expensive, yet robust application that leverages itself on SQL Server and Netscape Commerce Server, Metro allows users with any standard browser to access your workflows. Such access can be well worth the price, particularly for geographically dispersed organizations with lots of seats.

Other workflow options include the Ultimus Workflow Starter Kit with WebFlow, a product that is less costly than Metro and can use an existing E-mail infrastructure for routing; and Symantec's FormFlow 2.0, which facilitates forms handling by providing routing, application development, management, and security features, along with native access to SQL Server and Oracle databases.

Data Retrieval

Borrowing a technique from the manufacturing environment, many organizations are moving toward the concept of just-in-time information. Instead of using bulky computer printouts, executives are relying on EIS systems to retrieve the information they need—"drilling down" to the appropriate level of detail to support decision-making or planning. Intranet technology makes it relatively easy to provide this type of access to a wide variety of users dispersed throughout an organization. While it is common for today's users to access simple document-based data or a single database, in the near future they are likely to be accessing a data warehouse. A data warehouse, as defined by Kenn Orr, a pioneer in the database field, is "a facility to provide easy access to quality, integrated, enterprise data by both professional and non-professional end users."

Perhaps an example is the best way to explain how a data retrieval application functions: A Fortune 50 company replaced its traditional data retrieval system with a versatile EIS that links an HTML front-end server to PERL (Practical Extraction and Report Language) scripts that convert the hyperlink to an SQL command. The SQL command then embeds a URL in the variable from the HTML form. The EIS presents a summary screen of data organized by year and region. Users can retrieve more detailed information by drilling down from the summary screen—clicking on the year to retrieve a monthly breakdown, clicking on the region to retrieve results by individual offices in the region, or clicking on a cell to retrieve a detailed breakdown for a region in a specific year. The same data previously resided on a large Teradata machine, but users were required to submit written requests for printed reports, which produced huge volumes of largely out-of-date and often irrelevant data.

Connecting to the Database

There are two main approaches for integrating a Web server with the back-end database: third-party connectivity tools and database vendor extensions. Each option has a number of inherent advantages and disadvantages, which we describe in the following paragraphs.

Third-Party Connectivity Tools

These tools were the first applications to emerge in response to the problem of connecting the back-end database(s) to the Web server.

They are generally relatively small applications, often written in PERL or C++. Some of the newer connectivity tools are portable across differing databases, which is often a distinct advantage.

A few of the Web-based data retrieval tools that are currently available include:

◆ *NetDynamics from Spider Technologies (www.w3spider. com).* NetDynamics is a web/database application builder that provides corporate developers with a fast, automated environment for leveraging Java into business applications. NetDynamics integrates visual development, a Java application server, and scalable database access.

   NetDynamics is an open solution, supporting any Web server, any Web browser, any HTML editor, as well as all major database systems and ODBC-compliant databases on both UNIX and PC platforms.

◆ *Sapphire from Bluestone (www.bluestone.com/products/ sapphire).* Sapphire features a PowerBuilder-like interface and operates only with UNIX-based systems. It uses C, C++, and SQL stored procedures, and offers a range of tools for debugging and project management.

◆ *Cold Fusion from Allaire at (www.allaire.com).* Cold Fusion is a Web application development platform for Microsoft Windows NT and Windows 95 environments. It provides ODBC connectivity through its own DBML (database markup language) protocol.

Database Vendor Extensions

The software vendors' solution to the problem of connecting the back-end database(s) to the Web servers are extensions to the database API. These extensions, which are written specifically to facilitate such connectivity, work well if you are already using the particular database and have no need to connect to other databases. Their primary disadvantage, however, is that they tend to be tightly coupled and are often proprietary. For these reasons, the applications are often not portable to other environments.

Database Gateways are back-end processes that provide database access services to the Web server. These interface with the Web server via the Web server's proprietary API or the standard CGI. Database results are formatted into HTML, with embedded URLs.

Interfacing with a single database is straightforward. Data integrity and concurrency are handled by the database engine and don't require any special handling. Systems with a single database engine are free not only to read, but also to write and update information in the database. Errors caused by concurrent writes are reported by the database and passed on to the users without any special processing. Databases with particularly cryptic error messages may require an application program to translate errors into something that users can understand.

Databases

The following databases are often found at the back-end of Web servers. Some products and vendors are new, others are industry standards. We suggest thorough exploration of all these products before making a selection.

ORACLE

Oracle Corporation released its Oracle Applications for the Web product in mid-1996. This product, which is part of Oracle Applications, incorporates several new modules specifically designed for intra/Internet computing: Oracle Web Customers, Oracle Web Suppliers, and Oracle Web Employees. In addition to these modules, Oracle has announced the release of Oracle Workflow. Together, these products support secure business transactions both inside and outside the enterprise, on the Internet, and on corporate intranets.

Oracle WebServer 2.0 offers a scalable, secure, Web application platform. With its proprietary architecture, WebServer 2.0 delivers integrated access to both Oracle 7 Enterprise and Workgroup Servers, and also provides Web access to a range of application environments and services. It is suitable for publishing static documents or for developing sophisticated, data-driven Web applications using PL/SQL, Java, LiveHTML or other languages. WebServer 2.0 offers users a combination of easy access and flexible security facilities while supporting a variety of application development environments. It does not, however, offer a high degree of interoperability.

SYBASE

Sybase's web.sql product allows users to insert database instructions (e.g., SQL statements and PERL scripts) into HTML pages. These database queries elicit an electronic response that returns results to the Web server in the form of pure HTML text. This functionality enables Web pages that automatically generate personalized content for each user based on the predefined preferences. Sybase web.sql runs on Sun Solaris from Sun Microsystems, IRIX from Silicon Graphics, Inc., HP-UX from Hewlett Packard, and Microsoft Windows NT for Intel.

INGRES

Ingres's Jasmine, which is touted as representing the new generation in database technology, offers an object-oriented database that features a multimedia, Inter/intranet-enabled application development system. By enabling companies to process and display information in highly original ways, Jasmine is built to lower development costs and provide managers with the flexibility to respond to the most daunting business challenges.

INFORMIX AND ILLUSTRA (UNIVERSAL SERVER)

Informix, which is highly respected in the relational database arena, purchased Illustra, one of the leading object-oriented relational databases on the market in mid-1996. The Illustra Server is one of the industry's first DBMS products to efficiently handle a variety of data types (e.g., alphanumeric, character, text, video, images, and documents) within a single repository. Built from the ground up to deliver high-performance relational and object database management, Illustra embeds object-oriented (OO) capabilities in a relational model. The resulting synergy delivers capabilities that neither an object DBMS (ODMS) nor a relational DBMS (RDBMS) can provide. Although relational DBMS products have resolved many of the problems involved with managing commercial data (i.e., incorporating numbers and character strings), the technology does have difficulty handling the growing predominance of complex data types. Leading application architects are currently attempting to expand the definition of data to include additional complex elements, including diagrams, maps, images, sound, documents, time series, and multidimensional data.

In many ways, Illustra is the ideal back-end for a Web server that needs to handle complex data. This is due, at least in part, to its Datablade approach and to the fact that its API supports Java, making it possible to develop applications in Java. Datablades are modular search tools that can be custom-designed by the user or third-party developers. Datablades exist for Web, image, text, time series, and 2D/3D geometry. The image blade for example, can be used to search for all images that have sunsets and negative space (i.e., for placing ad copy). There are, however, some performance issues with Illustra's Datablade approach. Industry analysts are hoping that the problems will be resolved when Informix combines Illustra with the Informix RDBMS to create the "Universal Server," tentatively scheduled for release in late 1996. The Universal Server may, at least in theory, offer the best elements of OO and relational database technology.

ODBC

ODBC (Open Database Connectivity) is not actually a database but a Microsoft-promoted standard that provides a common API to multiple databases. ODBC incorporates a translation layer so that programs remain the same when used with different databases. When performance is important, the ODBC "pass through" option allows the developer to use database engine–specific SQL dialect, skipping the translation step and allowing the use of highly optimized SQL constructs peculiar to the specific dialect of SQL supported by the underlying engine.

MULTIPLE DATABASE ISSUES

Finally, while it is beyond the scope of this book to explore all of the issues involved with using multiple databases, it is important to mention that you'll need to consider issues related to synchronization, rollback, and backup and restore if you are using multiple databases.

Document Retrieval

Managing documents that don't belong in a traditional database system is an excellent intranet application. These can include traditional HTML pages, non-structured data such as text documents, spreadsheets and presentations, multimedia such as images, sounds and movies as well as interfaces to high-end imaging and document management systems such as FileNet and Documentum. Figure 11.2 illustrates how this type of application can fit into a relatively complex intranet application.

Nonstructured Data

Nonstructured data can include word processing documents, spreadsheets, and presentation slides. In general, your browser should be configured to open these files using the workstation

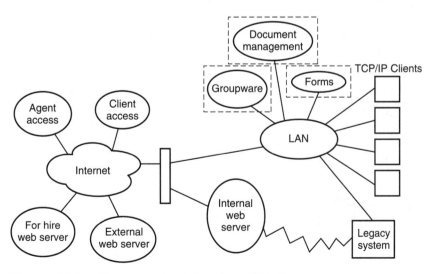

Figure 11.2   Document retrieval application.

default programs. If your program doesn't automatically convert the files, however, you may need a read-only viewer program such as Microsoft's Word Viewer or Adobe's Acrobat.

High-End Imaging/Document Management Systems

An intranet implementation project often goes hand-in-hand with an in-house imaging/document management initiative. Most document management product developers have announced and/or shipped Web-enabled versions of their packages. While the Web interface isn't intended to replace the scanning, indexing, or workflow aspects of the application, it does greatly facilitate users' search and retrieval of documents already in the system.

Some of the Web-compatible tools available for document retrieval include:

◆ *Documentum.*   The Documentum Server is a high-end, distributed document repository for managing business documents and their associated processes. It also accommodates other objects such as workflows, annotations, and business rules and associates them with the appropriate documents. Documentum uses its Accelera product to bridge the gap with the Web. Accelera integrates Web browsers and servers with the Documentum Server—providing secure access to business-critical documents stored in the Documentum document repository.

◆ *Odesta.*   Livelink Intranet from Odesta is a suite of tightly integrated intranet applications that allows organizations to find information, coordinate and control documents, and manage projects with work groups throughout the world.

Business-to-Business Communication/Electronic Data Interchange (EDI)

Business-to-business communication includes talking to sales agents (e.g., salespeople, distributors, bottlers) and suppliers, and usually incorporates Internet extensions to the X.12 EDI protocols. Figure 11.3 illustrates the conceptual Web diagram for this type of function. There are several products that facilitate the process. The Internet has lowered the bar for EDI. It is possible, for example, for suppliers to participate in an EDI network for as little as a few thousand dollars, as opposed to expenditures of more than a hundred thousand dollars with pre-Internet technology. The vastly lower cost of commitment is once again raising widespread interest in this application. EDI offers the opportunity to improve the flow of documents, payments, and goods between suppliers, manufacturers, and retailers—opening the possibility for lowering the costs involved in bringing products to market and thereby increasing profits.

Business-to-Consumer Communication/Electronic Commerce

This function presents the final logical step in the process of expanding the boundaries of interaction between an intranet information system and its users.

The efficiency of electronic commerce is best illustrated by the chart in Figure 11.4. The Internet provides a ubiquitous communi-

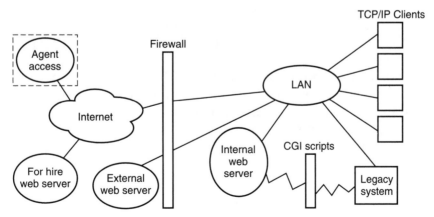

Figure 11.3   Business-to-business communication.

Traditional commerce

	Manufacturer	Exporter	Importer	Retailer	Client
Order	←	←	←	←	
Goods	→	→	→	→	
Funds	←	←	←	←	
Totals	12 processes (9 of which occur prior to sale), 4 shipments, 4 inventories				

Electronic commerce

	Manufacturer	Distributor (if any)		Client
Image	→	→		
Order	←	←		
Goods	→	→		
Funds	←	←		
Totals	8 processes (2 of which occur prior to sale), 2 shipments, 1 inventory*			

*There may be some "caching" of inventory for frequently ordered items

▭ Activity prior to sale

Figure 11.4 Comparison: traditional commerce versus electronic commerce.

cation channel that makes the theory of electronic commerce perfectly practical and desirable in today's highly competitive arena.

While some industry analysts predict that the electronic commerce market will reach $30 billion by the year 2000, government regulations and ongoing electronic commerce projects make it likely that this figure will be exceeded. Indeed, electronic commerce may be a logical outgrowth of your intranet, since the costs involved in extending the intranet infrastructure to the outside world are minimal. With earlier, traditional architectures, such costs were often prohibitive.

As you can see, a relatively minimal, add-on intranet can quickly grow into a sophisticated information Web like the one illustrated in Figure 11.5. This type of Web is, in itself, a strategic advantage in business and often key to maintaining a learning-based organization.

Security

Once again, while security is not an application in the traditional sense of the word, it is a popular use of the intranet. The long-

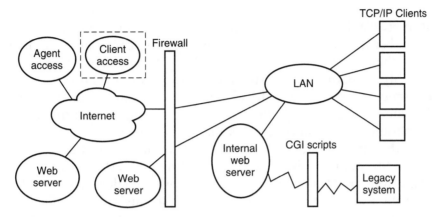

Figure 11.5 Sophisticated Web application.

sought goal of "Single Sign-On" is finally possible with an intranet. Single sign-on can be achieved by using client authentication and integrating the client authentication with the security built into the operating system and back-end applications. Once achieved, single sign-on has numerous advantages in that users need only remember one password. It is always advisable to avoid situations in which users have so many passwords to remember that they resort to writing them down and leaving them where other, unauthorized users may find—and use—them.

Considering the Past and the Future

Finally, in considering the back-end applications for your intranet, you'll obviously have to accommodate the existing applications that reside on your preintranet systems, typically mainframes. In fact, 90 percent of all corporate data currently resides on legacy systems. If you haven't already done so, refer back to Chapter 5 for a discussion of several of the methods for accessing data and applications that reside on legacy systems. Legacy-based applications may consist of almost anything—from databases to complex transaction systems—but you'll need to address a number of key issues in migrating the applications and converting the associated data from the legacy system to your intranet or, at a minimum, making the applications and data accessible to the intranet. We discuss a number of these issues in Chapter 12, but remember that such migration and conversion necessarily involve many complex considerations. If you've planned ahead, you're probably prepared for this step and know if you need outside assistance. If you haven't already considered using an outside service vendor to help with the conversion and migration process, you should make that determination now—before you actually begin the process of implementing the intranet. Even if there's some additional cost involved in migrating/converting your legacy system, it may well be worth the price. Federal Express, for example, was able to significantly reduce its customer service costs by linking its mainframe-based package tracking system to the Internet (see http://www.fedex.com).

And, of course, you'll also need to have a plan for future applications. For many organizations, object-oriented applications hold the key to future business processes. Object-oriented applications may be used in conjunction with traditional back-end applications or function as the application. There are essentially two major systems for distributing objects over the Web—Java and ActiveX. A number of other systems (e.g., NeXT Web Objects) are used to develop object-oriented Web applications. Again, if you haven't already read about object-oriented technology in Chapter 6, you probably want to do that before you finalize the back-end applications for your intranet.

CHAPTER TWELVE

IMPLEMENTING AN INTRANET

- ◆ Overview
- ◆ Guidelines for Testing
- ◆ Operations
- ◆ Help System Concepts
- ◆ Application Migration
- ◆ Data Conversions
- ◆ Connecting the Intranet to the Internet
- ◆ Performance Issues

Overview

Your intranet implementation project is nearing completion. You've finished the planning and design stages, dealt with those sticky questions of organization, selected your tools, developed your user interface, and decided on your intranet database. By this stage, hopefully, you've also developed new applications for the intranet and/or determined which existing applications you'll need to migrate to the intranet, and completed unit testing. So, what now? There are still a few steps that you need to take to prepare your production environment for the intranet implementation.

You will, for example, need to perform system tests on your database and applications, then consider some additional aspects of application migration and data conversion for the production environment. If you haven't already created help systems for your intranet users or determined how (or if) you're going to link your intranet to the Internet, you should deal with these issues before placing the intranet into production. Finally, there are some performance issues, such as scalability and contingency, that can be crucial to your intranet's current and future success.

Guidelines for Testing

Testing is the last step in a development effort and/or the first step in project implementation. As we discussed in chapter 8 (Intranet Development), application testing is typically divided into three phases:

1. *Unit testing.* Generally the final step in a development effort, unit testing is performed by the developer(s) to locate and resolve any obvious errors. A unit usually incorporates only one function or transaction.

2. *System testing.* The system testing is done by combining units and testing the entire application as a single system; it ensures that all components work together. Database testing, in which the functions of the database are checked out independently of other application components, is one example of a system test. All of the individual triggers, stored procedures, and views should have been unit tested individually by the developer or database administrator prior to system testing. System testing may be extended beyond database testing if/when other application components or "units" are added to the system.

3. *Integration testing.* Integration testing is testing performed on the system once all the applications components are installed in the production environment. Tests are performed that ensure the system is interacting with other systems and network components in the desired way. *Parallel testing,* the final step in the integration

testing, is performed by running the old system in parallel with the new system for a fixed period of time. Parallel testing lets the developer or administrator complete a shakedown of new procedures and compare the results from both systems to ensure that any problems with the old system are resolved and that the new system works as intended.

Test cases (i.e., the set of steps and data that test one aspect of an application) are cumulative, building upon one another—with unit test cases feeding into system test cases, and system test cases feeding into integration tests. Additional tests and cases are added at each level of development because some things, like interdependencies, can only be tested at the system or integration stages of implementation.

Testing routines vary by the complexity of the intranet application. Aspects that simplify testing include context independence, the browsers' ability to hide some errors, and the direct server-to-browser relationship. Aspects that complicate testing include techniques that *add context* to an intranet application by using fields within the forms to store context.

Because Intranet HTTP services are not session-based, any HTML request can come at any time. And, because most browsers cache forms for later use, the server can receive any form-based request at any time. This type of application can be described as *context free,* in that the application does not rely on context or any previously existing state. We'll discuss context in more detail to help clarify this concept.

Figure 12.1 illustrates the structure of a typical intranet application. The basis of the communication is a URL request and a response.

State and Context

An understanding of state and context is critical to testing an intranet application. *State* refers to the condition of a given situation in an application; for example, if the user has made a request from the database and is waiting for a response, that is the state at

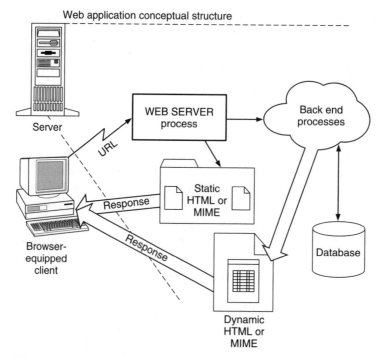

Figure 12.1   Web application conceptual structure.

that point in time. HTML and HTTP (Web) servers are state*less,* meaning that they do not track conditions of state. This can be very good in some cases, but also tricky for testing applications that require state information to track queries and the like.

Context refers to the circumstances surrounding an application's state with respect to each user request. In classic computer systems, the servers invariably save context information (i.e., security level, reference number, transaction number, session parameters, previous screen, etc.) during a user session from screen to screen, and menu to menu. Each of these types of information has one or more states associated with it, such as security level OK, 1, 2, 3, 4, . . . or NOT OK. The application behaves differently or refuses access to some screens until it reaches the proper state.

The World Wide Web servers that are the foundation of nearly all intranet applications do not maintain a session or have any concept of context. All screens (HTML pages) are equally accessible, regardless of state. There is no right or wrong way to navigate to any Web object, nor is there a preexisting state or context.

A few Web-based tools such as Parcplace VisualWave do, however, maintain a context with the user. An application process layer, which functions behind the Web server, maintains the session context. This layer must be ready for the unexpected since a user can send screens out of sequence or even send screens from a previous session.

Another way to track state and context information is with *cookies*—those text files in browsers that can save information from session to session. If you use this or another method to track state and context, keep this in mind when you design your test plans. The following discussion on testing simple and complex applications should give you some suggestions for what to watch.

Simple Intranet Applications

Simple intranet applications are static, HTML-based, and rely on the underlying server directory system for structure.

Testing basic intranet applications is very straightforward because of the context-free server architecture. In Figure 12.2, the components that do not participate in a simple intranet application are grayed out.

The following guidelines are useful to remember when designing a test plan for a simple intranet application:

♦ Don't depend on a specific page size or format in designing or testing an HTML page. Because browsers dynamically format HTML pages and vary in their formatting abilities, an HTML page may display differently than intended. Be sure to test each page with a variety of window sizes and resolutions to ensure its operability on any monitor.

♦ Follow a routine that ensures testing every link on every page. Note that there are management packages available that can help you identify broken links in a visual map of your HTML pages. Also check that the content of the page is accurately defined by the link (sometimes incorrect pages are associated).

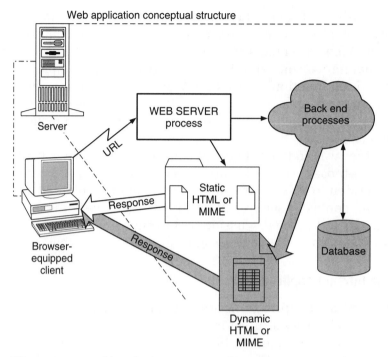

Figure 12.2   Simple intranet application.

- ◆ Test every link on a page only once for a specific browser or screen size. If you have links to the same page elsewhere, you need not go any deeper since there is no context carryover from previous pages.

- ◆ Be sure that you know which standard HTML levels and enhancements are supported by your users' browsers. Because each browser supports its own set of extensions and features, one browser may ignore some features that another will format properly, and a third browser may produce unpredictable formatting given the same feature code.

- ◆ Remember that browsers cache pages. Be sure to clear the memory and disk caches before each test cycle or you may test an old cached HTML page instead of its replacement. The reload button on most browsers causes the current page to be reread from the server. Be sure that this is the case before relying on this feature instead of clearing the cache.

♦ Retest the links to any URL that may have been modified. Modifying the URL of any object will cause some maintenance on each form that contains a link to that object. Be sure that your test plan identifies each form that should have been modified.

♦ Replace any URL that has been removed with a dead page. The *dead* page indicates that the URL was intentionally removed. Other servers, search indices, or pages beyond your control may directly reference the old page's URL. Always check this error condition, even though it is not in your application per se.

♦ Turn off the graphics on your browser (or use Lynx) to make sure there are alt-tags behind your graphics and that critical information is not embedded in them.

♦ If there are multiple connection rates in your organization (modems, ISDN, LAN), test the different configurations for appropriate connection and loading speeds, and so on, for your applications.

Simple Form-Based Intranet Applications

Form-based applications pass information to back-end processes or back-end servers through CGI or other server APIs.

While context is seldom necessary for simple applications (and the Web server does not maintain context in any case), forms introduce the concept of *user errors* and force you to deal with the additional complexity caused by such errors.

Be sure to consider the following additional guidelines when designing a test plan for simple forms-based applications:

♦ Whenever hidden fields maintain context, be sure to test the group of screens that initiate and use that context as a unit.

♦ Be sure that each possible user error for each field generates an appropriate error message. Good practice dictates that the error message page help the user recover from the error. You can do this by giving directions on using the *back arrow* to recover the screen with the offending information. This approach is preferable to a back-pointing URL that causes a complete redo of an empty screen.

◆ Be sure that saved HTML produces a valid request. Requests produced from HTML that has been tampered with should, at a minimum, cause benign errors.

◆ Be sure to include hidden fields when testing HTML and substitute bogus values for those fields as well as for all other fields.

Complex Intranet Applications

Logically enough, the more complex an application, the more complex the testing becomes. In most complex intranet applica-

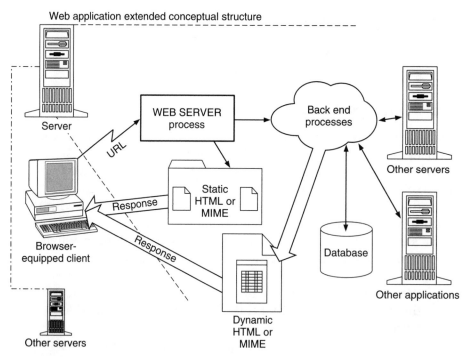

Figure 12.3 Complex intranet application.

tions, like the one illustrated in Figure 12.3, the real crux of the application lies behind the Web server linked to the user via CGI or server API. The test-design guidelines on the preceding pages will allow you to test the superficial support structure of HTML, but if the HTML is generated dynamically, you will also need to consider the following points in your test design:

- Create test cases that exercise the inclusion and exclusion of each HTML section. Be sure to include cases where all sections are included and all sections are excluded.
- Create test cases for each type of form request possible from any dynamically created forms.
- Test security and any other context-sensitive features that are supported by the Web server or maintained in the field codes.

If a session or other context is maintained by the back-end application, be sure to adhere to these additional guidelines:

- Test with multiple users at the same time.
- Save forms from one session and resubmit them out of sequence so that their context is invalid. Ensure proper error handling.
- Resubmit the form from one session during another session. Ensure proper error handling.

Also consider the application portion being serviced by the CGI or API program in your test design. Establish tests that can properly exercise the remainder of the application, including such aspects as:

- Correct implementation of formulas and calculations.
- Correct procedures to save and restore information, state, or context. This is especially important in the event of system or application shutdown.

◆ Correct error handling processes for out-of-resource conditions. This includes handles, memory, file space, sockets, directory entries, and anything else the application may consume.

Operations

After you've completed the testing procedures for your intranet applications, you'll need to be sure that the production environment is ready and serviceable for the intranet. Once the intranet is part of your production environment, ongoing operations will continue to consume resources. While some applications will use resources efficiently and not rely heavily on operational procedures, others may incorporate operational components that require regular attention and a considerable level of overhead. Be sure to prepare your production environment to compensate for these heavier processing loads, along with an expected high volume of network traffic.

Before you actually put the intranet into production, it's a good idea to review the existing IS infrastructure to ensure that it is compatible with the intranet architecture. Of course, you considered all of the necessary organizational and operations issues during the design and development phases of the intranet implementation project, but some of your application requirements may have changed in the interim. Also, because vendors are continually introducing new intra/Internet products or enhancing existing ones, some of the components that you've selected may have slightly different capabilities than you anticipated. Now is a good time to review those capabilities and ensure that they fit correctly into your architecture and meet your expectations.

Figure 12.4 presents a review of intranet components. (Refer back to Chapter 5 for more detailed information on these components and the various intranet services that they provide.) Client components include the IP stack, name resolution (DNS requester), browser/protocol interpreter, and add-ons. Infrastructure components on the other hand include such critical pieces as the DNS server (name resolution), the HTTP server at standard port, and the anonymous FTP server, as well as optional components like News and Mail servers, Secure server, HTTP server at custom port, FTP server, Telnet server, and Gopher server.

Client Management

As an administrator, you may have complete control or no control over the client side of the intranet. In either case, it is important to recognize the difference between setting standards and enforcing them. Users are often most comfortable with "recommendations" for the client side and generally more cooperative if they are encouraged (rather than forced) to adhere to corporate "standards." At a minimum, the administrator should have access to all of the standard (i.e., supported) versions of browsers for each platform that may perform the client function. The careful administrator should have a copy of all browsers that may be encountered in the environment. Be sure to note the HTML version supported by each browser, as well as any special features that differ among the various versions and releases.

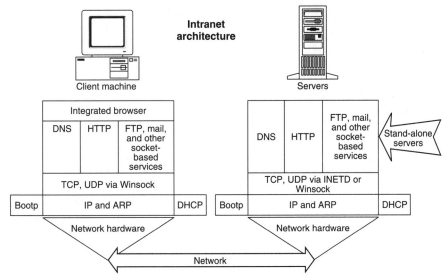

Figure 12.4   Intranet architecture.

Typical client configuration requirements include:

◆ IP stack, which may be part of the operating system release or a third-party add-on. In either case, the stack usually requires some configuration to match it to the network card(s) in the system.

◆ IP address, name servers address (one or more depending on stack capabilities), and gateway address, all of which can be managed via bootp and/or DHCP servers rather than by hard coding. If you choose the hard-coding route, however, be sure to budget for significant labor expense during upgrades since each client machine will probably need to be manually manipulated.

You will also need to install the browser software and configure it with the appropriate default home page and helper applications. In addition, you may want to add a beginning bookmark file and some local help pages.

Infrastructure Management

At a minimum, you should include the following services in your intranet architecture:

◆ IP address server (bootp or DHCP)
◆ Name server (DNS)
◆ Web server (HTTP)
◆ File server (FTP)

It is advisable to consider each of the various services as an independent server with its own setup and configuration. You may elect to provide these services using a single hardware platform, separate hardware platforms for each service, or multiple platforms for each service. This decision depends on the magnitude, the structure, and the capacity of the network. The size and number of intranet applications may also drive the number of servers. Finally, your choice of hardware platforms may also determine the number of users supported, and thus the number of platforms necessary to properly support the infrastructure.

THE IP ADDRESS SERVER: BOOTP OR DHCP

Bootp is a very low level protocol designed to allow network devices to learn critical information such as their own IP address and the address of their local segment's gateway to the rest of the network. Some devices even locate their boot image so they can retrieve it and boot up. Optional data within the bootp conversation can provide the location of the DNS servers and other useful information. Novell uses bootp as the resolution protocol in its LAN Workplace for DOS product and that product's associated IP stack. Sun Microsystems uses bootp for its workstations, and most network device vendors support bootp for their smart devices (e.g., routers and concentrators). Microsoft Windows 95 and Windows NT do not, however, support bootp because Microsoft elected to support DHCP instead.

Bootp administration requires the use of static addresses for each device on the network. The bootp database maps the unique hardware address (i.e., the media access control, or MAC number) on the network interface card (NIC) to its IP address in a one-to-one mapping relationship. Each device's unique address must be registered with the server before bootp can recognize and service the device's bootp requests.

For additional, detailed information on Bootp, refer to Internet Request for Comment (RFC) 951 and 1497. Appendix D contains a list of Internet RFCs and their Web site addresses.

Dynamic host configuration protocol (DHCP) is a newer and more comprehensive boot protocol which uses the bootp header as the basis for its header. DHCP is the resolution protocol chosen by Microsoft for use with its Windows NT and Windows 95 operating systems. Unfortunately, DHCP is not compatible with bootp in Microsoft's current implementation. Because many network devices cannot use DHCP for their own address resolution, most network administrators must provide support for both protocols (i.e., bootp and DHCP) for their networks.

The DHCP protocol statically (one-to-one) or dynamically allocates IP addresses. An address pool temporarily lends a dynamic address to a requesting device. The advantage of the dynamically allocated pool is that the administrator does not need to know the MAC addresses of all the devices being serviced. This is because a default configuration can handle an "unknown" device by allocating it an address from the default pool.

Servers use a static address to prevent confusion and to ensure that DNS is in sync. Clients can be dynamically addressed with little or no consequence caused by their address changing periodically, session-to-session, or day-to-day.

Multisegment networks must have either a DHCP or bootp server for each segment or the router on each segment must be configured to forward bootp packets to the server on another segment. Since DHCP and bootp share a bootp packet format, the routers configured to forward bootp packets can also forward DHCP packets.

Refer to RFC-1541 for more information on DHCP. RFC-1532, RFC-1533, and RFC-1534 discuss DHCP's enhancement of, and interoperation with, bootp.

NAME SERVER

The *name server* usually supports the *domain name system* (DNS) protocol. This is the Internet standard and the basis for resolving the name portion of the URL. Refer to RFC-1034 and/or RFC-1035 for further information on the DNS protocol.

Microsoft WINS.   Instead of adopting DNS, Microsoft developed its own name server protocol—WINS. The primary advantage of WINS is its synchronization with Microsoft's implementation of DHCP. A major disadvantage, however, is that Windows NT is presently the only operating system that provides WINS support, and then only for Windows 95 and NT clients. This situation is expected to change in the near future however. Largely because of the Internet explosion, Microsoft is expected to begin supporting DNS and should soon interoperate between WINS and DNS on NT servers.

Domain name system server.   The *domain name system server* (DNS server) supports the domain name system (DNS) protocol.

The DNS server resolves requests for name resolution by providing the IP address associated with the unique name. As we explained in chapter 1, names use the familiar dot format (e.g., www.microsoft.com) and can be either short-form or fully qualified. Short-form addresses skip some or all of the domain information. If the user and the requested name are in the same domain the following are equivalent:

```
trixy
trixy.dallas.bsginc.com
```

The name server assumes that the domain components are its default. While this shortcut has some benefit to users, application developers and systems administration staff should generally avoid using it in any code. Because fully qualified names always work, developers should be encouraged to use them in all intranet applications.

Similarly, it is important to register DNS Servers with each other. Figure 12.5 shows DNS servers cooperating with each other to resolve names from foreign domains. This infrastructure feature is one of the key reasons the Internet URL is so powerful.

Tips for using DNS to aid maintainability.   Although the usual convention is a one-to-one mapping between names and IP addresses, under some circumstances a single IP address can have multiple names. You can use this "trick" to allow one server to support the services usually handled by another server while the primary server is down, undergoing tests, or being serviced.

Another useful technique is to assign a different name for each service, so that you can split the server at a later date. Consider this approach whenever a single server supports more than one service or application; it causes minimal impact to the URLs embedded in applications, Web pages, bookmark files, and so forth.

Help System Concepts

Providing help for intranet users is a crucial issue to consider, since an adequate help system—along with efficient hypertext

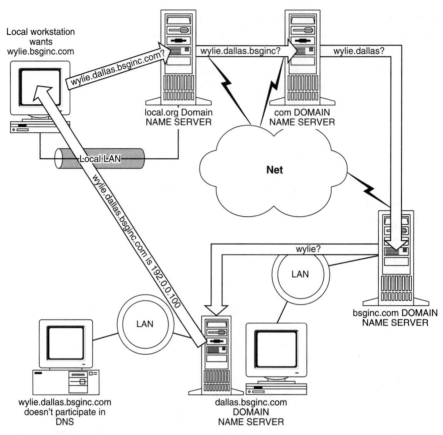

Figure 12.5   Domain name servers cooperate to resolve unknown names.

indexes and search mechanisms—can ensure user satisfaction. Perhaps one of the best features of the intranet is the ability to embed help as URL hot links inside almost any document. While the help pages can be simple or complex, users will find it particularly handy if, at the bottom of each help page, you provide a link to a help topic index. Because many documents can share the same help subsystem, it is advisable to spend time structuring the help pages rather than simply letting them evolve.

Hypertext Index

The *hypertext index* is an intuitive way to let users find the information they need, pursuing the necessary level of detail by drilling deeper into the index. Of course, an efficient hypertext index assumes that the help documents are fairly comprehensive and thoroughly indexed. It is also important to send the user to alternative help sources when such sources (e.g., help desks and telephone support) are available.

Help Desk Application Support

A well-crafted *help desk* offers a number of very real advantages for the help-desk operator. Ideally, the system should enable help-desk operators to log new tickets, search for similar problems by topic, and log their answers back to the user. A simple Web database application can meet this need. If the help desk is very large and/or complex, however, a help-desk package or custom application may be more productive. A Web-enabled help-desk database can save the help-desk staff considerable time and effort by permitting users to search the database themselves. In most cases, help-desk tickets can also be opened online or sent via E-mail to reduce the number of telephone calls.

Search Capability

Search capability is vital to helping users find the information they need. When documents are widely dispersed or involve particularly large volumes of data, search techniques offer the most practical means of locating specific information. Although full-text index techniques may seem like overkill, their ease of use and ease of administration are contributing to their current popularity; they are rapidly becoming the rule rather than the exception. The drawback, of course, is the size of the indices—these often run into the multimegabyte range. With the cost of data storage continuously dropping, however, the storage requirements may prove to be less of a concern than the need to keep information current and easily accessible.

Several search engines and techniques that originated on the Internet are finding their place in the corporate intranet as well. New search engines like Excite, as well as older standbys like Gopher and WAIS can be used to enhance intranet applications and make the proverbial task of looking for the needle in the haystack seem relatively quick and easy.

Application Migration

Most experienced developers would not even consider making changes directly to an application running in a production environment, much less perform development and testing in the production environment. Similarly, you will need to plan carefully to migrate new applications from the development and/or test environments into your intranet environment or to port existing applications into the intranet environment.

Although large, "glass-house" installations typically have separate environments for development, test, and production, as well as strict procedures for migrating code from one environment to the next, the migration process is seldom trouble-free, especially if you are dealing with complex applications. There are a number of things, however, that a developer can do to help smooth the migration process.

- Static HTML and embedded URLs should relate to the current directory rather than to the root directory. This type of file name can readily be moved from one location to another and from one server to another without making any changes to the URLs in the pages. Thus, it is advisable to use a filename like: *./apl/bullet.gif,* within the application rather than a filename like: */usr/local/netscape/myapps/apl/bullet.gif,* which relates to the root directory.
- Use a simple version control system like UNIX's Revision Control System (RCS) to produce *released* versions of all static files that go into an intranet application.

While it is certainly advisable to follow strict migration procedures when migrating complex intranet applications, the same strict adherence may not be necessary for simple intranet applications, and may in some cases seem like overkill.

Data Conversions

Back-end processes are not confined to Web server capabilities. Communicating with *legacy* systems (i.e., preexisting computer systems that must be interfaced through the Web server) is one of the primary uses of intranet technology. Data from legacy systems must typically be converted for use in an intranet application. Conversions range from simple transformations such as EBCDIC to ASCII and numeric to character, to complex cleansing of redundant or conflicting data.

While some legacy systems are directly accessible by users, this practice is usually discouraged to help ensure predictable performance. Because online and query systems don't generally mix well, it is common practice to copy data from a production system to a reporting database or data warehouse. The replicated database then becomes the target of the intranet applications. Conversion can be in real time when the query is made or can take place ahead of time, when the replicated database is being created; the latter is usually preferable from a performance standpoint. Of course, the replicated database can be updated or replaced periodically to ensure that the information remains current.

A number of software vendors, including Evolutionary Technologies, Prism, and Platinum Technologies, among others, currently offer legacy conversion tools. While these tools are relatively expensive, they are very helpful in any conversion process—particularly for large-scale data conversion. Gateway tools such as OmniSQL Server from Sybase, are useful for real-time conversions when the replicated data resides on the legacy hardware. Gateway tools should access a replica database rather than the operational database directly.

Connecting the Intranet to the Internet

While the intranet can be completely isolated from the Internet, much of the inherent utility of the browser and its associated tools is the ability to follow links beyond the bounds of the corporate intranet into the Internet as a whole. The advantages of connecting to the Internet—with its nearly unlimited resource base—make it generally advisable to provide an intranet/Internet boundary that is as transparent as possible.

Firewalls

No competent network administrator would hook the corporate network directly to the Internet without taking some precautions. A number of the early approaches to intranet/Internet computing didn't include firewalls, leading to some pretty horrific (and well-publicized) security breaches. Today, some type of firewall exists on even the most open network. The simplest *firewall* is a router that filters IP access and allows only certain, prespecified hosts (servers) to be visible from the Internet. (Chapter 5 contains additional information on firewalls and related, supplemental security techniques.)

Throughput is a frequent concern with firewalls since every Internet packet must pass through the "wall" to reach the intranet. In reality, however, because most companies have only a limited-bandwidth Internet connection (i.e., 1.5 Mbps or less), the firewall is not generally a bottleneck unless very elaborate filtering or proxying is being performed.

There are two common methods for securing the firewall: One is to make the techniques *secret* while the other is to make them *public*. Over time, most security techniques are found wanting in one way or another. Secret techniques often remain secret because they are defective in some way; knowing the "secret" gives away the keys to the universe. On the other hand, public techniques are open to complete scrutiny. If they are found lacking, they invariably get lots of negative publicity. Members of the Internet firewall community, however, are quick to correct security problems as they are identified; staying in touch with this user-community will enable you to reap the benefits of others' experience and solutions. In many cases, secret and proprietary techniques are based more on salesmanship than substance. The best candidate for a really secure firewall is one that has published code at its heart and whose maker, owners, and users have been diligent at finding and plugging holes.

Securing Servers

There are also a number of ways in which to secure servers on the Internet-side of the firewall. The prevailing security method is the use of *socket wrappers* (i.e., programs that monitor initial use of a socket). Socket wrappers can be used in a UNIX system to limit access to one or more ranges of IP addresses. They do not interfere with normal operation, but do prevent any IP address outside of the given range from accessing the host system. Wrappers can also be applied selectively to specific socket addresses, thereby allowing some protocols and services while denying others. You might, for example, deny FTP and Telnet sessions to anyone outside of your group, but allow HTTP-access to a much larger group.

Socket wrappers can also log authorized and unauthorized accesses. The unauthorized access attempt list is one of the best defenses from hackers—both inside and outside of the company. In most cases, an E-mail message to the administrator (or to the "root" user in a UNIX system) of the system attempting to gain unauthorized access will cause a fair amount of trouble for the offending user. Most administrators take this type of activity very seriously. If, as sometimes happens, the administrator and hacker are the same person, your message serves as a warning that you are aware of the attempted access and will not tolerate security breaches.

Use Tracking

Although use tracking may not be necessary within the intranet itself, most companies are interested in tracking the Internet traffic coming into their site. The Web server can track use overall while "counters" in the HTML pages can indicate the raw number of accesses against each page. These counters may be visible or invisible to the user. On UNIX systems, such statistics can be gathered to almost any level of detail. Similarly, FTP and other services can log which users transferred which files. This information can help you in your capacity, distribution, and expansion plans, as well as in content management.

Performance Issues

Of course, your choice of hardware and software for an intranet application is paramount to the success of that application. Be sure to leave some headroom for growth. In other words, don't select a platform unless it has at least 50 percent of its critical capacity in reserve—including its upgradability. Never start out with a configuration that is at its maximum capacity (or close to maximum capacity) right out of the box.

When performance begins to degrade, you need to understand where the bottleneck is located in your system. Likely bottlenecks, and potential solutions, include:

- ◆ *Network bandwidth on a remote segment—especially a T1 or ISDN link.*   Because it may be very costly to upgrade these circuits to a higher bandwidth, you may want to consider locating an additional server on the other end of the connection to help reduce the traffic.

- ◆ *Router throughput on the local router.*   Upgrading the router and collapsing the backbone into the router may be an effective remedy.

- ◆ *Network bandwidth on the local segment.*   Upgrading from Ethernet to 10base100 or FDDI may resolve this type of bottleneck.

- ◆ *Network interface card (NIC) throughput on the server.* You may want to consider adding network interface cards; most servers allow multiples.

- ◆ *Processing speed or memory capacity.*   These characteristics are often complementary—adding more memory is usually almost as effective as speeding up the processor. Adding additional processors may also be beneficial, but first be sure the application can take advantage of multiple processors.

◆ *System I/O capacity.*　Exceeding this limit may leave you with no recourse but to increase the number of computers in the system. To achieve greater flexibility, you may want to consider segmenting applications and services among multiple systems.

◆ *Disk capacity.*　Adding disk capacity is usually simple and relatively inexpensive.

Bottlenecks in the network must be resolved at their source. Too often, network specialists frustrate themselves and their customers by moving the problem from one place to another. Beware of the *hypothesis and test* process masquerading as overblown optimism. This can be costly and fruitless. Always ask yourself and the specialists "if this doesn't fix it, what are the other options?"

Stress and Volume Considerations

While it is difficult for most companies to effectively stress-test a system, many of the industry publications and manufacturers have spent a tremendous amount of time and money developing sophisticated test labs and procedures. In many cases, the benchmark programs and procedures to thoroughly stress- and volume-test hardware and software systems are available for a relatively low (or no) cost. Of course, the real cost of such testing is in the manpower and equipment required to perform the tests.

To compound the problem, Web servers with standard HTML documents are notoriously difficult to stress-test because they can cache requests. They may require literally hundreds of requests to keep from servicing them all from cached images, as well as hundreds of requests per second before any stress sets in.

While the monitoring tools from most UNIX vendors are text-based and rather crude, experienced UNIX network administrators can usually make them perform satisfactorily. A few vendors, including Hewlett-Packard, offer good monitoring tools and some products, such as Microsoft's Windows NT operating system, incorporate a limited monitoring capability that can be used during testing. Third-party or independent software vendors (ISV) are often a good source of monitoring tools for specific tests. Be sure to express your intent to use the tools for stress- and volume-testing purposes, and get assurances from the vendor of its serviceability in that area.

Contingency Planning

Contingency is one of the key words for success. When plans change or something unexpected happens, contingency planning pays off. The most basic contingency is the backup—a backup tape for data, and backup hardware for the critical server components—along with a clear procedure to ensure that they are implemented properly and can be called on quickly and efficiently when the need arises.

Of course, it is always advisable to thoroughly test the backup hardware and software, as well as the implementation procedure, before placing them into service. A flawed procedure or a malfunctioning backup component is actually more troublesome than no backup equipment or procedure because it lends a false sense of security—and invariably has dire consequences. Periodic dry runs or off-hour tests help prevent this type of tragedy.

One of the best contingencies is the use of multiple servers that can be configured to service each others' clients in case of emergency or overload conditions. This type of contingency often leads to redundant servers and replicated data. The servers are online and serviceable at the same time, and may share the client load. Switchover of clients can be manual or automatic, depending on the service, the operating system characteristics, and the type of equipment involved.

Equivalent servers are often distributed over a WAN for performance reasons. These servers can often be configured to cover for one another, although there is usually some degradation in service due to the limited bandwidth available over the WAN link. As a contingency, however, this arrangement is usually satisfactory for most applications.

Summary

So now your intranet is up and running! But you still face the day-to-day issues of managing it. Although intranets themselves are fairly easy to manage in and of themselves, in Chapter 13 we look at the long-term management issues of an intranet as part of a large, distributed, multiplatform environment.

CHAPTER THIRTEEN

MANAGING THE INTRANET

- ◆ Overview
- ◆ It's a Jungle Out There
- ◆ An Intranet Management Framework
- ◆ Intranet Systems Management
- ◆ Intranet-Specific Considerations
- ◆ Automating Intranet Management

Overview

In the October 2, 1995, issue of *The Wall Street Journal,* a front page article about one of the U.S. military's new leaders described the following scene:

> *"The U.S. Army's big rehearsal [for an upcoming mission] is in full swing. Two twin-rotored CH-47 Chinook helicopters thump into the grassy landing zone. An Apache attack helicopter, its 16 Hellfire missiles bristling, hovers just behind them. Overhead, two F-16 jets peel down the valley looking for a mortar emplacement. Dozens of flak-jacketed troops, their faces painted in green and black camouflage, run to the Chinooks. Radios crackle with military chatter. The short balding colonel surveys the tumult. 'Believe it or not,' he says with a grin, 'this all makes sense.'*
>
> *"It better—for his sake and America's."*

So concludes *Journal* reporter Thomas Ricks.

The corporate world faces a similar "believe it or not" scene with the same "it had better work" bottom line as we begin to bank on intranets for our entire enterprises. As we mix the vast array of new technology involved with client/server computing and intranets with old (i.e., 3–10 years) and really old (i.e., 10+ years) systems in big companies, we realize that the job of managing the ensuing chaos is one of today's greatest challenges.

Developing an intranet management framework is the first big step toward meeting the challenge. Such a framework must take into account the business and technology changes of the past—and coming—decade, while at the same time applying proven methods of procurement, management, and operations of intranet systems.

In other words, the approach to managing intranets is not one that can be created in isolation. Intranet management must be part of a comprehensive distributed systems management approach. Thus, this chapter discusses distributed systems management and intranet management together: the similarities, linkage points, and issues specific and/or new to intranets.

It's a Jungle Out There

Chaos is probably a good word for what the typical large company IT manager confronts. As we discussed in earlier chapters, the current decade has spawned a veritable explosion of new technology, with companies like Netscape, Open Market, and net.Genesis—that barely even existed a year ago—leading growth in whole new components of the IT industry. And, for a multitude of reasons—right and wrong—companies have been purchasing much of this new technology. Studies by Computer Economics and International Data Corporation indicate that approximately one-third of today's IT budgets are being spent on distributed computing goods and services, which includes intranet software and hardware.

The high cost of support for traditional systems combined with the high initial costs involved with legacy systems (i.e., mainframe and tightly coupled client/server architecture) contribute significantly to the rapid acceptance of intranet technology. Studies from Gartner Group and Morgan Stanley have indicated a trend since the early 1990s for increasing portions of IT budgets to go toward ongoing support. More recent Gartner Group studies in 1993 and 1994 confirmed that system purchase costs accounted for just 15 percent of the IT budget, with ongoing operational expenses consuming the other *85 percent.*

Intranet technology offers the opportunity to bring ongoing costs back under control, largely because:

♦ Much of the software used for intranet technology is either in the public domain (once considered to be unreliable but now quite robust and acceptable for business use) or at least relatively inexpensive.

♦ Configuring client computers is quite simple. Once they have a TCP/IP stack and a browser, the client computers can be configured over the network by an administrator or by the user clicking a button in the browser.

♦ The communications costs involved in monitoring and maintaining the network over a wide geographic area are much less than traditional systems due to the lower cost of a Virtual Private Internet (refer to the section on Communications in Chapter 3 for additional information).

♦ The commonality of the intranet interface greatly reduces the problems related to user inexperience, and the ability to link from one application to another helps to reduce help desk costs.

♦ The ability to use real-time conferencing windows to handle remote support such as those available at no cost from MUDs and MOOs (refer to Chapter 8 for additional information).

♦ Telepresence applications further facilitate remote support. Such applications are available from a number of sources, including Cornell University (CU-SeeMe), White Pine Software (Enhanced CU-SeeMe), Apple Computer (Quicktime Conferencing), and Connectix (Video-Phone).

- Users are closely involved in updating intranet sites.
- Security and passwords are significantly easier to manage in an intranet environment. With a single sign-on intranet, for example, a user can access all authorized applications with just one password. (Refer to Chapter 7 for additional information on a single sign-on password intranet.)
- Tools like "cookies" enable intranet managers to track user activity and preferred configurations, as well as to lock in certain settings (i.e., with current versions of Netscape Navigator), thus avoiding user confusion regarding unsupported settings.
- Products like InterTribe from Tribe Software are available to automate many of the functions of intranet maintenance, even from remote locations.
- Intranets offer the potential for using distributed components to facilitate the development of future applications from existing components. This capability is, perhaps, the most important factor in controlling IT expenditures over the long term.

In view of these potential cost savings, business organizations are beginning to consider the long-term effects of their technology decisions, thereby avoiding the short-term views that almost invariably positioned them for longer-term problems. Short-term decisions, such as shopping for lower-cost hardware, postponing projects, restricting application availability, and relying on end users and manufacturers to provide support, while seeming to have merit initially, only work against the IT organization's mandate of maximizing its value to the company.

And, none of these short-term decisions addresses core questions, such as:

- What specific scope support services are needed for an enterprise-wide intranet?
- What common tools and processes can/should be used to deliver services within cost?
- How should support costs for the intranet be recovered?

- What service levels and metrics are appropriate for an intranet?
- What are the intranet processes and policies for service improvements over time?

Identifying your organization's business goals for a technology project (as we discussed in Chapter 3) helps to ensure that your technology vision—including current and future investments—corresponds with your organization's goals for growth. However, the issue of *supporting* that technology once it's in place deserves at least the same attention as the implementation project.

An Intranet Management Framework

Developing an intranet management framework is the ounce of prevention that can avert the inefficient, millions-of-dollars pound of cure that short-term, inadequate, or outdated systems management approaches represent. The reality is that an intranet management framework is part of a distributed systems management framework. Rarely, if ever, will the intranet be built in a greenfield manner, where the intranet technology is being brought in first, without any type of integration to legacy host-based or client/server applications. Integration among old and new distributed technology is the norm; thus, it is a key requirement for a framework that handles all of the systems, including the intranet.

An effective distributed systems management framework, besides helping to avoid the problems (e.g., spiraling support costs) caused by short-term thinking, can have a major, positive impact on the business value of a company's IT investment. An effective distributed systems management framework and operation to support it can:

- Improve levels of service and response times
- Improve end user productivity and satisfaction
- Provide more effective financial control and flexibility for the IT investment
- Reduce overall distributed systems costs

Creating such a framework is the most important step you face once the intranet is put into production. In fact, putting an intranet into production can be a catalyst for developing a distributed systems management framework where one doesn't exist or is inadequate. The savvy intranet champion will press for a framework to be developed by using two important potential threats:

1. *The risk of network failure, which is closely aligned with the danger of intranet success.* In other words, if your intranet is successful, you can anticipate much heavier network traffic than preintranet levels, as well as a significantly larger portion of complex data types. These factors can easily overload a network that was designed for a lower volume of traffic and simpler data. A short-term fix for the problem is to restrict allowable data (i.e., prohibit complex data types). A better, longer-term solution is to plan for greater bandwidth on the internal LAN (and possibly on the local loops to your ISP). A strong management framework and automated tools can go a long way toward preventing this type of problem, as well as helping to deal with it if it does arise.

2. *The high cost of downtime.* Intranet applications are likely to support critical collaborative functions in most organizations, if not key decision-making activities. As more and more intranet applications provide these functions, as well as key transaction processing functions for the business, the cost of a server or network failure is likely to be extremely high. Fortunately, there are some relatively inexpensive ways to avoid these problems.

If the case for developing a systems management framework is successful, your challenge is to rapidly create a framework that can work for your entire enterprise. Developing such a framework is not magic and it's certainly not without its costs. You will need a real commitment from your organization's executive levels—from line-of-business leaders to the boardroom—as well as from the IT department itself.

To really make a framework pay off, you may need to change existing, inadequate approaches to systems management. You may, for example, need to dismantle existing organizational support structures and/or change long-standing relationships with vendors and third-party support organizations—changes that can result in some painful transition time as users and managers learn new processes.

Thus, commitment and speed are of the essence in developing such a framework. The *commitment* can come in a variety of ways. One of the best ways to ensure organization-wide support is to encourage the highest levels of company leadership to take the investment in a distributed systems management framework very seriously. To do this, you'll probably need to work out a gain/risk sharing plan that allows the company's leaders to clearly see the payoff for investing in a new framework.

The *speed* comes from working a plan, like the one illustrated in Figure 13.1, with a knowledgeable team that has the track record and incentive to develop an effective framework. While the team can be assembled entirely from within a company, many organizations choose to work with an IT services partner to design and implement a framework. Either way, the target timeframe for developing a management framework should be 60 to 90 days—depending on the size of a company and complexity of its operations.

Intranet Systems Management

Because of the relative newness of intranet technology, most of the existing approaches to systems management are deficient in some way for distributed systems management. For the most part, they focus on effective personal and workgroup management of resources but don't effectively tie these efforts into corporate, legacy systems management—resulting in duplicate support requirements and rogue procedures and methods.

A goal of systems management is to maintain technology in a state that is beneficial to the organization. When this is done correctly, systems management acts as the oil that keeps the cogs of

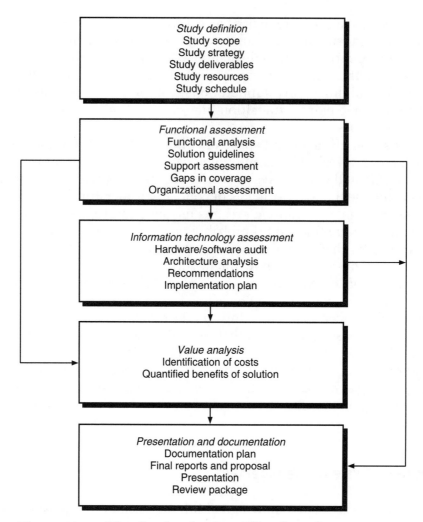

Figure 13.1   Plan for developing a distributed systems management framework.

the machine running smoothly. When done poorly, however, systems management is nothing less than an exercise in frustration for all concerned—IT, users, and management. Table 13.1 illustrates the two most common manifestations of systems management.

Clearly, option A is where your organization needs to be in order to keep or grow its competitive advantage. Although this book is

TABLE 13.1   Common Manifestations of Systems Administration

	A	B
A *system* is:	A group of devices that work together to serve some common purpose.	A lot of stuff accumulated over time that collectively serves some useful purpose when malfunctioning components are cajoled into operation.
Management of the system is:	The orderly control of complex matters in a proactive manner.	A group of well-intentioned individuals that spend their time running around handling crises while accomplishing very little of their original goal.

not about systems administration per se, you may want to review your existing systems management policies and procedures as you plan for your intranet management—particularly if your organization is large and widely distributed. You may also want to seek advice from true consultants in this area—knowledgeable individuals who concentrate and understand *process* as opposed to particular tools and/or platform brands. Be sure to pay proper attention to the three key components of systems management: human resources, organization, and procedure. See Figure 13.2.

Recommended Policies and Procedures

A lack of policies and procedures (or failure to enforce existing policies and procedures) is a major problem for many organizations that manage large, distributed IT systems, including intranets. Implementing a system requires more than just installing the necessary hardware and software and letting nature take its course. You also need to establish mechanisms to ensure that the system is functioning properly and contributing its full value to the organization.

   The following policies, procedures, and controls are the ones that we recommend for ensuring that distributed system activities proceed in an efficient and effective manner. While this is a rather thorough list, it is not all-inclusive. And, the listed items are not

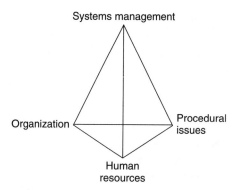

Figure 13.2   Key components of systems management.

requirements per se, but merely our suggestions for crafting a thorough management solution. We've tried to include just enough detail to start you in the right direction in managing your intranet as part of an integrated technology solution.

1. *Documentation.*   Prepare and maintain complete documentation of the system and all of its inherent components, including server hardware configuration, network cable diagrams, NIC listing by workstation, hardware/ software service contracts, hardware/software inventory, operating system configuration information, server and browser configuration information, and specific organizational policies and procedures as outlined in the following sections.

2. *Hardware and configuration maintenance.*   In addition to systems documentation, you will need complete maintenance information, including preventative maintenance logs, a spare parts inventory, and a reference of all hardware-specific setup and configuration disks and CDs (and their precise location). You will also need procedures to ensure that you notify all system managers and users of hardware upgrades or configuration changes in a timely manner. Try to use the fault tolerant features of the hardware and/or operating system to their

maximum extent to ensure the highest possible level of service.

3. *Mission-critical systems.*   Develop a complete list of all mission-critical systems and their related files, along with a list of applications that support daily operations. You will also need to prepare and maintain a daily, weekly, and monthly schedule of when specific applications must be run and a priority list of the applications and data that must be restored in the event of a disaster. Be sure to specify a minimal acceptable response time in the contracts with your hardware and software providers. In general, maintenance on mission-critical systems should be performed only by authorized personnel.

4. *Operating system implementation and maintenance.* Be sure to maintain hard copy configuration information for your operating system implementation. Your support personnel should know the exact location of original and backup operating system installation software. In addition, your maintenance procedures should specify when upgrades are required for the operating system, driver, and add-in modules. Also establish preset storage levels on the server(s) for your users.

5. *Security.*   After you've implemented all of the hardware and software techniques that seem necessary to safeguard your intranet, don't overlook simple security precautions such as housing your server(s) in a restricted area and/or locking the consoles to prevent use by unauthorized personnel. You'll also need to develop policies for protecting the sensitive data on your server(s) and workstations (i.e., assigning and modifying passwords, scanning for viruses, tracking user access, etc.).

6. *Fire protection.*   Take precautions to protect your hardware, software, and data from disasters such as fire. Be sure to equip the computer room(s) with smoke detectors that are tied to a 24-hour monitoring station or directly to the fire department. If possible, install a halon (or equivalent) fire suppression system. In any case, prohibit smok-

ing, minimize the use of flammable materials (e.g., carpets and wall coverings), and install fire extinguishers—and train your personnel in their proper use! You may also want to install an emergency power switch that lets you cut commercial power to the room.

7. *Communications.*   Establish policies and procedures for LAN/WAN, intra/Internet, and mainframe connectivity, as well as network management. Your policies should fully document the existence and location of all routers, bridges, and gateways in the system, as well as the various communication links. And, don't forget to include network cabling in your communications policies. You'll need to maintain a complete inventory of all cabling, along with a detailed network diagram that clearly labels components and locations.

   In addition, you'll need to regularly monitor the performance of the components in your communications system (e.g., NICs, modem banks, servers, etc.) to ensure that they're providing the maximum throughput. You can use operating system statistics, third-party utilities, or protocol analyzers to measure performance. You may also want to use dual ISPs and dual local connections (to different companies) to build fault tolerance into your communications system infrastructure.

8. *Backup/restore procedures and off-site storage.*   Establish backup and restoration procedures for your day-to-day operations. In general, these procedures should include schedules for backing up the data on the server(s) and workstations, as well as any on/off-site tape libraries (and rotating tapes). Be sure that your tape backup system is certified by the operating system vendor and includes such features as unattended backup and an error log. Your procedures should also identify the personnel responsible for the backup activities, including the alternates that are to perform the functions during periods of vacation or illness. It's usually a good idea to test your restoration facilities on a regular basis;

such testing can prevent nasty surprises in the event of a
real emergency!

The intranet introduces a number of additional opportunities for backup, including the use of server-based
scripts (or third-party utilities) that let you write
updated information to a tape drive as well as to the
server, and/or using the Internet to provide automatic
off-site data storage via real-time encrypted backup to
another geographical location.

9. *Business resumption planning.* Be sure that you have a
   comprehensive disaster recovery-business resumption
   plan in effect at all times. This plan should cover all
   departments that provide a support function for your
   organization and, of course, should be reviewed and
   approved by your organization's board of directors.
   Finally, remember to treat this plan as a living document—testing and modifying it on a regular basis to correspond with your technology and business needs.

   Again, intranet offers some additional options in this
   area. A client-based script can, for example, provide automatic switchover in the event of a major server failure. If
   your browser receives a DNS (domain name server) error
   reporting that a certain URL is unavailable, it can automatically check a local table for the backup URL and
   switch over to that server (which contains backup data, as
   determined by your backup and restoration procedures).

10. *Help desk, problem resolution.* Be sure to establish a
    set of procedures for dealing with user questions or
    problems as efficiently and effectively as possible. Be
    sure to document help desk position descriptions, hours
    of operation, after-hours support policies, and staffing
    and training requirements. It is also useful to establish a
    service-level agreement with the user community, as
    well as internal guidelines and goals for issue resolution.
    Also define methods for tracking incident calls and for
    escalating issues to a higher level in the support chain if
    necessary. Standardizing applications greatly helps to

reduce conversion activity among users and to limit the body of knowledge required by the help-desk staff.

The intranet also offers a number of powerful tools in this area, including real-time conferencing with MUDs or telepresence applications that allow the help-desk operator to appear in a window on the client's machine. In addition, many of the major help-desk application suppliers (e.g., Vantive and Scopus) are currently developing intranet extensions for their products.

11. *Administration and setup.*   You'll need a strategic plan to direct future LAN installation and growth in order to ensure consistency in implementation and WAN connectivity. Be sure to develop system administration policies and procedures for day-to-day activities such as setting up new users and/or directory structures, and for LAN hardware/software purchasing procedures. In addition, your organization should have procedures for reviewing proposed changes to the system and for ensuring that proposed changes correspond with long-range plans. Finally, your organization should have a clearly defined policy statement on compliance with software licensing agreements.

12. *Workgroup productivity.*   Try to standardize on a common user interface for the entire network. Such standardization can significantly reduce user training requirements, minimize reliance on the help desk, and increase user productivity. Do be sure, however, that training is available for all users and all applications and that the users have an opportunity for retraining on a regular basis, thereby sharpening their skills—which should reduce the load on help desk personnel.

Intranet-Specific Considerations

Because intranet management incorporates activities that are part of a comprehensive systems management framework, your distributed systems management framework must consider the multi-dimensional requirements of computing and address a broad life cycle of services. While all of the areas illustrated in Figure 13.3 are important in any technology implementation, a few have sub-points that deserve particular attention with respect to intranet management.

Planning

A renewed (or new) emphasis on change management is probably the most significant impact that an intranet has on the planning portion of the framework. When we speak of change management in this context, we're talking about two types of change brought about by the intranet implementation: changes in system configurations and changes in the way that people do their jobs and/or respond to the new systems.

We already know that some type of change management is necessary to introduce intranet applications to system users. (Refer to Chapter 4 for a detailed discussion on the potential impact of an intranet on traditional IS organizational structures.) One of the goals of good systems management is to create a structure that

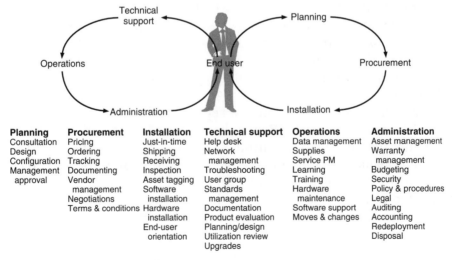

Planning	Procurement	Installation	Technical support	Operations	Administration
Consultation	Pricing	Just-in-time	Help desk	Data management	Asset management
Design	Ordering	Shipping	Network	Supplies	Warranty
Configuration	Tracking	Receiving	management	Service PM	management
Management	Documenting	Inspection	Troubleshooting	Learning	Budgeting
approval	Vendor	Asset tagging	User group	Training	Security
	management	Software	Standards	Hardware	Policy & procedures
	Negotiations	installation	management	maintenance	Legal
	Terms & conditions	Hardware	Documentation	Software support	Auditing
		installation	Product evaluation	Moves & changes	Accounting
		End-user	Planning/design		Redeployment
		orientation	Utilization review		Disposal
			Upgrades		

Figure 13.3   Scope of support services.

positively influences behavior, and in doing so, generates positive attitudes about the intranet. You might, for example, want to consider establishing a special "level 2" service center response team devoted to "intranet services." This team could function alongside the other standard level 2 support (LAN, hardware, applications) team in an organization.

Operations

An intranet adds several activities to the operations portion of a systems management framework, including

- Content management
- Link management
- Use measurement
- Performance management

It also places a new spin on both training and change control (i.e., moves and changes in the environment).

Traditional data management is primarily concerned with issues related to thorough backup and recovery procedures and/or to maintaining the data repository (data dictionary, etc.). Content management markedly escalates this task. Content must be replicated across multiple servers and sites. Large, sophisticated enterprises should consider indexing the content, which generally requires creating an index/crawler application to automate the function.

Also, content must not only be kept up-to-date, but also *look* like it's being kept fresh. (Remember, the cardinal sin of the Web, whether the Internet or an intranet: Don't be boring!) And finally, content management involves a new generation of users who take on quasi systems management responsibilities by staging their updated content in the place and time required to get to production servers. So, content management adds a number of considerations to operations.

The good news here is that object-oriented multimedia databases can greatly facilitate content management. These databases can manage the production process as well as keep track of versions—including versions of complex data types (e.g., images) as well as versions of text documents. A good tracking system is particularly important for complex data types such as images, since the version is not always immediately obvious. During the production process, for example, an image may be scanned, resampled, and sharpened—all of which can cause relatively subtle changes that are not obvious on viewing. Object-oriented multimedia databases also keep track of the relationships between the various elements (i.e., which image and/or sound is associated with which piece of text and on what page).

Like content management, link management generally represents an extension of existing data management issues for most operations. Given the statelessness of the Web (which we've discussed in earlier chapters), the tasks of keeping links current and accurate can be quite challenging in an enterprise with even medium-size Web servers. A 50-page (or more) content for a single server's application, much less 5 to 10 links to other server applications, can quickly become unruly. A growing Web server application, combined with links to vendor partners, suppliers, or even links to other servers on the Internet, rapidly adds cost and staff time to manage the links. Fortunately, link managers are being developed to help with this task.

Intranet use management goes beyond basic server use statistics. In intranet use management, you should focus on getting closer to demographically based use information about users for the various components of the intranet. This type of information lets systems managers effectively track which applications are getting the highest use and which ones serve particular user profiles—information that can be extremely valuable in determining the priority for adding or enhancing applications, changing the configuration of the supporting corporate network, and so forth.

Finally, an intranet adds to the requirements for performance management already performed by most operations areas. Specifically, because there is always a potential for link problems, as well as the likelihood for higher-volume network use, the task of gathering information about the performance of the intranet grows in importance. Accurate, timely performance information can help to identify intranet problem areas before they become critical and can point toward effective resolution.

For example, intranet-specific performance information can help you to recognize a need to reset user expectations. Figure 13.4 lists a number of the other intranet performance metrics that you may find useful in fostering a better user understanding of the intranet.

TRAINING

Don't underestimate the value of user training. Effective training—or the lack thereof—can literally make or break your intranet project. To ensure that you give user training the time and attention it deserves, begin by evaluating your user community. Obviously, your users are likely to vary widely in terms of experience and training requirements. You can't, for example, expect to provide the same level and type of training for the users in your accounting department—who are likely to have significant computer experience—as you do for the users in the benefits department—who may not know what a "mouse" is. At the same time, unless your organization is quite small, you probably can't break the user community into very small groups that accurately reflect their knowledge and ability. But, you probably can classify users in one of the following three major categories:

◆ *New mouse users.*   These are the people who may or may not have previously used a computer (although some may have experience with DOS-based systems). Typically, these users are unfamiliar with Windows and/or the Macintosh operating system, and think that GUI describes the consistency of chewing gum on hot pavement. You'll need to provide these users with rudimentary training, but the level of that training and the amount of background information that you provide (i.e., operating system theory) depends on the tasks that the users are expected to perform. You may, for example, confine training to the intranet interface and specific functions within key applications if the users need only perform a specific, limited set of tasks.

◆ *Intermediate users.*   These users typically have some experience (i.e., at least six months) using either Win-

Intranet Productivity	◆ New applications installed and made operational ◆ Number of users accessing/utilizing each application ◆ Number of training orientations completed ◆ Number of new seats installed ◆ Number of workstations supported per person/server
System Availability	◆ Servers (Web, mail, ftp, proxy, etc.) less planned outage ◆ Network operational less planned outage ◆ Turnaround time on new intranet service requests
Responsiveness	◆ Trouble calls handled within prescribed time limits ◆ Transition to new software/hardware done on schedule
Change/Add/Move/Delete Activity (CAM)	◆ Activity handled within prescribed time ◆ Number handled weekly/monthly (cumulative)
Management and Administration	◆ Semi-annual CSI ◆ Weekly, monthly progress reports ◆ Number of unresolved intranet service requests

Figure 13.4   Intranet performance metrics.

dows and/or the Macintosh operating system and feel confident about starting their computer every day and using it to help them perform their assigned job functions. In general, they are brave enough to explore a bit when they want to perform a new function and are willing to try out new software packages. Often, they have colorful designs for their "wallpaper," send and receive lots of E-mail, and have some limited experience surfing the Net. Your training for these users will focus on the new applications that are available through the intranet and helping them to understand the relationship between the old and new ways of obtaining and sharing information.

♦ *Super users.* These users often know more and better keyboard shortcuts than the manager of the IT department. They typically know all of the ins and outs of the E-mail system, understand attachments and embedded objects, and are willing and able to program macros for their spreadsheets. These users are also likely to purchase some of their own software (and surreptitiously install it on company computers). You'll probably need very minimal training for this type of user; they are usually very familiar with the Internet, know how to download files, and regularly participate in newsgroup discussions, and so on. You may, however, need to control the super user's enthusiasm for new programs by developing (and enforcing) policies to restrict software installation and/or content on the intranet.

After you've evaluated your user base, determine the system fundamentals that all users need to know and design a core curriculum. You can then add, subtract, or modify modules of information from the core curriculum to suit the needs of the specific user group. Of course, if you don't have the time or expertise to develop your own user training program or to disseminate the information to the various groups, you can contract out to a professional course developer, or use a training company.

There are a number of options for disseminating training information to your user community, including classroom training, computer-based training, self-study manuals, or any combination of methods. If you decide that you do need to provide classroom training, be sure to secure approval beforehand from organization executives and departmental managers, particularly if you're going to make the training mandatory. While classroom training can be very effective, it is also very time-consuming and can easily create scheduling nightmares.

If the majority of your users are fairly savvy, you may opt for brown-bag lunches where you can demonstrate the intranet. Be sure to set up some workstations in the lunchroom or lobby so users can try out the browser and links, and have your help desk or other support people available to help out with questions. A dry run of your training presentation (i.e., either classroom or brown-bag) using help desk personnel as your audience is often very helpful for anticipating user questions and formulating appropriate responses.

Regardless of the level or type of training that you decide to provide, don't forget to ask for feedback. Your users' initial excitement (or wariness) of the intranet is likely to incite comments. Don't let the initial user reaction go to waste! Provide your prospective users with evaluation forms or, even better, design a simple, form-based intranet application as part of your demonstration and "test drive."

CHANGE CONTROL

The process of managing changes to your intranet is much the same as in any other environment; it relies on the same processes of change request (i.e., prioritization and correlation), user notification and input, escalation, review by IT, review by user group, testing and efficacy assessment, tracking, and implementation. There is, however, one nice difference in intranet computing: If you are accustomed to a two-tier client/server architecture, you're likely to be delighted with the ease of deployment in an intranet environment. To make a change in an intranet application, you need only deploy the information to the server(s). Because the client browser looks to the server for nearly all information, you eliminate the need to individually modify hundreds of workstations or to change paths, config.sys files, and so forth.

One last cautionary note about change control—be sure to keep records. You'll eventually want to know what technologies were deployed when, to whom, why, and how, as well as their relative success or failure. What problems were problems resolved because of the change? What new problems were created? These metrics will help you to determine if your change control process is adequate, and if not, where it may be lacking.

Technical Support—The Modified Help Desk

The nature of your help desk will most assuredly change in the intranet environment—adding new capabilities along with some new issues. Specifically, you can expect the intranet to affect your help desk in the following ways:

◆ *Research and knowledge sharing.* Many of the features that are inherent to Inter/intranet technology (e.g., E-mail, newsgroups, and collaborative forums) will enable your help desk personnel to efficiently share their collective knowledge.

We recommend that you provide access to the Internet for your help desk staff—even if you don't provide it for the rest of your organization. A link to the Internet ensures easy access to vendors and discussion groups on the Web, enabling your staff to keep pace with technology and to provide up-to-the-minute answers to questions. This type of access is one of the greatest advantages of the Internet and offers tremendous potential benefit for your help desk.

◆ *Support for Internet and intranet technology.* Your help desk staff will need to be thoroughly familiar with the software and communications protocols (e.g., HTTP server, HTML document generation, indexing, and linking) that comprise your intranet, as well as with any changes or additions to the underlying system hardware.

◆ *Support for Internet and intranet applications.* Your help desk staff is likely to field an increased number of queries when you initially implement the intranet. The increase, which is likely to be short-lived, is largely attributable to the users' need for assistance in finding their way to preexisting applications that are moved to the intranet environment. The good news is that once users understand the mechanics of navigating the intranet, they rarely need further assistance.

Although help desk responsibilities vary according to the organization of the IT department and the intranet, the help desk application usually supports the help desk staff, the rest of the IT department, and any number of external groups. Figure 13.5 illustrates the entities with which the help desk typically interacts.

Note that the communication within your IT department (i.e., inside the circle in Figure 13.5) among your technical experts, your technical and development teams (typically level 2 support), and your help desk staff (level 1 support) should be constant and ongoing. In addition, your help desk may support one or more of the following groups outside of the IT department (and possibly outside of the organization as a whole):

- *Internal customers.*   Employees of the organization; these users typically access the intranet through LANs.
- *External customers.*   Individuals or businesses that have permission to access all or specific portions of your intranet. Many organizations are creating specialized intranet services for their customer base.
- *Vendors.*   The external businesses that supply goods or services to your organization. This category reflects the

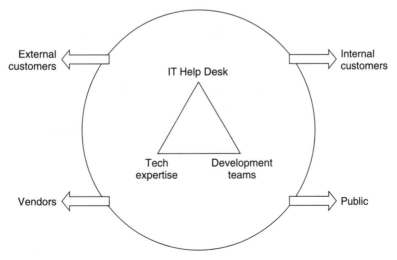

Figure 13.5   Help desk application interaction.

rising popularity of electronic commerce. Communicating with your vendors (i.e., placing orders, reconciling shipments, etc.) is a logical extension of intranet technology that may require support from your help desk.

◆ *Public.*   Individuals and businesses that may need to communicate with your organization to, for example, research information in your online public files. Federal Express is a good example of a company that allows the public (typically customers) to access its intranet via the Internet to track shipments.

For more information on help desks and their role in intranet technology, check out http://www.servicenews.com/reviews/ prrvtoc.htm for the Help Desk Product Review and the Help Desk Institute's site at www.HelpDeskInst.com.

Automating Intranet Management

Eventually, if not immediately, you will probably want to consider automating your intranet management activities. This automation is essential for several reasons:

◆ Leveraging management resources to spend more time on higher value-added, proactive tasks, as opposed to reactive, fire-fighting tasks

◆ Managing the overall expense of the intranet (remember that the vast majority of expense for IT is the ongoing management/enhancement costs!)

◆ Avoiding user anarchy and potential intranet disaster in fast-growing enterprises.

There's no question that product announcements will continue to flood the IT market during the next several years. Fortunately, it probably won't take vendors as long to develop and market credible intranet management tools as it did to introduce client/server management tools. This is partly because the systems management vendors that introduced client/server solutions have already begun to incorporate intranet-specific features in the existing products. To give you an example of what is available and what is likely to come in the near term, we'll look at a few of the approaches to automating intranet management.

Tivoli Systems

Tivoli Systems, which was purchased by IBM in 1996, now operates as the independent systems management division for IBM.

Tivoli bases its approach to intranet management on three major points:

◆ Distributed object technology

◆ An open standards–based approach

◆ Integrated management of existing client/server environments

In Tivoli's eyes, an intranet management solution must use distributed object technology to model the complex services, yet hide that complexity from the users. Tivoli created a proprietary object approach designed specifically for large-scale system management. This proprietary approach is a point of contention between Tivoli and companies like Computer Associates, which view Tivoli's method as "closed" and more expensive than the alternative—adherence to the SNMP standards. According to Tivoli, however, SNMP isn't adequate to manage complex environments.

In spite of its own proprietary approach, Tivoli does champion the use of industry standards in developing systems management products. Such standards can, according to Tivoli, relieve ISVs of the need to create individual product versions for each vendor service that uses a different API. Additionally, users need standards so they can buy products that are guaranteed to work together.

Finally, Tivoli's view of an integrated world is not unique. The company acknowledges that the traditional client/server world is not going to disappear in the face of intranets. For this reason, companies must have a tool that can manage everything in the existing environment, along with the continually developing, distributed technologies.

To respond to these requirements, Tivoli dubbed its intranet management approach net.TME. The foundation product of net.TME is net.Commander—a product that offers comprehensive management of the intranet application environment. Figure 13.6, which illustrates the net.Commander platform, is based on the TME (Tivoli Management Enterprise) architecture picture because net.TME is an Internet/intranet-enhanced version of TME—it performs a range of services, including deployment, availability, user access control, and automation for the intranets.

Tivoli's net.Commander tool facilitates intranet management by providing the following functions:

◆ Automatically discovers of all the servers and creates icons for them. It then gives the administrator dialogs that can be used to configure the servers. With TME, a

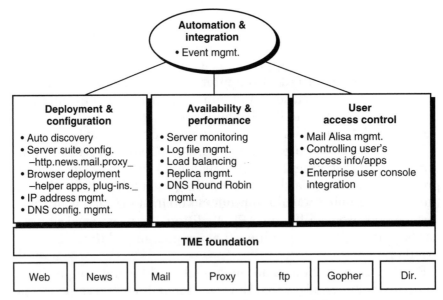

Figure 13.6   Tivoli's life cycle management of the intranet.

configuration profile can be pushed out to large numbers of servers.

◆ Provides file packages, including helper applications, for popular browsers. These packages go a long way toward resolving the difficulties in deploying large numbers of browsers in an intranet.

◆ Offers sentry monitoring collections for each of the Internet services.

◆ Uses DNS round-robin management to balance the load across multiple, identical Web servers.

◆ Provides user access controls via a document tree managed by the Web server. Users with browsers can browse the document tree. The administrator can control which users or groups of users can access which parts of the document tree.

Tivoli has indicated its intention to introduce an Internet management specification (IMS) to promote openness of intranet management. The company hopes to present the IMS, which it is currently developing in association with SunSoft, to the X/OPEN standards body for consideration as a standard management API for Internet services. Tivoli has a track record of establishing credible standards: It wrote the X/OPEN systems management standard and spearheaded the development of the application management standard (AMS), which addresses the management of clients.

The Tivoli approach is just one among several major vendors' approaches to automating intranet management. Other major contenders include Hewlett-Packard and Computer Associates Inc., both of which offer very capable products and a vision that backs up their Internet/intranet management offerings.

Hewlett-Packard

Hewlett-Packard's Fully Distributed Network Node Manager is actually an intranet-enabled version of its well-established network management system. Hewlett-Packard certainly has the experience and expertise to compete in the intranet market. The company recently unplugged its last mainframe computer—the final act in its own internal program to completely replace all of its existing legacy systems with an intranet! We expect Hewlett-Packard to introduce many more intranet-specific products as it continues on its own learning path in the intranet environment and develops hardware and software to meets its own—and its customers'—needs in the intranet arena.

Computer Associates

Computer Associates' Unicenter/Internet Commerce Enabled product builds on the company's Unicenter systems and network management platform. It brings many of the same tools that network managers now use to administer their private network to the intra/Internet environment, along with a number of specialized facilities for intranet event management, database monitoring, and security.

No matter which product or approach you choose to automate the management of your intranet, however, you should recognize that the automation tool may represent a greater financial investment than your initial intranet development effort. Be sure to keep that in mind when you're planning and budgeting for future intranet developments. Also, carefully consider the flexibility of the vendor's product line, as well as the stability of the company itself.

Now that your intranet is up and running smoothly, don't think that you've made all the decisions necessary for the next ten years—nothing could be farther from the truth! But, you now have a platform that truly can grow and change with your organization, significantly more than a host-based or two-tiered client/server architecture could. Unfortunately nothing is ever completely bug-free. Be sure to review Chapter 14 on Tips, Tricks, and Gotchas; it gives you some hints on how to avoid future problems as your intranet evolves to accommodate new requirements and technological changes.

CHAPTER FOURTEEN

TIPS, TRICKS, AND GOTCHAS

- ◆ Overview
- ◆ Lack of Planning
- ◆ Failure to Seek Expert Assistance
- ◆ Lack of a Management Framework
- ◆ Application Development Gotchas

Overview

There is no substitute for experience, and this maxim is just as true in the information technology business as it is elsewhere. While a small or limited information system can—at least in theory—be developed strictly from information resources, developing a large-scale, distributed system requires more than book knowledge. Experience is, without question, the best guide for handling the complexities of such a system. But, experience often involves learning by trial and error. In this chapter, we try to let you take advantage of other organizations' experience with intranet implementation projects—benefiting from their trials and learning from their errors.

Although the steps that we've outlined in this book should help you to design and implement a high-quality intranet that meets your current and future needs, we all know that actual execution rarely (if ever) goes according to plan. So, we've borrowed from the experiences of some of our clients and other companies that we know to give you some real-world advice. Although none of the organizations or situations that we describe in this chapter can exactly mirror your own environment or requirements, they are examples of the types of problems you may well encounter in your own intranet project. Obviously, if you can anticipate the types of problems you may face, you have a good chance of avoiding them altogether or, failing that, can resolve them with minimal interruption to the project. And, while horror stories are abundant in the information systems arena, we've tried to include some good ideas that are definitely worth sharing.

We've tried to organize the following scenarios into major problem areas (e.g., lack of planning, need for additional resources, etc.), but in reality, the categories overlap; failure to seek expert assistance, for example, may well represent a lack of planning. In fact, most of the problems that we see in intranet implementation projects are related to a lack of planning. So, once again, we suggest that you review the early steps in the implementation program and be sure that you have laid a proper foundation for your implementation project.

Lack of Planning

Many of the technologies related to intranet computing have a well-deserved reputation for simplicity. Indeed, simplicity is one of the advantages of an intranet, but just because the technology is relatively straightforward doesn't mean that the implementation project will be easy. Even if you're implementing a small intranet to determine its utility in your organization, you'll need to consider the planning steps that we outlined in earlier chapters. And, if you're contemplating a more complex intranet, with external links and mission-critical applications, you most definitely need to follow the planning steps, paying particular attention to your resource assessment and selection, organizational issues, and, of course, security issues.

Gotcha #1: Lack of Long-Term Planning

PROBLEM

Failure to plan for success.

EXAMPLE

A company began its intranet as a "skunk works" project with little organizational planning or thought about future development. But, in a remarkably short period of time, the intranet achieved surprisingly widespread popularity. In response to increasing user demands, company management began to establish links to partner sites and to the Internet. Intranet traffic increased considerably, along with numerous inquiries from potential customers and business partners interested in purchasing goods and/or services from the company. Thus, the organization discovered a new, low-cost channel for communicating valuable information to its business partners and potential customers.

But, the company never instituted a policy for managing the site, updating its content, or measuring its effectiveness. Even more serious, they failed to plan for the increased network traffic. The highly successful intranet soon became a victim of its own success, publishing outdated and/or inaccurate information and delivering poor performance as the increased traffic bogged down the entire network.

SOLUTION

Plan ahead! Even if you're only planning a "test run" to determine interest in an intranet, be sure to have a plan in place for logically expanding the project if there is widespread interest. And, even if you don't have immediate plans for linking to the Internet, be sure to plan for an eventual link. Review the planning steps that we outlined in Chapters 2 and 3 and be sure that you have the resources available to implement and manage a successful intranet. If necessary, seek outside help for developing an intranet that can meet your future needs as well as your immediate requirements. Finally, be sure to implement a management framework that addresses the issues of maintenance and content.

Gotcha #2: Forgetting Your Audience

PROBLEM

Failing to set realistic expectations and to explain the intranet in a manner that decision makers can understand.

EXAMPLE

When an IT department decided to initiate an intranet effort, it sought support from the CIO, presenting an implementation plan and budget for approval. The CIO, who was not particularly familiar with intranet technology but didn't want to appear ignorant on the subject, approved the budget as it stood. Unfortunately, his expectations for an intranet were based on the articles he'd read in the trade press and on some demonstrations he'd witnessed at IT conferences.

When the intranet project was complete and the first application delivered, the CIO saw only a speedy little application with minimal glitz instead of the RealAudio and virtual reality application that he was expecting. Not only was he disappointed, but the IT staff felt their efforts were unappreciated.

SOLUTION

Be sure to involve corporate management in the early stages of your project, making them aware of the real benefits that an intranet can offer to your organization. Use analogies to technologies that they know and understand (i.e., mainframes, two-tier client/server, ATMs, etc.) to explain the intranet concepts. Then, keep them informed of progress throughout the implementation process, making sure that they're aware of any trade-offs in speed of delivery, expense, performance, and utility. And, don't exaggerate the intranet benefits; if anything they should be pleasantly surprised by the capabilities of the intranet—not disappointed by its lack of features and functions.

Gotcha #3: Underestimating Use

PROBLEM

Server capacity is insufficient to handle demand/volume.

EXAMPLE

The IT department provides the organization with Web browsers and installs basic groupware software on a trial basis on a relatively small server running Windows NT. Users adapt rapidly to the groupware and the server is quickly overwhelmed, resulting in slow performance that hampers the system's popularity. As performance declines, users shy away from the system; it is soon underutilized—and even avoided—by the individuals and groups that initially embraced it.

SOLUTION

Plan ahead and be sure to leave some headroom for growth. Your choice of hardware and software for an intranet application is paramount to the success of that application. Don't select a platform unless it has at least 50 percent of its critical capacity in reserve—including its upgradability. Refer to chapter 12 for additional tips on performance issues and testing guidelines. Be sure to stress-test your system to ensure that it meets your current needs and never start out with a configuration that is at its maximum capacity (or close to maximum capacity) right out of the box.

Gotcha #4: Underestimating Complexity

PROBLEM

Assuming that raw technical ability is all that goes into a business solution.

EXAMPLE

A company that we know decided to jump on the intra/Internet computing bandwagon. Managers in the IT department researched the technology by reading numerous articles in the industry press; then, thoroughly convinced of the technology's benefits and inherent simplicity, they commissioned students at the local community college to build the intranet. While the development price was remarkably low, the resulting system was also incredibly inadequate. When the system was released for user testing, it was so badly received throughout the organization that the company abandoned the intranet effort altogether and tabled a number of related business initiatives.

Several of the company's business partners who had linked to the external portion of the intranet were livid when the project was terminated without warning. The company did an enormous amount of damage to its public image, which they had carefully cultivated for the past 50 years. The company's attempt to implement a low-budget intranet cost significantly more in the long term than a well-crafted project, even one with lots of professional expertise, could ever have cost.

SOLUTION

If you determine that you need outside assistance for your intranet implementation project, choose your advisors just as carefully as you would hire members of your internal staff. Be sure that they have experience that relates directly to your type of project and that they are capable of dealing with all facets of intra/Internet computing technology. Refer to Chapters 3 and 4 for additional information on determining your need for additional resources and selecting those resources.

Gotcha #4a: Selecting an Improper Architecture

PROBLEM

Improper selection of intranet architecture causes delays and additional expense.

EXAMPLE

A large retailer defined its intranet requirements for a relatively simple Content Distribution system. During the development process however, it became apparent that the company actually needed a Type 2 intranet design capable of handling database integration. The resulting change in intranet design plans caused a major delay in implementing the project, along with additional expenses for redesigning the architecture and selecting suitable components.

SOLUTION

Be sure that intranet requirements are clearly defined at the very beginning of the project. Following the initial steps of the BSG 12-Step Program (as we discussed in Chapters 2 and 3) can help to put the entire planning process into a logical sequence of events and ensure that all levels of the organization that will ultimately use the intranet are involved—from the onset—in defining its short- and long-term objectives.

Gotcha #5: Using Nongraphical Browsers

PROBLEM

Pages aren't designed to accommodate nongraphical browsers.

EXAMPLE

One company that we know designed a very successful intranet using a popular graphical browser. As the intranet expanded, however, additional users were connected, including a number of individuals with physical limitations who required a non-graphical browser (e.g., Lynx). When these users attempted to access information on the intranet, they discovered that much of it was embedded in graphics that they could not use. The company was faced with the prospect of redesigning its intranet to accommodate the physically disabled users and/or impending legal action if the system could not accommodate *all* users. It opted for a major rewrite of the system—at tremendous expense.

SOLUTION

When you're selecting a browser, consider the needs of all of your users—even those who may be added at some point in the future. And, use Alt Tags to place meaningful information behind your graphics; this information can be displayed whenever the graphic itself is not. It is also advisable to keep your text separate from the graphics, and be sure to test the intranet with *all* browsers, including the nongraphical ones.

Gotcha #6: Hard-Coding in the "Maintenance Boogeyman"

PROBLEM

Failing to plan for flexible growth, thereby incurring high maintenance costs.

EXAMPLE

A large corporation relies on traditional, hierarchical models for its intranet design initiative. The intranet is a success and quickly grows beyond all expectations. But, the hierarchical model is too rigid to allow for growth or necessary modifications. The "Maintenance Boogeyman" creates a nightmare of renaming and shuffling pages and information.

SOLUTION

Assume that you are going to be successful and that your intranet will grow like a weed. (Most well-planned and well-designed intranets do!) Design a modular Web that uses simple mapping such as "server aliases" to carve out modules that you'll be able to reorganize at will as requirements change. Check out the information on ORBs in chapter 6 to determine if some of the new and evolving object-oriented technologies are suitable for your intranet; then refer to chapters 7 and 8 for practical tips on designing and developing an intranet to meet current and future needs; and finally, turn to chapter 12 for guidelines on implementing your intranet.

Gotcha #7: "Me-Too" Mania

PROBLEM

Trying out new technology without business need.

EXAMPLE

IT developers in a major corporation were asked to develop some intranet applications to demonstrate how the medium could be used by the company. Taking advantage of the opportunity to explore new technologies, the developers overloaded the applications with frames, plug-ins, sound, and blinking text. Unfortunately, they failed to address any real business needs, focusing on the bells and whistles rather than utility of the applications. Company management viewed the applications as mere fluff and rejected a proposal to implement an intranet.

SOLUTION

Remember that advanced Web techniques and multimedia capabilities should enhance intranet applications, not dominate them. Review Step 1 in the 12-Step Program (Should We Implement?) and be sure that intranet applications correspond with your business values and lead toward defined business goals.

Gotcha #8: Skipping the Prototype

PROBLEM

Beginning development without taking time to prototype, research, and test technology options.

EXAMPLE

Working against a deadline, an IT department selected a technology set (i.e., Microsoft Front Page and IDC) and began to develop intranet applications without prototyping. Midway through the development effort, the team recognized that system performance would be completely unsatisfactory. They then determined—with direction from upper-level management—that the project required a complete redesign. They scrapped nearly all of their existing work, and started over again using C++ and working long overtime hours in an attempt to meet the original schedules. The project was eventually finished, but behind schedule and way over budget.

SOLUTION

Thoroughly research the tools that you're going to use to build your intranet, then take the time to "test-drive" those tools at the beginning of the project. Be sure to prototype the application(s), leaving plenty of time to make changes, if they're required. Taking the time to research and plan in the early phases of your project can save you enormous time and effort at the end of the project—when management and users are likely to be waiting anxiously for the results. If your initial choices are sound, you may be able to deliver a satisfactory product ahead of schedule.

Gotcha #9: Leveraging Resources

PROBLEM

Hiring one or two experts to lead a team of inexperienced developers.

EXAMPLE

Using the "producer/consumer" model, a company hired one really stellar C++ programmer and asked him to mentor a 30-person development team that was responsible for moving the organization from a traditional two-tier client/server architecture to an intranet environment. Although the programmer designed excellent class libraries and templates, they were misapplied. The intranet evolved into an almost useless hodgepodge of mixed objects and metaphors.

SOLUTION

When using the producer/consumer model described in Chapter 5, be aware that you'll need to begin with some very *smart* consumers who can build off of the producer's initial work. In the first implementation, the producers and consumers are tightly coupled; they really can't get along without each other. After this initial phase, use the more experienced consumers to mentor others and leverage the "products" across a large group.

Failure to Seek Expert Assistance

This category, which is closely related to a lack of planning and a tendency to underestimate the complexity of the implementation process, contributes heavily to unsuccessful intranet projects. Be realistic when you assess your in-house resources and/or acquire outside assistance; try to ensure that the "experts" on your implementation team have experience that relates directly to your intranet project in terms of size, complexity, and design. Remember, the individual members of your implementation team need not have experience in all areas, but collectively the team should have a thorough understanding of the underlying intranet technologies and the implementation issues that they're likely to face.

Gotcha #10: Lack of Expertise

PROBLEM
Assuming that just because someone has built a Web site he or she can roll out an enterprise-wide intranet.

EXAMPLE
A major corporation entrusted its intranet development to a small, internal group that had built a very successful intranet Web site. When the same group tried to implement an intranet, however, they encountered numerous technical and organizational problems. The implementation group handled the intranet project like an internal Web site, but failed to consider such major issues as internal integration and staff resistance. After one year, faced with considerable internal strife and user discontent, the company was forced to disband the internal intranet project group and seek assistance from a systems integrator, which essentially had to begin the project from scratch—starting with the all-important planning phase that the internal group had missed.

SOLUTION
Be sure to consider Step 2 in the 12-Step Intranet Implementation Program. Realistically evaluate your internal resources and determine what you can successfully accomplish in-house with the existing IS staff and expertise. Then, decide to either expand your in-house capabilities through training or hiring, or seek outside help in one form or another. In either case, look for solid experience with intranet implementation. Although intranets are closely related to the Internet (and share much of the technology), they involve a number of organizational differences as well as conversion and integration issues that can be critical to their success.

Gotcha #11: Legacy Wrappering

PROBLEM

Underestimating the difficulty of integrating legacy applications.

EXAMPLE

A company, following advice in the trade journals, decided to wrapper its legacy applications for use via the intranet. It hired a number of programmers to write JavaScript to access a Data General, key-indexed file system. However, they failed to consider that the application was running on an old version of the operating system (i.e., about 12 versions old). As a result, the coding volume expanded rapidly in an attempt to address incompatibility problems. In a remarkably short period of time, the project grew completely out of control, making a mockery of the time and budget estimates and failing to resolve the problem of integrating the legacy applications with the intranet.

SOLUTION

Get expert help! Don't believe that "quick and dirty" scripting can solve your legacy integration issues. Chapter 5 includes some suggestions that you may want to consider for integrating mainframe, legacy applications with an intranet, but it also includes our recommendation that you seek experienced assistance with this complex and critical process.

Gotcha #12: The Skill Mix Gotcha

PROBLEM

The need for a blend of technical expertise, business acumen, and creativity to design a successful intra/Internet application.

EXAMPLE

Of course ideally you should have all of these capabilities for any computer application, but the combination of skills is particularly critical in intra/Internet computing because of the easy, widespread accessibility of the applications and the visual nature of the medium. All too often, companies don't understand how these skillsets should combine in an application development effort and use developers with only one or two of the necessary skills, leading to disappointing products. We've all seen Web applications with one or more of the following characteristics:

1. Works really well, has great features, and is quite useful, but *looks* awful

2. Looks *great,* but every third link is broken, and it takes forever to load and run

3. Offers great business functions, but its performance is poor, and its design is less than pleasing to the eye

4. Looks great, and works okay, but has almost no business utility

SOLUTION

Again, be sure to realistically evaluate your staff's experience and capabilities and determine if you need additional resources to develop effective applications that incorporate all of the elements of business acumen, technical expertise, and design creativity. Consider all of these elements when you are assembling your intranet implementation team and, if necessary, find an outside consulting group or systems integrator that can bring the skillsets you need into the project.

Note. Although the most successful intranet projects have a confluence of all three skillsets, many systems can be considered "successful" without all three factors. Be sure to consider your own priorities and determine what (if anything) you're willing to sacrifice if time and/or budget constraints keep you from achieving all three.

Gotcha #13: Design Blunders

PROBLEM

Developers unfamiliar with Web design make obvious design blunders.

EXAMPLE

A company encourages its intranet development team to produce the initial pages for its Web site, without consulting a designer who is familiar with Web design. As a result, the initial pages on the Web site contain all of the necessary information, but are unattractive and difficult to read. The implementation team, unfamiliar with graphic design or the differences inherent in online presentation, incorporated numerous design errors, including busy backgrounds; flashy, but unreadable text colors; small print; unintuitive navigational controls; and never ending pages that required continuous scrolling. After one or two visits to the site, most users were discouraged and intranet use declined.

SOLUTION

It is advisable to include a graphic designer on your intranet implementation team. If that's not possible, contract with an experienced Web designer to create your basic design metaphors and templates or, at a minimum, have a knowledgeable designer review your basic designs and make suggestions. Then, be sure that your coders understand the basic design and navigation principles that we outlined in Chapter 10.

Gotcha #14: Advanced Feature Abuse

PROBLEM

Developers go overboard with design tricks.

EXAMPLE

Empowered to design Web pages for the new corporate intranet, a team of C programmers took full advantage of flashy design techniques, and incorporated a wild mix of colors and animation to present the company image. Instead of the Rembrandt-quality material they intended to produce, they ended up with pages that resembled Warhol on steroids.

SOLUTION

Again, consider the capabilities and experience of your in-house resources and don't hesitate to seek outside assistance for areas in which your team lacks experience. If you don't have an experienced graphic designer on the team, find a knowledgeable designer to review your Web page design. In any case, it's advisable to limit the number of graphics and advanced features on each page so the design features don't overwhelm the information on the page.

Gotcha #15: Breaking the Law

PROBLEM

Using proprietary materials without first obtaining legal permissions.

EXAMPLE

A member of senior management checks out the corporate Web site, and inquires why the popular cartoon characters that have been licensed as part of the company's marketing effort are not included on the site since they are part of the company "image." The characters are then added to the site. But, when the licensing agency discovers them there, it charges the company with breach of contract action because the medium (i.e., the Inter/intranet) is not covered in the use terms of the licensing agreement. As a result, the company is served with notice that it is in breach of contract; it is prohibited from using the artwork in any form and directed to cease and desist use in the Inter/intranet site.

In response, the site is immediately shut down to avoid further problems, causing great consternation to the marketing department and senior-level management. In addition, because the misuse of the artwork resulted in the cancellation of the media use contract, the company was forced to develop new marketing materials and incurred massive costs for reprinting and distributing the materials, as well as for cancellation of print, radio, and television advertising. Overall, the company incurred direct expenses of more than a hundred thousand dollars.

SOLUTION

Read Chapter 4 (Organizational Issues) for advice on how best to avoid legal snafus. Always seek advice of counsel regarding the information you publish on your intranet—particularly if the intranet is linked to the Internet!

Gotcha #16: Loss of Security in a Database Conversion Project

PROBLEM

Assuming that a conversion tool will accommodate security requirements.

EXAMPLE

During the process of testing InterNotes, a major pharmaceutical company converted one of its research databases to InterNotes and put it up on the corporate intranet. It wasn't until customers began to call with questions about the database that the developers realized that they had inadvertently posted a very proprietary database on the open Internet. Unfortunately, they had assumed that the security built into the InterNotes database would be automatically transferred to the HTML database during the conversion process.

SOLUTION

As a general rule, never assume anything about security! During a database conversion project, first convert the data, then apply the appropriate discretionary access controls. In nearly all cases, this will mean redefining or reimplementing the security controls from your original database.

Lack of a Management Framework

All too often, intranet problems begin—or are recognized—after the implementation project is complete and the intranet becomes part of the production environment. Then, a lack of firm, clearly stated policies for managing the intranet and its content can quickly doom all of the positive aspects of the project. Again, this relates back to your initial planning for the intranet. Many of the management issues—such as assigning responsibility for managing content and controlling use—should be addressed in your initial intranet implementation plan. But, if you don't address those issues in the early phases of your project, you're likely to face them after the intranet is implemented—they may be much more difficult to deal with at that point.

Gotcha #17: Version Matching

PROBLEM

Incompatibilities arising with new versions of software.

EXAMPLE

While this problem is not new to intra/Internet computing, the proliferation of new products and software releases for this environment, combined with easy availability via the Internet, does aggravate the situation.

One user we know downloaded the "latest and greatest" version of a browser program, resolving some bugs in the older version and adding a couple of new features he thought might be useful. Unfortunately, the latest version of browser software was compatible only with the "latest and greatest" version of a major application package. Furthermore, the organization was using an older version of that package in its production environment, with no plans for upgrading to the newer version in the foreseeable future because the current operating system didn't fully support the latest version of the application. So, our user couldn't take advantage of the latest version of browser software, but it took him some time (and required some assistance from IS) to identify the incompatibilities and revert to the original, company-approved version of the browser software.

SOLUTION

Be sure that your intranet management plan includes a provision for carefully evaluating new products and/or releases prior to installing them on the intranet. Your evaluation should not only determine if the new version or product offers a significant improvement in features and functions, but also what effect it is likely to have on other, related programs. Don't feel pressured to adopt every new release and new product that the vendors introduce. Wait until you're sure that you understand its effect on all other elements and can control that effect throughout the enterprise. Review chapter 13 for additional information on managing your intranet.

Finally, be sure that your users understand what products are approved for use on the intranet and the potential problems with installing untested, or nonapproved versions of products. This information should be clearly stated in your Intranet Usage Policy. (See chapter 4 for additional information on Intranet Organizational Issues.)

Gotcha #18: Testing (or the Lack Thereof)

PROBLEM

Insufficient integration testing.

EXAMPLE

Feeling pressured to provide instant gratification with a new intranet, a company installs new software and pieces together some applications. They perform only a cursory level of functional testing on the system and rely on the technical testing performed by the original developers at the unit level.

Upon release, enthusiastic users swarm to the new information on the intranet, only to find broken links, bottlenecks, and application errors. The help desk is overrun with calls and complaints. Both the IT department and intranet initiative lose credibility.

SOLUTION

Follow the testing guidelines that we described in chapter 12 and remember that testing is an ongoing process in an intra/Internet environment. Just because it isn't a separate line item on the workplan doesn't mean that it can be eliminated or even minimized. Be sure to include system and unit testing in your development plans and continually seek feedback from your users; they're the best source of information regarding the intranet utility and functionality.

Gotcha #19: Failing to Keep Current

PROBLEM

Dated material on the intranet is changed, but no one knows when or by whom.

EXAMPLE

A company begins to keep its policy and procedure information on the intranet, thereby streamlining its methods for updating and distributing information while saving thousands of dollars in printing and mailing costs. But, it fails to date the information on the intranet, making it nearly impossible for users to differentiate old policies from new ones; moreover, it fails to establish clear lines of accountability. There is no clear "audit trail" of changes, or clear responsibility for updating or verifying information on the intranet. In an effort to remedy the problem of outdated information on the intranet, management begins to erase old policies, making it impossible for users to reference them.

SOLUTION

Develop a set of procedures to control intranet content and to clearly designate responsibilities to departments and individuals. When revising documents on the intranet, be sure to archive any significant changes and provide access to the preceding version(s). All documents should be clearly dated—with the date of the original version and each subsequent revision—so that users can tell which version is current and, if necessary, can reconstruct the evolution of the information.

If some portions of your intranet change regularly, be sure to establish a schedule for revisions and assign responsibility— then stick to the plan. If, for example, you publish a weekly newsletter on the intranet, label it by date and volume, then indicate the date and volume for the next issue. With this approach, users will know when to expect new information. Refer to chapter 4 for tips on establishing an intranet use policy and to chapter 13 for guidelines on managing the intranet and its content.

Gotcha #20: Technology Cul-de-Sacs

PROBLEM

Betting on a short-term technology or product.

EXAMPLE

An IT department discovered some esoteric freeware that they liked and downloaded it from the Internet to try it out. Liking what they saw during the trial run, they incorporated the new software into their toolset and used it to build several applications. Unfortunately, while the company was happily taking advantage of the software, the vendor went out of business. Thus, the company was left without support or the prospect of future upgrades.

SOLUTION

Nothing is 100 percent certain (especially in the computer industry), but it is advisable to be conservative in your choice of hardware and software components. Try to select products from vendors that are likely to be around for awhile. At minimum, choose components that use a flexible design and ensure some degree of portability. Then, design your system to incorporate future changes (i.e., a distributed model is usually best).

Gotcha #20a: Failing to Adapt to Growth

PROBLEM

High demand for popular intranet sites resulted in an inefficient, fragmented solution.

EXAMPLE

A major Internet Service Provider (ISP) that was having a difficult time keeping up with rapidly increasing demands on its intranet resorted to a piecemeal solution using multiple servers and replicated data. As the system grew larger, the company began to experience major performance problems as files were continually copied and recopied among the server disk drives. In addition to problems with unnecessary disk fragmentation, the company was unable to efficiently allocate disk space on an as-needed basis.

SOLUTION

The company elected to take a somewhat radical step, replacing its 15 existing servers with a single Auspex NetServer. This step, which centralized all of the data on a highly-reliable, high-performance network file server, resolved the performance problems as well as difficulties with disk space allocation. The company's decision illustrates the point that some intranet solutions are outside of the pure Web architecture.

Application Development Gotchas

Building the intranet itself is only one part of the implementation project; you also need to be concerned with building or migrating the applications that are going to run on it. Be aware that this part of the project is just as ripe for errors as the intranet building process and can doom the future of your intranet just as quickly as a lack of solid design or good management techniques.

Gotcha #21: Performance Hits

PROBLEM

Perceived performance problems that are beyond the control of the application developers.

EXAMPLE

An intranet development team built an application using the best technology and tools available, but the application performs very poorly at remote sites. Research indicates that a number of performance variables contribute to the problem. In addition to the Web server, database, and modem (which the developers *can* control), performance is adversely affected by the line speed, ISP, backbone, and client PCs and modems, which the developers did not originally factor into the equation.

SOLUTION

In designing your applications, assume worst-case scenarios and test your application performance accordingly. Do everything you can to get the best quality service and system configuration before agreeing to specific performance targets, or at least set those targets according to a known system configuration. That is, be sure to consider how the client PCs and modems are equipped (e.g., machines with 16MB RAM and 28.8 Kbps modems).

Gotcha #22: Distributed Development

PROBLEM

Applications developed by various departments and/or regions that don't perform well (and sometimes don't work at all) when used in different environments.

EXAMPLE

A large, federation-style company empowered its worldwide offices to build their own intranet applications, figuring that the TCP/IP protocol alone would give them the portability and interoperability they needed. But, different parts of the corporation built applications in different ways, and selected proprietary tools that worked only on certain platforms. When the various regions and departments attempted to share applications or exchange information, they encountered major incompatibilities that required a massive effort to redesign and rebuild the applications.

SOLUTION

Be sure to establish standards and guidelines for your intranet throughout your organization. Then, select a design that ensures portability and require that all entities within your organization use tools that are compatible with a variety of platforms. Review chapter 4 for more information on setting standards, then see chapters 5, 7, and 9 for details on intranet architecture, design options, and tool selection.

Gotcha #23: Reinventing the Wheel

PROBLEM

Creating new applications where existing software can adequately address the same needs.

EXAMPLE

An IT group decided to build its own groupware applications for discussion forums, newsgroups, and project tracking. Although they produced good, solid programs, the programs are proprietary and require maintenance and upgrades that cannot be purchased from a vendor.

SOLUTION

Thoroughly research your options. If products are available to meet your needs—and your budget—it's usually better to buy than create in-house. Let someone else work out the bugs for you and focus your development efforts on applications that can't be bought off the shelf. This is particularly true in the intranet environment, where there's lots of really good software available for remarkably low prices.

Gotcha #24: The Bleeding Edge

PROBLEM

Using unproven technology to support mission-critical applications.

EXAMPLE

A group of IT developers fell in love with virtual reality. Knowing that VRML could potentially provide excellent applications for the company, they chose a high-profile application and devoted the next several months to trying to work out the bugs and kinks—all at ever rising expense. By the time they finished the application, it was so complex that it could not be supported by anyone other than the original development staff. The development investment was so costly, however, that the company was compelled to keep the application and use it. When members of the development staff threatened to leave the company, management was forced to negotiate with them to retain their knowledge.

SOLUTION

Confine the "bleeding edge" development efforts to so-called skunk works projects—at least until the underlying technologies are proven successful and are widely accepted. In general, use proven technologies and products for your mission-critical intranet applications and be sure that they can be supported outside of the development team.

Gotcha #25: Client Machine Quality

PROBLEM

Perceived performance issues on various client machines.

EXAMPLE

Developers used Pentium-120 machines equipped with 24MB of RAM to develop a new application. Although they checked remote access and screen size compatibility frequently during the development effort, when the application was deployed, they found that many users with old machines (e.g., 486/50 with 8MB or 16MB of RAM) go out of their way to avoid using it. Because the company accounting methods call for equipment depreciation of three years, a large portion of the users will have to put up with the poor performance for at least another year.

SOLUTION

A fast client machine can improve perceived system performance dramatically. Try to ensure that your intranet user community is equipped with high-quality machines so that the value of the intranet is not masked by poor machine performance. If you cannot ensure the quality of the client machines, keep your designs *very* light.

Gotcha #26: CGI Scripting versus API Calls

PROBLEM

CGI scripting is often slower than API calls.

EXAMPLE

When connecting to a database application, a company had to choose whether to use CGI scripting or API calls. Because most of the Web developers were comfortable with using the "open" CGI standard and had experience scripting in PERL, they chose that route. It wasn't until the application was tested by remote users that performance problems became apparent. The application couldn't pass the predefined response requirements.

SOLUTION

API calls are up to three times faster than invoking CGI scripts. Be sure to keep this in mind when application performance is critical (i.e., when they will be accessed from remote sites).

Gotcha #26a: Mistaking Ease of Use for Ease of Development

PROBLEM

Ease of use is usually inversely proportional to ease of development—but this rule isn't always apparent in a development environment.

EXAMPLE

A company vastly underestimated the time required to develop an application for a very large intranet with a large, varied user base. Because the application itself was relatively simple, the developers failed to plan appropriately to accommodate the large number of users with varying levels of interface requirements. Major delays were incurred in developing the multiple levels of abstraction required to maintain a consistent user presentation layer.

SOLUTION

It is very easy to confuse ease of use with ease of development. In reality, the reverse is usually true. Any application development project requires significant planning—even simple applications destined for a web environment. Planning for an intranet application may, however, differ from traditional project planning methodologies and employ some more pragmatic approaches for eliciting user requirements and testing application performance. Be sure to review the steps that we discussed in chapters 3 and 4 to understand the differences in planning and developing for a Web environment.

Gotcha #26b: The Merging of Content and Programming

PROBLEM

The boundary between content development and programming blurs in a Web development environment.

EXAMPLE

Web development often calls for a rare blend of logical and intuitive skills to bridge the traditional gap between content development and programming. An intranet project for a very design-sensitive site floundered badly when the programmers missed some of the fine design points that the client was extremely sensitive to.

SOLUTION

Try to involve designers at all stages of an intranet project or, as an alternative, be sure that your designers review all proposed screens very early in the implementation project (i.e., when you can still make changes without incurring major delays or expenses). Review some of the hints in Chapters 7 and 8 to fully understand all of the steps involved in designing and developing an intranet and encourage your programmers to read chapter 10 to gain a better understanding of design principles. Finally, if you happen to have any of those rare and valuable animals—programmers with a good sense of design—hold onto them at all costs!

DETERMINING CHANGE MAGNITUDE

The change magnitude tool described in this Appendix is intended to guide your selection of change management techniques by measuring the overall risk of a specific project. In other words, this tool can help you match the techniques to the risk and urgency of an impending project.

Change management techniques are a type of risk management applied to the "people" issues generally associated with major initiatives. Most IT projects aim to increase productivity and, often, quality. Intranet projects are no different. Even with all of the positive attributes of collaboration that intranets yield, productivity and quality typically decline for a period of time upon implementation. And, following the change, they gradually increase until they exceed their original metrics.

Change management's primary value lies in its ability to reduce the decline and duration of this productivity "trough" and increase the gain at the project's completion. While many variables can be addressed, fundamentally the benefits are accomplished through techniques and "interventions" (i.e., the "fancy" technical word used to describe actions taken to support a change) that minimize resistance and maximize commitment to the project's goals. Some of the basic variables addressed by change management are:

◆ Is there a clear vision of where this project leads and is the current situation described accurately?

◆ Is there a compelling rationale for discontinuing the current way of doing things and for choosing this project as the best remedy to achieve the vision?

◆ Is there a communications structure and plan in place to keep people informed and to maintain their sense of control as they live through the transition?

◆ Will people see the goals of this project in alignment with or in opposition to their personal goals and current abilities/skills?

◆ Does management have the skills and knowledge to "sponsor" the project and drive it forward?

◆ Does the project team have the necessary skills, track record, and political credibility to earn the organization's confidence?

◆ Does the organization's culture and recent history support or conflict with the goals of the project?

How deeply you should pursue such issues depends on the overall magnitude of the change and the risk it represents for your organization. The following questions should help to determine the magnitude of risk:

1. Given current day-to-day operations, will the new behaviors that are required to implement the change represent a *major or minor disruption* of people's expectations with regard to the organization?

2. Given the organization's history of change success/failure and the skills required for the project, is there a *high or low probability* that this initiative will exceed its budget and/or time schedule?

3. Do you consider this project a business imperative or an effort in which some degree of failure is acceptable? If the project exceeds budget or timelines, will the *cost to the organization be low or high?* In determining cost, be sure to consider the effect of failure on the organization's competitive position as well as on your staff's confidence in management's ability to lead.

The following steps are intended to guide you through a detailed review of these basic issues in order to determine the overall magnitude of a specific initiative.

What Is Change?

When we feel in control, we tend to be comfortable and functional in our given role (e.g., home, work). Control is a sense of equilibrium with our environment— being able to anticipate what is likely to happen and feeling comfortable with our expectations.

At work, control is usually based on a host of expectations about the ways in which things are done, when they are done, why they are done, and what's important or unimportant, as well as who does what, and who to consult if or when necessary. These expectations also include a belief that the future is likely to be much the same as the present and the recent past. Our sense of control is reinforced when our perceptions match our expectations. Change, however, is just the opposite.

Change disrupts our expectations and leads to a loss of control. To some degree, we are likely to feel uncertain about some or all of the familiar items that normally reinforce our sense of control. We lose perspective about job security and career path, and worry fruitlessly about where our friends will be, what a new environment will be like, if we have the skills to "win," and if the changes might require relocation, different or longer hours, less time for personal avocations, or potentially have a negative effect on family.

Change-related disruption, then, is a function of disrupting expectations with ambiguity (i.e., lots of questions and not many answers) or with specifics that are unexpected (i.e., positive and negative surprises). *Disruption* is a neutral term that applies to changes perceived as negative or positive. It's important to note that disruption is not related to how much money is spent or how many people are affected. Thus, an expensive project affecting the entire company is not a major change if employees expect it; the magnitude of the change is purely a function of disruptive impact on expectations.

Step 1: How Disruptive Is the Change?

Prior to any announcement of the forthcoming change, consider the general expectations of the people who will be affected. Characterize the degree of disruption these people are likely to feel after the change is announced by circling a response below.

LOW				MEDIUM			HIGH		
1	2	3	4	5	6	7	8	9	10
Very minor disruption to what normally occurs.				Significant disruption to what people are used to, although some things will stay the same.			Practically everything will be different. People will have difficulty understanding it all.		

SCORING

Determine the level of disruption you expect:

> LOW (1–3)   MEDIUM (4–7)   HIGH (8–10)
>
> What is the overall level of disruption?   L — M — H

Step 2: What Is the Cost if the Organization Fails?

Consider whether this project is a business imperative or an effort where some failure is acceptable. If, for example, you are planning an intranet to replace the entire executive information system (EIS) that the company's senior management now depends on for management information, the cost of failure could be significant. Consider the cost to the organization and to its business position if such a change is not implemented well or if it significantly exceeds the project budget and/or timelines.

In this discussion, we're using the term *organization* to refer to the group affected by the change. Thus, organization may refer to the company as a whole, or to a division or department within the company. If the group is the IS department, rather than the company as a whole, then the business-position cost for the IS department refers to the loss of potential business and the loss of perceived value for the IS department in the eyes of the rest of the organization.

As you consider potential costs, it may help to reflect on the following list:

◆ The current/anticipated problem or opportunity is not solved or exploited

◆ Time, money, and people resources are wasted

◆ Competitors improve their relative market positions

◆ Morale suffers and job security is threatened

◆ Senior management loses credibility and strategic imperatives are ignored

Characterize the potential costs to the organization of significantly exceeding the project's budget or timelines for each of the listed items by circling your response in the following table. Note that the table categorizes costs as organizational and business.

| | *LOW* | | | *MEDIUM* | | | | *HIGH* | | |
	L	L	L	M	M	M	M	H	H	H
Organization costs										
1. Management credibility	1	2	3	4	5	6	7	8	9	10
2. Ability to lead	1	2	3	4	5	6	7	8	9	10
3. Ability to attract, develop, retain quality people	1	2	3	4	5	6	7	8	9	10
4. Morale/future optimism	1	2	3	4	5	6	7	8	9	10
Business costs										
5. Competitive position	1	2	3	4	5	6	7	8	9	10
6. Growth potential	1	2	3	4	5	6	7	8	9	10
7. Profit potential	1	2	3	4	5	6	7	8	9	10
8. Corporate image/brand equity	1	2	3	4	5	6	7	8	9	10

SCORING

Total your responses and use the following guide to determine if the overall cost of failure is Low, Medium, or High:

LOW (8–27)   MEDIUM (28–59)   HIGH (60–80)

Note that the eight individual factors that determine your overall cost category have equal weights in the table. In reality, this may not be the case. If the factors in your situation are not of equal weight, reconsider the overall cost of failure and make sure that you're comfortable with the overall assessment. If you're not, move the total higher or lower as appropriate.

What is your overall cost of failure?   L — M — H

Step 3: What Is the Probability that the Project Will Fail?

During organizational change, there are *three key roles* that influence the risk of failure:

♦ *Sponsors* legitimize the change and provide resources via their position, power, and authority.

♦ *Agents* develop and execute implementation plans to achieve the change approved by the sponsors.

♦ *Targets* make the change real by changing the way they work (i.e., they change their behavior).

One other factor is vitally important to a project's chances for success—the organization's *culture*. Culture, in this context, is the set of beliefs, behaviors, and assumptions that define what is done within an organization and why. Culture also guides expectations of how things should be.

Characterize your assessment of the following factors by circling your response:

1. What is the level of risk due to the primary sponsors' lack of demonstrated commitment to this project's success?

LOW				MEDIUM			HIGH		
1	2	3	4	5	6	7	8	9	10
Sponsors will be visible and not accept anything less than success				Moderate support and interest			Sponsors will delegate, work on other issues, and just expect things to be done		

2. What is the level of risk due to the change agents (i.e., project team members') lack of political credibility, track record, and demonstrated skills in handling a project of this type?

LOW				MEDIUM			HIGH		
1	2	3	4	5	6	7	8	9	10
Agents are known for their experience, skills, and disciplined approach				Agents have a mix of balancing strengths and weaknesses			Agents may be perceived as weak and not know how to deal with this situation		

3. What is the level of risk due to the opposition of this projects' goals with the targets' personal goals and current abilities/skills?

LOW				MEDIUM			HIGH		
1	2	3	4	5	6	7	8	9	10
Targets feel willing and able to do what is expected				Targets are likely to have mixed reactions to this project			Targets may have trouble seeing what's in it for them and will resist this project		

4. What is the level of risk due to conflict between this project's requirements and the organization's culture and recent history?

LOW				MEDIUM			HIGH		
1	2	3	4	5	6	7	8	9	10
Project goals are very consistent with the existing culture				Some aspects of the culture support while others oppose this project			This project requires many behaviors and beliefs that directly contradict the existing culture		

Scoring: Total your responses and use the following guide to determine the overall probability of failure:

LOW (4–13)   MEDIUM (14–29)   HIGH (30–40)

What is your overall probability of failure? L — M — H

Step 4: Score Consolidation and Change Classification

Use the following tables to consolidate your scores and determine where your organization falls in the overall risk category.

	Enter an L, M, or H (to represent low, medium, or high risk)				
Step 1: Change disruption					
Step 2: Cost					
Step 3: Probability					
Totals	Lows ( )		Mediums ( )		Highs ( )

Change Category	Score Composition	Analysis
Category 1	No Highs and at least 2 Lows	Minor change: Some change management services may be needed
Category 3	Only 1 High or 3 Mediums	Significant change: A moderate package of change management services are probably needed
Category 5	No Lows and at least 2 Highs	Major, turbulent change: A broad range of change management services are urgently needed

You may want to review your answers to each step in this assessment tool to be sure you are comfortable with them. Remember, this tool is designed to estimate the magnitude of an impending change on an organization; it should be considered preliminary to gathering data on a more detailed level. It should, however, help to indicate the overall scope of change and urgency for change management support on behalf of a specific project in the early stages when such services are most useful.

INTRANET PROJECT WORKPLAN

Throughout this book we've emphasized that internet computing differs from traditional IT systems. Like the technologies that have preceded it, internet computing requires not only technical aptitude, but also functional and managerial expertise to be successful. The same types of problems that plague mainframe and two-tier client/server projects can certainly be observed in internet computing, but internet computing introduces a challenging new element: The speed of development is so rapid that Inter/intranet problems appear even earlier in the project lifecycle. While it might require six to twelve months in traditional client/server to find and define issues and problems, these same issues and problems now appear within weeks or even overnight. This inherent speed makes project management even more demanding than in traditional architectures.

Obviously, this situation also brings opportunity and challenges. The IT manager must be able to act quickly, ensure that requirements are being met, and not slow down his or her developers' progress. "Explosive growth" is probably the best way to describe intranet development, and management must be able to rise to the occasion and make it "effective explosive growth."

Clearly, requirements are still crucial. So is a project plan that provides structure to what otherwise would be mayhem. Functional analysts are perhaps more important than before, and they often are more involved than ever in the development itself. And although the project manager often needs to take a step back from the developers so that they can get busy, he or she still needs to use the tricks and tools that work in any system development. These include workplans, scope documents, requirements documents, technical and functional documentation, progress reports, and issues identification and resolution—all used to appropriate degrees based on the size and complexity of the work.

BSG detailed the following workplan to develop and build a large, complex, widely distributed intranet system for trading utilities. Notice that the plan incorporates requirements definition and functional specification phases. The time estimates for these tasks have been purposely left out due to the great variability directly related to issues like the skill and experience of the team members.

Depending on your project team, you may also need to add additional time to the architectural framework phase and testing procedures. Again, the amount of time and effort required will directly relate to the experience and skill sets of your implementation team. Even the most brilliant developers need hands-on experience to predict and address the issues that invariably arise in the construction of a complex system.

If, like us, you have a distributed development team (ours included active development in NYC, Dallas, and Seattle), be sure to budget time for your managerial and technical expertise to coordinate these pieces. Telephones and multiuser dialog environments are helpful for everyday issues, but face-to-face contact is still necessary at times. Hopefully, the rapid evolution of video conferencing may make this easier in the very near future!

Task #	Task	X-check TOTAL	Team 1	Team 2	Team 3	Team 4	Deliverable	Start	Date
CS	**Intranet Project NAME**	0	0	0	0	0	0 Client/Server System		
PI	**Project Initiation**	0	0	0	0	0	0 Project Initiation Report		
PSU	Project Start Up	0	0	0	0	0	0 Project Organization, Schedule,		
10	Recruit Project Sponsor						Project Organization		
20	Recruit Project Initiation Stage Manager						Project Organization		
30	Review Related Project Studies						Project Reference Documents		
40	Prepare Project Initiation Stage Schedule						Schedule		
50	Review Project Start Up						Project Reference Documents, Review Checklist, Schedule,		
PSPM	Project Scope - PM	0	0	0	0	0	0 Project Scope		
FSB	Project Schedule and Budgeting	0	0	0	0	0	0 Project Budget, Schedule,		
10	Determine Project Approach						Project Template		
20	Re-estimate Effort						Effort Estimate		
30	Revise Project Schedule						Schedule		
40	Revise Project Budget						Project Budget		
50	Document Project Process Success Criteria						Success Criteria		
PO	Project Organization	0	0	0	0	0	0 Project Organization, Training Requirements,		
10	Define the Project Organization						Project Organization Chart		
20	Determine Training Requirements						Training Requirements (if any)		
PCP	Project Control Procedures	0	0	0	0	0	0 Project Control Procedures		
10	Establish Quality Standards						Quality Standards		
20	Establish Quality Control Procedure						Quality Control Procedure		
30	Establish Progress and Process Control Procedures						Process Control Procedures, Progress Control Procedure,		
40	Establish Tolerance Parameters						Tolerance Parameters		
50	Establish Change Control Procedures						Change Control Procedure		
60	Establish Issue Resolution Procedure						Issue Resolution Procedure		
BC	Determine Project Reporting	0	0	0	0	0	0 Business Case		
10	Confirm Project Costs						Cost/Benefit Analysis		
20	Quantify Benefits						Cost/Benefit Analysis		
30	Analyze Risk						Risk Analysis		
40	Define Critical Success Criteria						Business Success Criteria		
50	Document Business Case						Business Case		
SETUP	Setup Administrative Environment	0	0	0	0	0	0 Set up administrative facilities		
10	Facilities - Office Space, Telephones, Fax, Parking, Security Pass, etc.								
20	Network Access - Cabling, Logon Id's, e-mail Access								

Code	Task				Deliverable
30	Development Hardware - Software Loaded and configured, printers		o		
50	Necessary Software purchased				
60	Back up and recovery procedures established				
70	Invoicing requirements documented				
PISA	**Project Initiation Stage Assessment**	o	o	o	**0 Project Initiation Report**
10	Stage End QA	o	o	o	Project Initiation Report
BPD	**Business Process**				**0 Business Process Report**
BPI	**Business Process Investigation/Analysis**	o	o	o	**0**
10	Review Project Documents and Source Material	o	o	o	
20	Review Data Model				DFD Diagram
30	Review current requirements				Data Model Diagram, Entity Description,
40	Gather Project Org chart				Notes and screen prints
50	Define other entity relationships				Organization Chart
60	Identify Outstanding Policy Issues				Business Process Map, Cross References,
70	Conduct JAD session (DFD, E/R, Tech framework)				Problem/Requirement List
					Problem/Requirement List
80	Review Results of Business Requirements				Requirements Model
90	Review Results of Business Process Investigation				Business Process Model, Data Flow Model, Data Model, Checklist,
BPA	**Confirmation**	o	o	o	**0 Business Process Model**
10	Develop Prototype				Data Flow Model
20	Set agenda to meet with groups				Data Model
30	Meet with Groups				Contact external sources, if required
40	Revise Approach/deliverables				Rollout Schedule
SEA	**Stage End Assessment**	o	o	o	**0 Stage Report**
10	Revise Schedule for Next Stage				Schedule
20	Conduct QA				Project Board Decision
CST	**Technical Architecture Definition**	o	o	o	**0 Stage Report, Technical Architecture,**
TAM	**Technical Architecture Vision**	o	o	o	**0 Technical Architecture Model**
10	Confirm Critical Technical Requirements				Problem/Requirement List
20	Select Critical Components (Web Server, Database Server, Firewall, etc)				Technical Architecture Cornerstone
30	Define Security Model				Integrate discretionary security
40	Review availability, survivability, recoverability requirements.				Technical Architecture Model
50	Define Standard Architecture Mapping				Partitioning Map
55	Define Systems Management Services				Systems Management Requirements
60	Define Backup strategy				Concurrency and Notification Scheme
70	Analyze Technical Risk				Risk Analysis
80	Review Results of Technical Architecture Modeling				Review Checklist, Technical Architecture Model,
DTE	**Development and Test Environment**	o	o	o	**0 Development Environment, Testing**

ID	Task					Deliverable
						Environment,
10	Establish Development Procedures					Development Procedures
30	Establish Test Strategy					Test Strategy
40	Establish Test Control Procedures					Test Control Procedures
50	Allocate Hardware and Software Resources					Hardware and Software Resources
60	Establish Internet Workspace					Development Environment, Testing Environment,
GUI	**HTML/Interface Standards**	0	0	0	0	0 **Application Style Guide**
10	Define End Users and Usability Requirements					User Definition
TAP	**Technical Architecture/ Hardware**	0	0	0	0	0 **Evaluation Report, Technical Architecture, Tech Architecture Model,**
0	Order Hardware/Software/Certificates					Bill of Material
10	Issue Access Certificates					Server installed
20	Pre-configure Firewall					Software Installed
30	Program ACS for development environment					Routers Installed
40	Install and Configure Database					
50	Establish version control system					
60	Install Firewall Software					Firewall
70	Establish interfaces to backend data					Firewall
80	Establish directory and Files structure					Pilot Application
90	Load SQL on secure server					Evaluation Report
100	Establish secure access path to SQL DB on Server					Technical Architecture, Technical Architecture Model,
110	Establish secure access path to SQL DB on remote					Review Checklist, Technical Architecture, Technical Architecture Model,
120	Integrate certificate based I & A to SQL calls					
130	Establish CGI architecture					
SEA	**Stage End Assessment**	0	0	0	0	0 **Stage Report**
10	Technical Stage QA					Schedule
CSE	**Application Engineering**	0	0	0	0	0 **Client/Server System**
APP	**Application Partitioning and Optimization**	0	0	0	0	0 **Physical Application Design**
10	Ensure Data/Transaction Consistency					Transaction/Entity Matrix
20	Finalize Data Model in Ervin					Data Model
30	Collect Volumetrics					Entity Description, Relationship Description, Transaction Specification,
40	Finalize Non Functional Requirements					Problem/Requirement List, Requirements Model,
41	* ownership of data					
42	* access to data from different locations					
43	* audit and control					
44	* security and recovery.					
50	Partition Design					Partitioning Map, Physical Application Design,

405

Code	Task						Deliverable
60	Design Physical Database	o	o	o	o	o	Physical Application Design
CLB	**Client Build**						0
10	Prototype Client						Prototype
15	Build Client HTML & CGI						Finish development
30	Create Client Unit Test Scripts						Test Script
40	Unit Test Client Components						Test Result
50	Review Results of Client Build						Review Checklist
SVB	**Server Build**	o	o	o	o	o	0
10	Build Database						Physical Database
20	Populate Database						Test Data
25	Develop Stored Procedures and Triggers						Stored Procedures
27	Create Common interface file						?
30	Build Database to Web Server Links						
40	Create Server Unit Test Scripts						Test Script
50	Other System Components						Test Result
60	Review Results of Server Build						Review Checklist
TD	**Test Planning**	o	o	o	o	o	0 Test Design, Test Plan,
10	Create Test Plan						Test Plan
20	Establish Test Environment						Testing Environment
30	Create Integration and System Test Scripts						Manual Test Script
40	Define Test Packages						Manual Test Package
50	Review Results of Testing Design						Review Checklist, Test Design, Test Plan,
IST	**Integration and System Testing**	o	o	o	o	o	0 System Build
10	Assemble the Application Build						System Build
20	Perform Integration and System Testing						Test Result
30	Review Results of Integration and System Testing						Review Checklist
SEA	Stage End Assessment	o	o	o	o	o	0 Stage Report
10	QA for Application Engineering						Schedule
CSD	**Distributed Deployment**	o	o	o	o	o	**0 Client/Server System**
ED	Education Development	o	o	o	o	o	0 Training Class, Training Materials, User Procedures,
10	Create Application User Guide						User Guide, User Procedures,
	Conduct Early-release Training Seminars						Training Session
	Create Administrators Guide						System Administrators Guide
20	Identify the Training Program Required						Training Requirements
30	Develop Training Materials						Training Class, Training Materials,
40							Process Quality Inspection Checklist[<Optional>,MS Wo
50	Review Results of Education Development						Review Checklist, System Administrators Guide, Trainin
							User Guide,
AT	**Acceptance Testing**	o	o	o	o	o	0 System Build, Test Result,
5	Create User Accounts						
10	Create Acceptance Test Scripts						Test Script
20	Pilot User Training and Procedures						Training Class, Training Class Assessment, Training Ma
							User Guide, User Procedures,

Code	Activity							Deliverable
30	Perform Acceptance Tests							Test Result
40	Correct System							Change Request, Review Checklist, System Build, Test Result,
50	Review Results of Acceptance Testing							
60	Complete Process Review							Process Quality Inspection Checklist[<Mandatory>,MS Word 6.0]
DP	Deployment Preparation	0	0	0	0	0	0	0 Management Procedures, Support Environment, Tech Environment, Working Environment,
10	Create Deployment Plan							Project Plan
20	Determine Systems Management Strategy							Management Procedures
30	Develop Job Scheduling Processes							Job Control Procedures
40	Establish Technical Environment							Technical Environment
50	Establish Working Environment							Working Environment
60	Establish Support Environment							Support Environment
70	Create Production Test Scripts							Test Script
80	Conduct Deployment Briefings							Briefing
90	Provide Developer Assistance							Training Class Assessment
SYSM	Systems Management	0	0	0	0	0	0	0 System Management Activities
SM	*Systems Management*	0	0	0	0	0	0	0
10	Develop Job Descriptions							
20	Confirm Service Levels							
30	Create Communications Plan							
40	Assist in Systems Testing and Rollout							
50	Finish Support Plan							
PM	Project Management	0	0	0	0	0	0	0 Project Plan
PM	Project Management	0	0	0	0	0	0	0
10	Quality Control							QA Plan
20	Progress Control							Status Reports and Time Reporting
30	Change Control							Change Control Process
40	Issues Management							Issue Resolution Process
50	Exception Situation							How to address Exceptions

APPENDIX C

INTERNET SERVICE PROVIDERS

Internet Service Providers (ISPs) provide connectivity between corporations (and individuals) and an Internet or intranet (in the case of virtual private Internets) node. ISP organizations range in size from small, local providers with one or two people operating out of a basement, to major multinational corporations.

The following list of ISPs focuses primarily on the large nationwide companies. To some extent, this is because many of the small, regional service providers are being acquired by the larger companies, or are being forced out of the market by the larger companies—many of which are offering low prices to gain market share. Costs and services vary considerably among the ISPs, often without the usual negative correlation. But, be sure to check the ISPs' reputation for service and dependability with your colleagues and associates. Also, you may want to check some of the Web sites that publish customer feedback information. Keep in mind, however, that some of the information on these sites is published by competitors, rather than actual customers and there is no way of knowing which is which. In any case, try to avoid long-term contracts because the prices are generally declining.

Name	Area	email	Phone#	Url	Services	Fees
ADP AUTONET	ALL-USA	avasher@autonet.net	(+1) (313) 995-6595 Customer Service (+1) (800) 829-2206	http://www.autonet.net/	Dedicated services up to T1 in 56K increments; DNS Service, Private Internet Services, Intranets; Nationwide Dial Services up to 14.4Kbps; WEB Hosting, Development, Facility Management	Call for pricing information
American Information Network	ALL-USA ALL-CANADA	all-info@ai.net	(+1) (800) 779-6938 (+1) (410) 715-6809	http://www.ai.net/	High-Bandwidth WWW/FTP Serving, Virtual Domain Service (T3/E3/DS3/OC3), Internet Connectivity, Internet Backbone Access, Realtime Internet Commerce, Credit Card Clearing, Secure Web Serving, Adult Site Service, Leased Lines, Dedicated Connections (ISDN, T1, PRI, BRI, SMDS), Frame Relay, Security Consulting, Equipment Sales	Contact for price quotes and latest promotions
ANS	ALL-USA	info@ans.net	(+1) (800) 456-8267 (+1) (703) 758-7700 (+1) (313) 677-7300 (+1) (914) 789-5300	http://www.ans.net/	ANS-56K -- Dedicated 56K circuit; ANS-T1 -- Dedicated 1.544 Kbps circuit; ANS-MegaT -- Dedicated 10 Mbps circuit; ANS-T3 -- Dedicated 45 Mbps circuit; ANS-VPDN -- Virtual Private Data Network; ANS-Interlock -- application layer firewall; ANS-InterServ -- turn-key Internet server solution; ANS-Resolve -- DNS (domain name system) service; Enterprise Dial -- 50,000+ V.34 modems nationwide; Web Hosting, Intranet solutions, & more...	Call for pricing information
AT&T	ALL-USA	dcs@attmail.com	(800) 248-2632	http://www.att.com/net/	Data Communication - Interspan Access Service, Frame Relay Service, ATM Service, On-Line Business Global Switched Digital Services	Call for pricing information
BBN Planet Corporation	ALL-USA	net-info@bbnplanet.com	(800) 472-4565	http://www.bbnplanet.com/	19.2 Kbps, 56Kbps, 128Kbps, 256Kbps, 384Kbps 768Kbps, T1 (1.54 Mbps), 10 Mbps, T3 (45 Mbps)	Call for pricing information
CERFnet	ALL-USA	info@cerf.net	(800) 876-CERF	http://www.cerf.net/	Frame Relay, Dedicated Systems, 24-hour customer support, Web Hosting. Lines up to T3 speeds.	112Kbps $500 Install, $600 monthly (including equipment) CERF 128 $3000 Install,

Company	Area	Email	Phone	URL	Services	Pricing
Delphi Internet Services Corp.	ALL-USA, ALL-CANADA	service@delphi.com	(+1) (800) 695-4005	http://www.delphi.com/	Dialup accounts. Online News, Sports, & Weather. Business and Financial Information; Downloadable software; multi-player games; Special interest groups. Full Internet access: FTP, Telnet, IRC, Lynx web browser. Personal home pages; corporate Website hosting.	$1600 monthly (including equipment and circuit) CERF T1 $3000 install, $2600 monthly (including equipment and circuit) Dial-up: $10/mo for 4 hrs then $4/hr $20/mo for 20 hrs then $1.80/hr
DIGEX	Call for Areas	sales@digex.net	(800) 99DIGEX	http://www.digex.net/	Leased Line up to T3; Frame Relay; Switched Multimegabit data service; Fiber Optic Network; Internet Management Service; Server Services; Hosting; International ISP Services; Security Solutions; Personal Connections; Education Services; Total System Solution	Call for pricing information
Diamond.Net	ALL-USA, +33, +49, +52, 314, 202, 703, 410, 214, 312, 816, 713, 404	info@dmnd.net	(+1) (314) 727-5596	http://www.dmnd.net/	OC3 (DS1, DS3); FTP/WEB hosting services available (Firewall Protection, Real time audio and video) Data vaulting Intranet	Burstable DS1 sustained usage: up to 128K - $1200 129K to 256K - $1700 257K to 512K - $2400 513k to 1.5M - $2800 Burstable DS3 sustained usage: 0M to 6M - $10,000 6.01M to 7.5M - $12,000 7.51M to 10.5M - $16,000 10.51M to 12M - $19,000 12.01M to 13.5M - $22,000 13.51M to 15M - $25,000 15.01M to 18M - $32,000 18.01M to 21M - $42,000 21.01M to 45M - $47,000
Global Enterprise Services, Inc.	ALL-USA, 800	market@jvnc.net	(800) 358-4437 x7325 (609) 897-7325	http://www.jvnc.net/	Shell, SLIP, PPP, ISDN, 56K, 128K, 256K, 512K, T1+	SLIP: $35/mo for 20 hrs, $2.50/hr extra, $29/setup; ISDN: $36/mo; Global 56K: $9500/year, $3000/setup; Standard 56K: $4300/year, $1000/setup; Global T1: $28,500/year, $5,000/setup; Standard T1: $22,000/year,

411

Provider	Coverage Areas	Email	Phone	Website	Services	Pricing
IBM Global Network	ALL-USA, ALL-CANADA, +27, +31, +32, +33, +34, +39, +41, +43, +44, +45, +46, +47, +49, +61, +64, +81, +90, +353 +357, +358, +599, +972	globalnetwork@info.ibm.com		http://www.ibm.com/global network/ http://www.ibm.com/global network/who.htm/ (Web info)	Dial access (575 access points), leased line access to T3, data security arrangements, LAN-to-Internet connectivity, content management, Web hosting.	$2500/setup Call for pricing information
IDT	Most-USA (44 states)	connect@ios.com	(201) 928-1000 (800) 245-8000	http://www.idt.net/	Dial Up Service Direct Connection Web Site Development	Call for pricing information
James River Group Inc	ALL-USA	internet@jriver.com	(+1) (612) 3392521	http://www.jriver.com/	Modem, ISDN, Frame Relay (28K to T1) access for business networks; Complete solution (e.g., pre-configured router and options including Web home page, POP Server email gateway, FTP Server, and ICE Block firewall).	Starting at $195 per month for full time 28K for unlimited PCs on a single network.
MCI (networkMCI)	ALL-USA	info@mci.com	(800) 955-5210	http://www.mci.com/	Direct Connect Access, HyperStream Frame Relay Access. Full range of internet services/dedicated lines.	Call for pricing information
Netcom	ALL-USA	businessinfo@netcom.com	(800) NETCOM1	http://www.netcom.com/	Online Business; up to T1 access; Domain Registration, Name Service, 24-hour customer support, news server service, web page service	Call for pricing information
OEM.NET	ALL-USA	info@oem.net	(+1) (617) 7406200	http://www.oem.net/	56K, 384K, T1, and T3 leased line access nationwide; Dial up and dedicated ISDN access in select areas	56K - $150/month, $500 setup (newsfeed additional); 384K - $600/month, $500 setup (newsfeed additional); T1 - $1000/month, $1000 setup (newsfeed additional); 10M - T3 - call for pricing; Dial-up 128K ISDN - $100/month; Dedicated ISDN - $300/month, $500 setup
PSI (Performance Systems International)	ALL-USA	info@psi.com	(800) 82PSI82	http://www.psi.com/	Individual: Interramp, Pipeline USA, UUPSI, BBS UUCP; Sun ResellerCorporate: LAN Dial, LAN-ISDN, InterFrame, InterMAN, PSI Cable, PSINET Services: Affinity Programs (for non-profit organizations), PSIWeb and Secure Connect	Varies according to service, call for details
Sprint	ALL USA	info@sprint.com	(800) 910-2418	http://www.sprintbiz.com/	Dedicated Access, Private Networks, X-25 packet switching, ATM, 24-hour customer support, Global Dial-Up Access, Frame Relay, Custom Linking	Call for pricing information.
UUNET Technologies, Inc.	Call for areas ALL-USA	info@uu.net	US - (+1) (800) 488-6384 or (+1) (703)	http://www.uu.net/	Dedicated Access - 56K through T3; Dial Access - Analog and ISDN;	Call for pricing information

412

Company	Area Codes	Phone	Email	URL	Services	Pricing
WebSpinners, Inc.	202, 215, 301, 302, 410, 540, 609, 610, 703, 717 ALL-USA	206-5600 Canada - (+1) (800) 463-8123 UK - (+44) (1223) 250-100 Germany - (+49) (231) 972-00 (+1) (410) 347-0800 (+1) (800) 909-SPIN	Sales@WebSpinnersInc.com	http://www.WebSpinnersInc.com/	Security Products and Services; Web and FTP Hosting Services; Consulting; Training; News; UUCP ISDN, 56K, fractional to full T1, T3. Complete Internet solutions for businesses include. design, host, & maintenance services. Billboards to secured commerce pages. Domain name registration. Hardware and software solutions for Internet servers, networks and small businesses	Call for pricing information
Zocalo Engineering	ALL-USA	(510) 540-8000	woody@zocalo.net	http://www.zocalo.net/	56K, 128K, 384K, T1, Frame-Relay, AppleTalk Routing	Call for pricing information

REQUEST FOR COMMENT (RFC) LISTINGS

The request for comment (RFC) procedure is a means of introducing standards to the Internet community. Members of the Internet community use this procedure as a forum for introducing new concepts, proposing new standards, or commenting on the adoption of standards. As such, RFCs cover both proposed Inter/intranet standards and established standards.

You can obtain full-text versions of all RFCs from a variety of sources. Selected ones are in PostScript and hypertext (HTML). Refer to the latest edition of the "Internet Architecture Board (IAB) Official Protocol Standards" RFC for current information on the state and status of standard Internet protocols.

The following URL lists all RFCs in reverse numerical order:

◆ http://nic.ddn.mil\LIBRARY/rfcind1.html

You may also want to try these additional URLs for selected RFCs:

◆ ftp://ftp.internic.net/rfc
◆ http://ds.internic.net/ds/dspg/intdoc.html
◆ http://www.es.net/hypertext/rfcs.html

RFC Summaries

The following paragraphs summarize the RFCs that we've specifically referenced in *Building the Corporate Intranet*. There are, of course, many other RFCs that apply to intra/internet computing. We recommend that you use one of the aforementioned URLs to review the full-text versions of these RFCs or others that may be of interest to you.

RFC1034.TXT
Domain Names—Concepts and Facilities

This RFC is an introduction to the domain name system (DNS). It omits many details that can be found in RFC-1035.

The domain system defines procedures for accessing the data and for referrals to other name servers. The domain system also defines procedures for caching retrieved data and for periodic refreshing of data defined by the system administrator.

Specifically, the domain system provides:

◆ Standard formats for resource data

◆ Standard methods for querying the database

◆ Standard methods for name servers to refresh local data from foreign name servers

RFC1035.TXT
Domain Names—Implementation and Specification

This RFC describes the details of the domain system and protocol. It assumes that the reader is familiar with the concepts discussed in RFC-1034.

The domain system is a mixture of functions and data types, including those that are official protocol and functions, and those that are still experimental. Since the domain system is intentionally extensible, new data types and experimental behavior should always be expected in parts of the system beyond the official protocol. The official protocol parts include standard queries, responses, and the Internet class RR data formats (e.g., host addresses).

RFC1055.TXT
A Nonstandard for Transmission of IP Datagrams
over Serial Lines: SLIP

The TCP/IP protocol family runs over a variety of network media: IEEE 802.3 (Ethernet) and 802.5 (token ring) LANs, X.25 lines, satellite links, and serial lines. There are standard encapsulations for IP packets defined for many of these networks, but there is no standard for serial lines. SLIP, Serial Line IP, is currently a de facto standard, commonly used for point-to-point serial connections running TCP/IP. It is not an Internet standard.

SLIP has its origins in the 3COM UNET TCP/IP implementation from the early 1980s. It is merely a packet-framing protocol: SLIP defines a sequence of characters that frame IP packets on a serial line. It provides no addressing, packet-type identification, error detection/correction, or compression mechanisms. It is, however, usually very easy to implement and is commonly used on dedicated serial links (and occasionally for dial-up) with line speeds between 1200 bps and 19.2Kbps.

RFC1081.TXT
Post Office Protocol, Version 3

This RFC suggests a simple method for workstations to dynamically access mail from a mailbox server and specifies a proposed protocol for the Internet community. It is based on RFC-918 (since revised as RFC-937).

The post office protocol, Version 3 (POP3) is intended to permit a workstation to dynamically access a maildrop on a server host in a useful fashion. Usually, this means that the POP3 is used to allow a workstation to retrieve mail that the server is holding for it. All messages transmitted during a POP3 session are assumed to conform to the standard for the format of Internet text messages (RFC-822).

RFC1082.TXT
Post Office Protocol, Version 3—Extended Service Offerings

This RFC suggests a simple method for workstations to dynamically access mail from a discussion group server, as an extension to RFC-1081 which deals with dynamically accessing mail from a mailbox server using the post office protocol, version 3 (POP3). This RFC describes extensions to the POP3, which enhance the service it offers to clients. This additional service permits a client host to access discussion group mail, which is often kept in a separate spool area, using the general POP3 facilities.

RFC1134.TXT
The Point-to-Point Protocol: A Proposal for Multiprotocol Transmission of Datagrams over Point-to-Point Links

This RFC defines the encapsulation scheme, the basic LCP, and an NCP for establishing and configuring the Internet protocol (IP; referred to as the IP control protocol, IPCP).

The point-to-point protocol (PPP) provides a method for transmitting datagrams over serial point-to-point links. PPP is composed of three parts:

1. A method for encapsulating datagrams over serial links.
2. An extensible link control protocol (LCP).
3. A family of network control protocols (NCP) for establishing and configuring different network-layer protocols.

RFC1157.TXT
A Simple Network Management Protocol (SNMP)

This RFC is a re-release of RFC-1098. It defines a simple protocol by which management information for a network element can be inspected or altered by logically remote users. Together with its companion memos that describe the structure of management information and the management information base, these documents provide a simple, workable architecture and system for managing TCP/IP–based internets and in particular the Internet.

The Internet Activities Board recommends that all IP and TCP implementations be network manageable. This implies implementation of the Internet MIB (RFC-1156) and at least one of the two recommended management protocols SNMP (RFC-1157) or CMOT (RFC-1095).

It should be noted that, at this time, SNMP is a full Internet standard and CMOT is a draft standard. Reference the Host and Gateway Requirements RFCs for more specific information on the applicability of this standard.

RFC1497.TXT
BOOTP Vendor Information Extensions

This memo is a status report on the vendor information extensions used in the bootstrap protocol (BOOTP). It represents a slight revision and extension of RFC-1048. This edition introduces Tag 18 for Extension Path.

The basic bootstrap protocol (RFC-951) dealt with the issue of assigning an Internet address to a client, as well as a few other resources. The protocol included provisions for vendor-defined resource information. This memo defines a (potentially) vendor-independent interpretation of this resource information.

RFC1521.TXT
MIME (Multipurpose Internet Mail Extensions) Part One: Mechanisms for Specifying and Describing the Format of Internet Message Bodies

This RFC is a revision of RFC-1341. It specifies an Internet standards track protocol for the Internet community.

STD 11, RFC-822 defines a message representation protocol which specifies considerable detail about message headers, but which leaves the message content, or message body, as flat ASCII text. This document redefines the format of message bodies to allow multipart textual and nontextual message bodies to be represented and exchanged without loss of information. This is based on earlier work documented in RFC-934 and STD 11, RFC-1049, but extends and revises that work.

In particular, this document is designed to provide facilities to include multiple objects in a single message, to represent body text in character sets other than US-ASCII, to represent formatted multifont text messages, to represent nontextual material such as images and audio fragments, and generally to facilitate later extensions defining new types of Internet mail for use by cooperating mail agents.

This document does *not* extend Internet mail header fields to permit anything other than US-ASCII text data. Such extensions are the subject of a companion document (RFC-1522).

RFC1522.TXT
MIME (Multipurpose Internet Mail Extensions) Part Two: Message Header Extensions for Non-ASCII Text

This RFC specifies an Internet standards track protocol for the Internet community. It describes an extension to the message format defined in RFC-1521 to allow the representation of character sets other than ASCII in RFC-822 (STD 11) message headers. The extensions described were designed to be highly compatible with existing Internet mail handling software, and to be easily implemented in mail readers that support RFC-1521.

RFC-1521 describes a mechanism for denoting textual body parts which are coded in various character sets, as well as methods for encoding such body parts as sequences of printable ASCII characters. This memo describes similar techniques to allow the encoding of non-ASCII text in various portions of a RFC-822 message header, in a manner that is unlikely to confuse existing message handling software.

RFC1532.TXT
Clarifications and Extensions for the Bootstrap Protocol

This RFC specifies an Internet standards track protocol for the Internet community and expends some aspects of the BOOTP protocol that were rather loosely defined in the original specification.

The bootstrap protocol (BOOTP) is a UDP/IP–based protocol that allows a booting host to configure itself dynamically and without user supervision. BOOTP provides a means to notify a host of its assigned IP address, the IP address of a boot server host, and the name of a file to be loaded into memory and executed.

The original BOOTP specification left some issues of the protocol open to question. It did not, for example, clearly specify the exact behavior of BOOTP relay agents (formerly called "BOOTP forwarding agents"). Also, some parts of the overall protocol specification conflict, and other parts are subject to misinterpretation. Further, the IEEE 802.5 Token Ring Network, which was developed since the introduction of BOOTP, presents a unique problem for BOOTP's message-transfer paradigm.

RFC1533.TXT
DHCP Options and BOOTP Vendor Extensions

This RFC specifies an Internet standards track protocol for the Internet community. The dynamic host configuration protocol (DHCP) provides a framework for passing configuration information to hosts on a TCP/IP network. Configuration parameters and other control information are carried in tagged data items that are stored in the "options" field of the DHCP message. The data items themselves are also called "options."

This document, which specifies the current set of DHCP options, will be updated as new options are defined. Each superseding document will include the entire current list of valid options.

All of the vendor information extensions defined in RFC 1497 can be used as DHCP options. The definitions given in RFC-1497 are included in this document, which supersedes RFC-1497.

RFC1534.TXT
Interoperation between DHCP and BOOTP

This RFC specifies an Internet standards track protocol for the Internet community. DHCP provides a superset of the functions provided by BOOTP. This document describes the interactions between DHCP and BOOTP network participants.

DHCP provides a mechanism for transmitting configuration parameters to hosts using the TCP/IP protocol suite. The format of DHCP messages is based on the format of BOOTP messages, so that, in certain circumstances, DHCP and BOOTP participants may exchange messages. This document specifies the ways in which DHCP and BOOTP participants may interoperate.

RFC1541.TXT
Dynamic Host Configuration Protocol

This RFC specifies an Internet standards track protocol for the Internet community. DHCP provides a framework for passing configuration information to hosts on a TCP/IP network. DHCP is based on the bootstrap protocol (BOOTP), adding the capability of automatic allocation of reusable network addresses and additional configuration options.

RFC1780.TXT
Internet Official Protocol Standards

This memo describes the state of standardization of protocols used in the Internet as determined by the Internet Architecture Board (IAB). This memo is an Internet standard.

The Internet Architecture Board maintains this list of documents that define standards for the Internet protocol suite. (See RFC-1601 for the charter of the IAB and RFC-1160 for an explanation of the role and organization of the IAB and its subsidiary groups—the Internet Engineering Task Force (IETF) and the Internet Research Task Force (IRTF). Each of these groups has a steering group: the IESG and IRSG, respectively.)

The IETF develops standards with the goal of coordinating the evolution of the Internet protocols. (Refer to RFC-1602 for a definitive description of the Internet standards process.)

The majority of Internet protocol development and standardization activity takes place in the working groups of the IETF. Protocols that are to become standards in the Internet go through a series of states or maturity levels (proposed standard, draft standard, and standard) involving increasing amounts of scrutiny and testing. When a protocol completes this process it is assigned a STD number (reference RFC-1311).

To allow time for the Internet community to consider and react to standardization proposals, there is a minimum delay of 6 months before a proposed standard can be advanced to a draft standard, and a 4-month delay before a draft standard can be promoted to standard.

RFC821.TXT
Simple Mail Transfer Protocol

The objective of simple mail transfer protocol (SMTP) is to transfer mail reliably and efficiently. SMTP is independent of the particular transmission subsystem and requires only a reliable ordered data stream channel. A particularly important feature of SMTP is its capability to relay mail across transport service environments.

RFC951.TXT
Bootstrap Protocol (BOOTP)

This RFC suggests a proposed protocol for the ARPA-Internet community. It describes an IP/UDP bootstrap protocol (BOOTP) that allows a diskless client machine to discover its own IP address, the address of a server host, and the name of a file to be loaded into memory and executed.

The bootstrap operation can be thought of as consisting of two phases. This RFC describes the first phase, which can be considered "address determination and bootfile selection." After this address and filename information is obtained, control passes to the second phase of the bootstrap where a file transfer occurs.

RFC977.TXT
Network News Transfer Protocol:
A Proposed Standard for the Stream-Based Transmission of News

NNTP specifies a protocol for the distribution, inquiry, retrieval, and posting of news articles using a reliable stream-based transmission of news among the ARPA-Internet community. NNTP is designed so that news articles are stored in a central database allowing a subscriber to select only those items he wishes to read. Indexing, cross-referencing, and expiration of aged messages are also provided.

GLOSSARY

ACS. Asynchronous communications server. A series of dial-up modems for use on a network. Also referred to as a terminal server.

ActiveX. Microsoft's answer to Java. Allows distributed objects over the Internet.

alpha version. An early test version of a software package. May still have programming errors or "bugs."

Alta Vista. Well known search engine with the largest number of URLs. Maintained by Digital Equipment.

anchor. Synonym for hyperlink.

anonymous FTP. FTP (file transfer protocol). A standard set of tools for downloading files across the Internet. Anonymous FTP refers to the technique of providing downloads to users who do not have accounts on a given system.

applet. A small application that performs a specific task, such as the Cardfile and Calculator in Microsoft Windows.

archie. An archiving tool that helps find specific files on the Internet.

ARPANet. A predecessor of the Internet. Started in 1969 with funds from the Defense Department's Advanced Projects Research Agency (DARPA).

authoring tools. Software application that enables programmers to integrate multimedia components into interactive applications.

backbone. Internet connection/transfer mainlines at speeds over 45 Mbps. NFS-Net, which was a government-funded link between supercomputers, was the primary Internet backbone for many years (it has now been commercialized).

bandwidth. Transmission capacity of Internet lines. Amount of data "traffic." Historically, bandwidth restricted the Internet's ability to deliver all the information requested. With fiber-optic cables, however, the bandwidth is essentially limitless.

beta version. Newly released version of software package, fairly well tested and debugged, though not entirely complete.

bookmark. In a Web browser, such as Microsoft Netscape, a bookmark is a way to save the current link, so that you won't have to type in the complete address the next time you want to visit the same site.

bounce. Used to describe what happens to E-mail when it is sent to an incorrect address, formatted incorrectly, or if the recipient no longer has an account on his server. The "bounced" message will generally be sent to you, complete, with some header information that can help determine what went wrong.

bridge. Something that connects two networks so that they appear to be a single larger network.

browser. Software that enables users to "browse" through the World Wide Web. Netscape Navigator and Microsoft's Internet Explorer are the most well known browsers.

brownout. A system overload in which the network is reduced to crawling, nearly unusable speeds.

bps. Bits per second. Data transfer speeds. Also Tbps, Gbps, Mbps (Trillion (T-), Million (G-) and Thousand (M-) bits per second respectively). Ethernet connection is either @56K or 1 Mbps. A backbone is 45 Mbps.

cache. Stores information where it can be accessed quickly. A Web browser, such as Netscape Navigator, stores pages, sounds, URLs, images in caches where they can be easily retrieved. As the user "backs" through the links, the pages are retrieved quickly, saving the time of a reload.

certificate. A digitally signed, encrypted document that is exchanged during an SSL encryption session. The certificate contains information about the client or server, including the public key. The certificate itself is digitally signed by the certificate authority (CA). Certificates follow a standard format, known as X.509.

certificate authority. A mutually trusted server that contains certificates. These certificates which, based on the cryptographic tools used, cannot be forged, are passed on to clients and servers to provide authentication and encryption mechanisms.

CGI. Common gateway interface. A customizable vehicle to receive queries from the WWW, submit them to "back-end programs" such as mailers, search engines, or databases, then return HTML documents that can be displayed by the browser.

client/server. An architecture in which the client (personal computer or workstation) is the requesting machine and the server is the supplying machine. Servers can be high-speed microcomputers, minicomputers or even mainframes. The client provides the user interface and may perform some or all of the application processing. A database server is a computer that maintains the databases and processes requests from the client to extract data from or update the database. An application server is a computer that provides additional business processing for the clients

daemon. A background process, generally in the UNIX operating system. Daemons are designed to work behind the scenes, performing routine tasks like moving E-mail to the proper directory.

DES. Data encryption standard. IBM developed DES under contract to the U.S. government in the mid-70s. Since then it has become the most widely used private key encryption algorithm.

dial-in. An Internet account that can connect a PC to the Internet. The account is accessed by having the PC software application dial in to an Internet Access or Service Provider (IAP or ISP). The software connects with the ISP and establishes a TCP/IP link to the Internet that enables software to access Internet information. The PC that accesses a dial-in connection needs either a modem (via a phone line) or a terminal adapter (TA) to connect via an ISDN line.

digital signature. Generally used in conjunction with public-key encryption. The encryption part ensures that no one but the intended recipient can read the message. The signature function gives the recipient assurance that the sender is really who he says he is, because he provided his private key—thus 'signing' the document.

domain. The extension in the host name that identifies the host. There are six hosts: .com (commercial), .edu (educational), .gov (governmental), .mil (military), .org (organization), and .arpa (ARPA.) If the host is outside the United States, there is a two letter country code at the end of the host URL.

domain name registration. The domain name of an Internet site must be registered with the InterNIC. For example, Widgetz Inc. might register the URL: "www.widgetz.com".

domain name server. DNS is a computer on the Internet that translates between Internet domain names, such as "microsoft.com" and the Internet numerical addresses, such as 192.123.32.1

dot. Internet vernacular for the period that separates names and organizations. One would read "gates@microsoft.com" out loud as "Gates at Microsoft dot com."

dot file. A file on a UNIX public-access system that alters the way you or your messages interact with that system. For example, the .login file contains various parameters for such things as the text editor you get when you send a message.

download. Copy a file from a host system to your computer. There are several different methods, or protocols, for downloading files, most of which periodically check the file as it is being copied to ensure no information is inadvertently destroyed or damaged during the process.

dynamic rerouting. A method of addressing information about the Internet so if one route is blocked or broken, the information can use another route.

DTD. Data type definition. Specification for allowing the layout of documents to be displayed within a browser

E-mail. Electronic mail. It is often used as a verb as well.

encrypt. A method of encoding data utilizing sophisticated algorithms. Modern encryption algorithms, such as DES and RSA, can quickly transform information into secured gibberish that cannot be read without the encryption key(s).

FAQ. Frequently asked questions, and more important, answers. FAQs for thousands of subjects are available on the Internet.

FDDI.   Standard for data transmission of optical fiber cables (at rate of 100 million bps, twice the speed of a T3).

finger.   A way of getting a short piece of information about someone on the Internet—if they allow it.

firewall.   Hardware and/or software that protects a LAN or intranet from Internet hackers. It separates network into two or more parts, restricting outsiders. Private/sensitive information is kept within "firewall."

forms.   A form is a dialog with the user of a browser, allowing users to enter information to a Web server. This generally requires a program on host server to handle data.

FQDN.   Fully qualified domain name. The "official" name assigned to a computer. Organizations register names such as "ibm.com". They then assign unique names to their computers like "dank.ibm.com".

FTP.   File transfer protocol. One of the major utilities used to work the Internet. There are countless files throughout the Internet that can be downloaded free of charge using FTP. See also anonymous FTP.

gateway.   A host computer that connects one network with another and translates communications protocols between them.

GIF.   Graphic interchange format. A bit-mapped image format that was developed by CompuServe. It does not compress the image size as well as some newer formats, such as JPEG.

Gopher.   A file retrieval system on the Internet that is menu-based, unlike traditional FTP, which requires the user to enter commands.

hacker.   To the general public, this term refers to someone who breaks into computers. Originally, it meant a programmer or analyst who enjoyed pushing the edge of the envelope in terms of hardware or software, often coming up with clever solutions. Old-style hackers refer to computer pirates as crackers, although the term has not been widely used outside of the industry.

handshake.   An exchange of protocol information between two modems or communications devices.

history list.   A list of document titles and URLs retained in memory by a browser.

hit.   A hit generally refers to each accessed page in a site. If a user calls up "www.yahoo.com" a hit is completed. Each link clicked is another hit. In the Excite search engine, a hit refers to search results.

home page.   The first page that browsers see of the information that you post on your computer attached to the World Wide Web. The home page is a "welcome" page. It typically contains a table of contents to more information that a visitor (browser, surfer, etc.) can find at your site by clicking onto hypertext links you've created. See also, HTML, Internet, and WWW.

HotJava.   The Web browser developed by Sun Microsystems using a cross-platform, object-oriented language called Java. Java gives users the ability to write small programs that can be embedded into a Web page.

hotlist.   On a Web browser, a collection of bookmarks.

HTML.   Hypertext markup language. This is the authoring software language used on the Internet's World Wide Web. HTML is used for creating World Wide Web pages. The linking of phrases to another section of text is called hypertext.

HTTP.   Hypertext transfer protocol. A client/server protocol used for information sharing on the Internet. It is the basis of the World Wide Web (WWW).

hyperlink.   A way to connect two Internet resources via a simple word or phrase on which a user can click to start the connection.

hypermedia.   Richly formatted document with a variety of information types, including text, audio, movies, and images.

Internet.   The Internet is made up of thousands of interconnected networks in more than 70 countries. Originally developed for the military, much of the Internet today is used for academic and commercial research. Users have access to unpublished data, journals, and bulletin board services. It is also widely used as a worldwide electronic mail system.

E-mail connection to the Internet is available through online services such as CompuServe, BIX, and America Online. Internet computers use the TCP/IP communications protocol. The Internet is connected to all types of computer networks worldwide via gateways that convert TCP/IP into other protocols.

image map.   Refers to an image in HTML document with parts of an image acting as links to other pages or information.

intranet.   A TCP/IP network, generally with restricted access to/from Internet, managed by a corporation promoting shared resources between employees.

IAP/ISP.   Internet Access Provider/Internet Service Provider. Generally, an IAP offers dial-up access to individual customers while an ISP offers larger-scale Internet services, primarily dedicated lines. IAPs/ISPs have trunk line connections, and resell the access.

IRC.   Internet relay chat. Currently, a tool with limited use that allows "users" to join "chat" channels and exchange typed messages. When the Internet improves its bandwidth, it will soon carry voice and images (full-color, live-action video and audio). Already IRC can be a valuable business conferencing tool, providing adequate voice communication.

InterNIC.   The Internet Network Information Center, a repository of information about the Internet. Located in northern Virginia, it is federally funded.

IP.   Internet protocol. A routing scheme that uses the concept of "virtual links" to connect from point A to point B by routing through any of an infinite number of possible connections. If one link is broken, IP will route itself through alternative links.

ISAPI.   Microsoft's Internet Server application programming interface. Allows for multithreading.

ISDN.   Integrated services digital network. ISDN is a set of communications standards that enable a single phone line or optical cable to carry voice, digital network service, and video. ISDN may eventually replace the current twisted-wire copper phone lines.

Java. A language developed by Sun from the shoulders of C++. Java stripped some of the C++ libraries and added some Web-designed functionalities. Allows for distributed objects over the Internet. Often is used for animation and action within Web sites. With Java, applets can play on any graphical browser that is Java-capable.

JPEG. Joint photographic experts group. Format for images, utilizing compression for full-color and grayscale images. Does not handle black and white images or video.

leased line. A full-time, dedicated, leased connection to Internet.

lurk. To read messages in a Usenet newsgroup without ever posting anything.

mailing list. A conference in which messages are delivered right to your mailbox, instead of to a Usenet newsgroup. A server automatically forwards messages sent to one centralized address to all subscribers of the mailing list.

mail server. A computer on the Internet that provides electronic mail services. A mail server sends out messages for you using SMTP.

MIME. Multipurpose Internet mail extensions. MIME is a set of Internet functions that extends normal E-mail capabilities and enables computer files to be attached to E-mail. MIME formats might be word processing files, spreadsheets, images, sound clips, and software applications you can send via E-mail.

mirrorsite. Due to Internet population growth, some sites are duplicated in other locations, often unknown to the user, diverting traffic from a heavily used site.

Mosaic. The first Windows-based HTML browser that took full advantage of the graphical capabilities of HTTP. It was developed by the National Center for Supercomputing at the University of Illinois.

MPEG. Motion picture experts group is a digital movie format.

navigation. Refers to the way in which a user moves through a site.

Netiquette. A set of commonsense guidelines for not annoying others. For example, TYPING IN ALL UPPERCASE LETTERS IS CONSIDERED SHOUTING.

Netscape Navigator. A Web browsing software product developed by NetScape Communications Corporation. NetScape was written by many of the same people who wrote the original graphical Web browser, Mosaic.

network. A communications system that links two or more computers. It can be as simple as a cable strung between two computers a few feet apart or as complex as hundreds of thousands of computers around the world linked through fiber-optic cables, phone lines and satellites.

newsgroup. A Usenet conference.

NIC. Network information center. A storage area for information about a particular Internet server.

NIS.   Network information services. Formerly known as the Yellow Pages, is a facility used on UNIX networks to administer a group of computers as if they were one.

NNTP.   Network news transfer protocol. The mechanism by which newsgroups are collected and distributed.

NSAPI.   Netscape's application programming interface.

packet.   A piece of information sent across a network. Each packet contains the sender's address and the recipient's address, among other things.

packet switching.   Method to move data, by which information is divided up in chunks (i.e., packets) for transmission.

page.   A document or piece of information in HTML available from the WWW.

PEM.   Privacy enhanced mail. An E-mail scheme that uses public-key encryption to secure and digitally sign E-mail messages.

Ping.   An Internet utility that allows one to test a connection. Ping returns the amount of time it took to reach the host (in milliseconds) and sometimes can even tell you the number of connections, or hops, it took to get there.

.plan file.   On a UNIX system, a way for users to publish a few lines of information about themselves. When other users FINGER this user, what is returned is the contents of the .plan file.

POP.   Post office protocol. An E-mail server for users of SLIP or PPP accounts.

PoP.   Point of Presence. The point at which a phone system is connected to the phone provider's backbone.

post.   To compose a message for a Usenet newsgroup.

Postmaster.   The common address for the mail administrator at a given site.

PostScript.   A page description language developed by Adobe Systems.

PPP.   Point-to-point protocol, a scheme for connecting two computers over a phone line. Similar to, but faster than, SLIP.

prompt.   Mechanism by which a computer asks (and waits) for information from a user.

protocols.   Computer rules that provide uniform specifications easing the communication between hardware and operating systems.

proxy.   The technique firewalls use to pass information back and forth to the Internet. Instead of allowing users to connect directly to the Internet, the firewall intercepts requests, examines them, and then passes them through in a more controlled manner. Firewalls can make decisions about which proxies to pass based on the authentication of the user.

private key encryption.   An encryption scheme like DES that requires both the sender and receiver to have knowledge of the secret "key," upon which the data is encrypted. Also known as symmetric cryptography.

public key encryption.   An encryption scheme like RSA that does not require both the sender and receiver to share the secret "key," upon which the data is encrypted. Also known as asymmetric cryptography.

Quick Time.   A method of storing video and audio information in digital format. Developed by Apple Computer Corp.

README.   Generally listed as REAME.TXT or REAME.1ST, these are explanatory files on FTP servers. Users will download this small text file first, which can help them decide if they want to spend the time and effort downloading anything else. Copyrights and disclaimers are often included.

RFC.   Request for comments. A series of documents that describe various technical aspects of the Internet.

router.   Connects two or more networks, including networks that use different types of cables and different types of speeds, using IP.

RSA.   Both an encryption algorithm and a company in California (RSA Data Security) that sells products based on RSA cryptography. RSA is a public-key algorithm, meaning that one does not have to know the private key of the recipient to encrypt a given document.

RTF.   Rich text format, a text format incorporating additions such as boldface, underlining, and italics.

server.   A computer that can distribute information or files automatically in response to specifically worded E-mail requests.

SGML.   Standard generalized markup language. The foundation of HTML, provides guidelines for the development of formatting display languages.

Shareware.   Software distributed freely through the public domain, yet author expects compensation.

shell account.   A software account that allows you to use someone else's Internet connection. It's not the same as your own account. You connect to a host computer and use the Internet through the host computer's connection.

SHTTP.   Secure hypertext transfer protocol. An extension to HTTP developed by EINET technologies, allowing encrypted and authenticated browsers to exchange information without threat of eavesdropping.

.sig file.   A file that, when placed in your home directory on your public-access site, is automatically appended to every Usenet posting you write. Sometimes, .signature file.

SLIP.   Serial line internet protocol. A popular way for home users, or businesses without Internet connections, to use a modem and receive full Internet connectivity (albeit slowly).

snail mail.   A derogatory term for the U.S. Postal Service. As opposed to E-mail.

SMDS.   New standard for very high speed data transmission.

SMTP.   Simple mail transfer protocol, the method by which Internet mail is passed from server to server.

socket. The virtual conversation between your computer and another on the Internet. One may have more than one socket going at a time (i.e., one for FTP and one for Telnet).

Solaris 2.0. A multitasking, multiprocessing distributed computing environment from SunSoft for SPARC computers, 386s and up and the PowerPC. Solaris 2.0 for SPARC machines is backward compatible with Solaris 1.0, and includes the SunOS 5.0 operating system (based on UNIX SVR4), Sun's ONC networking products (NFS, NIS, etc.), OpenWindows (Sun's version of X Windows) and Sun's Open Look graphical interface with DeskSet utilities that provide multimedia mail and drag-and-drop capability.

SPARCstation. A high-speed workstation or server built by Sun Microsystems, Inc.

SSL. Secure sockets layer (SSL) open protocol developed by Netscape that encrypts data passed along the Internet. It works by encrypting a consumer's financial information from his or her PC to the financial institution.

Sysadmin. The system administrator.

Sysop. The system operator.

T1. An Internet backbone line that carries up to 1.544 million bits per second (1.536 Mbps).

T3. An Internet backbone line that carries up to 45 million bits per second (45 Mbps).

TA. Terminal adapter. An electronic device that interfaces a PC with an Internet host computer via an ISDN phone line. Sometimes called "ISDN modems." TAs are not modems, however, since they are digital.

TCP/IP. Transmission control protocol/Internet protocol. The particular system for transferring information over a computer network that is at the heart of the Internet.

Telnet. An Internet-based terminal emulation session; allows you to access other computers interactively.

terminal emulation. A defined relationship between the keyboard keystrokes, the characters on the screen, screen colors, and so forth. To connect with another computer interactively, both must be addressing the same terminal emulation.

terminal server. A series of dial-up modems for use on a network, with software that allows remote users to access internal computers. Also referred to as an asynchronous communications server.

thread. An article posted to a Usenet newsgroup, along with follow-up messages.

TIFF. Tagged image file format is an image format often used by Apple Macintosh computers.

UNIX. The operating system used to write most of the programs and protocols that built the Internet. The name was created by programmers who felt they had become "eunuchs" in the language development process.

upload.   Copy a file from your computer (called the remote computer) to a host system.

URL.   Uniform resource locator. An address on the World Wide Web. It consists of the protocol to use, followed by the characters "://" and then points to the Internet address of the desired host. For example, http://www. coca-cola.com references a World Wide Web page, and would require a browser like Mosaic or Netscape to read the information. ftp://ftp.microsoft.com on the other hand, references Microsoft's FTP server.

Usenet.   A system of thousands of newsgroups.

user name.   On most host systems, the first time you connect you are asked to supply a one-word user name. This can generally be any combination of letters and numbers.

UUCP.   Unix-to-Unix CoPy. A method for transferring Usenet postings and E-mail that requires far fewer net resources than TCP/IP, but which can result in considerably slower transfer times.

UUNET.   A nonprofit organization that runs a large Internet site that links the UUCP mail network with the Internet and has a large FTP file archive.

Veronica.   A program that allows a user to find information on Gopher menus within Gopher documents. "Very Easy Rodent-Oriented Net-wide Index to Computerized Archives."

WAIS.   Wide area information servers. A distributed information retrieval system sponsored by Apple, Thinking Machines and Dow Jones. Users can locate documents by keyword searches.

Web browser.   A utility used to peruse documents on the World Wide Web of the Internet. See also, WWW and Mosaic.

WinSock.   Short for Windows Socket, is a standard way for Microsoft Windows programs to work with TCP/IP.

WWW.   World Wide Web. An Internet service that links documents by providing HyperText links from server to server. It allows a user to jump from document to related document no matter where it is stored on the Internet. World Wide Web client programs, or Web browsers, such as Mosaic and Cello, allow users to browse "the Web."

WWW documents are structured with format codes and hypertext links using the hypertext markup language, or HTML. A home page is created for each server with links to other documents locally and throughout the Internet. The Web has become a centerpiece of Internet activity, because its documents can contain both text and graphics, and it is quickly turning the Internet into an online shopping mall.

X.509.   The standard format for Certificates.

Z39.50 Protocol.   Name of National Information Standards Organization (NISO) that defines an application level protocol by which a computer can query another computer and transfer results.

ZIP.   Open standard for PC file compression.

INDEX